Essentials of NIH Toolbox® Version 3 Cognition Tests

Essentials of Psychological Assessment Series

Series Editors, Alan S. Kaufman and Nadeen L. Kaufman

Essentials of CAS2 Assessment
by Jack A. Naglieri and Tulio M. Otero

Essentials of Child and Adolescent Psychopathology, Second Edition
by Linda Wilmshurst

Essentials of Cognitive Assessment with KAIT and Other Kaufman Measures
by Elizabeth O. Lichtenberger, Debra Y. Broadbooks, and Alan S. Kaufman

Essentials of Conners Behavior Assessments™
by Elizabeth P. Sparrow

Essentials of Creativity Assessment
by James C. Kaufman, Jonathan A. Plucker, and John Baer

Essentials of Cross-Battery Assessment, Third Edition
by Dawn P. Flanagan, Samuel O. Ortiz, and Vincent C. Alfonso

Essentials of DAS-II® Assessment
by Ron Dumont, John O. Willis, and Colin D. Elliott

Essentials of Dyslexia Assessment and Intervention
by Nancy Mather and Barbara J. Wendling

Essentials of Evidence-Based Academic Interventions
by Barbara J. Wendling and Nancy Mather

Essentials of Executive Functions Assessment
by George McCloskey and Lisa A. Perkins

Essentials of Forensic Psychological Assessment, Second Edition
by Marc J. Ackerman

Essentials of Gifted Assessment
by Steven I. Pfeiffer

Essentials of IDEA for Assessment Professionals
by Guy McBride, Ron Dumont, and John O. Willis

Essentials of Individual Achievement Assessment
by Douglas K. Smith

Essentials of Intellectual Disability Assessment and Identification
by Alan W. Brue and Linda Wilmshurst

Essentials of KABC-II Assessment
by Alan S. Kaufman, Elizabeth O. Lichtenberger, Elaine Fletcher-Janzen, and Nadeen L. Kaufman

Essentials of KTEA™-3 and WIAT®-III Assessment
by Kristina C. Breaux and Elizabeth O. Lichtenberger

Essentials of MCMI®-IV Assessment
by Seth D. Grossman and Blaise Amendolace

Essentials of Millon™ Inventories Assessment, Third Edition
by Stephen Strack

Essentials of MMPI-A™ Assessment
by Robert P. Archer and Radhika Krishnamurthy

Essentials of MMPI-2® Assessment, Second Edition
by David S. Nichols

Essentials of Myers-Briggs Type Indicator® Assessment, Second Edition
by Naomi L. Quenk

Essentials of NEPSY®-II Assessment
by Sally L. Kemp and Marit Korkman

Essentials of Neuropsychological Assessment, Second Edition
by Nancy Hebben and William Milberg

Essentials of Nonverbal Assessment
by Steve McCallum, Bruce Bracken, and John Wasserman

Essentials of PAI® Assessment
by Leslie C. Morey

Essentials of Planning, Selecting, and Tailoring Interventions for Unique Learners
by Jennifer T. Mascolo, Vincent C. Alfonso, and Dawn P. Flanagan

Essentials of Processing Assessment, Second Edition
by Milton J. Dehn

Essentials of Psychological Assessment Supervision
by A. Jordan Wright

Essentials of Psychological Testing, Second Edition
by Susana Urbina

Essentials of Response to Intervention
by Amanda M. VanDerHeyden and Matthew K. Burns

Essentials of Rorschach® Assessment
by Tara Rose, Michael P. Maloney, and Nancy Kaser-Boyd

Essentials of Rorschach Assessment: Comprehensive System and R-PAS
by Jessica R. Gurley

Essentials of School Neuropsychological Assessment, Third Edition
by Daniel C. Miller and Denise E. Maricle

Essentials of Specific Learning Disability Identification, Second Edition
by Vincent C. Alfonso and Dawn P. Flanagan

Essentials of Stanford-Binet Intelligence Scales (SB5) Assessment
by Gale H. Roid and R. Andrew Barram

Essentials of TAT and Other Storytelling Assessments, Second Edition
by Hedwig Teglasi

Essentials of Temperament Assessment
by Diana Joyce

Essentials of Trauma-Informed Assessment and Interventions in School and Community Settings
by Kirby L. Wycoff and Bettina Franzese

Essentials of Treatment Planning, Second Edition
by Mark E. Maruish

Essentials of WAIS®-IV Assessment, Second Edition
by Elizabeth O. Lichtenberger and Alan S. Kaufman

Essentials of WISC®-IV Assessment, Second Edition
by Dawn P. Flanagan and Alan S. Kaufman

Essentials of WISC-V® Assessment
by Dawn P. Flanagan and Vincent C. Alfonso

Essentials of WISC-V Integrated Assessment
by Susan Engi Raiford

Essentials of WJ IV® Cognitive Abilities Assessment
by Fredrick A. Schrank, Scott L. Decker, and John M. Garruto

Essentials of the Tests of Dyslexia
by Nancy Mather, R. Steve McCallum, Barbara J. Wendling and Sherry M. Bell

Essentials of WJ IV® Tests of Achievement
by Nancy Mather and Barbara J. Wendling

Essentials of WMS®-IV Assessment
by Lisa Whipple Drozdick, James A. Holdnack, and Robin C. Hilsabeck

Essentials of WNV™ Assessment
by Kimberly A. Brunnert, Jack A. Naglieri, and Steven T. Hardy-Braz

Essentials of Working Memory Assessment and Intervention
by Milton J. Dehn

Essentials of WPPSI™-IV Assessment
by Susan Engi Raiford and Diane L. Coalson

Essentials of WRAML2 and TOMAL-2 Assessment
by Wayne Adams and Cecil R. Reynolds

Essentials of WRAML3 and EMS Assessment
by Wayne V. Adams, David V. Sheslow, and Trevor A. Hall

Essentials of Evaluating Bias in Intelligence Testing
by Craig L. Frisby

Essentials of WJ V™ Assessment
by Erica M. Laforte, Nancy Mather, and W. Joel Schneider

Essentials of NIH Toolbox® Version 3 Cognition Tests
by Julie N. Hook, Amy Kovacs Giella and Erica M. LaForte

Essentials

of NIH Toolbox®

Version 3 Cognition Tests

Julie N. Hook

Amy K. Giella

Erica M. LaForte

WILEY

Published by John Wiley & Sons, Inc., Hoboken, New Jersey.

Library of Congress Cataloging-in-Publication Data applied for:

Paperback: 9781394310753

Cover Design: Wiley
Cover Image: Robert/stock.adobe.com

Set in 10.5/13pt Adobe Garamond Pro by Straive, Pondicherry, India

SKY10165983_081926

DEDICATIONS

To my daughter, Helena, you mean the world to me and, to my family, especially my mom, thank you for all your support.

J.N.H.

With all my love, I dedicate this to Hailey, who has indisputably made my world brighter. With the curiosity, limitless energy, and hilariously unexpected remarks only five-year-olds can muster, she never ceases to bring me overwhelming joy, laughter, and gray hairs. May your future be prosperous, safe, and brimming with happiness. To Thomas and my family for supporting me through all of life's hurdles. To a healthy, peaceful world filled with kind hearts and compassion.

A.K.G.

To my husband, George, and my children, Connor and Lucy, I am grateful for your unwavering support and constant encouragement. I would also like to acknowledge several individuals who have played a pivotal role in shaping my career and guiding me with their wisdom and mentorship: Richard Woodcock, Kevin McGrew, Fredrick Schrank, David Dailey, Nancy Mather, Barbara Wendling, and Richard Gershon. I am forever grateful for the impact you've had on my personal and professional growth.

E.M.L

CONTENTS

FOREWORD

It is with both pleasure and pride that I write this foreword to *Essentials of the NIH Toolbox® Version 3 Cognition Tests*. The book represents the culmination of nearly two decades of innovation, interdisciplinary collaboration, and a relentless commitment to democratizing access to high-quality cognitive measurement tools across the lifespan.

The NIH Toolbox, from inception, was envisioned as a robust system that would:

- Cover a broad age range (initially 3–85+ years, more recently validated to age 90, and expanded to include infancy and early childhood with the NIH Baby Toolbox)
- Assess individual differences and change over time
- Feature brief and practical assessments to be used in a broad range of settings
- Offer digitally based administration with automated scoring
- Utilize modern psychometric approaches, including Item Response Theory (IRT) and Computer Adaptive Testing (CAT), where appropriate.

Emphasis was also placed on cultural and linguistic adaptation from the outset, ensuring availability in both English and Spanish with careful review to support equity in measurement.

The Cognition domain, the focus of this volume, was a cornerstone of this effort to create a unique core suite of tests that could be flexibly deployed across a wide range of research and clinical applications.

THE JOURNEY FROM VERSION 1 TO VERSION 3: AN EVOLUTION IN PRECISION AND POWER

Version 1 of the NIH Toolbox in 2012 marked the first deliverable sponsored by the National Institutes of Health (NIH) Neuroscience Blueprint, which strives to accelerate transformative discoveries in brain function in health, aging, and disease. It was immediately adopted into several major research initiatives, including the Adolescent Brain Cognitive Development (ABCD) Study. The original Cognition Battery included seven core measures, each carefully designed and normed across the lifespan, with adjustments available for age, language, and level of education.

Version 2 (2015) expanded Toolbox technology to the iPad in response to user requests to make the measurement system more portable while at the same time improving the accuracy of recording response time. Version 2 was ultimately adopted for use in over 1,200 institutions.

Version 3 (2023), the centerpiece of this book, represents the most comprehensive revision of the NIH Toolbox to date. Not merely an update, it reflects a full rethinking and reengineering of the application interface based on input from users as well as updates to the measures in the Cognition domain.

Highlights of Version 3 include:

- **Expanded constructs:** Additional cognitive measures were created, validated, and normed, including enhanced measures of delayed memory and visual reasoning. Academic achievement measures will be added in 2026.
- **Updated normative data:** A new normative sample was collected, updated to align with the demographics of the US 2020 Census.
- **Redesigned application:** An easier-to-use interface providing for/enabling improved workflows.

Essentials of the NIH Toolbox® Version 3 Cognition Tests arrives at a critical juncture in cognitive science and neuropsychological assessment. As interest grows in scalable, standardized, and technologically enabled assessments, it is more important than ever that users fully understand not only how to administer these tools but also how they were developed, what they measure, how to interpret their scores, and how to apply them.

The authors of this volume are each deeply familiar with the conceptual foundations and technical specifications of the Toolbox, providing readers with a clear, accessible, and authoritative guide. Each test is presented with precision, contextualized within its theoretical origins and empirical support. Of equal importance, they provide users with real-world examples of how these tests can be deployed, adapted, and interpreted across diverse research designs and clinical questions.

Having led this project since its inception, I am especially pleased to see how the NIH Toolbox has grown from a vision into a continuously evolving platform that will support future generations of researchers, clinicians, educators, and public health professionals. These tools, as shared in *Essentials of the NIH Toolbox® Version 3 Cognition Tests*, are more accessible and interpretable than ever before. This book should be viewed not only as a guide to Version 3 but also as an invitation to fully engage with the NIH Toolbox in new and creative ways.

A NOTE OF GRATITUDE

The scale of this project was massive and required the collaboration of over 250 experts nationwide across domains and within subdomains—each noted leaders in their respective fields. The NIH Toolbox is the product of this collective intelligence and tireless collaboration of extraordinary researchers, clinicians, software engineers, and data scientists, each of whom contributed a pivotal part of this project over the past two decades. I would like to both formally and personally offer my gratitude to my colleagues at Northwestern University along with coinvestigators at dozens of academic and clinical organizations worldwide, succeeding teams of science, project, and contract officers at the National Institutes of Health (NIH), and the tens of thousands of individuals who participated in pilot testing, norming studies, and field trials. I also extend my thanks to the authors of this volume for capturing the essence of our work with such clarity and depth.

To the readers of this book—whether you are new to the NIH Toolbox or a longtime user—I hope you find within these pages not just information, but inspiration. The science of cognition is one of the most dynamic and impactful domains of human inquiry. With tools like those described in this volume, we are better equipped than ever before to explore, understand, and enhance the workings of the human mind.

Richard C. Gershon, PhD
Principal Investigator: NIH Toolbox, NIH Baby Toolbox, Mobile Toolbox
Professor of Medical Social Sciences
Division Chief, Outcome and Measurement Science
Professor of Health and Biomedical Informatics
Feinberg School of Medicine
Northwestern University

SERIES EDITOR'S PREFACE

In the *Essentials of Psychological Assessment Series*, we have attempted to provide the reader with books that deliver key practical information in the most efficient and accessible manner. Many books in the series feature specific topics in a variety of domains, such as specific learning disabilities, social-emotional learning, neuropsychological assessment, cross-battery assessment, and adaptive behavior assessment. Books in this category are intended for professionals in psychology and education—and for graduate students in these or related disciplines—who are involved with any aspect of assessment and intervention. A second category of books in this series, such as *Essentials of Bayley™–4 Assessment*, is devoted to a single test. Books in this category offer a concise yet thorough review of an instrument, with special attention given to the details of administration, scoring, interpretation, application, and tips for best practice of the test. Students can rely on series books in both categories for a clear and concise overview of the important assessment tools and key topics in which they must become proficient to practice skillfully, efficiently, and ethically in their chosen fields. Experienced clinicians will feel equally at home with this series in their efforts to remain on the cutting edge of new research and new instruments (including revisions of old ones) in an array of diverse fields.

Wherever feasible, visual cues highlighting key points are utilized alongside systematic, step-by-step guidelines. Chapters are focused and succinct. Topics are organized for an easy understanding of the essential material related to a particular test or topic. Theory and research are continually woven into the fabric of each book, but always to enhance the practical application of the material, rather than to sidetrack or overwhelm readers. With this series, we aim to challenge and assist readers interested in psychological assessment to aspire to the highest level of competency by arming them with the tools they need for knowledgeable, informed practice. We have long been advocates of "intelligent" testing—the notion that numbers are meaningless unless they are brought to life by the clinical acumen and expertise of examiners. Assessment must be used to make a difference in the child's life or the adult's life—or why bother to test? All books in the series—whether devoted to specific tests or general topics—are consistent with this credo. We want this series to help our readers, novice and veteran alike, to benefit from the intelligent assessment approaches of the authors of each book.

In *Essentials of the NIH Toolbox Version 3 Cognition Tests*, Drs. Hook and LaForte and Ms. Giella provide important insights into cognition and cognition testing as they detail administration procedures, guidance on score interpretation, and existing and potential clinical applications for the NIH Toolbox® Version 3 (V3) Cognition suite of tests. The NIH Toolbox® V3 Cognition domain builds upon the strong foundation of the two previous versions of the NIH Toolbox, as well as nearly two decades of NIH Toolbox research. The NIH Toolbox is among the first neuropsychological assessment tools to combine modern psychometric theory with digital technology, resulting in a comprehensive, psychometrically sound platform that features over 80 tests that measure over a dozen constructs across four key domains: Cognition, Emotion, Motor, and Sensation. The NIH Toolbox® V3 app streamlines these tests, user interface, and scores. This *Essentials* edition explores the V3 updates to the Cognition tests, including the new normative data, streamlined workflows, and standardized administration. Early-career and seasoned examiners who are familiar with assessment in general, and neurobehavioral cognitive testing in particular, will discover a wealth of information within these thorough, yet straightforward, pages. In addition to the NIH Toolbox® V3 Administration Manual and NIH Toolbox® V3 Technical Manual, this *Essentials* edition is a foundational collection of materials and insights that will assist examiners in the selection and administration of the tests and psychometricians in understanding the history, development, interpretation, and real-world uses of these tests.

Alan S. Kaufman, PhD, and Nadeen L. Kaufman, EdD,
Series Editors,
Neag School of Education, University of Connecticut

ALPHABETICAL LISTING OF CONTRIBUTING AUTHORS

Richard C. Gershon, PhD, is a nationally recognized leader in health measurement science and digital assessment innovation. A Professor and Division Chief at Northwestern University Feinberg School of Medicine, Dr. Gershon specializes in Item Response Theory and Computerized Adaptive Testing across cognitive, emotional, sensory, and motor domains. He has led the development of numerous National Institutes of Health (NIH) initiatives, including the NIH Toolbox, NIH Infant and Toddler Toolbox, PROMIS Technical Center, and Mobile Toolbox. Currently, he serves as PI or co-PI on projects focused on cognitive aging, intellectual disabilities, pediatric health, and EHR integration. Throughout his career, Dr. Gershon has contributed to over 70 NIH, DoD, and foundation-funded studies advancing patient-reported and performance outcome measurement.

Amy K. Giella, PMP, is a project manager at the Feinberg School of Medicine at Northwestern University, specializing in the development, translation, and implementation of digitally administered assessments. With over 14 years of experience in psychological test administration and development, she has led the creation of support materials, including manuals, help articles, administration videos, and digital training courses. She played a central role in the restructuring, development, quality assurance, and release of the NIH Toolbox® V3 app, as well as the design and delivery of its accompanying support materials.

Bruno Giordani, PhD, is a clinical neuropsychologist and tenured professor at the University of Michigan, holding appointments in Psychiatry, Neurology, Psychology, and the School of Nursing. His work spans decades of research and clinical practice focused on cognitive and behavioral health across the lifespan, with particular emphasis on dementia, sleep, neuroimaging, and cross-cultural neuropsychology. As Associate Director of the Michigan Alzheimer's Disease Research Center, he leads multicenter initiatives that prioritize real-world patient outcomes and novel biomarkers of disease.

Julie N. Hook, PhD, MBA, ABPP, is a board-certified clinical neuropsychologist and Research Associate Professor at Northwestern University's Feinberg School of Medicine. Drawing on more than 20 years of experience in psychological test development across both industry and academia, she has been at the forefront of advancing digitally administered assessments to improve accessibility, efficiency, and impact in research, education, and clinical practice. Further, she led the development and launch of NIH Toolbox® Version 3, directing the redesign and enhancement of its app, website, e-learning, and customer service platform to meet evolving scientific and user needs.

Anson Kairys, PhD, is a clinical neuropsychologist and Assistant Professor of Psychiatry at the University of Michigan, where his work focuses on cognitive functioning in chronic pain and neurodegenerative conditions. His research integrates traditional assessment methods with digital tools to enhance early detection and personalized intervention. He is a K23-funded investigator developing novel approaches to cognitive assessment using neurophysiological and mobile health technologies.

Erica M. LaForte, PhD, is an applied psychometrician and the owner of Applied Measurement Solutions, LLC. Her career in test development spans nearly 30 years. Her areas of research interest include the application of the Rasch model to item development, test score interpretation, and validation; computer-adaptive testing; test score equating and linking; and the application of psychometric principles to solve practical measurement challenges. In her former role at Northwestern University, she served on the scientific team for the NIH Toolbox, and she co-edited the NIH Toolbox® Version 3 Technical Manual. Additionally, Dr. LaForte worked in various research and development capacities on the *Woodcock-Johnson III* and the *Woodcock-Johnson IV*, and co-authored the *Woodcock-Johnson V*.

Abigail B. Sivan, PhD, is a clinical psychologist whose research interests span a diverse range of topics in pediatrics and neuropsychological assessment. As a Research Associate Professor in Medical Social Sciences at Northwestern University, she focuses primarily on the development of training materials for the Environmental Children's Health Outcome Study, the NIH Toolbox, and the NIH Baby Toolbox. Dr. Sivan has also led key initiatives to translate the NIH Toolbox Cognition measures into Arabic and Hebrew, supporting broader access and cultural relevance in global assessment efforts.

ACKNOWLEDGMENTS

The authors wish to acknowledge with deep appreciation the visionary leadership and scientific direction of Dr. Richard C. Gershon in guiding the NIH Toolbox and the foundational role of Dr. Molly V. Wagster as Lead Project Officer on the original contract and as a steadfast supporter of this measurement initiative throughout the years.

We extend special recognition to the faculty and staff in the Department of Medical Social Sciences, Feinberg School of Medicine, Northwestern University, for their sustained contributions to the development and implementation of the NIH Toolbox. We also acknowledge the researchers and collaborators from institutions nationwide (and across the globe) whose expertise and commitment have guided this project from its inception through its current version. More than two decades of collaboration, planning, research, data collection, programming, norming, analysis, quality assurance, and user support have culminated in a scientifically validated and reliable suite of assessments spanning the human lifespan.

FUNDING AND INSTITUTIONAL SUPPORT

Primary funding for the conception and development of the NIH Toolbox was provided through the NIH Blueprint for Neuroscience Research (HHS-N-260-2006-00007-C) and the Office of Behavioral and Social Sciences Research (OBSSR) of the National Institutes of Health (NIH). The Principal Investigator was Richard C. Gershon, PhD, Division Chief for Outcome and Measurement Science, Department of Medical Social Sciences, Feinberg School of Medicine, Northwestern University. The Lead Project Officer was Molly V. Wagster, PhD, Chief, Behavioral and Systems Neuroscience Branch, Division of Neuroscience, National Institute on Aging, NIH.

The NIH Blueprint for Neuroscience Research represents a collaborative framework among multiple NIH Institutes and Centers, including the National Center for Complementary and Alternative Medicine (NCCAM); National Eye Institute (NEI); National Institute on Aging (NIA); National Institute on Alcohol Abuse and Alcoholism (NIAAA); National Institute of Biomedical Imaging and Bioengineering (NIBIB); Eunice

Kennedy Shriver National Institute of Child Health and Human Development (NICHD); National Institute on Drug Abuse (NIDA); National Institute on Deafness and Other Communication Disorders (NIDCD); National Institute of Dental and Craniofacial Research (NIDCR); National Institute of Environmental Health Sciences (NIEHS); National Institute of General Medical Sciences (NIGMS); National Institute of Mental Health (NIMH); National Institute of Neurological Disorders and Stroke (NINDS); and the National Institute of Nursing Research (NINR).

Additional support for the NIH Toolbox was provided through the following federally funded initiatives:

- A Cognitive Test Battery for Intellectual Disabilities (NICHD 1R01HD076189-01A1)
- ARMADA: Advancing Reliable Measurement in Alzheimer's Disease and Cognitive Aging (NIA/U2CAG057441)
- ECHO PRO Research Resource: A Developmentally-Based Measurement Science Framework for Assessing Environmental Exposure and Child Health (NIH 1U24OD023319-01)
- MyCog: Rapid Detection of Cognitive Impairment in Everyday Clinical Settings (NINDS UG3NS105562)
- National Children's Study (HHSN275201200007l)
- NIH Infant and Toddler Toolbox (75N94019D00005)
- The Mobile Toolbox for Monitoring Cognitive Function (NIA 1U2CAG060426-01)

These projects collectively extended the reach and application of the NIH Toolbox, fostering innovation in digital cognitive assessment and expanding its utility across diverse populations and developmental stages.

EDITORIAL ACKNOWLEDGMENTS

The authors express sincere appreciation to John Wiley & Sons Inc., as well as the Wiley editorial team for their expert guidance throughout the publication process: Darren Lalonde, Executive Acquisitions Editor; Nathanael Mcgavin, Managing Editor; and Christina Weyrauch, Assistant Editor. The authors are particularly grateful to Drs. Alan S. Kaufman and Nadeen L. Kaufman for their exemplary stewardship of the Essentials book series.

CLOSING REMARKS

The NIH Toolbox represents a truly collaborative endeavor. Now in its third iteration, it continues to expand its reach and impact globally. The authors extend their gratitude to all who have used, contributed to the development of, or sustained interest in advancing the NIH Toolbox. It has been a privilege to contribute to the documentation of these assessments within this distinguished series.

One

NIH TOOLBOX® HISTORY AND DEVELOPMENT

Julie N. Hook
Amy K. Giella
Abigail B. Sivan

OVERVIEW

Traditional cognitive batteries, while robust, are often time-intensive and costly. Recognizing this, the National Institutes of Health (NIH), through the Blueprint for Neuroscience Research, initiated an ambitious effort to develop a common set of tools capable of measuring neurological and behavioral functions across the lifespan. This initiative led to the creation of the NIH Toolbox for the assessment of neurological and behavioral function—a milestone in digital cognitive measurement.

In 2006, the NIH Toolbox contract was awarded to develop a set of brief, psychometrically sound, and royalty-free tests that would allow for greater ease when comparing the results of neurobehavioral and neuropsychological studies (Gershon et al., 2010). After six years of development, the NIH Toolbox measurement system was released. It included a suite of tests that allowed for assessment across the lifespan (aged 3–85+) and focused on four fundamental areas of neurobehavioral functioning, including: (1) cognition, (2) motor, (3) sensation, and (4) emotion. Since its inaugural release in 2012 as a web-based system, it was reconceptualized and rereleased as an Apple iPad app in 2015. This repositioning as an app allowed for both a more flexible and an easy-to-use test administration and data collection system.

Rapid Reference 1.1

Psychometrics is a field of study focused on measuring mental processes, including theory and techniques.

In 2023, the NIH Toolbox Version 3 (V3) was released as a new iPad app with improved user interface (UI) and user experience (UX) capabilities, making it more user-friendly with streamlined test instructions and updated scoring algorithms. The NIH Toolbox V3 iPad app was initially released in English and Spanish. In addition, select Cognition tests are now available in separate language apps, which include Arabic, French, Hebrew, Italian, and Spanish, plus more translations on the horizon.

Rapid Reference 1.2

User interface (UI) focuses on the visual elements and interaction with the product's interface (e.g., buttons and layouts).

User experience (UX) is how someone interacts with the product overall (e.g., product usability or how intuitive the design is to use).

VERSION 1 (V1) DEVELOPMENT

The NIH Toolbox was launched under the NIH Blueprint for Neuroscience Research, a multiagency effort that began in 2004 to accelerate the pace of discovery in brain research.

Rapid Reference 1.3

The NIH Toolbox is a direct response to the problem of instrument heterogeneity, a key barrier to reproducible science.

The NIH Blueprint for Neuroscience Research is a collaborative effort among the NIH Office of the Director and 12 NIH institutes and centers that support research on the nervous system (National Institute of Neurological Disorders and Stroke, n.d.). The participating institutes, centers, and offices include:

- National Center for Complementary and Integrative Health (NCCIH)
- National Eye Institute (NEI)
- National Institute on Aging (NIA)
- National Institute on Alcohol Abuse and Alcoholism (NIAAA)
- National Institute of Biomedical Imaging and Bioengineering (NIBIB)
- Eunice Kennedy Shriver National Institute of Child Health and Human Development (NICHD)
- National Institute on Drug Abuse (NIDA)
- National Institute of Dental and Craniofacial Research (NIDCR)

- National Institute of Environmental Health Sciences (NIEHS)
- National Institute of Mental Health (NIMH)
- National Institute of Neurological Disorders and Stroke (NINDS)
- Office of Behavioral and Social Sciences Research (OBSSR)

The NIH Blueprint is aimed at advancing research and discoveries in brain function, including disease, health, and aging, and to accelerate discoveries in neuroscience research and is focused on initiatives that were too large an undertaking for any one NIH institute. For more information about the NIH Blueprint, please refer to neuroscienceblueprint.nih.gov. Since 2004, the Blueprint has invested over $615 million to support these aims (NINDS, n.d.). An example of a supported large-scale program includes the Human Connectome Project, which has advanced our understanding of both the brain and ways to treat brain disorders. The Blueprint funds training efforts as well as research resources and tools, such as the NeuroBioBank, which includes a collection of post-mortem brain tissue that can be used to study neurological, developmental, and psychiatric disorders.

One issue with traditional neurobehavioral assessment tools is that they frequently vary in methodology. Take, for example, two tests of processing speed; they could both use different items, test designs, scoring methods, and normative data. With all these possible differences, it can make it difficult to compare scores when different tests are used. This can hinder the comparability of findings across studies, as well as limit meta-analytic power. Further, these issues can become more pronounced in longitudinal and multisite research when different tests are used.

VERSION 1 DEVELOPMENT

In 2006, the development of the NIH Toolbox began when the Blueprint awarded Dr. Richard Gershon, principal investigator, a contract to develop a suite of assessment tools to address the need of developing a standardized set of instruments to assess neurobehavioral functioning. This project lasted six years and included input from over 250 scientists and about 80 institutions.

The framework for the NIH Toolbox was created by performing an extensive literature review and interviewing or surveying around 100 experts (Nowinski et al., 2013). From this work, the following domains and subdomains were identified (Table 1.1).

There were several other factors that drove the selection of tests for inclusion in the NIH Toolbox, and these factors included:

- appropriate for use across the age span (ages 3–85 years),
- ability to use in diverse settings and groups,
- no fees for intellectual property use,
- strong reliability and validity findings (i.e., psychometric soundness), and
- brevity in assessment.

Table 1.1 NIH Toolbox Version 1 Domains and Subdomains

Domain	Subdomain	References
Cognition	Attention, episodic memory, working memory, expressive and receptive language, executive function, and processing speed	Weintraub et al. (2013)
Emotion	Psychological well-being, stress and self-efficacy, social relationships, and negative affect	Salsman et al. (2013)
Motor	Balance, dexterity, strength, endurance, and locomotion	Rine et al. (2013), Reuben et al. (2013)
Sensation	Audition, vision, vestibular, olfaction, pain, and gustation	Coldwell et al. (2013), Cook et al. (2013), Dalton et al. (2013), Dunn et al. (2013), Varma et al. (2013), and Zecker et al. (2013)

Administration of the core set of tests in each domain needed to be 30 minutes or less, so all four core test domains (Cognition, Emotion, Motor, and Sensation) could be administered in 2 hours or less. Test instructions needed to be understandable to examinees with low literacy, and tests needed to allow for the assessment of people from diverse backgrounds. Further, tests needed to assess typical functioning rather than being specific to functioning associated with a specific disorder or disease. For example, a test specific to the assessment of one particular disorder, like autism, was not considered. However, a test of cognitive function that could assess typically developing cognition, in addition to being sensitive to cognitive issues associated with autism or other disorders, was selected.

Across all four domains, 1,391 measures were reviewed. After the downward selection based on the criteria listed herewith, 48 tests remained. This smaller group was then reviewed by expert working groups covering: (1) culture, (2) language, (3) accessibility, (4) use in pediatrics, and (5) use in geriatrics. Tests then underwent further evaluation when needed and were examined in validation studies of 450–500 participants using criterion measures in their respective domains and subdomains (see Akshoomoff et al., 2013; Weintraub et al., 2014; Zelazo et al., 2014). For instance, validity studies for the Cognition tests included the *Wechsler Adult Intelligence Scale* IV (WAIS; Wechsler, 2008), *Delis Kaplan Executive Function System* (D-KEFS; Delis et al., 2001), and *Peabody Picture Vocabulary Test, 4th Edition* (PPVT-4; Dunn & Dunn, 2007). Next, tests were identified to see if they were suitable for administration and scoring via computerized adaptive testing (CAT) and item response theory (IRT). Because these techniques require more participants, this resulted in 16,000 participants being assessed as part of validation, calibration, and field test studies.

After test selection and refinement, there was a large national standardization study conducted in English and Spanish with 4,859 participants. Ages ranged from 3 to 85 years and were representative of the 2010 US population based on geographic location, socioeconomic status, ethnicity/race, and sex assigned at birth (see Casaletto et al., 2015 for more details). Normative scores were collected and calculated for each year from 3 through 17 years and then in the following age bands: 18–29, 30–39, 40–49, 50–59, 60–69, 70–79, and 80–85 years (Beaumont et al., 2013).

In 2012, version 1 of the NIH Toolbox was launched as a validated test suite for online use. To use version 1, examiners frequently needed a laptop with two auxiliary keyboards and mice and monitors. Other specialized equipment was also required for non-cognition domain tests in sensation and motor.

Neuropsychological Test Design

The NIH Toolbox introduced several groundbreaking features in its test battery. It stands among the first fully digital collections of norm-referenced neurobehavioral assessments, with the added distinction of being co-normed across various tests and functional domains. These measures were crafted using innovative statistical methodologies, enabling administration in under five minutes for most tests while preserving strong psychometric integrity. Importantly, the tests were designed to evaluate a broad spectrum of neurobehavioral functioning, rather than focusing on specific clinical conditions.

Digital Norm-Referenced and Co-normed Testing

Norm-referenced tests evaluate an individual's performance by comparing it to that of a defined reference group. For the NIH Toolbox, this group consists of a representative sample of community-dwelling adults and children from across the United States (as described herewith). While the value of co-norming, especially in fixed batteries, has been supported by some experts for enhancing cross-test comparability (e.g., Russell, 2004), others have questioned its necessity (Rohling et al., 2015). To that end, the NIH Toolbox accommodates both fixed and flexible testing formats. Examiners can administer the standard core battery in each domain or customize assessments by selecting individual tests across domains, with all options benefiting from co-norming.

Item Response Theory and Computerized Adaptive Testing in the NIH Toolbox

A key strength of the NIH Toolbox lies in its efficiency, with most tests completed in five minutes or less. This is largely due to the integration of IRT and CAT (Cella et al., 2007). In fact, the NIH Toolbox was among the first neurobehavioral assessment tools to utilize these advanced psychometric approaches.

To use IRT, the trait being measured must vary along a continuum (i.e., one can possess more or less of it), and test items must vary in difficulty along that continuum. This setup allows individuals to be accurately placed based on their level of the trait. Developing a CAT requires assembling a large pool of potential items. These items undergo rigorous evaluation and calibration to determine their measurement properties. In the NIH

Toolbox's development, over 16,000 individuals completed early versions of items assessing cognition (e.g., vocabulary and reading), emotion, and vision. Only items that met strict quality standards, such as showing no gender-based bias, were retained in the final item banks.

When a CAT test is administered to an examinee, the test algorithms select items from the item bank to estimate the individual's ability level. The CAT algorithm uses preset rules, such as starting difficulty, test length, precision thresholds, and how much item difficulty can change between questions (Gershon, 2005; Gershon et al., 2003). For example, when administering the NIH Toolbox Picture Vocabulary test to an adult, the first item is chosen based on the person's education level. If they respond correctly, the next item is harder; if not, an easier one is given. The test continues until the result reaches the desired level of precision. On average, about 22 items are needed to achieve a standard error of 0.75 or lower.

VERSION 2 (V2) DEVELOPMENT

To improve mobility and simplify test administration, in 2015, the NIH Toolbox was relaunched as an iPad app. As part of this relaunch, an equivalency study was conducted, and scoring algorithms in the V2 iPad app were updated for several timed cognitive assessments to account for device-specific differences. The normative data provided in Casaletto et al. (2015) became the gold standard. Users who wanted to continue using the V1 (the web version) were informed that the normative data was updated but not integrated on the web platform; V1 web users interested in the updated norms needed to apply formulas manually or use the Python Norming Program. Then-current NIH Toolbox V2 users and future users were encouraged to begin new studies or data collection on the iPad only (i.e., not the web version), as the V2 iPad app was updated with the new normative formulas, and old data collected in the V2 app was automatically rescored with the new formulas when that data was reexported. Those interested in using both the V1 web version and the V2 iPad app version were alerted to some score discrepancies that were identified for some tests, and formulas were provided so users could utilize the Python Norming Program to rescore the data and align the scores with the V2 iPad app version.

Rapid Reference 1.4

When the decision was being made to select a more portable device, one of the reasons Apple's iPad was selected was that Apple had a more tightly controlled "ecosystem." For example, developers had fewer device variations and operating system versions to account for, making it easier to ensure compatibility and consistent performance across Apple devices.

Cognition Domain Access, Use, and Structure

While the NIH Toolbox assessments are examiner-administered (versus self-administered), the degree of examiner involvement varies. For instance, in the Cognition domain, the List Sorting Working Memory test relies on the examiner to judge the accuracy of an examinee's spoken response. The examiner, using an external keyboard, scores and records the examinee's response. In contrast, the Picture Vocabulary test is automated, administered, and scored by the app with minimal examiner input.

The Cognition domain offers recommended core batteries tailored to the participant's age, recognizing that not all assessments are suitable for young children. Examiners have the flexibility to administer individual tests, design custom batteries across domains, or use the preset/preconfigured core Cognition battery. All test data is scored and saved directly on the iPad used for administration. This means examinee data does not need to be uploaded or transferred elsewhere, as it is scored locally on the iPad. Examiners can optionally export score reports or raw data files (i.e., CSV spreadsheets) and can even print score reports directly from the app, if desired.

Access to the NIH Toolbox Cognition Battery requires completion of a credential verification process, in alignment with professional guidelines outlined in the *Standards for Educational and Psychological Testing* (American Educational Research Association et al., 2014). These standards emphasize that test users must demonstrate appropriate levels of training, knowledge, and experience to ensure ethical and accurate use of psychological assessments.

In accordance with these principles, NIH Toolbox Cognition tests are classified as *Level C* measures, which is the highest classification level used in test security protocols (APA, 2002). As a comparison, this is the same level of credential requirements that the Wechsler Intelligence Scales (Wechsler, 2008) would require. Level C assessments require users to possess a doctoral degree in psychology, education, or a closely related field, or to hold current state licensure or national certification to practice independently in a relevant professional capacity. Furthermore, users must have formal training in the administration, scoring, and interpretation of standardized assessments. Individuals who do not meet these qualifications must be supervised by a qualified professional to ensure test integrity and ethical standards are upheld.

Restricting access to these assessments also serves to protect the validity and reliability of the measures by preventing overexposure of test content. Exposure to specific test items or procedures may lead examinees to respond in a way that undermines the purpose of the test, such as exaggerating impairments to appear impaired or rehearsing responses to inflate apparent ability (Ben-Porath, 2012). This concern is especially relevant in neuropsychological and high-stakes assessments, where test preparation or prior knowledge can significantly alter outcomes (Bush et al., 2005).

In V2, the Cognition Battery included seven core tests, which contribute to the calculation of three composite scores for individuals aged 7–85: *Total Cognition Composite*, *Fluid Cognition Composite*, and *Crystallized Cognition Composite*.

For younger participants aged 3–6 years, the *Early Childhood Cognition Composite* is provided as a developmentally appropriate alternative to the Total Cognition Composite. All individual tests and composite scores are norm-referenced.

Rapid Reference 1.5

A composite score comprises two or more tests. It is a summary score.

A complete listing of the V2 Cognition tests and composites is provided in Table 1.2.

Version 2 Scoring and Normative Considerations

The NIH Toolbox Cognition Battery V2 generated a comprehensive set of scores at both the individual test and composite level scores, which included raw scores (or ability estimates, such as theta scores for CAT-administered tests), uncorrected standardized scores, age-corrected standardized scores, and fully demographically adjusted T-scores.

Table 1.2 Version 2 NIH Toolbox Cognition Tests by Age and Subdomain

			Normed Composite Scores			
Test Name	Subdomain	Ages	Early Childhood (3–6 years)	Fluid (7+ years)	Crystallized (7+ years)	Total (7+ years)
Dimensional Change Card Sort	Executive function	3–85	X	X		X
Flanker Inhibitory Control and Attention	Attention and executive function	3–85	X	X		X
List Sorting Working Memory	Working memory	7–85		X		X
Pattern Comparison	Processing speed	7–85		X		X
Picture Sequence Memory	Episodic memory	3–85	X	X		X
Picture Vocabulary	Receptive language	3–85	X		X	X
Oral Reading Recognition	Expressive language	3–85			X	X
Auditory Verbal Learning (Rey)	Immediate recall	8–85	Supplemental tests Only raw scores available			
Oral Symbol Digit	Processing speed	8–85				

The demographic correction model accounts for age, sex assigned at birth, educational attainment (or maternal education for participants under 18), and self-identified race/ethnicity (Gershon et al., 2013). To produce valid norm-referenced composite scores, all contributing subtests for a given composite must be administered in their entirety.

At the test level and the composite level, examiners receive raw scores (or thetas for CAT-administered tests), uncorrected standardized scores, age-corrected standardized scores, and a fully demographically corrected T-score (including sex assigned at birth, age, education [or mother's level of education for examinees below 18 years], and ethnicity). To obtain norm-referenced composite scores, all tests that comprise that composite must be administered.

In V2, the uncorrected standard scores compared the examinee's response to everyone in the normative sample (i.e., almost 5,000 people aged 3–85 years). The advantage of the standard score, compared to a raw score, is that it provides a common metric and distribution, allowing for comparison across any of the NIH Toolbox tests. When selecting scores, the uncorrected standard score would be most useful in a longitudinal study to track change over the lifespan or comparisons with a matched control group. However, a disadvantage of the uncorrected standard score is that it can be difficult to determine whether scores are unusual for an individual or group; it may even be difficult to understand whether a change over time was greater than or less than expected.

Rapid Reference 1.6

Standard scores have a mean of 100 and a standard deviation of 15.

The age-corrected standard scores reflect the level of a characteristic the examinee had compared to others in that age band. These scores can be useful in showing the measure of a characteristic in relation to the examinee's age. They can be used to interpret the change over time expected for that age group. For example, one might expect that a typically developing child would acquire a larger volume of vocabulary words over a five-year period than a typical adult. So, in this example, the age-corrected score for this child on the Picture Vocabulary test would likely show a greater change over time for an adult. One disadvantage of age-corrected standard scores is that they do not consider other characteristics of community-dwelling individuals that could affect cognitive ability, such as education. For instance, two 30-year-old adults who took the Picture Vocabulary test; one got a high-average score on a Picture Vocabulary test, and the other had a low-average age-corrected standard score. One may theorize a

CAUTION 1.1

Remember that when reviewing an age-corrected standard score, the examiner should understand what the age band is. For example, a child may be part of a 1-year normative age band versus an adult who could be part of a 10-year normative age band.

biological cause for this difference when it could be that the high-average scorer has a doctorate in English, while the latter had only completed some high school.

In version 2, the fully demographically corrected *T*-score was based on age, education (parent education for children), sex at birth, and ethnicity, and it is useful in detecting changes or acquired impairments due to medical conditions. It also allows for a judgment to be made as to whether the resulting score is unusual for an individual. However, this score is a poor estimate of the absolute level of a characteristic being measured. Please note that some researchers and clinicians do not believe that ethnicity should be used in score calculation, suggesting that any ethnic differences are more likely due to socioeconomic differences (Gasquoine, 2009; Rea-Sandin et al., 2021).

Rapid Reference 1.7

A T-score has a mean of 50 and a standard deviation of 10.

Theoretical Framework

The development of the cognition tests was anchored in the Cattell-Horn-Carroll (CHC) theory of cognitive abilities, one of the most empirically supported frameworks in modern psychometrics (Neisser et al., 1996; Schneider & McGrew, 2018). This model conceptualizes intelligence as a hierarchical structure, where general cognitive ability (g) is subdivided into broad abilities, most notably fluid and crystallized intelligence.

Fluid cognition refers to the capacity for problem-solving, reasoning, and novel information processing. These skills tend to decline with age and are sensitive to neurological insult (Horn & Cattell, 1967). In the NIH Toolbox, fluid cognition is assessed using five tests: Dimensional Change Card Sort, Flanker Inhibitory Control and Attention, List Sorting Working Memory, Pattern Comparison Processing Speed, and Picture Sequence Memory.

In contrast, crystallized cognition encompasses accumulated knowledge and verbal abilities—skills that are more stable over the lifespan and often used to estimate premorbid functioning (Lezak et al., 2012). There are two NIH Toolbox tests in this area, which include Oral Reading Recognition (ORR) and Picture Vocabulary (PV).

Factor Structure and Construct Validity

The internal structure of the V2 Cognition Battery has been validated through multiple factor analytic studies across both normative and clinical populations. Initial studies by Mungas et al. (2013) established the construct validity of the test battery in healthy children and adults. Among children aged 3–7 years, a three-factor structure—vocabulary, reading, and fluid abilities—was supported. For older children (aged 8–15), a five-factor model emerged, encompassing vocabulary, reading, episodic memory, working memory, and executive functioning/processing speed. These findings were consistent with the intended constructs and aligned with CHC theory. In adults (aged 20–85), these researchers found support for a similar five-factor model that included reading, vocabulary, episodic memory, working memory, and executive functioning/processing speed (Mungas et al., 2014).

Moreover, studies in clinical populations have reinforced these findings. For example, Tulsky et al. (2017) confirmed the five-factor model in individuals with acquired brain injuries, including traumatic brain injury (TBI) and stroke, showing robustness of the factor structure in the presence of neurological conditions. In addition, Ma et al. (2020) evaluated the structure of the V2 Cognition Battery in a sample ranging from cognitively intact older adults to those with mild cognitive impairment and dementia. Their findings supported a two-factor model distinguishing fluid and crystallized cognition, in line with the CHC framework, and demonstrated good construct validity across clinical severity levels.

Fluid Cognitive Abilities

The NIH Toolbox Cognition Battery evaluates fluid cognition through five core tests: Dimensional Change Card Sort (DCCS), Flanker Inhibitory Control and Attention (Flanker), List Sorting Working Memory (LSWM), Pattern Comparison Processing Speed Test (PC), and Picture Sequence Memory (PSM). Each test was designed to assess foundational constructs of fluid intelligence, including attention, executive functioning, episodic memory, working memory, and processing speed. These constructs are integral to daily cognitive function and are sensitive to developmental and neurodegenerative changes across the lifespan (Carlozzi et al., 2015; Zelazo et al., 2014).

Attention

Attention, a critical cognitive construct, supports numerous higher-order functions, including learning, memory, and executive processes. The Flanker task, adapted from Eriksen and Eriksen (1974), measures selective attention and inhibitory control. Examinees determine the direction of a central stimulus flanked by congruent or incongruent distractors. This adaptation is based on the Attention Network Test and has demonstrated robust psychometric properties in both child and adult populations (Fan et al., 2002; Rueda et al., 2004). Visual and auditory cues enhance task comprehension for younger children. Performance is evaluated based on accuracy and reaction time, and the test typically requires under three minutes to administer.

Executive Function

Executive functions enable goal-directed behavior, including planning, shifting between tasks, and inhibiting inappropriate responses. The DCCS, originally derived from Luria's rule-use paradigms (Frye et al., 1995), assesses cognitive flexibility. Participants match stimuli based on changing rules (i.e., color or shape), simulating real-life task-switching demands. For young children, the task is scaffolded with additional visual and auditory cues. Zelazo et al. (2014) demonstrated convergent validity of the Flanker and DCCS tests with the D-KEFS Color-Word Interference subtest and found strong discriminant validity relative to vocabulary assessments.

Episodic Memory

Episodic memory refers to the ability to recall information tied to a specific context or experience and is vulnerable to decline from age or neurological injury (Squire, 2004). The PSM test uniquely evaluates visual episodic memory across a broad age range using culturally neutral image sequences. Performance is based on the participant's ability to recall and reproduce the correct sequence of thematically linked pictures. Bauer et al. (2013) highlighted the relevance of medial temporal structures in episodic memory, and validation studies (e.g., Carlozzi et al., 2015) showed strong correlations with standard episodic memory tasks such as the Rey Auditory Verbal Learning Test.

Working Memory

Working memory supports short-term storage and manipulation of information and is essential for reasoning, comprehension, and learning (Baddeley, 2003). The LSWM test presents visual stimuli (e.g., animals and foods) and asks participants to reorder them based on a size hierarchy. Difficulty increases as list lengths expand and as additional stimulus categories are introduced. Convergent validity has been established with traditional measures such as WAIS-IV Letter Number Sequencing and the PASAT (Tulsky et al., 2014). Research confirms that working memory capacity increases significantly from early childhood through adulthood (Alloway et al., 2006; Dempster, 1981).

Processing Speed

Processing speed is the rate at which individuals perceive, interpret, and respond to stimuli. It is sensitive to neurological dysfunction and aging (Coyle et al., 2011). The PC task requires participants to quickly judge whether two visual stimuli are identical, providing a simple but effective index of cognitive speed. The test, validated by Carlozzi et al. (2015), showed strong convergence with the WAIS-IV Processing Speed Index and demonstrated expected age-related performance declines.

Crystallized Cognitive Abilities

Crystallized cognition encompasses language-based knowledge and skills acquired through experience, which are assessed by two tests—Oral Reading Recognition (ORR) and Picture Vocabulary (PV). These measures assess expressive and receptive language, respectively, using IRT-calibrated item banks and CAT to enhance efficiency and precision (Gershon et al., 2014).

Expressive Language

Reading and expressive language are measured through ORR, which is a test of single-word reading ability. Word selection was based on psycholinguistic properties such as frequency and phonological complexity (Gershon et al., 2014). Validation research demonstrated high correlations with the WRAT-4 Reading subtest and low correlations with nonlanguage cognitive tasks, supporting the test's construct specificity.

Receptive Language

Receptive language involves the comprehension of structured verbal information. PV assesses receptive vocabulary by presenting a spoken word and requiring the participant to select the corresponding image from four pictured options. Items are carefully constructed based on linguistic difficulty, translatability, and age appropriateness (Dale & O'Rourke, 1976; Gershon, 1988). Distractors vary in semantic and phonemic similarity to ensure a range of difficulty. Validity studies confirmed strong correlations with the PPVT-4 and low correlations with unrelated measures, such as visuospatial memory (Gershon et al., 2014).

VERSION 3 (V3) DEVELOPMENT

The NIH Toolbox Version 3 iPad app was released in 2023 to researchers and clinicians. Compared to V2, the updated V3 app provides users with improved UI and UX capabilities, user-friendly administration features, streamlined test instructions, and updated scoring algorithms.

The NIH Toolbox initiated a normative update beginning in 2021 to enhance population representativeness of the normative sample in response to the 2020 US Census data (US Census Bureau, 2021). The V3 app includes the integration of an additional composite score and several new measures, including delayed recall tasks, a visual reasoning (VR) measure, and a processing speed test adapted for young children. Previously unnormed supplementary tests, such as the Oral Symbol Digit and Auditory Verbal Learning Test (AVLT), were normed and included in the updated Cognition domain.

Overview: Renorming V3 Cognition Tests

As part of the comprehensive update to the Cognition domain, the team prioritized renorming to address changes in cognitive performance across generations—an effect widely known as the Flynn effect. This gradual rise in average cognitive test scores over time is thought to result from improvements in factors such as education, healthcare, and environmental stimulation. Without updated norms, test scores can become misaligned with current population benchmarks, leading to overestimated or inaccurate interpretations. Moreover, transitioning from different modes of administration may introduce differences in UX that could affect performance. In keeping with the *Standards for Educational and Psychological Testing* (AERA et al., 2014), test publishers are expected to update normative data regularly to maintain the accuracy and relevance of score interpretations as populations and testing conditions evolve.

The NIH Toolbox V3 Cognition domain norming study was conducted between June and September 2021, involving a nationally representative sample of 3,956 participants.

This included 2,248 children aged 3–17 and 1,708 adults aged 18–90 and older. The primary objectives of the study were to:

- Expand the Cognition domain by introducing new tests to enhance construct coverage;
- Revise existing measures to address user-identified concerns related to floor and ceiling effects, as well as age-specific reliability;
- Update normative data to better reflect the current US population in terms of sex assigned at birth, race, ethnicity, and education;
- Implement continuous norming procedures to reduce limitations associated with broad age-group "binning;"
- Recalibrate as many tests as possible using a unified, IRT-based change-sensitive score (CSS) metric to improve sensitivity to developmental and clinical change over time.

The norming study was conducted in collaboration with a private market research firm under the supervision of researchers at Northwestern University. Data collection took place at 12 sites across all four US census regions, ensuring national representation by including at least one location per census division.

The market research firm was responsible for hiring and training examiners, recruiting participants, and conducting assessments in their office facilities. A "train-the-trainer" model was used: Northwestern University staff conducted a five-day in-person training with lead trainers, who were then certified through video-recorded practice sessions. These certified trainers went on to train and certify local examiners at each testing site.

Examiners collecting external validity data received additional training in administering both the NIH Toolbox and standardized measures available through Pearson's Q-Interactive platform. Prior experience with Q-Interactive was required, and a refresher session was provided by Northwestern University staff.

Participants were recruited from the firm's national database via phone and email, based on demographic quotas specified by Northwestern University. These quotas ensured that the sample reflected the US population in terms of age, sex assigned at birth, race, ethnicity, and education (or parent education for children). All testing was conducted in controlled office environments across the participating sites (Table 1.3).

Updates to the V3 App

Although the primary objectives of NIH Toolbox V3 were to streamline the Cognition tests and collect new normative data, the NIH Toolbox team embraced the opportunity to improve the tests and the platform overall.

To this end, the platform underwent a full restructure of the examiner interface, with more efficient workflows and a new sidebar that allows examiners to quickly and easily navigate the main sections of the V3 app. See Figure 1.1.

Table 1.3 Version 3 NIH Toolbox Cognitive Tests by Age and Subdomain

Test Name	Subdomain	Ages	Normed Composite Scores				
			Early Childhood CFPS (3–6 years)[a]	Early Childhood (4–6 years)	Crystallized (7+ years)	Fluid (7+ years)	Total (7+ years)
Dimensional Change Card Sort	Executive function	4–85		X		X	X
Flanker Inhibitory Control and Attention	Attention and executive function	4–85		X		X	X
List Sorting Working Memory	Working memory	5–85				X	X
Pattern Comparison	Processing speed	5–85				X	X
Picture Sequence Memory[a]	Episodic memory	3–85		X		X	X
Picture Vocabulary	Language	3–85	X	X	X		X
Oral Reading Recognition	Language	7–85			X		X
Speeded Matching[a]	Processing speed	3–6	X	X			
Visual Reasoning[a]	Executive function	3–85	X				
Face Name Associative Memory Exam[b]	Associative and Delayed Memory	18–85					
Rey Auditory Verbal Learning[b]	Immediate Recall and Delayed Memory	5–85	Not currently included in a composite				
Oral Symbol Digit[b]	Processing Speed	5–85					

[a] Tests or composites that were newly added or had a significant update in V3.

[b] Tests that were normed in V3, but were not previously normed.

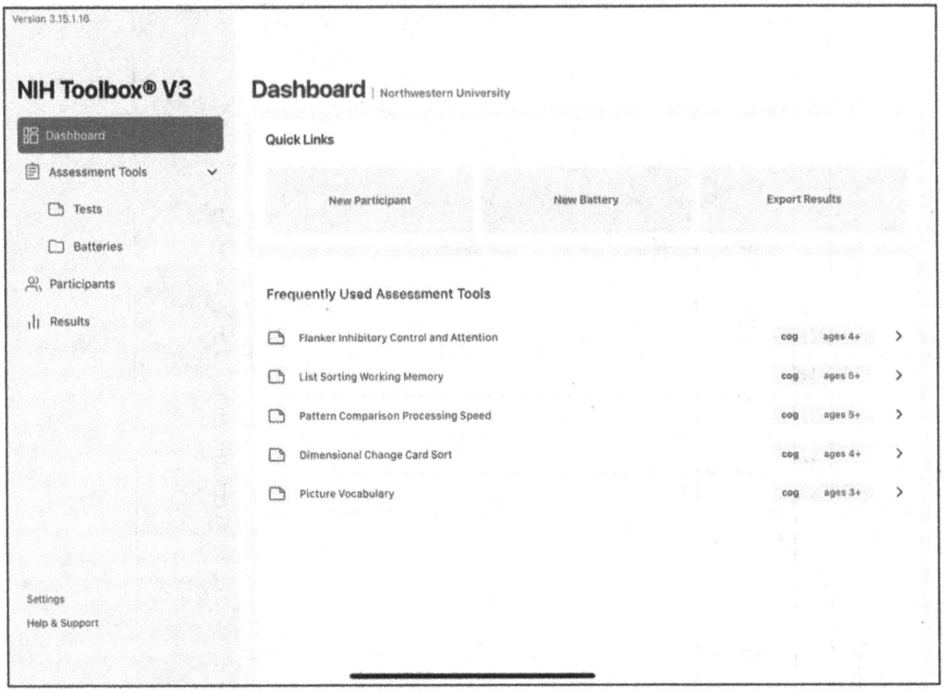

Figure 1.1 NIH Toolbox V3 Examiner Interface. Source: From NIH Toolbox V3. Copyright 2025 Toolbox Assessments, Inc. Reproduced with permission from NIH Toolbox V3/ Toolbox Assessments, Inc.

Additional features were added to the examiner interface to make the selection of tests easier, such as the addition of test cards (i.e., an expandable box/card describing the test). Also, outside materials or equipment needed to properly administer the tests are identified in multiple places to ensure examiners can prepare before seeing the examinee.

In addition to the examiner interface, the instructions and workflows of the Cognition tests were streamlined. These changes were tested in a pilot study and were revised as needed to support the psychometric quality of the Cognition tests. After the test workflows were updated, the NIH Toolbox team evaluated and updated the UX for a more consistent administration experience across tests.

- V3 test names were shortened by removing "NIH Toolbox," "Test," and the age (except for tests that have age-specific versions). For instance, the V2 test name "NIH Toolbox Oral Reading Recognition Test Age 3+" was renamed "Oral Reading Recognition" in V3.
- When psychometrically justifiable, multiple test versions were evaluated, streamlined, and merged into one version for all relevant ages (e.g., the three age-specific versions of Dimensional Change Card Sort in V2 are now one DCCS test that is appropriate for ages 4+).

- Instructions were updated to be clearer and easily understandable, even to the youngest examinees. Instructions, which were sometimes printed on the screen, sometimes played via prerecorded audio, and sometimes read aloud by the examiner, are now presented as text on the screen and played via prerecorded audio (with a few exceptions for unique administration procedures). Presenting the instructions via the test's audio additionally bolsters a uniform examinee experience.

When administering NIH Toolbox V3 tests, a title screen appears before that test's first instruction screen. V3 title screens introduced colored banners to indicate that test's domain (e.g., all Cognition tests have a red banner), as well as icons to indicate if/what additional materials or equipment is required to administer that test. This is a helpful reminder for examiners to arrange the equipment as needed prior to beginning that test.

The test interface itself has been made consistent where possible, including one background color and text in the same font and size across all tests. "Next," "Play again," and "Back" buttons were added where appropriate to help the examiner navigate each test. The "Touch and hold to continue" button was changed to "Slide to continue." The administrator's gesture, which is used during test administration to pause the test, was changed to address user feedback that V2 examinees, on occasion, accidentally performed the administrator's gesture when responding to live items.

Updates to the V3 Cognition Tests

For the V3 Cognition tests, there were updates and changes made to the existing tests from V2 to improve the workflows and psychometric properties. A listing of each test follows.

Dimensional Change Card Sort (DCCS)

DCCS measures executive functioning. Examinees are shown two cards and are asked to select the one that is either the same shape or the same color as the card in the middle of the screen.

In NIH Toolbox V2, DCCS had three separate age-specific tests (NIH Toolbox Dimensional Change Card Sort Test Ages 3–7, NIH Toolbox Dimensional Change Card Sort Test Ages 8–11, and NIH Toolbox Dimensional Change Card Sort Test Age 12+), which were restructured into a single Dimensional Change Card Sort test that is appropriate for ages 4+. The instructions and routing workflows were simplified so that all examinees, regardless of age, see the same instructions, navigate the same pre-switch and post-switch items, and take the same live items. According to LaForte et al. (2024), the V3 pilot study collected data down to 36 months of age, and it was found that many of the three-year-olds' response accuracy was at chance or lower, thus justifying the lower recommended age limit to change from three to four years and the removal of the V2 experimental downward extensions of DCCS.

The test images were redrawn to update the look and feel, but the content itself remained the same (i.e., balls and trucks). When needed, image colors were changed to avoid any issues for examinees with colorblindness. For example, the blue and yellow images were changed to blue and orange to address blue-yellow colorblindness.

Rapid Reference 1.8

Color blindness is the inability to differentiate certain colors. In the United States, red-green is the most common color blindness, followed by blue-yellow.

The DCCS test was also updated so that the target dimension is now presented visually in the middle of the screen and via audio (e.g., the audio says the word "Shape," while "SHAPE" is displayed as text on the screen). The star previously presented in the middle of the screen for V2 was removed. In addition, "Home Base"—a piece of paper with a small circle on it that was placed in front of the iPad for V2 DCCS—was removed and is no longer used in V3.

To improve the usability of the tests, user feedback was also incorporated into the V3 redesign. One example of this incorporation was offering a further drill-down of performance scores on timed tests. Although this information was available in V2, it was not easily accessible, as the examiner would need to export a data file from the app, import that data into another database, and then calculate these scores. To make this more user-friendly in V3 for applicable tests, such as the DCCS, new process scores were added to the score report at the test level. These scores include:

- median response time per item,
- commission errors (i.e., number of incorrect responses on live items), and
- omission errors (i.e., number of items on which the examinee does not respond/times out).

Face Name Associative Memory Exam (FNAME)

FNAME is an assessment of delayed visual and associative memory. FNAME and FNAME Delay were marked as experimental measures in V2, were not included in the Cognition domain, and only offered raw scores. In V3, FNAME and FNAME Delay are supplemental tests in the Cognition domain and produce normative scores derived from the NIH Toolbox V3 norming sample, as well as process scores for each of the FNAME Delay sections (i.e., Faces Seen Before, First Name Letter, and Face-Name Matching).

FNAME assesses a person's ability to learn and recall the association between unfamiliar faces and names—an ecologically valid and cognitively demanding task that heavily relies on the integrity of the medial temporal lobes, especially the hippocampus (Rentz et al., 2011). This memory test has two parts. The first is the learning trial, in which the

CAUTION 1.2

Even though FNAME is one test, in the NIH Toolbox V3 app, the FNAME test will appear as if it is two separate (but associated) tests: FNAME and FNAME Delay. This was done in order to allow the examiner to add the learning trial first and then add the delayed recall portion of the test later in the assessment.

examinee is presented with 12 pictures of faces paired with names, one at a time. After a 5- to 25-minute delay, FNAME Delay asks examinees about those face-name pairs to test their memory of the prior learning trial.

From V2 to V3, other changes to the FNAME tests included an overall UI update to make it consistent with the other Cognition tests. Instructions and workflows were streamlined. The response options for FNAME were also changed from "Fits" and "Doesn't Fit" (as in, does this name "fit" the face in the picture?) to "Easy" or "Hard" (as in, will it be easy or hard to remember the face-name pair?).

Flanker Inhibitory Control and Attention (Flanker)

Flanker is a test of executive function. This test shows five fish that point either left or right, and examinees must quickly and accurately tap the button (either right or left) that matches the way the fish in the middle is pointing.

The three age-specific versions of V2 Flanker (NIH Toolbox Flanker Inhibitory Control and Attention Test Ages 3–7, NIH Toolbox Flanker Inhibitory Control and Attention Test Ages 8–11, and NIH Toolbox Flanker Inhibitory Control and Attention Test Age 12+) were combined into one V3 Flanker Inhibitory Control and Attention test. Streamlined instructions and routing workflows allow examinees aged 4 and older to take the same version of the test, with the same practice items and the same live items. LaForte et al. (2024) found that many three-year-olds in the V3 pilot study exhibited an at-chance or lower response accuracy, thus justifying the lower recommended age limit to change from 3 to 4 and the removal of the V2 experimental downward extension of Flanker.

Depending on which version of Flanker V2 examinees took, they either saw pictures of fish, black arrows, or both; V3 streamlined this so that all examinees see pictures of fish with black arrows over them. The number of live items increased from 20 to 30, with the first 20 items being identical to V2, and eight congruent (i.e., all five fish point the same way) and two incongruent (i.e., the middle fish points in the opposite direction) items were added. To make the test a bit less predictable, the delays between the fixation star and the live item were made variable (e.g., sometimes 0.3 second, sometimes 1.0 second; LaForte et al., 2024). V3 also implemented a time limit for live items; if there is no response within 10 seconds, the test automatically moves to the next item.

As with DCCS, the "Home Base"—a piece of paper with a small circle on it that was placed in front of the iPad for V2 Flanker—was eliminated and is no longer used in V3.

Similarly, based on user feedback, V3 Flanker introduced new process scores for congruent items [median response time per item and commission errors (i.e., number of congruent trials that are answered incorrectly)] and for incongruent items (i.e., median response time per item).

List Sorting Working Memory (LSWM)

LSWM is a measure of working memory. The first part (1-List) presents a series of foods or animals, then asks the examinee to say all of them back in size order, from smallest to biggest. The second part (2-List) presents lists of food and animals, which examinees must say back in size order, starting with the foods first, then the animals.

The two age-specific versions of LSWM in V2 (NIH Toolbox List Sorting Working Memory Test Ages 3–6 and NIH Toolbox List Sorting Working Memory Test 7+) were combined into one LSWM test. To facilitate a single version that is appropriate for examinees aged 5 and older, instructions were streamlined, workflows were reorganized, and age-based start points were introduced. Age-based start points paired with streamlined basal and ceiling rules help reduce administration time. As part of the streamlining of this test for inclusion in V3, the practice items were standardized, so regardless of age, everyone sees the same two practice items per List, and they have two attempts to answer each practice item correctly.

Rapid Reference 1.9

Basal and ceiling rules are standardized testing procedures used in psychological and educational assessments to determine starting and stopping points within a test, ensuring efficiency and accuracy in measuring an individual's abilities.

- Basal rule refers to the point at which it is assumed the test-taker would have answered all previous (easier) items correctly. Once a basal is established—typically by answering a set number of consecutive items correctly—the examiner can skip earlier items and credit them as correct, reducing unnecessary testing of clearly mastered content.
- Ceiling rule indicates the point at which it is assumed the test-taker would answer all subsequent (more difficult) items incorrectly. Once a ceiling is reached—often defined as a set number of consecutive incorrect responses—the examiner discontinues the subtest to prevent frustration and preserve time.

LSWM has two items at each sequence length (e.g., two items in 1-List that contain four pictures). In V2, answering the first item of each sequence length correctly moved the examinee immediately to the next sequence length; the second item of any sequence length was only administered if the first was answered incorrectly (e.g., answering the first three-picture item correctly moves to the four-picture item; an incorrect response moves to the second three-picture item). The V3 norming study showed that the difficulty often varied between the items of each sequence length, which suggested that administering both items of the sequence may improve the test's precision. This led to the change in V3 that, regardless of the examinee's response, both items of each sequence length are administered (LaForte et al., 2024).

A cross-cultural comprehensibility review was also done for the V3 update. As part of this review, two images were identified as not being easily recognized globally. Therefore, the Blueberry in V2 was replaced with Bean in V3, and the Pumpkin in V2 was replaced with Cake in V3. Notably, all images were redrawn in a uniform art style to ensure visual continuity throughout the test.

During the V2 redesign process, users reported that examinees were often unclear about when a list had ended. Some participants began responding before all the food or animal items had been presented, while others waited unnecessarily, expecting additional items. To resolve this issue in V3, a chime was added at the end of each list to clearly signal that the list is complete, and the participant may begin responding.

Oral Reading Recognition (ORR)

ORR measures reading decoding skills. Words are displayed as text on the iPad screen, one at a time, and the examinee must say the word aloud. The examiner manually scores the pronunciation as correct or incorrect by typing "1" or "0" on a wireless keyboard.

The ORR instructions underwent minor edits, and they are now presented as text on the screen and via prerecorded audio. ORR items were recalibrated, but the words themselves remain the same. The recommended age range for ORR was raised from ages 3+ to ages 7+.

As a CAT, the start points in V2 were changed from routing by age through 17 years to routing by age for examinees 7–18 years old; examinees 19 years and older are routed by education.

Oral Symbol Digit (OSD)

OSD measures processing speed without a manual motor component (i.e., only a verbal response is required). Examinees are given a two-sided, laminated "Oral Symbol Digit Examination Sheet." Side 1, used for practice, displays a grid pairing the numbers one through nine with corresponding symbols, along with a separate grid of unpaired symbols. Examinees use this side to become familiar with the task before starting the actual test. Side 2 contains the live test: a grid consisting of 13 rows, each with 11 symbols.

Rapid Reference 1.10

When examiners are approved for C-level access to Cognition tests via the NIH Toolbox website, the Oral Symbol Digit Examination Sheet will be available online for download.

OSD in V3 includes normed scores (unlike V2), and the age range was extended from ages 8 and older to ages 5 and older.

OSD administration differs from other Cognition tests; instead of seeing each item on the iPad screen, examinees look at the Oral Symbol Digit Examination Sheet for practice and live items. As a more hands-on test, instruction audio is not prerecorded for OSD. Instead, the examiner refers to the iPad screen for examiner-specific directions and instructions. Black text on the screen indicates instructions that the examiner should read aloud to the examinee (e.g., "Now you try the rest for practice. Say each number out loud so I can hear you."). Blue, italicized text represents examiner-specific notes or directions for the examiner (e.g., "Tap each word the participant says to mark it as correct.").

V2 had 144 items, with 18 symbols per row across 8 rows, which did not align with the examiner's view of 9 items across each row in the app. Unless the examiner was closely following the examinee, and the examinee made very few mistakes, it could be difficult for V2 examiners to track examinees' progress and accurately report which items were correct versus incorrect. V3 addressed the misalignment of items by having the same 11 by 13 grid on the OSD Examination Sheet and the examiner's view in the app. This equivalency makes it much easier for V3 examiners to follow along.

Pattern Comparison (PC)

PC is a test of processing speed. In this timed test, examinees are shown two pictures at a time and must quickly tap the "Yes" button if the two images are the same or tap "No" if the two pictures are not the same.

For V2, the two age-specific versions of PC (NIH Toolbox Pattern Comparison Processing Speed Test Ages 3–6 and NIH Toolbox Pattern Comparison Processing Speed Test Age 7+) were restructured into one PC test. The smile and frown face buttons children aged 3–6 used in V2 were replaced, and in V3, all PC examinees have "Yes" and "No" response buttons. Instructions were streamlined and are read by prerecorded audio in V3. Further, the V3 pilot study indicated that the youngest examinees did not perform better than chance, so the age range for PC in V3 is ages five and older. For a replacement processing speed test for younger children, please refer to the Speeded Matching test.

To ensure that the PC test remains a pure measure of processing speed (minimizing the influence of other cognitive abilities such as memory, language, or executive function), the test was carefully redesigned with simplicity and clarity in mind. Specifically, the visual items were redrawn and enhanced in both quality and resolution to make it quicker and easier for examinees to determine whether two images are the same or different (LaForte et al., 2024). This refinement reduces perceptual ambiguity and cognitive load, allowing the task to focus solely on rapid visual discrimination. Importantly, while the artwork was improved for visual clarity, the underlying item content remained consistent across versions (e.g., a tree in V2 remains a tree in V3), ensuring continuity in test structure while optimizing ease of use. This design principle reflects the broader goal of a processing speed task: to assess how quickly individuals can perform simple, automatic decisions without engaging (or at least minimizing the engagement of) higher-level reasoning or interpretation.

The audio prompt preceding each practice item was shortened in V3 to a concise and direct question: "Are these the same?" In V2, the practice phase included seven items for examinees aged 3–6 and six items for those aged 7 and older. A discontinue rule was applied, whereby examinees who responded incorrectly to two trials on two separate items did not proceed to the live test. In V3, this structure was streamlined: all examinees, regardless of age, complete the same three practice items, with up to two attempts permitted for each. Importantly, the discontinue rule was eliminated—regardless of performance on the practice items, all examinees proceed to the live items.

Three of the practice items removed in V3 were incorporated into the live item pool, increasing the total number of test items from 130 in V2 to 133 in V3. Additionally, the time limit for the test was reduced from 85 seconds in V2 to 80 seconds in V3.

Scoring procedures were also updated: the examinee's dominant hand no longer influences scoring. A new process score was introduced in V3, capturing the median response time per item to provide a more nuanced index of processing speed.

Picture Sequence Memory (PSM)

PSM is a computerized measure of episodic memory, designed to assess the ability to learn and recall the temporal order of visual information. During each trial, a sequence of images is presented one at a time in the center of the screen, accompanied by brief prerecorded phrases that describe the scenes. As each image is shown, it moves to a small box surrounding the display area. Once the full sequence has been presented, the images are scrambled and returned to the large center box. The examinee is then prompted to reconstruct the sequence by dragging the images back into their original order.

In V2, PSM included three forms (A, B, and C), each with four age-specific versions tailored for ages 3–4, 5–6, 7, and 8+, resulting in a total of 12 separate PSM tests. In V3, the structure was streamlined by collapsing the age-specific versions within each form. Consequently, each form now exists in a single version—Form A and Form B—while Form C was retired.

A primary enhancement in V3 was the automation of test routing to more closely align sequence difficulty with the examinee's developmental level. Routing is initially determined by the examinee's age, which assigns age-appropriate practice item(s) and an initial live test item. Subsequent routing is based on the examinee's adjacent-pairs score (i.e., the number of correctly ordered pairs in the sequence). For example, a four-year-old taking PSM Form A will view two practice items, followed by the Fair 6 item (a six-picture sequence with a fairground theme). Based on performance:

- An adjacent-pairs score of 0 leads to the Park 3 item (three-picture sequence) presented twice,
- An adjacent-pairs score of 1–3 results in a second administration of Fair 6, and
- An adjacent-pairs score of 4–5 advances the examinee to the Park 9 item (nine-picture sequence) presented twice.

Thus, the initial test item is determined by age, while the subsequent item(s) and sequence length are tailored to performance.

In V2, each form featured a unique thematic narrative—Form A (Park), Form B (Fair), and Form C (Farm). In V3, themes are standardized for routing purposes: Form A begins with the Fair theme, and Form B begins with the Park theme. The examinee's performance on the first item determines whether they continue with the same theme or transition to another. Forms are counterbalanced to ensure comparable difficulty levels across administrations.

Unlike other tests in the Cognition domain that rely on fixed response options, PSM is highly interactive, requiring examinees to tap and drag images into their chosen sequence order. In V2, training was examiner-led, involving scripted instructions and physical demonstrations. In V3, this training was standardized through animated instructional sequences with synchronized audio, which can be replayed as needed until the examinee demonstrates comfort with the task demands.

Additional refinements in V3 include streamlined audio instructions and a simplified post-shuffle prompt. Examinees aged 3–5 receive two practice items, while those aged 6 and older receive one practice item. Regardless of age, each practice item allows for two trials. If the examinee responds incorrectly on all trials of all practice items, the test is discontinued.

Picture Vocabulary (PV)

PV is a measure of receptive vocabulary, administered as a CAT. During each item, the examinee hears a target word through the iPad's speaker and is asked to select the image—among four options—that best represents the meaning of the word.

The word pool in V3 remains unchanged from V2, and most of the corresponding images were retained. However, several outdated visuals were updated with more contemporary images to enhance relevance and clarity. One item was removed due to ambiguity, as it contained two plausible correct responses. The child-directed audio prompt used in V2 (e.g., "Touch the picture of . . .") was eliminated in V3; live items now present only the target word, streamlining the task and reducing linguistic scaffolding.

All items were recalibrated in V3, and difficulty parameters were updated using refreshed response data. For examinees aged 18 years and younger, the test uses age to determine the starting item. For those aged 19 and older, routing is based on the examinee's education level—a slight revision from V2, which used education level for examinees 18 and older.

Rey Auditory Verbal Learning Test (RAVLT)

RAVLT assesses immediate verbal learning and recall. Examinees listen to a prerecorded list of 15 words and are then prompted to verbally recall as many words as they can remember. This process is repeated over three trials. The RAVLT Delay task, introduced in V3, measures delayed recall by asking the examinee to recall the same 15 words following a delay of 5–25 minutes.

Rapid Reference 1.11

Similar to the FNAME test, RAVLT appears as two separate (but related) tests in the V3 app—RAVLT as the learning trial and RAVLT Delay as the delayed recall trial. This was done to assist in administration flexibility when using the app, and this should be treated as one test.

Both RAVLT and RAVLT Delay now generate norm-referenced scores. Additionally, the age range for RAVLT was extended in V3 to include examinees as young as five years old (compared to ages 8 and older in V2), enhancing developmental coverage. RAVLT Delay in V3 produces normed scores for examinees aged 12 and older.

To improve task clarity, a chime was added at the end of each word list to indicate when examinees may begin responding. This change addresses prior feedback from V2, where participants occasionally responded prematurely or delayed their responses due to uncertainty about the list's completion.

In V2, responses were stored in a bitwise format, complicating data analysis. In V3, each word is scored individually as correct or incorrect for each trial, facilitating cleaner item-level data analysis.

Speeded Matching (SM)

SM is a test of processing speed for children aged 3–6 years, in which examinees view a target image centered on the screen and must quickly identify which of the four comparison images matches the target.

In V2, SM was considered experimental and was not formally included in the Cognition domain. In V3, SM was fully integrated into the Cognition domain and contributes to two composite scores: the Early Childhood Cognition Composite and the Early Childhood Cognition—Crystallized-Fluid-Processing Speed—Composite. The test now generates normed scores as well as a median response time metric.

Several updates were made to enhance usability and scoring. Entry of the examinee's dominant hand is no longer required for administration. Instructions are now delivered via audio, with only minor modifications to wording. The practice item fail rule was revised: the test now discontinues after eight incorrect responses to practice items, up from four in V2. Additionally, the response window for live items was reduced from 120 seconds to 90 seconds, reflecting a more efficient design aligned with the test's focus on speed.

Visual Reasoning (VR)

VR is a newly introduced measure in V3 that assesses executive functioning and nonverbal reasoning. Examinees aged 3 and older are shown a visual stimulus in the center of the screen and asked to select from multiple choices the image that best completes or corresponds to it. Item formats vary and may include selecting the missing piece in a matrix, completing a visual sequence, or choosing the most similar image.

VR was developed specifically for V3 to expand the Cognition domain's coverage of higher-order cognitive processes, particularly in reasoning and problem-solving. For the youngest examinees aged 3–6, VR is included in the Early Childhood Cognition Battery—Crystallized-Fluid-Processing Speed (CFPS).

Updates to V3 Cognition Test-Level and Composite-Level Scores

Whether used in education, clinical, or research settings, score selection should be guided by the assessment's intended purpose. Many of the scores and composites used in V2 were pulled forward into V3, though there were also some changes that are reviewed here.

Like in V2, the V3 raw scores can differ in scale and distribution and may reflect computed values or be derived from IRT models rather than simple tallies. One key advantage of raw scores is that they closely reflect the examinee's observed performance, making them potentially useful for tracking change over time. However, raw scores are limited in that they do not allow for straightforward comparisons across different NIH Toolbox measures and can be challenging to interpret in isolation. Without a normative reference or benchmark, it is difficult to determine whether a raw score represents strong or weak performance.

The V3 age-adjusted standard scores indicate how an individual's performance compares to a nationally representative sample of peers within the same age group, based on 2020 US Census benchmarks (US Census Bureau, 2021). These scores provide valuable context by accounting for typical age-related expectations, making them especially useful for assessing developmental trends or tracking meaningful changes in performance over time.

In V3 Cognition, the fully corrected scores used in V2—which adjusted for age, sex, education, and race/ethnicity—were not retained. Instead, V3 Cognition provides age- and education-adjusted T-scores. The decision was made to focus on age and education, which remain two of the most robust predictors of cognitive performance and offer a more parsimonious yet meaningful basis for comparison across individuals. One drawback of the age- and education-adjusted T-score is that certain group-specific variations may not be fully captured, such as the impact of socioeconomic status, which is an important contextual factor known to influence cognitive outcomes.

The inclusion of a CSS is new to V3. The CSS is derived from IRT and is specifically designed to track meaningful changes in an individual's performance over time. Unlike traditional norm-referenced scores that compare an individual's performance to that of a demographic peer group, the CSS is calculated directly from the raw test performance and reflects change in the individual's underlying ability or trait. Because it is not adjusted relative to age or other demographic norms, the CSS provides a clearer picture of actual improvement or decline.

Norm-referenced scores may only reflect a person's rank within a group, whereas the CSS captures true within-person change, independent of group performance trends.

For example, an individual might demonstrate a four-point increase in their CSS over one year, from Time 1 to Time 2. However, if their reference peer group showed an average increase of five points during that same period, the individual's adjusted score at Time 2 would actually be lower relative to their peers—effectively obscuring their true individual improvement. This highlights the unique value of the CSS for monitoring personal growth, especially in developmental or intervention-based contexts. To maintain consistency across Cognition measures in the NIH Toolbox, the

CSS has a standardized reference point: a value of 500 corresponds to the median performance level of 10-year-olds from the norming sample. While not norm-referenced, this shared anchor supports interpretability across tests.

V3 COGNITION COMPOSITE SCORES

The V3 offers two composite scores geared toward younger children and three for older children through adulthood. These composite scores offer standard scores similar to the individual tests.

Early Childhood Cognition Battery—Crystallized-Fluid-Processing Speed (CFPS)

New to V3, the Early Childhood Cognition Battery—CFPS is tailored for children aged 3–6, with extended normative data available for up to age 8.5 years. This composite includes tests of executive function, processing speed, and language development:

- Picture Vocabulary
- Visual Reasoning
- Speeded Matching

Administering the complete set of live items across these assessments yields an Early Childhood Cognition CFPS Composite score, offering a concise measure of cognitive performance across these targeted domains.

Early Childhood Cognition Composite

The Early Childhood Cognition Composite is designed to be developmentally appropriate for children between the ages of 4 and 6. However, extended normative scores are available for children up to age 8.5. This composite evaluates core areas of early cognitive development, including attention, episodic memory, executive function, processing speed, and language. The following tests are included:

- Picture Vocabulary
- Flanker Inhibitory Control and Attention
- Dimensional Change Card Sort
- Picture Sequence Memory
- Speeded Matching

When all live items from each of these assessments are administered, an Early Childhood Composite score is generated, reflecting general cognitive functioning in this age group. Of note, the V2 Early Childhood Cognition Composite went down to age 3, but due to the streamlining and renorming of these tests, some of the start ages changed and were no longer determined to be appropriate for age 3.

Total Cognition Composite

The Total Cognition Composite is recommended for individuals aged 7 years and older, though it can be used with children as young as 6, generating extended normative data for that younger subset. This battery offers a broad assessment of cognitive functioning, covering domains such as attention, episodic memory, executive function, language, processing speed, and working memory.

The Total Cognition Composite comprises the Fluid and Crystallized Composites:

- Fluid Composite tests
  - Dimensional Change Card Sort
  - Flanker Inhibitory Control and Attention
  - List Sorting Working Memory
  - Pattern Comparison Processing Speed
  - Picture Sequence Memory
- Crystallized Composite tests
  - Oral Reading Recognition
  - Picture Vocabulary

Completion of all live items across the tests results in three composite scores—Fluid Cognition Composite, Crystallized Cognition Composite, and Total Cognition Composite—which provide a comprehensive profile of cognitive abilities.

V3 ACCESSIBILITY AND CROSS-CULTURE APPLICABILITY UPDATES

Keeping in line with the NIH Toolbox's core tenet of maximizing accessibility, the V3 updates were made with careful attention to reducing barriers across diverse users and settings. These updates reflect a continued commitment to inclusivity through clearer instructions, improved UIs, and refinements that support administration across varied age groups, educational backgrounds, and clinical populations.

Building on the V2 foundation, V3 placed a focus on accessibility and usability for both examiners and participants. Design and usability experts were consulted to ensure that both the examiner interface and participant-facing screens align as closely as possible with current accessibility standards. Particular attention was paid to the requirements outlined in Section 508 accessibility guidelines (Rehabilitation Act of 1973, 1998). Accessibility compliance levels—categorized as A, AA, or AAA—were considered throughout the design process. These standards were addressed through thoughtful design features such as consistent layout, appropriate contrast ratios, readable sizing, and proportional visual elements.

In the NIH Toolbox tests—particularly the DCCS, where color is one of the key matching dimensions—drawings were carefully evaluated for accessibility using color analysis tools. Colors were mapped onto a color wheel and reviewed to ensure that individuals with color vision deficiencies could still accurately distinguish between categories.

Special attention was given to avoiding color pairings that may be indistinguishable to those with red-green or blue-yellow color blindness. Adjustments to hue, saturation, and brightness were made as needed, and simulations were used to confirm that all examinees, regardless of color perception, could engage with the task as intended.

As part of the NIH Toolbox V3 development, some measures underwent expert cultural review to ensure greater sensitivity and relevance across diverse populations. Feedback from users and administrators was actively incorporated to enhance clarity, reduce cultural bias, and promote global usability. In addition, insights gained from current and prior translation efforts played a key role in shaping revisions to language, imagery, and instructional content, thus fostering broader cultural acceptance and supporting more equitable administration across varied linguistic and cultural contexts.

USE OF THE NIH TOOLBOX AND FUTURE DIRECTIONS

Since its introduction in 2012, the NIH Toolbox has become an increasingly valuable resource across a wide range of settings, including research, clinical practice, and education. Initially developed to support large-scale research studies, the NIH Toolbox has evolved into a versatile platform used in both applied and translational contexts. Its broad lifespan coverage—from early childhood through older adulthood—combined with brief administration times and digital delivery, makes it especially well-suited for diverse applications. For example, in educational environments, the Cognition tests have been used to monitor developmental trajectories and identify learning needs. In clinical settings, they support neuropsychological screening, intervention planning, and outcome tracking. In research, the NIH Toolbox has become a core component of numerous national and international studies such as the Human Connectome Project (Human Connectome Project, n.d.), the Adolescent Brain Cognitive Development (ABCD) Study® (Thompson et al., 2022; National Institutes of Health, 2015), and the Environmental Influences on Child Health Outcomes (ECHO) program (Blaisdell et al., 2022; Gillman & Blaisdell, 2018).

A recent scoping review by Fox et al. (2022) documented over 280 published studies using the NIH Toolbox in clinical populations. Among these, the Cognition Battery was the most frequently employed, appearing in about 80% of studies. Of these 225 studies that used the NIH Toolbox Cognition tests, half were focused on neurological disorders; however, clinical applications span psychiatric conditions, cancer, and other chronic diseases, with growing interest in populations with intellectual and developmental disabilities (Fox et al., 2022). This expansion is supported by targeted resources such as the *NIH Toolbox Version 3 Supplemental Administration Manual for Intellectual and Developmental Disabilities* (McKenzie et al., 2023). In addition to Cognition-focused studies, Fox et al. (2022) also identified 49 studies that referenced NIH Toolbox Emotion tests, 29 studies that used NIH Toolbox Motor tests, and 16 studies that utilized NIH Toolbox Sensation tests from 2008 to 2020. This shows that although Cognition testing is undeniably the primary focus of clinical testing when using the NIH Toolbox, tests in the Emotion,

Motor, and Sensation domains have also been utilized in nearly 100 other clinical studies alone in the meta-analysis of the Fox et al. (2022) review, further emphasizing the NIH Toolbox's relevance as a versatile platform for a wide array of uses.

As demand grows for scalable, reliable, and lifespan-sensitive measures, the NIH Toolbox is uniquely positioned to meet these needs. Its flexibility and scientific rigor make it a strong candidate for continued integration into clinical trials, educational practice, and health systems aiming to monitor cognitive and behavioral function over time. With each iteration, the NIH Toolbox continues to align with emerging priorities in neuropsychology, education, neuroscience, and personalized care—bridging gaps between research and practice in a rapidly changing landscape.

TEST YOURSELF

1. **Updates to the NIH Toolbox V3 Cognition domain prioritized renorming to address changes in cognitive performance across generations.**
   True or False
2. **Which of the following tests are new to NIH Toolbox V3?**
   (a) Flanker Inhibitory Control and Attention
   (b) Visual Reasoning
   (c) Picture Sequence Memory
   (d) Oral Reading Recognition
3. **The Crystallized Composite includes the Oral Reading Recognition and Visual Reasoning tests.**
   True or False
4. **Which of the following formats was NOT an objective for the new NIH Toolbox V3 app?**
   (a) Creating a test suite available on iPads, Android tablets, and computers
   (b) Improving the user interface and user experience
   (c) Updating test scoring and implementing new normative data
   (d) Streamlining the Cognition tests and updating their workflows
5. **When was NIH Toolbox V3 released?**
   (a) 2012
   (b) 2015
   (c) 2021
   (d) 2023
6. **What are the four domains in the NIH Toolbox?**
   (a) Cognition, Emotion, Intelligence, Motor
   (b) Cognition, Intelligence, Personality, Sensation
   (c) Cognition, Motor, Sensation, Speech
   (d) Cognition, Emotion, Motor, Sensation

7. **NIH Toolbox Cognition tests utilize item response theory (IRT) and computerized adaptive testing (CAT).**
   True or False
8. **Which of the following statements is true of the NIH Toolbox?**
   (a) Version 1 was available on computers via a downloadable, local software system.
   (b) Version 1 was available as a paper-and-pencil test kit.
   (c) Version 1 was available on computers via the web.
   (d) Version 1 was available on computers and iPads.
9. **The new Early Childhood Cognition CFPS Composite includes which of the following tests?**
   (a) Picture Vocabulary, Speeded Matching, Visual Reasoning
   (b) Speeded Matching, Pattern Comparison Processing Speed, Picture Vocabulary
   (c) Flanker Inhibitory Control and Attention, Picture Vocabulary, Picture Sequence Memory
   (d) Picture Sequence Memory, Speeded Matching, Visual Reasoning
10. **The Fluid Cognition Composite is new to NIH Toolbox V3.**
   True or False

Answers: 1. True; 2. (b); 3. False; 4. (a); 5. (d); 6. (d); 7. True; 8. (c); 9. (a); 10. False

REFERENCES

Akshoomoff, N., Beaumont, J. L., Bauer, P. J., Dikmen, S. S., Gershon, R. C., Mungas, D., & Heaton, R. K. (2013). NIH toolbox cognitive battery (CB): Composite scores of crystallized, fluid, and overall cognition. *Monographs of the Society for Research in Child Development, 78*(4), 119–132.

Alloway, P. A., Gathercole, S. E., & Pickering, S. J. (2006). Verbal and visuospatial short-term and working memory in children: Are they separable? *Child Development, 77*(6), 1698–1716.

American Educational Research Association, American Psychological Association, & National Council on Measurement in Education. (Ed.) (2014). *Standards for educational and psychological testing*. American Educational Research Association.

American Psychological Association (APA). (2002). *Ethical principles of psychologists and code of conduct*. https://www.apa.org/ethics/code

Baddeley, A. (2003). Working memory and language: An overview. *Journal of Communication Disorders, 36*(3), 189–208.

Bauer, P. J., Dikmen, S. S., Heaton, R. K., Mungas, D., Slotkin, J., & Beaumont, J. L. (2013). NIH Toolbox Cognition Battery (Cb): Measuring episodic memory. *Monographs of the Society for Research in Child Development, 78*(4), 34–48.

Beaumont, J. L., Havlik, R., Cook, K. F., Hays, R. D., Wallner-Allen, K., Korper, S. P., ... Gershon, R. (2013). Norming plans for the NIH toolbox. *Neurology, 80*(11_supplement_3), S87–S92.

Ben-Porath, Y. S. (2012). Interpreting assessment data: Ethical and practical considerations. In J. N. Butcher (Ed.), *Oxford handbook of personality assessment* (pp. 144–161). Oxford University Press.

Blaisdell, C. J., Park, C., Hanspal, M., Roary, M., Arteaga, S. S., Laessig, S., ... Program Collaborators for Environmental influences on Child Health Outcomes. (2022). The NIH ECHO Program: Investigating how early environmental influences affect child health. *Pediatric Research, 92*(5), 1215–1216.

Bush, S. S., Ruff, R. M., Troster, A. I., Barth, J. T., Koffler, S. P., Pliskin, N. H., ... Silver, C. H. (2005). Symptom validity assessment: Practice issues and medical necessity. *Archives of Clinical Neuropsychology, 20*(4), 419–426.

Carlozzi, N. E., Beaumont, J. L., Tulsky, D. S., & Gershon, R. C. (2015). The NIH toolbox pattern comparison processing speed test: Normative data. *Archives of Clinical Neuropsychology, 30*(5), 359–368.

Casaletto, K. B., Umlauf, A., Beaumont, J., Gershon, R., Slotkin, J., Akshoomoff, N., & Heaton, R. K. (2015). Demographically corrected normative standards for the English version of the NIH toolbox cognition battery. *Journal of the International Neuropsychological Society, 21*(S1), 378–391.

Cella, D., Gershon, R., Lai, J.-S., & Choi, S. (2007). The future of outcomes measurement: Item banking, tailored short-forms, and computerized adaptive assessment. *Quality of Life Research, 16*(S1), 133–141.

Coldwell, S. E., Mennella, J. A., Duffy, V. B., Pelchat, M. L., Griffith, J. W., Smutzer, G., & Hoffman, H. J. (2013). Gustation assessment using the NIH Toolbox. *Neurology, 80*(11 Suppl. 3), S20–S24.

Cook, K. F., Dunn, W., Griffith, J. W., Morrison, M. T., Tanquary, J., Sabata, D., ... Gershon, R. C. (2013). Pain assessment using the NIH Toolbox. *Neurology, 80*(11 Supplement 3), S49–S53. https://doi.org/10.1212/WNL.0b013e3182872e80

Coyle, T. R., Pillow, D. R., Snyder, A. C., & Kochunov, P. (2011). Processing speed mediates the development of general intelligence (g) in adolescence. *Psychological Science, 22*(10), 1265–1269.

Dale, E., & O'Rourke, J. (1976). *The living word vocabulary: The words we know: A national vocabulary inventory*. Field Enterprises Educational Corp.

Dalton, P., Doty, R. L., Murphy, C., Frank, R., Hoffman, H. J., Maute, C., & Slotkin, J. (2013). Olfactory assessment using the NIH Toolbox. *Neurology, 80*(11 Suppl. 3), S32–S36.

Delis, D. C., Kaplan, E., & Kramer, J. H. (2001). *Delis-Kaplan executive function system (D-KEFS)*. Pearson.

Dempster, F. N. (1981). Memory span: Sources of individual and developmental differences. *Psychological Bulletin, 89*(1), 63–100.

Dunn, L. M., & Dunn, D. M. (2007). *Peabody picture vocabulary test* (4th ed.). Pearson.

Dunn, W., Griffith, J. W., Morrison, M. T., Tanquary, J., Sabata, D., Victorson, D., & Gershon, R. C. (2013). Somatosensation assessment using the NIH Toolbox. *Neurology, 80*(11 Suppl. 3), S41–S44.

Eriksen, B. A., & Eriksen, C. W. (1974). Effects of noise letters upon the identification of a target letter in a nonsearch task. *Perception and Psychophysics, 16*, 143–149.

Fan, J., McCandliss, B. D., Sommer, T., Raz, A., & Posner, M. I. (2002). Testing the efficiency and independence of attentional networks. *Journal of Cognitive Neuroscience, 14*(3), 340–347.

Fox, R. S., Zhang, M., Amagai, S., Bassard, A., Dworak, E. M., Han, Y. C., … Gershon, R. C. (2022). Uses of the NIH Toolbox® in clinical samples: A scoping review. *Neurology. Clinical Practice, 12*(4), 307–319.

Frye, D., Zelazo, P. D., & Palfai, T. (1995). Theory of mind and rule-based reasoning. *Cognitive Development, 10*, 483–527.

Gasquoine, P. G. (2009). Race-norming of neuropsychological tests. *Neuropsychological Review, 19*, 250–263.

Gershon, R. (1988). *Index of words in the Johnson O'Connor Research Foundation, Inc. Vocabulary item bank.* Johnson O'Connor Research Foundation Human Engineering Laboratory.

Gershon, R. (2005). Computer adaptive testing. *Journal of Applied Measurement, 6*(1), 109–127.

Gershon, R., Cella, D., Dineen, K., Rosenblom, S., Peterman, A., & Lai, J. S. (2003). Item response theory and health-related quality of life in cancer. *Expert Review of Pharmacoeconomics and Outcomes Research, 3*(6), 783–791.

Gershon, R., Cella, D., Fox, N. A., Havlik, R. J., Hendrie, H. C., & Wagster, M. V. (2010). Assessment of neurological and behavioral function: The NIH Toolbox. *Lancet Neurology, 9*(2), 138–139.

Gershon, R., Cook, K. F., Mungas, D., Manly, J. J., Slotkin, J., Beaumont, J. L., & Weintraub, S. (2014). The language measures of the NIH toolbox cognition battery. *Journal of the International Neuropsychological Society, 20*(6), 642–651.

Gershon, R., Wagster, M. V., Hendrie, H. C., Fox, N. A., Cook, K. F., & Nowinski, C. J. (2013). Responding to the needs of the neurology research community: introduction to the NIH toolbox for the assessment of neurological and behavioral function. *Neurology, 80*(11 Suppl. 3), S2–S6.

Gillman, M. W., & Blaisdell, C. J. (2018). Environmental influences on child health outcomes, a research program of the NIH. *Current Opinion in Pediatrics, 30*(2), 260–262.

Horn, J. L., & Cattell, R. B. (1967). Age differences in fluid and crystallized intelligence. *Acta Psychologica, 26*, 107–129.

Rehabilitation Act of 1973. (1998). *Title number 29 U.S.C. §794d.* https://www.section508.gov/

Human Connectome Project. (n.d.). *About the HCP*. Retrieved July 30, 2025, from https://www.humanconnectome.org/

LaForte, E. M., Hook, J. N., & Giella, A. K. (2024). *National Institutes of Health (NIH) Toolbox® V3 technical manual.* Toolbox Assessments. Inc.

Lezak, M. D., Howieson, D. B., Bigler, E. D., & Tranel, D. (2012). *Neuropsychological assessment* (5th ed.). Oxford University Press.

Ma, Y., Carlsson, C. M., Wahoskie, M. L., Blazel, H. M., Chappel, R. J., Hohnson, S. C., … Gleason, C. E. (2020). Latent factor structure and measurement invariance of the NIH toolbox cognition battery in an Alzheimer's disease research sample. *Journal of International Neuropsychologic Society, 27*(5), 412–425.

McKenzie, F. J., Drayton, A., Shields, R. H., Dakopolos, A., Glassman, D., Kaat, A., Coleman, J., Thompson, T., Sansone, S., Riley, K., Berry-Kravis, E., Gershon, R. C., & Hessl, D. (2023). *National Institutes of Health Toolbox® V3 cognition battery supplemental administration manual for intellectual and developmental disabilities: A guide on administration and scoring standards [Supplemental material]. NIH Toolbox.* https://nihbabytoolbox.org/wp-content/uploads/2023/07/NIHTB-V3-CB-IDD-Supplemental-Manual_07052023.pdf

Mungas, D., Heaton, R., Tlsky, D., Zelazo, P. D., Slotkin, J., Blitz, D., … Gershon, R. (2014). Factor structure, convergent validity, and discriminant validity of the NIH toolbox cognitive health battery (NIHTB-CHB) in adults. *Journal of the International Neuropsychological Society, 20*, 579–587.

Mungas, D., Widaman, K., Zelazo, P. D., Tulsky, D., Heaton, R. K., Slotkin, J., & Gershon, R. (2013). NIH Toolbox cognition battery (CB): Factor structure for 3–15 year olds. *Monographs of the Society for Research in Child Development, 78*(4), 103–118.

National Institute of Neurological Disorders and Stroke. (n.d.). *NIH blueprint overview flyer* [PDF]. US Department of Health and Human Services. Retrieved July 24, 2025, from https://www.ninds.nih.gov/sites/default/files/documents/NIH_Blueprint_Overview_Flyer_508C.pdf

National Institutes of Health. (2015). *Adolescent brain cognitive development study.*

Neisser, U., Boodoo, G., Bouchard, T. J., Jr., Boykin, A. W., Brody, N., & Ceci, S. J. (1996). Intelligence: Knowns and unknowns. *American Psychologist, 51*(2), 77–101.

Nowinski, C. J., Victorson, D., Debb, S. M., & Gershon, R. C. (2013). Input on NIH Toolbox inclusion criteria: Surveying the end-user community. *Neurology, 80*(11 Suppl. 3), S7–S12.

Rea-Sandin, G., Korous, K. M., & Causadias, J. M. (2021). A systematic review and meta-analysis of racial/ethnic differences and similarities in executive function performance in the United States. *Neuropsychology, 35*(2), 141–156.

Rentz, D. M., Amariglio, R. E., Becker, J. A., Frey, M., Olson, L. E., Frishe, K., … Sperling, R. A. (2011). Face-name associative memory performance is related to amyloid burden in normal elderly. *Neuropsychologia, 49*(9), 2776–2783.

Reuben, D. B., Magasi, S., McCreath, H. E., Bohannon, R. W., Wang, Y. C., Bubela, D. J., & Gershon, R. C. (2013). Motor assessment using the NIH Toolbox. *Neurology, 80*(11 Suppl. 3), S65–S75.

Rine, R. M., Schubert, M. C., Whitney, S. L., Roberts, D., Redfern, M. S., Musolino, M. C., & Slotkin, J. (2013). Vestibular function assessment using the NIH Toolbox. *Neurology, 80*(11 Suppl. 3), S25–S31.

Rohling, M. L., Miller, R. M., Axelrod, B. N., Wall, J. R., Lee, A. J. H., & Kinikini, D. T. (2015). Is co-norming required? *Archives of Clinical Neuropsychology, 30*, 611–633.

Rueda, M. R., Fan, J., McCandliss, B. D., Halparin, J. D., Gruber, D. B., Lercari, L. P., & Posner, M. I. (2004). Development of attentional networks in childhood. *Neuropsychologia, 42*, 1029–1040.

Russell, E. W. (2004). The operating characteristics of the major HRNES-R measures. *Archives of Clinical Neuropsychology, 19*, 1043–1061.

Salsman, J. M., Butt, Z., Pilkonis, P. A., Cyranowski, J. M., Zill, N., Hendrie, H. C., & Cella, D. (2013). Emotion assessment using the NIH toolbox. *Neurology, 80*(11 Suppl. 3), S76–S86.

Schneider, W. J., & McGrew, K. S. (2018). The Cattell-Horn-Carroll theory of cognitive abilities. In D. P. Flanagan & E. M. McDonough (Eds.), *Contemporary intellectual assessment: Theories, tests, and issues* (4th ed., pp. 73–163). Guilford.

Squire, L. R. (2004). Memory systems of the brain: a brief history and current perspective. *Neurobiology of Learning and Memory, 82*, 171–177.

Thompson, R. C., Montena, A. L., Liu, K., Watson, J., & Warren, S. L. (2022). Associations of family distress, family income, and acculturation on pediatric cognitive performance using the NIH Toolbox: Implications for clinical and research settings. *Archives of Clinical Neuropsychology, 37*(4), 798–813.

Tulsky, D. S., Carlozzi, N., Chiaravalloti, N., Beaumont, J. L., Conway, K., & Mungas, D. (2014). NIH Toolbox cognition battery (NIHTB-CB): Measuring working memory. *Journal of the International Neuropsychological Society, 20*(6), 599–610.

Tulsky, D. S., Holdnack, J. A., Cohen, M. L., Heaton, R. K., Carlozzi, N. E., Wong, A. W. K., & Heinemann, A. W. (2017). Factor structure of the NIH Toolbox cognition battery in individuals with acquired brain injury. *Rehabilitation Psychology, 62*(4), 435–442.

U.S. Census Bureau. (2021). *2020 Census data*. U.S. Department of Commerce. https://www.census.gov/programs-surveys/decennial-census/decade/2020.html

Varma, R., McKean-Cowdin, R., Vitale, S., Slotkin, J., & Hays, R. D. (2013). Vision assessment using the NIH Toolbox. *Neurology, 80*(11 Suppl. 3), S37–S40.

Wechsler, D. (2008). *Wechsler adult intelligence scale IV*. Harcourt Assessment.

Weintraub, S., Dikmen, S. S., Heaton, R. K., Tulsky, D. S., Zelazo, P. D., Bauer, P. J., & Gershon, R. C. (2013). Cognition assessment using the NIH Toolbox. *Neurology, 80*(11 Suppl. 3), S54–S64.

Weintraub, S., Dikmen, S. S., Heaton, R. K., Tulsky, D. S., Zelazo, P. D., Slotkin, J., & Gershon, R. (2014). The cognition battery of the NIH toolbox for assessment of neurological and behavioral function: Validation in an adult sample. *Journal of the International Neuropsychological Society, 20*(6), 567–578.

Zecker, S. G., Hoffman, H. J., Frisina, R., Dubno, J. R., Dhar, S., Wallhagen, M., & Wilson, R. H. (2013). Audition assessment using the NIH Toolbox. *Neurology, 80*(11 Suppl. 3), S45–S48.

Zelazo, P. D., Anderson, J. E., Richler, J., Wallner-Allen, K., Beaumont, J. L., Gershon, R., … Weintraub, S. (2014). NIH toolbox cognition battery (CB): Validation of executive function measures in adults. *Journal of the International Neuropsychological Society, 20*(6), 620–629.

Two

GENERAL EXAMINER GUIDELINES

Amy K. Giella
Julie N. Hook

Standardized cognitive assessments are only as reliable and valid as the rigor with which they are administered. Examiner error, inconsistent instructions, or misinterpretation of behavior can significantly impact results, which can therefore diminish the quality of data, introduce bias, and ultimately impair scientific or clinical conclusions. As a modern, computer-assisted suite of measures, the NIH Toolbox Cognition tests reduce some sources of human error through automation but still require examiners to follow standardized guidelines. This chapter outlines the essential examiner behaviors, attitudes, and practices needed to ensure consistent, high-quality cognitive testing, regardless of the population or setting.

EXAMINER QUALIFICATIONS AND TRAINING

Minimum Qualifications

The administration of the NIH Toolbox Cognition tests does not require licensure as a clinical neuropsychologist, but it should be conducted by trained personnel with the understanding of:

- basic cognitive and developmental psychology,
- principles of standardized test administration,
- ethics and confidentiality in assessments, and
- sensitivity to individual differences (e.g., age, culture, and disability).

In clinical settings, administration is typically performed by trained research assistants, psychometrists, or clinicians under appropriate supervision (if needed). In research contexts, paraprofessionals may be trained in administering standardized protocols. Regardless of prior experience, all examiners (i.e., those who administer the tests to examinees) must be familiar with and properly trained in administering NIH Toolbox tests.

Training Components

There are many different elements involved with learning to administer digital tests. The examiner should not only understand the tests themselves but also know the basics of the hardware and software that those tests run on. The more familiar an examiner can become with the test(s) and/or measurement system prior to the actual testing, the more confident the examiner will be, allowing them greater time to focus on putting the examinee (e.g., patient, student, and participant) at ease. Prior to administering the tests to a live examinee, it is recommended that the examiner perform the following five steps:

1. Review and understand equipment setup.
2. Participate in didactic instruction.
3. Practice administering tests.
4. Undergo a competency assessment.
5. Engage in periodic retraining.

Let's review each in more detail to gain a deeper understanding of what is expected.

Review and Understand Equipment Setup

Proper setup is a critical foundation for administering the NIH Toolbox assessments with precision and consistency. This includes not only preparing the digital platform (e.g., iPad configuration, software installation, and updates) but also ensuring the testing environment is appropriate (e.g., quiet, well-lit, and free from distractions).

Examiners must review a list of all the tests they will be administering and confirm they have all necessary materials in advance, including any required accessories (e.g., List Sorting Working Memory Answer Sheet). The iPad and wireless keyboard (required for the List Sorting Working Memory and Oral Reading Recognition tests) should be fully charged and connected prior to the testing session.

Attention to physical space, seating arrangement, and examiner posture relative to the examinee is essential for minimizing confounding variables and supporting standardized test delivery. Ensure the examinee's chair is comfortably positioned center to the iPad and at an appropriate distance from the screen. Ensure the room's lighting is adequate, and background noise (e.g., ticking clocks) is minimized. A well-prepared environment enhances data quality and examinee engagement.

Download and set up the NIH Toolbox V3 app. Users interested in the NIH Toolbox can explore the app for free, but collected data is not saved without a valid subscription. Examiners MUST ensure their app has a valid subscription prior to administering the tests to examinees and collecting data. Review the different areas in the app, including Tests, Participants, and Settings. Examiners should

CAUTION 2.1

Assessment data is not without a valid subscription. Examiners should never collect data prior to first activating a valid subscription on that iPad, in that app.

know how to perform basic functions such as creating a new participant, creating a new assessment, and accessing score reports or exports. Furthermore, the examiner should know how to perform tasks that may be needed during an assessment, such as pausing the assessment using the administration gesture (i.e., placing three fingers on the screen and swiping left) or adding a note to record any important information about the testing.

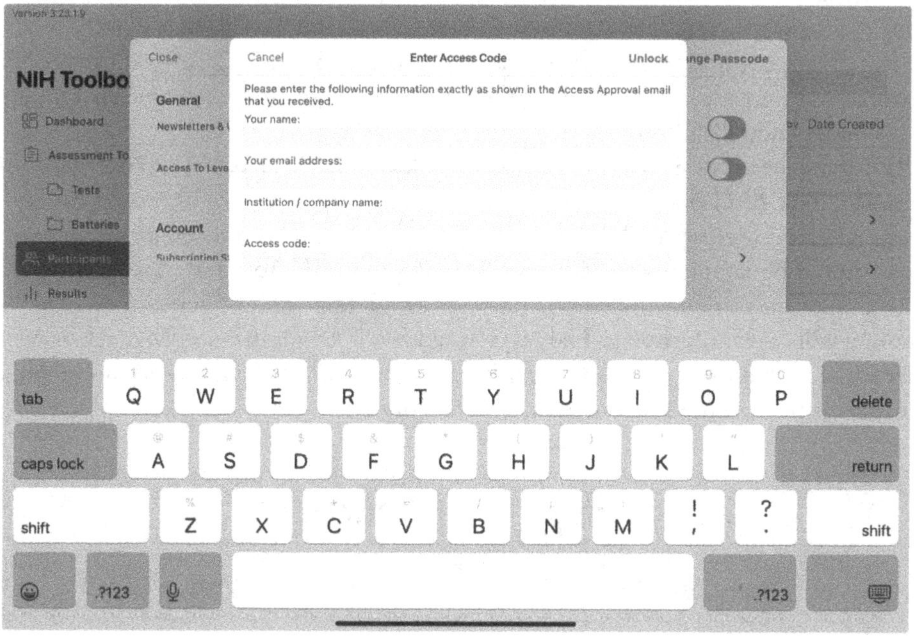

Prior to using the Cognition tests, the examiner must apply online (https://resources.nihtoolbox.org/) and be approved for C-level access to be able to unlock and use the Cognition tests in the app. After the examiner has been approved, they will receive a C-level access code, which must be entered in the app. Once that code is entered into the app, the examiner will be able to add all the Cognition tests to assessments and administer them. Without this C-level access code entered in the app, only the tests in the Emotion, Motor, and Sensation domains will be accessible.

Please note that once the app is set up, including the purchase of a subscription and entering the Cognition access code, the examiner should regularly check for iOS and app updates whenever there is access to the Internet. It is important to keep the iPad's

DON'T FORGET 2.1

Remember that the C-level access code is separate from the app subscription purchase. To be able to score tests and save data, the app must be purchased. This can be done via the in-app purchase or by contacting customer service for a license (email: help@nihtoolbox.org).

operating system (i.e., iOS) and the app up to date. Prior to any administration, confirm that all background notifications (e.g., email alerts) are silenced so they will not interrupt the testing session.

Participate in Didactic Instruction

Examiner training begins with a thorough review of materials that introduces the theoretical underpinnings of the NIH Toolbox V3 tests. Specifically, the examiner should learn about the basic structure (e.g., computer adaptive test, and fixed form), workflow of the test (e.g., Instructions, Practice Items, Transition to Test, and Live Items), construct being measured (e.g., processing speed and executive functioning), and psychometric properties (e.g., validity and reliability).

Reviewing materials such as this *Essentials* book and the *NIH Toolbox V3 Administration Manual* (Hook & Giella, 2023) will offer the examiner detailed information about all aspects of administering the NIH Toolbox V3 Cognition tests. The examiner, at a minimum, should be familiar with "Chapter 2: Using the NIH Toolbox® App," "Chapter 3: General Administration Guidelines," as well as all test sections relevant to what the examiner will be administering. The NIH Toolbox V3 Administration Manual, as well as other supplemental materials (e.g., Oral Reading Recognition Pronunciation Guide), are available for free at https://resources.nihtoolbox.org/.

Rapid Reference 2.1

Examiners can download a free copy of the NIH Toolbox V3 Administration Manual, as well as other supplemental materials and helpful resources from the "Toolbox Learning and Resources" section at resources.nihtoolbox.org.

Examiners should also review relevant test material in the NIH Toolbox V3 self-guided courses that are available online at https://resources.nihtoolbox.org/. As part of the series of self-guided lessons, the examiner can watch "How to" videos about the examiner interface features (e.g., how to create a participant and how to export results), view administration videos on specific tests, and read highlighted key points about the administration of each test. At the end of each module, the examiner can also take a self-assessment quiz to test their knowledge and monitor their progress in understanding the material. Although it is not required to complete these online courses, they are a valuable resource and can help bolster examiners' understanding of the material prior to administering the tests.

Practice Administering Tests

Practicing the test administration can occur in conjunction with or following the didactic instruction. In fact, some examiners find it helpful to reference each test section in the *NIH Toolbox V3 Administration Manual* (Hook & Giella, 2023) while going through the corresponding test in the app. This process helps the examiner understand the workflows and nuances of each test that they will be administering. Doing the practice in parallel will also assist in understanding how the test is structured (e.g., Instructions, Practice Items, Transition to Test, and Live Items) and what the examinee is expected to do during each section.

Regardless of which order is preferred, the examiners should engage in hands-on practice to reinforce procedural fluency. Examples of practice scenarios could include both guided role-play with a training supervisor or self-directed mock administrations with peers. Through repetition, trainee examiners will gain confidence and develop mastery in test navigation, prompt delivery, and error handling.

For examiners new to the NIH Toolbox or new to cognitive testing, feedback from experienced supervisors can help refine technique, clarify uncertainties, and correct deviations from standard protocol. Furthermore, practicing across a variety of simulated scenarios prepares examiners for the range of real-world examinee behaviors they may encounter, thus promoting adaptive competence with standardized guidelines.

In fact, the examiner is encouraged to perform several mock administrations prior to their first real administration. To circumvent avoidable issues, the examiner should never administer the tests for the first time in a real examinee setting. This is particularly important for anyone new to digital assessments and unfamiliar with the NIH Toolbox or neuropsychological testing. Even examiners who have ample experience administering paper-and-pencil measures, but not digital administration, should plan to mock-administer the NIH Toolbox V3 tests several times prior to testing their first examinee.

If the examiner intends to administer the NIH Toolbox V3 tests to examinees of a particular age (e.g., school-aged children), it would be ideal for the examiner to first mock-administer the relevant tests to an examinee close in age to that target demographic. By training with a demographic as close as possible to a targeted examinee pool, examiners can better anticipate and respond to potential examinee comments or interruptions. For instance, practicing administration with young children is likely to help the examiner communicate more fluidly with children, ask more frequently if restroom or drink breaks are needed to avoid test interruptions, and redirect strayed attention with age-appropriate instruction. Alternatively, if the target population is older adults, running mock administrations with individuals closer to that demographic can help the examiner practice how to welcome the examinee to the testing session, and perhaps more perceptively notice and smoothly address examinee embarrassment in the event that the examinee believes they are doing poorly on the given task.

During these mock administrations, the examiner should pay close attention to the app and the administration manual to ensure the administration is as smooth as possible. For instance, certain screens should be demonstrated by the examiner; examiners should be aware of which screens require them to gesture or respond, which screens are intended for the examinee, and whether they or the examinee should tap the button to move to the next screen. To help distinguish mock assessments from the real assessments, examiners should label the assessment names clearly (e.g., "Mock Examinee A," "Practice Assessment 2").

After the examiner is ready for real administrations, these mock examinees and assessments can be archived so they are not visible in the Participants list or included in the export files.

Undergo a Competency Assessment

Before administering the NIH Toolbox independently, examiners (especially new examiners) should pass a competency assessment. This can be accomplished by having an examiner-in-training record their "mock" administration for later review by a colleague who could provide pointers or advice about the examiner's performance (e.g., recommending more frequent eye contact, speaking more slowly with younger children, offering more general "well done" feedback). This type of review can vary in scope but usually includes judging the examiner's performance against a standardized rubric, evaluating factors such as adherence to the protocol, and professionalism. That is, the examiners should demonstrate technical proficiency and the ability to manage issues with testing (e.g., connecting the Bluetooth keyboard to the iPad), answer examinee questions, and address unexpected responses while maintaining the fidelity of the assessment. Only after successful completion of this phase should examiners contribute data to clinical or research studies.

Rapid Reference 2.2

Before administering their first NIH Toolbox V3 assessment to a real participant, examiners must first review all relevant materials, mock-administer all relevant tests on their own, and then administer the full range of relevant tests to mock examinees (e.g., colleagues and friends) to ensure they fully understand the test workflows and relevant supplemental materials (e.g., how to input responses on the wireless Bluetooth keyboard), and how to deliver any potentially relevant response feedback (e.g., saying, "Tap only one picture at a time").

Engage in Periodic Retraining

To maintain high standards of data integrity, periodic retraining is recommended for all NIH Toolbox examiners. This ensures consistency across time, helps correct drift from the protocol, and incorporates possible updates to the tests, battery, or examiner interface. Examiners should be reminded to export data frequently, and we strongly recommend that relevant administrators and/or data analysts periodically review incoming data to confirm that data is being collected and exported as expected. Review of common administration errors or interactive discussion with team members also tends to be helpful to ensure each examiner understands and abides by their study's or institution's expectations. Particularly in long-term studies or clinical settings with high staff turnover, ongoing training is vital for preserving scientific rigor. Retraining also helps reinforce examiner accountability and supports continuous improvement in assessment quality.

SETTING AND ENVIRONMENT

Testing should occur in a location that supports focus and minimizes distractions. This is particularly important when testing may be done in school-based or mobile testing environments, such as at an examinee's home, as these environments may be more prone to noise or distractions.

An ideal testing environment is in a comfortable room that is free of distractions. Examinees should feel relatively relaxed, confident, and ready to give their best effort to the assessment. Though the following considerations are not a comprehensive list of every consideration that should be taken, they serve as a helpful guide to examiners to help them become more cognizant of the testing environment and its surroundings.

Cognitive testing can be considered personal, and many examinees would not want to take tests in public settings or with an examiner with whom they do not feel comfortable. Regardless of examinee preference, it is ideal for all testing sessions to be conducted in an enclosed space that is free of observers (except, perhaps, for parents of young test takers, or a supervisor of a training examiner).

Outside distractions should be reduced as much as possible to avoid unexpected interruptions. Ideally, the testing room should be located away from noisy equipment and main hallways where people might have loud conversations. If that is not possible, it may help to communicate with neighbors prior to administration by circulating a notice via email or bulletin board, or by placing a "Do Not Disturb: Testing in Progress" sign on the outside of the door. If distractions are expected at certain times (e.g., school bells signaling the end of the school day), it would be ideal to avoid testing during those times or scheduling breaks around those expected interruptions.

Additional visual or auditory distractions in the testing room should also be reduced. For example, too many signs, posters, pictures, figurines, ticking analog clocks, etc., may be distracting and potentially impact the examinee's performance. If the room has windows that open onto distracting environments, such as a busy street or sidewalk, the examiner should close the windows and blinds to reduce visual and auditory disruptions. If there is a doctor's office television that is set to circulate information, that television should be turned off when the examinee is in the room.

Both the examiner and examinee should silence notifications from electronic devices such as phones, computers, or smartwatches. As much as possible, all technological interference should be reduced or eliminated.

In addition to the examiner silencing their personal cell phone and computer, the examiner should also silence all other notifications that might interrupt the test administration, including silencing alerts and notifications from the iPad. Ensure the iPad on which the

> **DON'T FORGET 2.2**
>
> Any notification or alert that flashes or makes a sound during the testing session could easily distract the examinee. Silence all notifications during all administrations, including any that may come from the examinee's phone or smart watch.

testing will be performed has any pop-up messages (e.g., email notifications and iOS updates) disabled to prevent distractions. Automated alerts, such as background updates and enabling mail (which may receive large attachments), may impede test timing, especially if they transpire during a timed test, such as Pattern Comparison Processing Speed. If possible, disable any background notifications and automated updates on the iPad to prevent examinee distraction and potential test interference. In general, it is good practice to check for iOS and app updates on a weekly basis, as that allows examiners to install updates in a timely manner, when it is most convenient (i.e., not immediately before an examinee arrives for testing).

Food and drinks should be avoided immediately before or during testing, if possible, as seeing or smelling food or drinks might distract the examinee. For instance, food odors unagreeable to the examinee may be distracting, while pleasant scents may make the examinee hungrier and therefore distract them from the tests. That said, it is a good idea to have tissues and perhaps small bottles of water available, in case the examinee requires them. It is acceptable to take snack breaks as needed, as long as snacks are consumed away from the testing table.

Providing a comfortable chair will help examinees remain attentive for longer periods of time. Chairs that swivel may be distracting, while stationary seats that allow the examinee to rest their feet flat on the floor are ideal. The table or workspace should be at a height that is appropriate for the examinee. For instance, having a child sit at an adult-sized table might be intimidating or distracting, while seating an adult at a low table might be inappropriate, degrading, or uncomfortable. If children are seated at an adult-sized table, offering a step stool on which to rest their feet will prevent their legs from dangling and potentially distracting them.

Examiners should be prepared to accommodate persons with special needs, such as those who require wheelchair accessibility. Should the examinee wish to remain in their wheelchair, they should be able to do so, without that accommodation causing distraction. If the wheelchair does not fit comfortably under the table, if the person must be positioned at a strange angle to fit, or they are too far to comfortably reach the iPad, that participant may be distracted while taking the assessment, therefore potentially having them complete the assessment at a disadvantage compared to individuals who do not rely on a wheelchair. When possible, it is helpful to understand the target population's needs, as well as individual needs that may be brought to light during the intake questionnaires.

If it is possible to adjust the room temperature, the examiner should ensure it is at a comfortable level. If the room temperature is out of the examiner's control and temperatures tend to vary to extremes, it may be helpful to alert the examinee prior to the assessment (e.g., "the room tends to be cold, so you may want to bring a sweater").

Examiners should be seated in a position beside the examinee that allows them to comfortably see the iPad screen and demonstrate certain instructions, without crowding or sitting too close to the examinee. The examinee should be seated comfortably, directly facing the center of the iPad, and able to easily reach the screen. Examiners might consider the examinee's handedness (i.e., dominant hand) and sit on the opposite side of the examinee to avoid competing for space (e.g., if the examinee is right-handed, the examiner might sit to the left of the examinee).

Generally, scoring is performed within the app, and the examinee is not cued into whether they answered correctly or incorrectly. However, three tests in the Cognition domain have materials external to the iPad, two of which are relevant to scoring the test, and the examiner should therefore shield those materials from the examinee's view. The List Sorting Working Memory and Oral Reading Recognition tests are administered on the iPad but have external answer sheets, which the examiner can reference and use to manually key in the examinee's response on an external Bluetooth keyboard. The answer sheets and keyboard should be positioned in such a way that the examinee cannot see the correct answer or what the examiner keys in.

The Oral Symbol Digit test, on the other hand, has the examinee answer verbally while looking at a paper outside the app, and the examiner enters the responses directly on the iPad screen in the app. In this case, the iPad screen should be turned away from the examinee to ensure they cannot see the examiner's entries on the iPad screen.

Rapid Reference 2.3

Examiners should ensure the testing environment is as free of distractions as possible by conducting testing sessions away from loud hallways and busy parking lots; ensuring silence as much as possible by removing loud items such as analog clocks and putting up "Testing in Progress" signs. Limiting visual distractions such as open blinds that look onto busy streets or excessive trinkets on the examiner's desk, and providing comfortable, age-appropriate tables and chairs can help to elimiate potential distractions.

In sum, when possible, examiners should sit next to and not across from the examinee, ensuring they can view the examinee's behavior without influencing their performance. For instance, the examiner should be positioned in a way that can monitor the examinee's genuine attention, as well as notice disingenuous responding (e.g., unfocused gaze, repeatedly glancing away from the iPad screen during live items, pattern-based responding incongruent with the test items).

A checklist for the ideal setting environment should include:

- a quiet, private, and well-lit room,
- a table and chair at an appropriate height for the examinee (particularly important for young children),
- minimal noise and visual distraction,
- uninterrupted use of the iPad during the testing by turning off automatic reminders, push notifications, email alerts, etc., and
- confirming all necessary materials and equipment are present, connected (e.g., wireless Bluetooth keyboard is paired with the iPad), and fully charged.

APPOINTMENT CONSIDERATIONS

Proper preparation and scheduling of cognitive testing sessions are critical to ensuring the comfort of the examinee and the quality of the data that is collected. Examiners must consider several logistical, clinical, and interpersonal factors when planning these appointments. This section outlines key considerations to support optimal testing outcomes.

Clinical Evaluations: Clarifying the Referral Question

A clear understanding of the referral question is foundational to any neuropsychological or cognitive assessment. Examiners must ensure they know precisely why the individual is being referred for testing and what clinical or research questions need to be addressed. For example, a referral might seek to determine if a child has a learning disability or to clarify an individual's cognitive functioning in the context of a known neurological condition. If the referral question is vague or absent, it is the examiner who should seek clarification if possible. This may mean contacting the referring physician or school counselor to seek more information as to the purpose of the evaluation. The information can inform test selection and administration strategy, in addition to helping guide interpretation and reporting.

Alternatively, if the examinee is being recruited as a participant in a clinical trial, those responsible for recruitment are generally the ones tasked with confirming the examinee meets all relevant inclusion criteria (e.g., appropriate age and relevant diagnosis) and that the examinee does not meet any exclusion criteria (e.g., examinee currently taking certain medications).

When possible, examiners should confirm prior to test administration that they have obtained all relevant information and that the examinee is eligible for testing (e.g., approved by health insurance and meets inclusion criteria).

Communicating Expectations

Many people associate cognitive testing with overly challenging questions, which makes some anxious about poor performance or being judged by the examiner. When scheduling the appointment, it is essential to communicate clearly with the examinee about what to expect. Providing a brief overview of the session can help demystify the process, reduce anxiety, and improve rapport. For instance, the examiner might explain:

> Thank you for agreeing to participate. During this appointment, we will discuss some of your medical history, and then I will guide you through a series of tasks. These may feel a bit like games; some are easy, and others are meant to be more challenging. Most people don't get everything right, and that's okay. The entire session should take about 30 to 45 minutes, and if you'd like, I can coordinate with your referring provider to make sure they receive the results so they can review them with you in more detail.

Setting expectations in this manner normalizes potential difficulty, enhances engagement, and establishes trust. It also creates a safe environment conducive to optimal effort and cooperation. It also informs the examinee that they will not immediately receive results, and that they'd need to speak with their referring provider for more information about their testing performance and results; understanding this expected delay in obtaining results may help reduce anxiety (e.g., "this person can't judge me as harshly because they won't immediately see how poorly I performed").

Logistical Planning and Individualized Scheduling

Whenever possible, scheduling should accommodate the examinee's physical, cognitive, and emotional needs. Several factors should be considered:

- **Time of day:** Whenever feasible, align the appointment with the examinee's optimal cognitive period (e.g., mornings for individuals with fatigue and avoiding nap times for young children).
- **Medication schedules:** Try to avoid scheduling sessions during times when taking medications that may alter alertness, such as medications that may cause drowsiness. If the examinee requires medication at a specific time during the administration, try to time that around natural breaks between tests. If that is not possible, note any test interferences in the administration notes.
- **Life logistics:** Inform the examinee how long they can expect the session to last, so they have a realistic expectation of the required time commitment. When possible, sessions should not coincide with personally stressful or time-constrained events (e.g., needing to leave to pick up children from school or day care). Such external pressures can detract from optimal attention and performance.

Examinees should be asked to bring any essential items such as glasses, hearing aids, snacks, water, medications, or referral documents. If documentation was not collected beforehand, a list of current medications and relevant medical history should be obtained at the time of the appointment. Further, if the examinee requires glasses to see the test material clearly or hearing aids to understand the tests, these should be worn during the testing, unless otherwise noted in the NIH Toolbox V3 Administration Manual (Hook & Giella, 2023). Failure to use them may invalidate the test. For example, without their required eyeglasses, an examinee may not do well simply because they couldn't clearly see the test materials; in effect, that administration would be a test of vision and not one of cognition. If the examinee forgets their glasses, hearing aids, or any other required devices, the examiner should note this in the administration notes and be aware of this when interpreting results.

At times, there are questions as to whether an examinee should take their medication before the evaluation, particularly if the medication were to alter cognitive performance. Before requesting any change in the examinee's medication routine, it is a good rule of thumb to consult the referring physician.

Financial Transparency

If applicable, insurance coverage and any potential out-of-pocket expenses should be disclosed in advance of the appointment. The examiner should ensure that the examinee is aware of all aspects of the appointment prior to the visit, including costs. Financial transparency helps reduce stress and support a more trusting relationship. For research studies, if the examinee is receiving compensation for participation, this should be clear.

Verifying Information

Despite best practices, administrative errors or outdated information are not uncommon. Prior to testing, examiners should verify the accuracy of the examinee's personal and medical information. This includes confirming the individual's name, date of birth, demographic details, current medication regimen, and any significant medical history. This verification should be completed either before the appointment or at the beginning of the session to ensure all the relevant contextual variables are correct for interpretation and documentation.

ESTABLISHING AND MAINTAINING RAPPORT

Establishing rapport is a critical component of cognitive and neuropsychological assessment. Rapport can influence examinee engagement, effort, comfort, and overall data validity. A well-prepared examiner can create an environment that supports optimal performance, minimizes test anxiety, and discourages malingering or disengagement. This section outlines the principles and best practices for building rapport across diverse populations, grounded in empirical research and clinical wisdom.

Fundamentals of Rapport Building

In testing contexts, a strong rapport can increase examinee effort and reduce anxiety, both of which are known to affect neuropsychological test performance (Suchy & Miller, 2023). Examiners must aim to be professional, approachable, and supportive while maintaining appropriate boundaries.

> **Rapid Reference 2.4**
>
> Rapport refers to the positive interpersonal connection between examiner and examinee that fosters trust, comfort, and cooperation.

Examiners should begin each interaction with a warm greeting and maintain a balance between professionalism and friendliness. While the examiner should avoid appearing overly casual or disinterested, they must also avoid rigid or authoritarian behavior that could cause the examinee to feel judged or scrutinized. Topics such as politics, religion, or contentious personal matters should be avoided, while more neutral subjects, such as hobbies, pets, or daily activities, can be useful topics of discussion to help ease tension.

Examiners should always strive to remain professional; however, they might modify the way they approach the examinee based on the examinee's age, attitude, and demeanor. For instance, to help put them at ease, examiners might be a bit friendlier and spend a few extra minutes chatting with an apprehensive four-year-old versus a confident teenager. That same overly friendly and talkative approach might annoy that eager teenager or a more reserved individual, who might find casual conversation tedious. Therefore, it is important for examiners to adopt a professional, yet friendly, interaction with the participant and fluidly adjust their approach to best suit the examinee.

Communicating Expectations with Clarity

Before test administration begins, the examiner should clearly explain what the session will involve. This can be done in a supportive and nonthreatening manner, such as: "Today, we're going to do a few tasks. Some may feel like puzzles or games. These will help us better understand how you think about things. Some tasks may be challenging, and that's okay. The tests were designed so that you wouldn't know everything."

Note that during communication about the tests, overexplaining can backfire at times. When possible, avoid giving extreme details about the reason for the referral or about the cognitive constructs being measured, as this may increase examinee anxiety, encourage non-credible performance, or lead to biased responses, particularly in children or individuals seeking external validation (Hersen & Thomas, 2007). For example, it would be inappropriate to reveal too much information about a specific test structure by saying: "This is a timed test that measures executive function based on how quickly and accurately you respond to items."

Reducing Technological Anxiety

NIH Toolbox V3 is currently available only as an iPad-based app, and as such, it is crucial to ensure the examinee is comfortable with touchscreen technology. If any signs of hesitation are observed, the examiner should administer the "Touch Screen Tutorial," which is a simple but effective tool found close to the bottom of the app's test list. The Touch Screen Tutorial asks examinees to use their finger to tap three specific targets on the screen. Since

> **DON'T FORGET 2.3**
>
> The Touch Screen Tutorial is located at the bottom of the NIH Toolbox V3 test list and is appropriate for all ages. To add the Touch Screen Tutorial, create a new assessment, tap "Add Tools," then scroll down to the "N/A" section, and select "Touch Screen Tutorial." When reviewing the list of tests (before saving the assessment and beginning it), ensure that the Touch Screen Tutorial is positioned at the top of the list so it is the first to be administered to the examinee.

the majority of the NIH Toolbox V3 Cognition tests rely on the examinee to select the appropriate response button, adding the brief Touch Screen Tutorial can help boost the examinee's confidence and minimize discomfort with the testing device and response interface. If hesitation persists, the examinee is welcome to take the Touch Screen Tutorial more than once, and the examiner can reassure the examinee that they will have a chance to practice each task before the real test items begin.

Creating a Comfortable Testing Environment

As mentioned in a previous section on Settings and Environment, the testing environment should be quiet, well-lit, and free from distractions. Both the examiner and the examinee should silence their mobile devices and place them out of sight. Like the examinee, the examiner should remain fully engaged, avoiding phone use, answering emails, or reviewing paperwork unrelated to the session. Maintaining a consistent, calm presence without distractions reassures the examinee and communicates that their time and effort are respected.

Language should be developmentally appropriate. Avoid clinical jargon or overly complex instructions. For children, don't use words that would be too complicated for them to understand, and consider using a more playful tone or game-like descriptions, such as, "Let's play a thinking game and remember to try your best." With adults, on the other hand, speak clearly and respectfully without being patronizing. This adaptation of communication style to match the developmental level of the examinee is an essential skill in psychological practice (Sattler, 2024).

Monitoring Engagement and Fatigue

Throughout the session, the examiner should continually monitor the examinee's motivation, affect, and engagement. Look for signs of fatigue, frustration, or boredom, particularly during longer test batteries. Breaks should be offered between tests when appropriate. These may include restroom visits, a few moments for the examinee to refresh themselves with a snack, or simply have a few minutes to rest. Breaks during individual tests should be avoided unless necessary. This is especially true in timed tasks, as a break may invalidate results. That is, the delay between FNAME and FNAME Delay, as well as the delay between RAVLT and RAVLT Delay, should be no less than 5 minutes and no greater than 25 minutes; allowing a break between those tests might invalidate them if the delay is too short, too long, or if the examinee was subjected to additional memory load. Consider documenting any unscheduled breaks in the assessment notes; this documentation will become of increasing importance if the unscheduled break could have impacted the test results (e.g., extreme emotional response to a test item, resulting in failure to respond).

Engaging in light conversation during breaks between tests can serve to renew rapport and provide the examinee a mental or emotional reset. These short breaks might be all that is needed to encourage continued effort. However, examiners should be sensitive to the examinee's demeanor. Some individuals may benefit from social interaction, while others, who tend to be more introverted, may find it taxing (Sommers-Flanagan & Sommers-Flanagan, 2022). Use of clinical intuition informed by training and experience should guide the examiner's decision-making process on how to best engage each individual examinee.

Conclusion of Testing

At the conclusion of testing, thank the examinee for their time and effort. Express appreciation for their participation and, if necessary, reassure them that the tasks were designed to be challenging. For example, the examiner might encourage the examinee by saying, "These tests are designed to be challenging and have items of all different types of difficulty. The important part is that you gave your best effort."

It is important that the closing interaction gives the examinee a sense of accomplishment and dignity, regardless of their performance. If parents or caregivers are present, they should also be thanked and reassured about the appointment as appropriate.

Results

Although the scoring algorithms in the NIH Toolbox automatically score the tests when the assessment is completed, care should be taken before sharing results directly with the examinee during the testing session. That is, the NIH Toolbox app provides numerical scores for each test, but an interpretation of the resultant test scores must be conducted in a broader clinical context, integrating history, referral questions, and behavioral observations. In other words, the examiner should not immediately show the score report to the examinee because those values (e.g., an age-adjusted standard score of 81 on the Dimensional Change Card Sort test) will have little meaning without proper interpretation from a trained professional; or worse, the examinee might interpret the values on their own and come to inaccurate conclusions (e.g., my National Age-Adjusted Percentile was 20 on that test, so that must mean I am in the top 20% of the nation).

> **CAUTION 2.2**
>
> Examiners should never show examinees their test results immediately upon completing their assessment. Professionals trained in interpreting test results must first review the scores, administration notes, and all relevant examinee background information before determining whether the examinee's performance during that administration was as expected, and what in particular those results allude to.

The final discussion of results and implications should be deferred to a licensed clinical or referring provider; in many cases, the clinical provider is not always the one administering the tests. Thus, the clinical provider should establish guidelines about what to do if the examinee requests immediate feedback. The examiner could say: "I understand you are curious about your results, but unfortunately, I can't provide feedback at this time.

The results need to be reviewed and interpreted by Dr. X, who will go over them with you in the context of your full evaluation during your follow-up appointment."

In the instance that the NIH Toolbox was taken as part of a research study, the principal investigator or study lead should establish guidelines as to how to address the request for results. It is important to address these examinee expectations early on, as it could avoid confusion and tension later after the study has already begun. For example, the research study might be focused on group-level data, and individuals are therefore not meant to receive their scores. Again, it is best to discuss this prior to their participation to avoid any misunderstandings.

FEEDBACK DURING THE EVALUATION

Appropriate and consistent feedback during cognitive testing is essential for maintaining examinee engagement, minimizing anxiety, and ensuring valid performance. Within standardized assessment protocols, like the NIH Toolbox, feedback must be carefully given to both preserve the psychometric integrity of the testing while supporting the examinee throughout the session.

Balancing Encouragement with Standardization

Examiners should follow the administration guidelines provided by the *NIH Toolbox V3 Administration Manual* (Hook & Giella, 2023) to ensure standardization across testing environments. However, clinical flexibility is sometimes needed to sustain motivation, particularly in lengthier batteries or with examinees who appear anxious, fatigued, or uncertain about their performance.

The goal of all examiner feedback should be to encourage task persistence and reduce emotional reactivity, without disclosing information about the accuracy of the examinee's responses or offering any cues that may bias test performance. Research suggests that examiner demeanor, including being kind and friendly, coupled with neutral encouragement, can support examinee engagement, particularly in younger or more vulnerable populations (Sattler, 2024). Gently offering basic encouragement (e.g., "You're doing great") to examinees who are frustrated or discouraged may be the difference between them continuing or their refusal to complete the current test (or even the rest of the assessment).

Types of Effective Feedback

Neutrality

Examiners should refrain from giving corrective or evaluative feedback during the live test items, unless specifically directed to do so in the NIH Toolbox V3 Administration Manual. This includes avoiding any facial expressions, body language, or tone of voice that may reveal whether an answer is right or wrong. For example, wincing, smiling, raising eyebrows, or nodding can all influence examinee behavior, often unconsciously (Hersen & Thomas, 2007).

Table 2.1 Situational Examples

Scenario	Appropriate Feedback	Notes
A child pauses after making an error	"Nice work. Let's see what comes next."	Encourages persistence without highlighting the error
An adult sighs or groans after a difficult task	"That one was tricky. Thanks for sticking with it."	Normalizes difficulty and emphasizes effort
An examinee is losing motivation midway through a long session	"You're doing a great job focusing. We're making good progress."	Reinforces engagement and provides a sense of progress with the end in sight
After a break, before resuming testing	"Let's jump back in. You're doing well so far."	Sets a positive tone for resuming work

Encouragement Without Evaluation

Feedback should be supportive and general. Use phrases that reinforce effort, persistence, and comfort without implying judgment. Some examples include (Table 2.1):

- "You're doing great. Keep going."
- "Thanks for working so hard on this."
- "Keep with it. You are doing just fine."
- "Keep going. You're doing a good job. Stay focused."

Avoid Overpraising

Encouragement can be helpful, but excessive praise is not appropriate. This is especially true for individuals who are sensitive to performance pressure. If an examiner repeatedly says "Excellent!" or "Perfect!," then this can unintentionally raise expectations or increase anxiety. It may also lead to inflated effort on noncritical tasks or disengagement when difficulty increases (Hersen & Thomas, 2007). In other words, when an examiner repeatedly overly emphasizes praise (e.g., "You're doing so great!"), it may begin to sound disingenuous or fake, especially when the examinee recognizes they guessed on the previous response and is quite confident the response was incorrect; hearing praise after a clearly incorrect response may further discourage or disengage the examinee (e.g., "He knows I'm failing but still continues to praise me like a child; he just wants to rush me to through the end of the test and doesn't care if I pass or fail.").

Individual Differences

Not all examinees respond to feedback in the same way. Children may benefit from more frequent encouragement, while adolescents or adults may prefer a more professional tone. For example, individuals with anxiety or low frustration tolerance may benefit from reassurance to complete difficult tasks. Examiners should strive to understand the examinee's posture, demeanor, and countenance to determine whether that examinee might benefit from a few words of additional encouragement or potentially perform more favorably without them.

Types of Feedback to Avoid

Examiners should avoid providing feedback that may unintentionally skew results, reduce reliability, or compromise the validity of individual test scores (Suchy & Miller, 2023).

- **Judgmental feedback:** "That wasn't right," or "You missed that one."
- **Hints or cues:** "Are you sure you want that answer?" or "I'd think twice about that one."
- **Exaggerated praise:** "That was the best answer that I have ever seen!" or "I've never seen anyone answer that item so quickly before," particularly if the examinee didn't answer correctly.

Nonverbal Feedback

As indicated earlier in the "Neutrality" of feedback subsection, examiners should be aware of their nonverbal behavior such as facial expressions, gestures, or posture which can impact an examinee's behavior during testing. Facing the examinee and maintaining eye contact while speaking with them can encourage engagement, while outright staring is likely to make the examinee uncomfortable. It may be the case that what the examiner said sounded neutral, but their facial expressions conveyed a different meaning. For example, raised eyebrows, nodding, smiling, or sighing may unintentionally signal to an examinee that their response was correct or incorrect. This may be particularly important to be aware of when assessing children or individuals who have a high need for approval or reassurance, as these individuals may rely more heavily on examiner cues for guidance (Sommers-Flanagan & Sommers-Flanagan, 2022). To preserve standardization and test validity, examiners should remain conscious of their body language and facial expressions and maintain a calm and open posture.

In sum, feedback is a great tool for supporting examinees through the assessment process. When used correctly, it can foster rapport, motivation, and optimal engagement. The examiner, however, must be aware of the boundaries of appropriate verbal and nonverbal feedback within the standardized testing context to ensure that the scores are reflective of the examinee's abilities and not inadvertently influenced by extraneous variables.

BEHAVIORAL OBSERVATION

Even with digital tests, like the NIH Toolbox, there is no substitute for examiner observation. Behavioral observations can provide essential context for interpreting performance.

The examiner should be attuned to:

- fatigue or inattention (e.g., yawning, restlessness, and wandering eyes),
- motor disturbances (e.g. tremor at rest, while doing a task, or both),
- complaints of visual or auditory problems (e.g., excessive squinting and frequently asking the examiner to repeat instructions), but report that they don't use glasses or hearing aids,

- overly emotional reactions (e.g., giving up easily, verbal expressions of distress), and
- external interruptions or distractions (e.g., yelling in the hall, car alarm during live items).

The observations should be documented in the notes function on the app, as they can aid in interpretation, particularly when results may appear inconsistent or atypical.

LANGUAGE AND CULTURAL CONSIDERATIONS

The NIH Toolbox V3 tests were developed and normed in English, in the United States; examiners should consider this when using these tests with individuals who are not from the United States or with whom English (US) is not their native or primary language. The NIH Toolbox was designed to be inclusive and has undergone review in different cultural settings and languages. The NIH Toolbox team engaged international and intercultural experts to highlight items that may be inappropriate in certain cultures or regions. Some changes were made to the NIH Toolbox V3 tests to accommodate their feedback, though it is recognized that the final version might still contain some cultural and linguistic nuances, especially when administered to international examinees.

Choice of language in which the test is administered should be determined prior to the examinee coming into the session. For example, if the examinee is fluent in Spanish and requires administration of the NIH Toolbox V3 en Español, the examiner may not be able to comply if they themselves don't speak Spanish. For a comprehensive list of available translations, please refer to https://nihtoolbox.org/get-the-toolbox/.

If translators are needed (e.g., the examiner is not fluent in Spanish), the examiner must decide if this method of test administration will yield results that they can use. It may be that a supervisor or licensed clinical neuropsychologist should be consulted to understand best practices. Notably, it is better to obtain a translator that is available through a third party, such as translation services (e.g., available at some hospitals). Using a family member should be avoided as they may influence the results. That is, they might deliberately translate an item in a non-exact way to assist the examinee's understanding or inadvertently translate the instructions with a slightly altered meaning, which might shift the examinee's perception of the task (and therefore not necessarily test exactly the same construct as an examinee who takes the same test without a translator).

Examiners who choose to administer NIH Toolbox V3 English tests to examinees outside of the United States and in a language other than English (US) must consider that even if the examinee is completely fluent in English or if a regionally appropriate translation is available, their cultural references may inadvertently impact their responses. For instance, while translating the NIH Toolbox V2 Dimensional Change Card Sort test into Swahili and Dholuo, cognitive interviews revealed that younger native-speaking children had difficulty conceptualizing "shape" (Duffey et al., 2022). In this case, the examinees' responses and, therefore, scores may be impacted differently and/or measure a different construct than a child of the same age who grew up in the United States, which might subsequently be less of a test of executive function and more of a test of understanding the prompts.

Unique dialects might also inadvertently impact the examinee's responses. For example, someone who grew up in the United Kingdom might understand someone native to Australia perfectly, despite some words, phrases, and their accents being different. Though this might not be noteworthy in casual discussions and interactions, the difference in dialect might unexpectedly alter the examinee's understanding of the instructions and/or items. Similarly, someone from Spain might be able to communicate fluently with someone who grew up in Puerto Rico, though some wording or references might be more difficult to understand. Even if casual conversations between those individuals are perfectly understandable, that does not guarantee each person's understanding of the test instructions and content is the same as someone from the normative sample (i.e., an English speaker in the United States).

Another notable difference in translated content is that although English (US) does not have a formal/informal distinction, many other languages and cultures have distinctly different ways in which the examiner would speak with adults or those with whom they are unfamiliar (i.e., formal language) versus how they speak with children, family, and friends (i.e., informal language). For instance, an instruction in DCCS in English, regardless of the examinee's age, is "Now you try;" regardless of age, all examinees see and hear the same instructions. That same instruction in Spanish is, "Ahora inténtelo usted" for adults aged 18 and older, and "Ahora inténtalo tú" for examinees aged 17 and younger. Though formal versus informal distinctions are unlikely to impact the examinee's understanding of the instructions and task, it may be worth noting this linguistic difference when administering and/or interpreting results.

In summary, it is important to be aware that cultural norms can influence communication, test-taking behavior, and perceptions of cognitive testing. The examiner should avoid judgment or misattribution when encountering unfamiliar behavior.

HANDLING NONCOMPLIANCE

If an examinee becomes significantly unruly or uncooperative and is performing below expected levels due to factors unrelated to cognitive abilities (e.g., severe anxiety and conduct disorder), the examiner should attempt gentle redirection to return the examinee's full attention to the task. The examiner should always avoid coercion or shaming; regardless of the reason for or nature of the examinee's noncompliance, they should always be treated with respect. Should the examinee continue to be unwilling or unable to continue testing, the examiner should end the session and document the reason for early termination or incomplete data.

In the event the testing session is ended prematurely, the examiner should add a test-level note in the app to indicate why the examinee did not complete that test or why the assessment ended early. Generally, more information is ideal, especially if looking back on notes from months prior, or if the results are interpreted by someone other than the person who administered the test. For instance, it would be more helpful to see, "Examinee refused to continue; he reported that he did not sleep well last night and was running late, so he did not have enough time to eat lunch prior to assessment. Asked to reschedule, if possible," than to see, "Examinee refused."

DON'T FORGET 2.4

Incomplete or invalid administrations should be flagged in the app with a note. Detailed notes can be referenced and used to better understand unexpected scores or missing data.

TESTING WITH SPECIFIC POPULATIONS

Administering cognitive tests requires not only the knowledge of standardized testing procedures, but also developmental sensitivity to ensure that examinees are able to respond to the best of their abilities.

Assessing Children

Children can present unique challenges during cognitive testing due to variability in development level, attention span, motivation, and comfort with being in a highly structured situation. While the NIH Toolbox V3 is designed to be engaging and developmentally appropriate, examiners should be cautious to take extra steps to engage children.

Before starting a testing session with a minor, examiners need to obtain legal consent from the child's parent or legal guardian. While obtaining the child's assent, or agreement to participate in testing, is not legally required, it is important to assist in rapport building and engaging the child in testing.

Selection of words and framing tasks as activities or games versus tests may more effectively engage children and make the situation less intimidating (Sattler, 2024). Without changing the instructions for tests, it may help guide the examinee into the task with the mindset that they're about to "play a special game" (instead of "we're going to take some tests"). As much as possible, the examiner should err on the side of having a friendly, animated tone and being flexible while still maintaining professional boundaries.

Brief verbal praise, stickers, short movement breaks, or playful conversation between tests can help maintain motivation and engagement. Behavioral research shows that immediate reinforcement (e.g., stickers or a favorite topic of discussion) can help maintain engagement with young children (Hersen & Thomas, 2007). For example, offering wiggle breaks at the end of certain tests might help motivate younger examinees. It is the examiner's responsibility to engage the examinee and maintain their interest as much as possible. Asking about the child's favorite television show, superhero, or game can often go a long way to reinvigorate them between tasks. Younger, active children often benefit from "showing off their dance moves," doing a few in-place jumping jacks, taking a short walk around the hallway, or being offered a small ball to hold and squeeze while not responding to live test items.

For young children, a parent or guardian may remain in the testing room, provided they are seated quietly away from the testing area and refrain from giving cues or feedback. With this positioning, the parent or guardian would be able to provide periodic encouragement if needed, without disrupting the test administration. External interference, such as a parent directing the examinee, may invalidate the results, so it is important for the examiner to monitor for subtle coaching behaviors and document any interference. If their presence is disruptive, the examiner might need to ask the parent or guardian to leave the room until the testing session is over. It is also possible that older children may prefer to take the assessment alone, in which case the examiner should try to accommodate those wishes.

Children with high activity levels may benefit from brief gross motor activities like jumping jacks. These strategies align with sensory integration principles, helping regulate arousal and optimize cognitive engagement (Sattler, 2024).

Assessing Adults

Adults tend to expect more formal or structured interactions. Examiners should try to tailor communication to match individual preferences or cultural norms.

Address adults by title and surname unless invited to use a first name. That is, the examiner should generally address the examinee formally, such as "Mrs. Smith" instead of "Jane." While some may feel this is too rigid, it is often better to err on the side of being more formal than being perceived as unprofessional or disrespectful. Remember that a calm and confident tone helps with maintaining the examinee's comfort.

Some adults may be more sensitive or prone to embarrassment regarding their performance and might treat the tests less seriously to buffer themselves from disappointing results. Examinees who do this should be encouraged to try their best. It may be helpful to remind the examinee that the tests are designed in a way that even top-performing examinees rarely get every item correct. Just because an item or a test is very difficult does not mean that the examinee is doing poorly, and that is by design.

Examiners should avoid discussing the examinee's performance outside of practice items. Examiners should address such concerns with general feedback, such as, "You are doing fine. Try your best."

Assessing Participants with Diminished Cognitive or Physical Capacity

For all populations, but especially for examinees with diminished cognitive capacity, examiners should speak clearly and slowly. The *National Institutes of Health Toolbox Cognition Battery Supplemental Administration Manual for Intellectual and Developmental Disabilities: A Guide on Administration and Scoring Standards* (McKenzie et al., 2023) is a great resource for using the NIH Toolbox V3 tests with people with intellectual disability, and is free to download from https://resources.nihtoolbox.org/.

When testing individuals with reduced cognitive capacity, sensory deficits, or motor impairments, examiners should make every effort to ensure accessibility while maintaining standardization. However, in certain circumstances, the examiner might wish to make exceptions to the standardized procedures to obtain assessment results. If this is done, the examiner should add detailed test notes in the app regarding what changes were made or how the examination was non-standardized. For example, though not part of a standard administration, it would be acceptable for an examinee to use a Speech-Generating Device if they require that to effectively communicate—provided the examinee only uses it to produce their response and not otherwise storing data in the device to assist with answering the test (e.g., on a world list learning task, saving the words so they would be available at recall).

Examiners should introduce themselves at the beginning of the testing session and broadly remind the examinee what they will be doing and why they are taking these tests. Look for indications that the examinee understands, such as a verbal response or nodding. Slow down if you notice the examinee seems to have trouble keeping up. Some examinees might process things at a slower pace, so speaking and demonstrating tasks more slowly might be helpful, even if it prolongs the testing session.

Ensure the testing environment is safe and accommodating for people with special needs, such as wheelchairs. As much as possible, remove obstacles that might put the examinee at risk of falling and ensure they can easily reach the iPad and any relevant forms they might need to fill out.

Consider that medication use or time of day may impact the examinee's performance. For example, if the examinee is generally more alert during the morning, that would be the ideal time for testing. If the examinee needs to take a specific medication at noon, testing should not be scheduled around that time.

Examinees with visual deficits should wear any corrective lenses they normally wear for reading. If they normally wear corrective lenses but do not have them at the time of testing, that should be recorded in the administration notes. And, depending on how severely impaired the examinee's vision is, that testing session may be considered invalid, and the examiner may choose to discontinue the testing.

If the examinee has sensory impairments, it may help to speak slowly and clearly, and increase the iPad's volume. Some examinees rely on lip reading, so examiners should keep their hands away from their faces and turn to the examinee directly while speaking.

Listen to any concerns the examinee might have and pay close attention to what the examinee does not say outright (e.g., agitated body language, irritability, and dejected expression). Some examinees may be more easily fatigued, more prone to physical distress, or exhibit higher levels of stress than other examinees and not want to draw attention to something they might deem a deficit. Provide positive reinforcement and continue to encourage them throughout the assessment, without sounding patronizing. Provide breaks as needed.

CONCLUDING RECOMMENDATIONS

In this section, general testing recommendations and best practices are highlighted. Remember that while the NIH Toolbox is designed to be "easy to use," there is no substitute for knowing and practicing tests prior to using them; they require the examiner to first familiarize themselves and practice administering each test prior to seeing their first real examinee.

This chapter discussed the following:

- **Preparation:** Review all materials in advance. Examiners should conduct mock administrations until comfortable with the app interface and scripted instructions. Confidence and preparation enhance examiners' feelings of credibility, and this is easily sensed by the examinee.
- **Appointment considerations:** Those who are responsible for scheduling the appointment should be fully aware of what types of testing the examinee will face, and without revealing too much, the scheduler should inform the examinee of the requirements (e.g., bring corrective lenses or hearing aids, if applicable).
- **Technical readiness:** Ensure all software is updated, all electronics are fully charged, and Bluetooth accessories are synced (if the keyboard is needed). Have materials, such as the NIH Toolbox V3 Administration Manual, on hand and in order of administration.
- **Establish rapport:** Examinees who feel comfortable and confident tend to respond better, and in a way that more accurately reflects their true ability level. Trusting the examiner is among the first steps toward establishing rapport and ensuring a successful test administration.
- **Respect the examinee:** If the examinee refuses a test, offer encouragement and an opportunity to reengage, but don't overly pressure them.
- **Feedback during evaluation:** Examiners should be sufficiently trained to anticipate examinee feedback, commentary, and noncompliance, and to have a standardized method to reorient such examinees or otherwise acknowledge if/when prematurely end the assessment.
- **Documentation:** Use the NIH Toolbox app's note function to record behavioral observations, task interference, refusals, or irregularities during administration. Specific notes are invaluable for later interpretation (e.g., fire alarm went off during the Flanker test and it was discontinued).
- **Closing the session:** Make sure to thank the examinee for engaging in the testing session. Normalize that the items on the test were designed to be hard, and that the examinee did a great job.

TEST YOURSELF

1. Which of the following is not required when scheduling a testing session?

(a) Clarifying the referral question/reason for testing so the examiner understands the impetus for the assessment

(b) Telling the examinee that they need to physically bring all their current medications so staff can confirm the medication names and dosages on the bottle labels against what is recorded in the system

(c) Describing what the testing session will entail so the examinee has a clear expectation of what will transpire during the appointment

(d) Verifying the examinee's information (e.g., name, date of birth, and relevant medical history)

2. Which of the following is the examiner responsible for during testing sessions?

(a) Maintaining the examinee's physical safety

(b) Maintaining a good rapport with the examinee

(c) Being cognizant of the examinee's mental state

(d) All of the above

3. Examiners should respect the examinee's refusal to take a test or assessment.

True or False

4. Examiners should add notes to the app and on their testing protocol if something out of the ordinary occurs during the testing session.

True or False

5. Examiners should only rely on the examinee's ability to inform the examiner when they are distressed; the examiner does not need to ask them if they are okay.

True or False

6. Which of the following is the most appropriate introduction to a testing session?

(a) "Hello. My name is __. Today, we will be working on some tasks that will help me better understand the complaints you've recently expressed to your primary care physician."

(b) "Hello. My name is __. Thank you for your time today. Today, we will work on some tasks that help me see how deeply you have been impacted by your recent fall and the extent of your concussion."

(c) "Hello. My name is __. Thank you for your time today. I see that you've recently expressed concerns about your memory, so we're going to see how much that is actually a cause for concern."

(d) "Hello. My name is __. Today, we will be evaluating the attention and executive function issues you mentioned previously. Doing poorly on these tasks is more likely to give me reason to prescribe __."

7. **When the examinee is fatigued or losing interest, the examiner should force them to continue until the test is over.**
   True or False
8. **Which of the following is the most explanatory note to enter for an abnormal administration?**
   (a) "Examinee was distracted."
   (b) "Examinee was very wiggly."
   (c) "Examinee was distracted. Upon questioning, she revealed that her mother would prohibit ice cream if she performed poorly today."
   (d) "Examinee was impatient for the assessment to end."
9. **Examiners should address their child and adult examinees in the same way.**
   True or False
10. **Examinees who normally use corrective lenses (i.e., glasses and contacts) should use those during test administration.**
    True or False

Answers: 1. (b); 2. (d); 3. True; 4. True; 5. False; 6. (a); 7. False; 8. (c); 9. False; 10. True

REFERENCES

Duffey, M. M., Ayuku, D., Ayodo, G., Abuonji, E., Nyalumbe, M., Giella, A. K., … McHenry, M. S. (2022). Translation and cultural adaptation of NIH toolbox cognitive tests into Swahili and Dholuo languages for use in children in Western Kenya. *Journal of the International Neuropsychological Society*, *28*(4), 414–423. https://doi.org/10.1017/S1355617721000497

Hersen, M., & Thomas, J. C. (2007). *Handbook of clinical interviewing with children.* SAGE Publications.

Hook, J. N., & Giella, A. K. (2023). *National Institutes of Health (NIH) Toolbox® V3 administration manual.* Toolbox Assessments, Inc.

McKenzie, F. J., Drayton, A., Shields, R. H., Dakopolos, A., Glassman, D., Kaat, A., … Hessl, D. (2023). *National Institutes of Health Toolbox® Cognition battery supplemental administration manual for intellectual and developmental disabilities: A guide on administration and scoring standards.* University of California.

Sattler, J. M. (2024). *Assessment of children: Cognitive foundations and applications* (7th ed.). Jerome M. Sattler Publisher, Inc.

Sommers-Flanagan, J., & Sommers-Flanagan, R. (2022). *Clinical interviewing* (6th ed.). Wiley.

Suchy, Y., & Miller, J. B. (2023). *Neuropsychological interviewing of adults.* Oxford University Press.

Three

HOW TO ADMINISTER AND SCORE THE NIH TOOLBOX® COGNITION TESTS

Julie N. Hook
Amy K. Giella

NAVIGATING THE NIH TOOLBOX V3 APP

Setting Up the App

The NIH Toolbox V3 app is free to download from the App Store. Users can explore the app for free, but an active subscription is required to save any data and view test results. For current subscription information, please visit NIHToolbox.org. The first time the app is opened, the user must create an eight-digit passcode that will be required to access the app each time it is opened and after assessments are completed. It is important to keep this passcode safe. If users lose or forget the passcode, they will need to email the NIH Toolbox Help Desk (Help@NIHToolbox.org) for support.

CAUTION 3.1

It is important to store and keep the eight-digit passcode safe. Users cannot access the app without it.

In accordance with the Standards for Educational and Psychological Testing developed jointly by the American Psychological Association et al. (2014), Cognition tests require special access. To gain access to the Cognition tests, examiners must submit for a credential review, which can be done for free at Resources.NIHToolbox.org. Approved examiners will gain access to Cognition test support materials online, and they will need to separately enter their credentials (which are given at the time of approval) in the NIH Toolbox V3 app, in the *Access to Cognition* section in the app's Settings.

Participants

After the NIH Toolbox V3 app has been set up (e.g., app has a valid subscription and access to Cognition tests has been verified), the examiner can create participants and assessments. To create a participant, the examiner should tap on the *Participants* button on the left sidebar, then tap the *New Participant* button at the bottom corner. A unique participant identifier (PID) and the participant's date of birth are required fields. All other fields are optional, though some scores cannot be calculated without certain information. For instance, age- and education-adjusted *T* scores cannot be calculated without the participant's education level. Some tests—such as Oral Reading Recognition (ORR), Picture Vocabulary (PV), and Visual Reasoning (VR)—require the participant's education level (and parent's education, if the participant is younger than 19 years of age) to route the participant to the appropriate live item start point during administration.

CAUTION 3.2

Take care with entering the Participant Identifier, as this cannot be changed after the participant has been created.

Assessments

An assessment is a test or tests that is/are administered to a participant/examinee. Some examiners administer a wide range of tests as part of a general evaluation, while others select tests that measure a more specific set of constructs. After a participant has been created in the app, the examiner can create an assessment and add any test from any domain. When selecting tests, it is important to note the appropriate age ranges displayed beside each test; although it is possible to administer tests to participants beyond the appropriate age range, some scores will not be calculated.

Results

Tapping on the *Results* button on the left sidebar in the app displays each assessment's information. Each assessment card displays the participant's identifier, name, assessment name, completion date, status (i.e., not started, in progress, and completed), and whether that assessment's data has been previously exported. It is possible to view each assessment's data by tapping on the individual icons to the right of each assessment card, or by tapping the *Select* button at the top of the screen and selecting any/all assessments.

Types of Data Files

NIH Toolbox assessment data is presented in either PDF form or CSV format. The *Score Report* is available only as a PDF and includes information about a specific assessment for a specific participant. It includes demographic information, test-level scores, composite-level scores (if applicable), and notes entered by the examiner for that assessment. Score Reports are a great way for the examiner to view and interpret a participant's performance during that particular assessment.

Alternatively, examiners can view the data in CSV (i.e., spreadsheet) format via the export files. There are three types of export files, each containing different types of information, which can be linked using the PID. The *Registration Export* details the participant demographics, app version, firmware version, and iPad version. The *Scores Export* contains information and scores at the test-level, such as test-level change-sensitive scores (CSSs), the time the assessment began and ended, and whether there were any interruptions during a test. The *Item Export* includes item-level information, such as responses, scores, and response times for each item. An alternative, rotated view of the Registration Export, Scores Export, and Item Export is available as Narrow Structure files. Narrow Structure files are most often used by analysts and databases to create filtered and/or pivoted datasets. That is, the Narrow Structure file contains much of the same information, just a different structure.

Rapid Reference 3.1

NIH Toolbox Result Formats	
Score Report	**Exports**
Available only in PDF format	Available only in CSV format
Displays information for a specific assessment	Displays information for any assessments that are selected by the examiner
Presents demographic information, test-level scores, and composite-level scores	Presents demographic information, app and iPad details, test-level scores and details, and item-level scores and details
Information is produced in a single, comprehensive file	Information is produced separately in CSV files

Export Options

The Score Report PDF can be viewed directly on the screen in the app, and it can be emailed to any email address.

There are five ways to view the CSV export files. *Email* allows the examiner to email the files to any email address. *iPad File Sharing* allows the examiner to transfer files directly from the iPad to a computer via a cable. *Upload to iCloud* allows the examiner to export the files to the iCloud that are associated with the Apple ID signed into that iPad. *Upload to Web Server* allows the examiner to send the files directly to an existing location on the web. Examiners can also view results directly on the screen to quickly check for anything of note. Please remember that the user must set up their preferred export method on their iPad.

Data Security

The NIH Toolbox has several levels of security to protect collected data. The NIH Toolbox app requires the iPad to have a passcode, and sensitive parts of the app are locked behind an eight-digit app passcode. In other words, to view any examinee data, the person must know

CAUTION 3.3

It is critical to note that data (e.g., participants, assessments, collected data, and results) in the NIH Toolbox are stored in the app. If the app is deleted or the iPad is lost, that data cannot be recovered. NIH Toolbox users should regularly export and back up their data to avoid major data loss.

the iPad passcode and the NIH Toolbox V3 app passcode. Collected data is stored directly on the device, in the app, and can only be exported if the app administrator first navigates to the app's Settings and permits any of the export options listed earlier. Three of the export options—iPad File Sharing, Upload to iCloud, and Upload to Web Server—send data directly to the examiner's external system. The email export option allows the examiner to encrypt the files as an additional security measure.

The NIH Toolbox V3 Administration Manual (Hook & Giella, 2023) provides a wealth of information about setting up and using the app. All examiners, clinicians, data collectors, and administrators should read the NIH Toolbox V3 Administration Manual prior to administering tests to become familiar with best practices and administration procedures.

ADMINISTRATION OVERVIEW

Administration of the NIH Toolbox V3 Cognition tests is streamlined to be as easy and straightforward as possible for both the examiner and the examinee. All NIH Toolbox V3 Cognition tests are administered via an iPad, though three tests (i.e., List Sorting Working Memory, Oral Reading Recognition, and Oral Symbol Digit) also use external materials, such as a wireless keyboard or external answer sheet that can be accessed for free on NIHToolbox.org. During administration, a title screen is presented before each test, which depicts any additional materials or equipment that might be required for that test. This helps orient the examiner to the upcoming task and acts as a reminder to have the designated materials at hand for that test. Figure 3.1 shows the icons/materials and equipment that are needed for various tests in the Cognition domain.

With a few exceptions, the workflow of each test is generally the same. First, the task is introduced to the examinee so they can understand what they will be expected to do, and some tests may include a more detailed demonstration of the task. Then, the examinee has the opportunity to respond to a few practice items, which will present feedback based on their responses (e.g., "Good job!" for correct responses, or "These pictures are the same, so you should tap YES," for incorrect responses). The practice items and feedback are designed to help the examinee see what types of live items will be presented and how to respond correctly to them. Next, there is typically a transition screen that summarizes the task once more and allows the examinee to confirm they are ready to begin the live test items. After this transition, the examiner begins the live items. Responses are recorded and automatically scored within the NIH Toolbox V3 app, and results are available immediately following a fully completed assessment (e.g., tests were not incomplete due to skips or pauses).

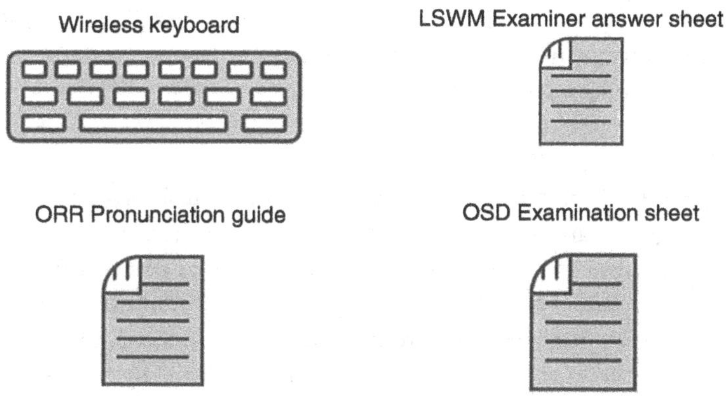

Figure 3.1 Title Screen Icons for Cognition Domain Tests. Note. LSWM = List Sort Working Memory; ORR = Oral Reading Recognition; OSD = Oral Symbol Digit.

Test instructions were written to be simple and precise, so the tasks are as straightforward as possible. For each test, instructions are the same across all ages, so it was critical during the development of these tests to ensure a 3-year-old could understand the tasks as well as an 89-year-old. Attention was also given to future test translations into languages other than native English. Thus, it was even more important for the wording to be precise so that direct translations could be easily understood across languages and cultures.

To decrease variability across administrations, the Cognition tests were designed to be as automated as possible, while still allowing the examiner some control to pause, return to the instructions or practice items, replay instructions, and move the test to a later point in the administration. Although test instructions are the same for all ages, some tests have different starting points that are based on the examinee's age or age/education. For instance, a 20-year-old will begin the List Sorting Working Memory test's live items at a greater difficulty than a 7-year-old. Item routing is done automatically in the background, though examiners have the option to override the start points for select Cognition tests if they believe an examinee should be tested at a higher or lower level.

TESTS

Dimensional Change Card Sort

Dimensional Change Card Sort (DCCS) measures mental flexibility and is a test for examinees aged four and older that takes around four minutes to complete. DCCS measures executive functioning by asking examinees to quickly shift between two dimensions: shape and color. Before each item is presented, a word is displayed on the screen and read aloud via prerecorded audio—"SHAPE" or "COLOR"—then a target image is presented in the middle of the screen, with two buttons at the bottom of the screen. Depending on the word that was just presented, the examinee must select, as quickly as possible, which of the bottom images matches the target image's shape (ball or truck) or color (orange or blue). Speed and accuracy are factors in scoring, so quick and accurate responses produce high scores.

Administration

A series of instructions, practice items, trial items, and transitions guides the examinee through the task's expectations before moving on to the live items.

The first set of instructions prepares the examinee to "play some games." In the "color game," the examinee should choose the picture from the bottom that is the same color as the target picture in the middle of the screen. After the instructions, the examinee is given five practice items where they should match rabbits or sailboats by color—either white or brown. These practice items are the only time in DCCS when the examinee hears feedback. The audio either says, "That's right!" and moves to the next practice item, or it says, "This is the same color, so you should choose this picture," while a blue box blinks around the correct picture. If the examinee answers four or five practice items incorrectly, the test ends.

After the practice items, the colors change from brown and white to orange and blue, and the shapes change from rabbits and sailboats to balls and trucks. There are two sets of trial items to help orient the examinee before the live items. First, the color trials direct the examinee to select the picture at the bottom of the screen that is the same as the target picture at the middle of the screen (that is, either orange or blue). After these instructions, five trial items are presented. Regardless of whether the examinee answers correctly, the test automatically moves to the next item after the examinee responds, or after 10 seconds without a response.

Next, the test introduces the "shape game," where examinees are asked to select the response that is the same shape as the picture in the middle of the screen (that is, either ball or truck). After these instructions, five shape trial items are presented. Regardless of whether the examinee answers correctly, the test automatically moves to the next item after the examinee responds, or after ten seconds without a response.

After the shape trials, there is a transition screen that summarizes the task. When the examinee is ready, the examiner can move the purple "Slide to continue" button across the screen to move on to the live items. If the examinee is not ready, the examiner can take a moment to either replay the audio on that screen or briefly summarize the task for the examinee.

There are 30 live items of orange and blue balls and trucks. Before each item, the word "SHAPE" or "COLOR" is presented on the screen and via audio to prime the examinee which of the two buttons to select. The test automatically advances to the next item after ten seconds without a response. After all 30 items are administered, the test ends.

Scoring

DCCS produces item-level scores (i.e., correct or incorrect) and response times. At the test level, DCCS produces the following scores: CSS, CSS standard error, age-adjusted standard score, age-adjusted standard score standard error, age- and education-adjusted

T score, age- and education-adjusted *T* score standard error, age-adjusted national percentile, and computed score. Additionally, DCCS calculates the median response time for all completed live items. The commission error score is the number of incorrect responses on the live items. The omission errors score is the number of live items the person did not respond to or ran out of time on.

The DCCS test is included in two preset batteries: Cognition Battery and Early Childhood Cognition Battery. DCCS scores are used to calculate the Fluid Composite, Total Cognition Composite, and Early Childhood Composite.

Face Name Associative Memory Exam and Face Name Associative Memory Exam Delay

Face Name Associative Memory Exam (FNAME) measures delayed visual and associative memory for examinees aged 18 and older. The FNAME, learning trial, and FNAME Delay are listed in the app as separate tests but are intended to be administered in the same assessment, with a 5- to 25-minute delay between them. During this delay, examiners should select activities that will not interfere with the delayed recall of this material, such as another test like VR, or allowing the examinee to take a break. FNAME introduces the task, then presents 12 faces paired with names, one at a time. FNAME Delay has three parts that ask the examinee about the faces and names they saw earlier: examinees must select which faces were shown before, select the first letter of the person's name, and identify the person's name from three options. FNAME takes around three minutes to administer and FNAME Delay takes about four minutes to administer. Examinees who can remember the pictures and the names associated with them receive higher scores.

Administration

FNAME has one instruction screen, a practice item, a transition, and then 12 items.

The FNAME instructions tell the examinee via text on the screen and audio played through the iPad's speakers that they will be shown pictures of faces with names below them, and that the examinee should quickly decide whether it will be easy or hard for them to remember the face-name pairs. The practice item on the next screen shows a picture of a woman, her name printed underneath the picture, and two buttons at the bottom: *Easy* and *Hard*. The examinee should tap either the *Easy* or the *Hard* button to indicate whether they think it will be easy or hard to remember the face and the name that is associated with it. Regardless of the examinee's response, the picture and the name remain on the screen for five seconds, then the test automatically advances to the transition screen. The transition screen tells the examinee they will see more pictures of faces paired with names, and that they should try to remember the name that goes with each face. When the examinee is ready, the examiner can slide the purple button to the right to begin the live items.

The 12 live items in FNAME are presented one at a time, and each remains on the screen for five seconds before automatically moving to the next item. There are six male faces and six female faces that vary in race and age, shown in alternating orders (i.e., male, female, male, and female). After all 12 face-name pairs have been displayed, the last screen in FNAME reminds the examinee that they will be asked about the faces and names later.

After FNAME ends, the NIH Toolbox V3 app begins an internal timer. After FNAME and before FNAME Delay, the examiner should provide an activity that does not impact the examinee's recall of the test items. For example, the examiner could administer non-memory-related tests or allow the examinee to take a break to use the bathroom or eat a snack. If the examiner attempts to begin FNAME Delay too early or too late (i.e., sooner than 5 minutes or after 25 minutes have elapsed), a message appears, telling the examiner that it is too soon or too late to administer FNAME Delay. The examiner is given the option to continue with FNAME Delay, skip FNAME Delay, or stop the assessment. If FNAME Delay is administered too soon or too late, the examiner should note this as a non-standard administration.

> **DON'T FORGET 3.1**
>
> After FNAME has been completed, there must be a delay of 5–25 minutes before FNAME Delay should be started.

FNAME Delay has three parts, and each part has instructions, a practice item, a transition screen, and then 12 live items. FNAME Delay begins with the instructions for *Faces Seen Before* (FSB) presented as text on the screen and via recorded audio played through the iPad's speakers. The examinee is reminded of the faces and names they saw earlier, and that now they must select the faces they have already seen. The practice item presents three pictures in a row, one of them being the same picture of the woman from the FNAME practice item. The test automatically advances to the next screen when the examinee taps one of the three faces or after five seconds have elapsed. There is no feedback to inform the examinee if they answered correctly or incorrectly. The following transition screen tells the examinee they will do some more, and they should quickly select the face they saw earlier. When the examinee is ready, the examiner slides the purple button to the right to begin the 12 live items. Each live item has three pictures of people that look similar (e.g., similar color shirt, similar haircut), but only one of the pictures is the same as the one shown in FNAME. If the examinee does not respond within five seconds, the next item appears.

After the FSB portion of FNAME Delay, examinees see and hear instructions for the *First Letter of Name* (FNL) items. The instructions tell the examinee to tap the first letter of the person's name. The practice item shows the picture of the same woman in the previous practice items, and a grid of 24 letters in alphabetical order. The test automatically advances to the next screen when the examinee taps a letter or after ten seconds have elapsed. There is no feedback to inform the examinee if they answered correctly or incorrectly. The following transition screen tells the examinee they will do some more, and they should quickly select the first letter of that person's name. When the examinee is ready, the examiner slides the purple button to the right to begin the 12 live items. If there is no response within ten seconds, the next item appears.

The third and final portion of FNAME Delay is *Face-Name Matching* (FNM). The instructions tell the examinee to select the person's name. The practice item shows the same picture of the woman in the previous practice items, and three names below the picture, one of which is correct. The test automatically advances to the next screen when the examinee taps a name or after five seconds have elapsed. There is no feedback to inform the examinee if they answered correctly or incorrectly. The following transition screen tells the examinee they will do some more, and they should quickly select each person's name. When the examinee is ready, the examiner slides the purple button to the right to begin the 12 live items. If there is no response within five seconds, the next item appears.

Scoring

FNAME produces item-level response times. At the test level, FNAME produces a raw score. FNAME Delay produces item-level scores (i.e., correct or incorrect) and response times. At the test level, FNAME Delay produces the following scores: raw score, theta, theta standard error, CSS, CSS standard error, age-adjusted standard score, age-adjusted standard score standard error, age- and education-adjusted *T* score, age- and education-adjusted *T* score standard error, and age-adjusted national percentile. Additionally, FNAME Delay calculates the number of correct responses per trial.

FNAME and FNAME Delay are not included in any preset batteries or composite scores.

Flanker Inhibitory Control and Attention

Flanker Inhibitory Control and Attention (Flanker) can be administered to examinees aged four and older and takes about three minutes to complete. Flanker measures attention, inhibitory control, and executive function. Five fish with arrows over them are shown in a row on the screen. The fish/arrows either always point in the same direction (i.e., left or right), or the fish/arrow in the middle points in the opposite direction of the other arrows (e.g., four of the fish point left, but the fish in the middle points right). Below this row of fish are two buttons—one with an arrow pointing left and one with an arrow pointing right—and the examinee is asked to select the button that corresponds to the direction the middle fish/arrow is pointing. Speed and accuracy are factors in scoring, so quick and accurate responses produce high scores.

Administration

A series of instructions, practice items, and transitions guides the examinee through the task's expectations before moving on to the live items.

On the first screen, the instructions are written out and read aloud via audio. The instructions let the examinee know that they will see a row of fish, and they must choose the button that corresponds with the direction the fish in the middle is pointing. The next few screens demonstrate how to respond when there are congruent items (i.e., all fish/arrows pointing the same way) and incongruent items (four fish/arrows point one way while the middle fish/arrow points the opposite way).

After the instructions, there is a brief transition screen that tells the examinee that they will practice the task next, and they should keep their focus on the middle of the screen. Then, five practice items are presented. Before each practice item, a star appears in the middle of the screen, and then the practice item is immediately presented. The star is meant to center the examinee's attention on the middle of the screen, which is exactly where the middle fish/arrow appears milliseconds later. If the examinee answers the practice item correctly, the audio says, "Great job!" and moves to the next practice item. If the examinee answers the practice item incorrectly, the audio says, "The middle fish is pointing this way, so you should choose this button," while a circle appears around the middle fish/arrow and the correct button blinks; then the test will automatically move to the next practice item. If the examinee answers four or five practice items incorrectly, the test ends.

After all practice items have been administered, a transition screen shows text and plays corresponding audio to remind the examinee they should keep their eyes on the star in the middle of the screen, and to respond as quickly and accurately as they can. If the examinee is ready, the examiner can move the purple "Slide to continue" button across the screen to move on to the live items. If the examinee is not ready, the examiner can take a moment to either replay the audio on that screen or briefly summarize the task for the examinee.

There are 30 live items, which are presented in a fixed order; that is, the same fish/arrow sequence is presented in the same order for every administration. The test automatically advances after the examinee taps one of the response buttons or after ten seconds without a response. After all 30 items are administered, the test ends.

Scoring

Flanker produces item-level scores (i.e., correct or incorrect) and response times. At the test level, Flanker produces the following scores: CSS, CSS standard error, age-adjusted standard score, age-adjusted standard score standard error, age- and education-adjusted *T* score, age- and education-adjusted *T* score standard error, age-adjusted national percentile, and computed score. Additionally, Flanker calculates the median response time for all completed live congruent items and all completed live incongruent items. The commission error score is the number of incorrect responses on the live congruent items. The omission errors score is the number of live items the person did not respond to or ran out of time on.

The Flanker test is included in two preset batteries: Cognition Battery and Early Childhood Cognition Battery. Flanker scores are used to calculate the Fluid Composite, Total Cognition Composite, and Early Childhood Composite.

List Sorting Working Memory

List Sorting Working Memory (LSWM) is a test that measures working memory and generally takes around seven minutes to administer. This task requires examinees aged five and older to watch and remember the foods and animals as they appear visually on the screen and are named via the iPad's audio, then the examinee should say them back in size order. In the first part (i.e., 1-List), examinees must mentally and verbally arrange either foods or animals from smallest to biggest. In the second part (i.e., 2-List), examinees are shown a series of foods and animals, then are asked to say the foods back from smallest to biggest, and then the animals from smallest to biggest. LSWM is not a timed test, so examinees can take as much time as they need to mentally rearrange the foods and animals. The examiner follows along with the *NIH Toolbox V3 List Sorting Working Memory Examiner Answer Sheet*, then scores the examinee's verbal response via an external Bluetooth keyboard by keying "1" for a correct response or "0" for an incorrect response. The LSWM Answer Sheet is available for free at NIHToolbox.org to users who have been approved for access to Cognition tests.

DON'T FORGET 3.2

LSWM requires the examiner to enter examinee responses on a Bluetooth keyboard, and should use the LSWM Answer Sheet as a guide to score responses.

Administration

A series of instructions, practice items, and transitions guides the examinee through the task's expectations before moving on to the live items. The test is structured in two parts: 1-List and 2-List.

The test begins with the 1-List instructions, which tell the examinee, "You will see some pictures one at a time on the screen. When you hear the chime, tell me the pictures you just saw in size order from smallest to biggest." There are two practice items, each with two opportunities/trials for the examinee to answer correctly. If the examinee answers the practice item correctly, the audio says, "That's right!" and moves to the next practice item. If the examinee answers the practice item incorrectly, corrective feedback appears and plays through the iPad's speakers. If the examinee answers all four practice item trials incorrectly, the test ends. If the examinee answers at least one practice item trial correctly, a transition screen summarizes the task and allows the examinee the opportunity to ask any questions. When the examinee is ready, the examiner can slide the purple button to the right to begin the live items.

There are 12 live items in 1-List, increasing in difficulty from two-picture sequences up to seven-picture sequences. That is, the easiest items have two pictures (e.g., a horse and a dog), and the most difficult items have seven pictures of foods or animals. The examinee's age determines their starting item; kids aged 5 to 8 begin with a two-picture sequence, and people aged 9 and older begin with a four-picture sequence.

Items are presented by showing the food or animal picture with the name printed below it, while the audio says the name of the food or animal. After all pictures in the item have been presented, the iPad plays a chime sound to indicate all pictures have been presented, and it is time for the examinee to respond. There is a letter at the bottom of the iPad screen which corresponds to the *NIH Toolbox V3 List Sorting Working Memory Examiner Answer Sheet*; the examiner uses this key with the answer sheet to determine if the examinee's response is correct. After the examiner keys the score into the Bluetooth keyboard (i.e., "1" for correct, "0" for incorrect) and presses the spacebar, the test automatically moves to the next item. Basal and ceiling rules are built into the test to automatically route the examinee to the next appropriate item until they have attained the appropriate basal level and the ceiling level (i.e., responded incorrectly to two items of the same sequence length).

After the 1-List live items, instructions for the 2-List task are presented. In 2-List, examinees are shown foods *and* animals, and they must repeat them back in size order, starting with foods, then animals. For instance, if the examinee sees a frog, a pineapple, and a tiger, they should repeat back, "pineapple, frog, tiger." Like in 1-List, there are two practice items, each with two opportunities/trials to answer correctly, then there is a transition screen. 2-List has 12 live items that are structured much like 1-List. Examinees aged five to eight begin with a two-picture sequence, people aged nine to 14 begin with a three-picture sequence, and examinees 15 and older begin with a four-picture sequence. The examiner must use the Bluetooth keyboard to note correct and incorrect responses, and, like 1-List, the test's built-in basal and ceiling rules route the examinee to the appropriate items until the basal and ceiling have been reached and the test ends.

Scoring

LSWM produces item-level scores (i.e., correct or incorrect). At the test level, LSWM produces the following scores: raw score, theta, theta standard error, CSS, CSS standard error, age-adjusted standard score, age-adjusted standard score standard error, age- and education-adjusted *T* score, age- and education-adjusted *T* score standard error, and age-adjusted national percentile.

The LSWM test is included in the Cognition Battery. LSWM scores are used to calculate the Fluid Composite and Total Cognition Composite.

Oral Reading Recognition

Oral Reading Recognition (ORR) is for examinees aged seven and older and measures the examinee's ability to read and decode individual words on the screen and orate them with the correct pronunciation. This is not an assessment of the examinee's ability to understand the meaning associated with a given word. As a computerized adaptive test (CAT), ORR generally takes four minutes to administer from the first instruction screen through all live items. For each item, examinees are shown a single word on the screen, and they must say the word aloud. The examiner must listen and evaluate whether the pronunciation is correct. On an external Bluetooth keyboard, the examiner must press "1" if the response is correct or "0" if the response is incorrect. If the examinee's response is correct, a more difficult word is presented next. If the word is not pronounced correctly, an easier word is presented next. For examinees who perform very poorly on this test, a single letter may be presented. If the examinee has difficulty naming individual letters, the CAT may present an array of numbers and a letter, asking the examinee to point to the letter. The test automatically ends when 20–35 items have been presented. Accurate pronunciations produce high scores.

Prior to administering ORR, the examiner must download and extensively review the supplemental files that are freely available on www.nihtoolbox.org. That is, the examiner must know how to pronounce all the words in ORR to correctly score the examinee, as it is a CAT-based test, and any words can be presented. The examiner can review the words through the downloadable sound files and the written *Oral Reading Recognition Pronunciation Guide*, which indicates the correct pronunciation. Also, prior to beginning the test, the examiner must pair the wireless Bluetooth keyboard with the iPad.

DON'T FORGET 3.3

ORR requires the examiner to enter examinee responses on a Bluetooth keyboard, and should use the Oral Reading Recognition Pronunciation Guide as a guide to score responses.

Administration

The instructions are presented on the screen and played through the iPad's speakers. The examinee is informed that they will see some letters and words, and they should read each letter or word out loud. The instructions inform the examinee that it's okay if they are unfamiliar with the word or its meaning; they should just read the word aloud to the best of their ability. There are no practice items for ORR.

After the instructions, the test immediately moves to the live items. For examinees aged 3 to 18, their age is used to determine the difficulty of the first live item they see. For examinees aged 19 and older, their education (i.e., less than high school, completed high school, some college, four-year college degree or higher) is used to determine the difficulty of the first live item they see. Each of the examinee's responses determines the difficulty of the next item that is presented. Items are not timed, so the examinee has as much time as they need to evaluate the word and how to correctly pronounce it.

This test does not listen to or automatically evaluate the examinee's verbal response. For each item, the examiner must press "1" or "0" on the wireless keyboard to let the test know if the response was correct or incorrect, then press the spacebar to enter/submit the response. It is important for the examiner to have the wireless keyboard at hand, though hidden or obstructed from the examinee's view, so the examinee cannot discern what the examiner types on the keyboard. The examiner can go back one item by pressing the left (back) arrow if they accidentally entered the incorrect response/score, or if the examinee immediately self-corrects. It is not possible to go back more than one item at a time.

The test ends when at least 20 items have been administered, and the standard error of the ability estimate falls below 0.44 logits (LaForte et al., 2024, p. 21).

Scoring

ORR produces item-level scores (i.e., correct or incorrect), theta, and theta standard error. At the test level, ORR produces the following scores: theta, theta standard error, CSS, CSS standard error, age-adjusted standard score, age-adjusted standard score standard error, age- and education-adjusted *T* score, age- and education-adjusted *T* score standard error, and age-adjusted national percentile.

The ORR test is included in the Cognition Battery. ORR scores are used to calculate the Crystallized Composite and Total Cognition Composite.

Oral Symbol Digit

Oral Symbol Digit (OSD) measures processing speed in examinees aged five and older. Examinees look at a grid of symbols printed on the paper *NIH Toolbox V3 Oral Symbol Digit Examination Sheet* on the table in front of them. Each symbol is paired with a number (one through nine), and the examinee must say the number associated with each symbol as quickly as they can within 120 seconds. The examiner uses the iPad to mark correct responses. Quick and accurate responses yield high scores. OSD takes around three minutes total to administer.

DON'T FORGET 3.4

OSD requires the NIH Toolbox V3 Oral Symbol Digit Examination Sheet.

Administration

A series of instructions, practice items, and transition guides the examinee through the task's expectations before moving on to the live items.

The examiner must angle the iPad away from the examinee so they cannot see the screen. Then, the examiner should place the *NIH Toolbox V3 Oral Symbol Digit Examination Sheet* in front of the examinee with Side 1 facing up. Side 1 has a grid of symbols paired with numbers and a separate grid of only symbols. Side 1 is used as a tool to introduce the instructions, then to demonstrate and practice the task.

Unlike other NIH Toolbox V3 Cognition tests, OSD requires the examiner to actively demonstrate the instructions with an external supplemental material (i.e., *OSD Examination Sheet*). Since each examiner does this at a different speed, there is no prerecorded audio for this test. Instead, the instructions on the screen tell the examiner what to read aloud and when they should point to specific places on the *OSD Examination Sheet.*

The instructions ask the examinee to look at the symbols at the top of the page (i.e., the top row of the first grid). Using the instructions written on the iPad screen, the examiner explains, and points when appropriate, that each symbol is paired with a number (e.g., "O" is paired with the number 6). Before moving on, the examiner should confirm that the examinee understands the symbol-digit pairs.

Then the examiner asks the examinee to focus on the second grid (i.e., the row of symbols only) and say the number that is paired with each symbol across the row. For instance, the first symbol is "O," so the examinee should look at the grid above, see that "O" is paired with 6, then say "6" aloud. The examinee should do this for all nine practice items. The examiner should say, "That's right!" for correct responses, and provide corrective feedback for incorrect responses. When the examinee is ready, the examiner reads a summary of the task, reminding the examinee that they should say the number that matches each symbol, as quickly and accurately as possible, moving across the top row, then moving to the next row, until the iPad's timer indicates the test is over.

Then, the examiner turns the *OSD Examination Sheet* over. Side 2 has the same grid of symbols paired with numbers at the top, and below that is a grid of 13 rows, 11 symbols across. The examiner should tap "Next" on the iPad, then tap the "Start Test" button at the bottom of the screen to begin a 120-second timer. As the examinee moves across the row, saying each number, the examiner follows along on the iPad, which shows the same grid of symbols paired with the correct number. For each item the examinee says correctly, the examiner taps that item on the screen to mark it as correct. Self-corrections should be marked as correct. The total number of correct responses appears in real time at the bottom of the screen. Incorrect or skipped items should not be tapped (i.e., remain unselected and marked incorrect). When 120 seconds have elapsed, the iPad beeps and the examinee should stop the task. A message appears on the screen, allowing the examiner to either continue marking responses that were provided before the 120-second time limit, or to end the test.

Scoring

OSD produces item-level scores (i.e., correct or incorrect). At the test level, OSD produces the following scores: raw score, theta, theta standard error, CSS, CSS standard error, age-adjusted standard score, age-adjusted standard score standard error, age- and education-adjusted *T* score, age- and education-adjusted *T* score standard error, and age-adjusted national percentile.

OSD is a supplemental test that is not included in any preset batteries or composite scores.

Pattern Comparison Processing Speed

Pattern Comparison (PC) Processing Speed is a measure of the speed at which the examinee processes information. This test is appropriate for examinees aged five and older and takes around three minutes to administer. For each item, two pictures of equal size are presented on the screen, with two buttons at the bottom (*Yes* and *No*). The two pictures are either identical or have a slight difference between them. The examinee must compare the pictures as quickly as they can and determine whether the pictures are the same by tapping either the *Yes* or *No* button. Speed and accuracy are factors in scoring, so quick and accurate responses produce high scores.

Administration

A series of instructions, practice items, and transitions guides the examinee through the task's expectations before moving on to the live items.

When the test begins, the instructions tell the examinee that there will be two pictures on the screen, and the examinee should decide if those pictures are the same or not the same. If the two pictures are the same, the examinee should tap the *Yes* button that is on the bottom of the screen. If the two pictures are not the same, the examinee should tap the *No* button at the bottom of the screen.

After the instructions, the examinee is given three practice items where they should indicate whether the two pictures are the same or not the same. These practice items are the only time in PC when the examinee will hear feedback. The audio will say, "That's right!" if the examinee selects the correct response. If the examinee answers incorrectly, the audio will either say, "These pictures are the same, so you should tap 'Yes,'" or "These pictures are NOT the same, so you should tap 'No'." During any corrective feedback, the correct response button (i.e., *Yes* or *No*) blinks. Regardless of performance on the practice items, all examinees move forward to the transition screen, which informs them they will do some more, and they should go as fast as they can without making mistakes. When the examinee is ready, the examiner slides the purple button all the way to the right to begin the live items.

The examinee must quickly and accurately answer as many of the 133 live items as they can within the allotted 80 seconds. For each item, the examinee must tap the *Yes* button if the pictures are the same or the *No* button if the pictures are not the same. The test automatically advances to the next item after ten seconds without a response. After 80 seconds have elapsed or all 133 items have been administered, the test ends.

Scoring

PC produces item-level scores (i.e., correct or incorrect) and response times. At the test level, PC produces the following scores: raw score, theta, theta standard error, CSS, CSS standard error, age-adjusted standard score, age-adjusted standard score standard error, age- and education-adjusted *T* score, age- and education-adjusted *T* score standard error, and age-adjusted national percentile. Additionally, PC calculates the median response time for all completed live items.

The PC test is included in the Cognition Battery. PC scores are used to calculate the Fluid Composite and Total Cognition Composite.

Picture Sequence Memory

Picture Sequence Memory (PSM) is a seven-minute assessment of episodic memory for examinees aged three and older. Pictures and brief associated audio are presented, one at a time, then are scrambled together in the middle of the screen. The examinee must drag each picture to the boxes along the left, bottom, and right sides of the screen, in the order they were presented. The examinee's age and performance determine how many sequences and how many pictures they will see. Placing the pictures back in the same order they were presented yields high scores.

There are two parallel forms—PSM Form A and PSM Form B—which examiners can use in reliability studies. The main difference between PSM Form A and PSM Form B is the order in which the two themes are presented. The Fair theme has pictures related to a fair or festival, such as eating a hot dog, playing a game, and going on a ride. The Park theme has pictures such as laying out a blanket, riding a bike, and going for a walk.

Administration

First, a brief instruction screen introduces the examinee to the task, then an animated demonstration shows the examinee how to move the images that appear in the yellow box in the middle of the screen to the smaller boxes along the sides of the screen. Examinees who are three to five years old are shown two practice items, while examinees aged six and older see a single, slightly longer practice item. Examinees have two opportunities/trials to answer each practice item correctly. If they respond correctly to at least one trial, they move to a transition screen, then to the live items.

The PSM form and the examinee's age determine how many pictures they see on the first live item, and their performance on that first item determines how difficult the next items are. For example, a four-year-old will see six Fair theme pictures, and if they perform well, they will be shown nine Park theme pictures. As another example, a 30-year-old taking Form B will see 15 Park pictures, and if they place most items back in the incorrect order, that examinee will see nine Fair pictures next. When the examinee finishes placing all the pictures from the middle yellow box into the boxes around the edges of the screen, they are asked if they are finished or if they would like to make any changes. When the examinee confirms they are done with the first item, the test automatically calculates the adjacent-pairs score (i.e., how many pictures were placed in the correct sequential order, even if they're not in the correct location). The adjacent-pairs score determines which sequence the examinee is given next. Examinees can see anywhere from two to four live items/sequences, then the test ends.

Scoring

PSM produces item-level scores (i.e., correct or incorrect) and response times. At the test level, PSM produces the following scores: theta, theta standard error, CSS, CSS standard error, age-adjusted standard score, age-adjusted standard score standard error, age- and education-adjusted *T* score, age- and education-adjusted *T* score standard error, and age-adjusted national percentile.

The PSM test is included in two preset batteries: Cognition Battery and Early Childhood Cognition Battery. PSM scores are used to calculate the Fluid Composite, Total Cognition Composite, and Early Childhood Composite.

Picture Vocabulary

Picture Vocabulary (PV) is a measure of receptive vocabulary and language for examinees aged three and older. As a CAT, PV generally takes three minutes to administer from the first instruction screen through all live items. For each item, examinees are shown four pictures on the screen while the prerecorded audio plays the target word. Then, the examinee must tap on the picture that best represents the word, while the three other pictures serve as distractors (e.g., homophones). For example, one item's target word is "pillars" and displays the following four pictures: a puddle on the ground, a caterpillar, a chimney (single pillar atop a roof), and pillars of a building. If the examinee selects the correct picture, the test moves to a more difficult item. If the examinee selects an incorrect picture, an easier item is presented next. The test automatically ends when 20–35 items have been presented.

Administration

After being introduced to the task, examinees have the opportunity to respond to two practice items, then are shown a brief transition before moving on to the live items.

The instructions on the first screen inform the examinee that they will hear a word and see four pictures on the screen, and that the examinee should tap the picture that shows what the word means. The first instruction screen also orients the examinee to the *Play again* and *Back* buttons, which they can use during the live items. The *Play again* button repeats the target word via audio for the item, and the *Back* button allows the examinee to go back to the previous item to change their last answer.

Two practice items follow the instruction screen. The audio asks the examinee to touch the picture of a banana. If the examinee selects the correct image out of the four pictures on the screen, a checkmark and blue box appear around the picture, and the audio says, "That's right!" If the examinee selects an incorrect image, a red box appears around the selected picture while a blue box appears around the correct picture, and the audio says, "This is a banana. Let's try again." The examinee can try again and again until they select the correct picture, then the next practice item is presented. The examinee must select the correct picture before the test moves forward.

After the practice items, a transition screen informs the examinee that they will be shown more items and then briefly summarizes the task. When the examinee is ready, the examiner can slide the purple button to the right to begin the live items.

Age is used in examinees aged 3–18 to determine the difficulty of the first live item they see. For examinees aged 19 and older, their education (i.e., less than high school, completed high school, some college, four-year college degree or higher) is used to determine the difficulty of the first live item they see. Each of the examinee's responses determines the difficulty of the next item that is presented. Items are not timed, so the examinee has as much time as they need to consider the options and to replay the audio of the target word. The *Back* at the top of the screen allows the examinee to go back to the previous item only to change their answer; they cannot go back more than one item at a time. The test ends when at least 20 items have been administered, and the standard error of the ability estimate falls below 0.44 logits (LaForte et al., 2024, p. 24).

Scoring

PV produces item-level scores (i.e., correct or incorrect), response times, theta, and theta standard error. At the test level, PV produces the following scores: theta, theta standard error, CSS, CSS standard error, age-adjusted standard score, age-adjusted standard score standard error, age- and education-adjusted *T* score, age- and education-adjusted *T* score standard error, and age-adjusted national percentile.

The PV test is included in three preset batteries: Cognition Battery, Early Childhood Cognition Battery, and Early Childhood Cognition Battery—CFPS. PV scores are used to calculate the Crystallized Composite, Total Cognition Composite, Early Childhood Composite, and Early Childhood CFPS Composite.

Rey Auditory Verbal Learning and Rey Auditory Verbal Learning Delay

Rey Auditory Verbal Learning (RAVLT) measures verbal learning and memory for ages five and older. RAVLT and RAVLT Delay are listed as separate tests in the app, but are intended to be administered in the same assessment, with a 5- to 25-minute delay between them. During this delay, examiners typically administer a test that does not burden memory (e.g., Visual Reasoning) or allow the examinee to take a break. RAVLT presents a recorded list of 15 words that are played through the iPad's speakers, then the examinee is asked to say all the words they can remember. The same list of 15 words is presented two more times for a total of three trials, and each time the examinee must say as many words as they can remember. After a 5- to 25-minute delay, the examinee is asked to freely recall as many of those 15 words as they can remember. RAVLT takes around three minutes to administer, and RAVLT Delay takes one minute to administer. Examinees who can remember more of the 15 words receive higher scores.

Administration

On the first screen, the examinee sees and hears instructions that tell them to listen and remember the list of words that will be presented to them. Then, the examiner should turn the screen away from the examinee so they cannot see it. On the next screen, the examiner taps the "Play" button, then the iPad speaker plays 15 words at a rate of one word per second. After the last word, a chime sound plays from the iPad to inform the examinee that the list is over, and they should start saying as many of the 15 words as they can. The examiner interacts with the iPad screen by tapping each word the examinee answers correctly. Self-corrections should be marked as correct, but similar words (e.g., "home" instead of "house") should be marked as incorrect. RAVLT presents the same word list a total of three times and allows the examinee to respond after each word list is presented. Then, the test ends.

After RAVLT ends, the NIH Toolbox V3 app begins an internal timer. After RAVLT and before RAVLT Delay, the examiner should do something that does not tax the examinee's memory; administering non-memory-related tests or taking a bathroom or snack break are recommended. If the examiner attempts to begin RAVLT Delay too early or too late (i.e., sooner than 5 minutes or after 25 minutes have elapsed), a message appears, telling the examiner that it is too soon or too late to administer RAVLT Delay. The examiner is given the option to continue with RAVLT Delay, skip RAVLT Delay, or stop the assessment. If RAVLT Delay is administered too soon or too late, the examiner should note this as a non-standard administration.

RAVLT Delay has an instruction screen that reminds the examinee that they heard a list of 15 words earlier. The examiner should again turn the screen away from the examinee so they cannot see it, then the examiner should navigate to the next screen, which has the list of 15 words from before. The examiner should tap all the words that the examinee recalls. When the examinee is done, the examiner ends the test.

Scoring

RAVLT and RAVLT Delay produce item-level scores (i.e., correct or incorrect). At the test level, RAVLT and RAVLT Delay produce the following scores: raw score, theta, theta standard error, CSS, CSS standard error, age-adjusted standard score, age-adjusted standard score standard error, age- and education-adjusted *T* score, age- and education-adjusted *T* score standard error, and age-adjusted national percentile. Additionally, RAVLT calculates the number of correct responses per trial.

RAVLT is not included in any preset batteries or composite scores.

Speeded Matching

Speeded Matching (SM) is a test appropriate for examinees aged three-six, though normative data is available for children up to eight and a half years old. SM presents an image in the middle of the screen and four images at the bottom of the screen. The images are simple, single-color line drawings of different animals. The picture color is always the same within each item. An item may have a line drawing of a blue cat in the middle of the screen, and line drawings of a blue dog, blue cat, blue horse, and blue donkey at the bottom. The examinee is directed to tap on the picture that is the same as the one in the middle of the screen. SM measures processing speed and takes just three minutes to administer. Quick and accurate responding yields high test-level scores.

Administration

SM begins by presenting a picture in the middle of the screen and four pictures that act as buttons at the bottom of the screen. Since this is a test for young children, the instructions are played through the iPad's speaker only (i.e., no text on the screen). The audio recording says, "Look at this picture." A box around the middle picture blinks, then stops to draw the child's attention. "Tap the picture down here," boxes around the bottom four pictures blink, then stop, "that looks the same." As a demonstration, the examiner is meant to indicate the correct picture, then tap it. Then the audio says, "Now you try it. Use only one finger to tap." Only the correct picture is active at this time, so the only way for the test to move forward is for the examinee to select the correct picture.

After the instructions and demonstration, the practice items are introduced. A brief transition screen says, "Now let's try some more!" There are four practice items, each with two trials/attempts to respond correctly. Audio and visual animations orient the examinee on the first practice item, asking them which pictures on the bottom of the screen are the same as the one in the middle of the screen. If the examinee taps the correct picture, the audio says, "Great job!" If the examinee answers any practice item incorrectly, corrective feedback is provided, and the examinee is given one more opportunity to answer that item correctly. If the second attempt is correct, the audio says, "Great job!" If the second attempt is incorrect, the audio says, "These pictures are the same," then a box appears around the picture in the middle of the screen and the matching picture at the bottom. After the examinee responds to each practice item, the appropriate feedback is played (i.e., praise or corrective prompts), then the test automatically advances to the next item. If the examinee answers each trial of all four practice items incorrectly (i.e., eight incorrect responses on the practice items), the test ends.

After all practice items are presented (and if the examinee answered at least one practice trial correctly), a transition screen appears. The transition screen reminds the examinee via text and audio that they should choose the picture that is the same as the one on top, and they should go as fast as they can without making mistakes. When the examinee is ready, the examiner can slide the purple button all the way to the right to begin the live items.

The examinee must tap on one of the four pictures at the bottom of the screen, then the test automatically advances to the next live item. The examinee has 90 seconds to respond to as many of the live items as they can, then the test ends.

Scoring

SM produces item-level scores (i.e., correct or incorrect) and response times. At the test level, SM produces the following scores: raw score, theta, theta standard error, CSS, CSS standard error, age-adjusted standard score, age-adjusted standard score standard error, and age-adjusted national percentile. Additionally, SM calculates the median response time for all completed live items.

The SM test is included in the Early Childhood Cognition Battery—Crystallized-Fluid-Processing Speed (CFPS). SM scores are used to calculate the Early Childhood CFPS Composite.

Visual Reasoning

Visual Reasoning (VR) is an assessment of executive function in nonverbal and visual reasoning, and can be administered to examinees aged three and older. VR has images in the middle of the screen, generally displayed in a pattern, sequence, or puzzle. For easier items, the examinee must choose which of the response options at the bottom of the screen looks most like the picture(s) in the middle of the screen. For example, if there is a pencil in the middle of the screen and the response options are a loaf of bread, a fish, a pen, and a banana, the examinee should pick the pen because, of the available options, it is most like the pencil in the middle of the screen. More difficult items have a missing component, and the examinee must choose which of the response options best completes the sequence or puzzle. More difficult items often include grids of geometric shapes and colors that form a pattern which the examinee must identify, then pick the response option that best completes the pattern. If the examinee responds correctly, the test moves to a more difficult item. If the examinee selects an incorrect option, an easier item is presented next. As a CAT, VR generally takes seven minutes to administer, and the test automatically ends when 20–35 items have been administered.

Administration

A series of instructions, practice items, and transition guides the examinee through the task's expectations before moving on to the live items.

First, the instructions appear as text on the screen and are played via a prerecorded audio file. The instructions tell the examinee that they will see a picture in the middle of the screen and some pictures at the bottom; the examinee should select the option from the bottom that is most like the picture in the middle of the screen or shows the missing picture.

Then, three practice items are presented, each demonstrating a different type of live item (e.g., "which picture looks most like the target" and "which picture completes the sequence or pattern"). Examinees are given two opportunities to answer each practice item correctly. If they respond correctly, the audio says, "That's right!" and the test automatically moves to the next item. If the examinee taps an incorrect option, animations and corrective audio explain which is the correct answer, then allow the examinee to answer once more. After all three practice items are administered, a transition screen summarizes the test. If the examinee answers all six practice item trials incorrectly, the test ends. When the examinee is ready, the examiner begins the live items.

Ages is used for examinees aged 3–18 to determine the difficulty of the first live item they see. For examinees aged 19 and older, their education (i.e., less than high school, completed high school, some college, four-year college degree or higher) is used to determine the difficulty of the first live item they see. Each of the examinee's responses determines the difficulty of the next item that is presented. Although the test is not timed, a prompt appears if 60 seconds have elapsed without the examinee picking an answer; however, the examinee can spend as much time as they would like on each item. The test ends when at least 20 items have been administered, and the standard error of the ability estimate falls below 0.44 logits (LaForte et al., 2024, p. 31).

Scoring

VR produces item-level scores (i.e., correct or incorrect) and response times. At the test level, VR produces the following scores: theta, theta standard error, CSS, CSS standard error, age-adjusted standard score, age-adjusted standard score standard error, age- and education-adjusted *T* score, age- and education-adjusted *T* score standard error, age-adjusted national percentile.

The VR test is included in the Early Childhood Cognition Battery—Crystallized-Fluid-Processing Speed (CFPS) (Ages 3–6). VR scores are used to calculate the Early Childhood CFPS Composite.

Scoring

A number of different scores are provided for the NIH Toolbox Cognition tests and composites. Different types of scores provide different information about an individual's performance on the NIH Toolbox tests and composites. For example, a norm-referenced score describes an individual's relative standing in a group of peers but is less useful for describing relative change in ability between two time points. Test users should select the metric(s) that are most appropriate for the interpretation(s) they are making from the NIH Toolbox scores.

A raw score is an unadjusted score. For the FNAME Delay, OSD, RAVLT, and SM tests, the raw score represents the total number of test items the participant answers correctly. For the LSWM test, the raw score is the total number of lists the participant correctly responds to, plus one point for each unadministered sequence below the basals in the 1-List and 2-List portions of the test. No raw scores are reported for the ORR, PV, DCCS, Flanker, PSM, or VR tests.

A computed score is a special type of raw score that takes into account the participant's speed and accuracy in answering the test items. Computed scores are reported only for the DCCS and Flanker tests.

A theta score is a metric derived from Item Response Theory (IRT), which is a type of statistical analysis used in test development. Unlike raw-score scales, theta scales are equal-interval metrics. This means that a change of 1 theta point has the same meaning across the entire scale range. Theta scores are reported for all tests except DCCS and Flanker. A typical range of test theta scores on the NIH Toolbox is −8.0 to +8.0, but varies by test. Although theta scores can be useful for tracking growth or decline over time, they are less interpretable than CSSs because they can be negative and can contain decimals.

Like a theta score, a change-sensitive score (CSS) is also an IRT-based metric. CSSs are provided for all NIH Toolbox Cognition tests and composites. The CSS score is simply a linear transformation of the theta score, where CSS = 500 + (9.1024 * Theta). The resulting value is rounded to the nearest integer to remove decimals. This transformation produces scores that are always positive integers, making them easier to explain and interpret; a typical range of CSS on the NIH Toolbox tests and composites is approximately 400–600, but varies across the battery. As its name implies, the CSS is the recommended metric for use cases where the amount of change over time (i.e., growth or decline) is of interest. Because it is an equal-interval metric (like tick marks on a ruler), differences in CSS can be compared within and across examinees. For example, if one examinee shows an increase of 5 CSS points from pre- to posttreatment and another examinee shows an increase of 10 points during the same timeframe, then it can be stated that the second examinee showed twice as much growth as the first examinee. This type of interpretation cannot be made with raw scores, computed scores, or any of the norm-referenced scores provided in the NIH Toolbox.

An age-adjusted standard score is a norm-referenced score that describes an individual's performance relative to their same-age peers in the NIH Toolbox V3 norming sample. It is based on a normal distribution of CSSs where the mean is set equal to 100 and the standard deviation is set equal to 15. Age-adjusted standard scores are useful for describing the performance of an individual, or comparing the performance of multiple individuals, at a single point in time. Because age-adjusted standard scores are computed by comparing an individual's score to the distribution of scores from same-age peers, changes over time can only be interpreted in the context of the individual's relative standing in the reference group. For example, it could be possible for an individual to display growth in an ability from pre- to posttreatment (as evidenced by a positive change in CSS from Time 1 to Time 2) but to obtain a lower age-adjusted standard score at Time 2 than at Time 1. In this scenario, the individual's own rate of growth between Time 1 and Time 2 was outpaced by the reference peer group's rate of growth, resulting in a lower relative standing for the individual at Time 2. For this reason, norm-referenced standard scores are not recommended for comparing performance across time points.

An age-adjusted national percentile is another way of describing an individual's performance relative to their same-age peers. Age-adjusted national percentiles are reported on a scale of 1–99 and can be interpreted as the percentage of same-age peers in the population who would obtain a score that is equal to or less than the individual's obtained score. Like age-adjusted standard scores, age-adjusted national percentiles are useful for describing the performance of an individual, or comparing the performance of multiple individuals, at a single point in time. The same cautions and recommendations that apply to age-adjusted standard scores apply to age-adjusted national percentiles.

An age- and education-adjusted *T* score is similar to an age-adjusted standard score, with two differences that are implied in the score name. First, these scores describe an individual's performance relative to their same-age peers in the NIH Toolbox V3 norming sample who also have the same level of education. Second, age- and education-adjusted *T* scores are reported on a *T* score metric, with a mean of 50 and a standard deviation of 10. Age- and education-adjusted *T* scores are only reported for adults aged 22 and older in NIH Toolbox V3 Cognition tests. The same cautions and recommendations that apply to age-adjusted standard scores apply to age- and education-adjusted *T* scores.

Error is inherent in all test scores; the standard error of measurement (SEM) quantifies the amount of variation in a distribution of observed test scores that is due to measurement error. A large standard error implies that a test score has less precision, or reliability, than a test score with a smaller standard error. Any observed test score is an estimate of the "true" score; the ±1 SEM interval around an observed test score provides a range within which the "true" score lies, with 68% probability. NIH Toolbox V3 provides standard errors of measurement for the theta score, CSS, age-adjusted standard score, and age- and education-adjusted standard score.

TEST YOURSELF

1. **Sensitive information in the NIH Toolbox app is protected behind an eight-digit passcode.**
   True or False
2. **When creating a participant in the app, what fields are required?**
   (a) Participant Identifier
   (b) Participant Identifier and Date of Birth
   (c) Participant Identifier, Date of Birth, and Education
   (d) Participant Identifier and Age
3. **Each test has a recommended age range.**
   True or False
4. **Which of the following formats is assessment data available in?**
   (a) CSV
   (b) PDF
   (c) .png
   (d) Word
5. **Which of the following are important for the examiner to remember?**
   (a) Regularly export data
   (b) Keep the eight-digit app passcode safe
   (c) Some tests require additional materials or equipment
   (d) All of the above
6. **Examiners have the option to pause assessments during administration.**
   True or False
7. **Change Sensitive Scores are not provided for all Cognition tests and composites.**
   True or False
8. **Which of the following scores is ideal for tracking change over time?**
   (a) Raw score
   (b) Theta score
   (c) Change-sensitive score
   (d) Age-adjusted standard score
9. **Which of the following scores is not provided for NIH Toolbox Cognition tests?**
   (a) Raw score
   (b) Age-adjusted national percentile
   (c) Age- and education-adjusted *T* score
   (d) Fully adjusted *T* score
10. **Some NIH Toolbox Cognition tests require the examiner to key in the examinee's responses on a Bluetooth keyboard.**
    True or False

Answers: 1. True; 2. (b); 3. True; 4. (a and b); 5. (d); 6. True; 7. False; 8. (c); 9. (d); 10. True

REFERENCES

American Educational Research Association, American Psychological Association, & National Council on Measurement in Education. (Ed.) (2014). *Standards for educational and psychological testing.* American Educational Research Association.

Hook, J. N., & Giella, A. K. (2023). *National Institutes of Health (NIH) Toolbox® V3 administration manual.* Toolbox Assessments, Inc.

LaForte, E. M., Hook, J. N., & Giella, A. K. (2024). *National Institutes of Health (NIH) Toolbox® V3 technical manual.* Toolbox Assessments, Inc.

Four

HOW TO INTERPRET THE NIH TOOLBOX® COGNITION SCORES AND COMPOSITES

Erica M. LaForte
Amy K. Giella
Julie N. Hook

BACKGROUND AND CONTEXT FOR NIH TOOLBOX SCORE INTERPRETATION

The National Institutes of Health (NIH) Toolbox provides several different types of scores at the test and composite levels. Each score metric provides different information to describe test results (see Figure 4.1). Raw scores, computed scores, theta scores, and change-sensitive scores (CSSs) provide different ways to describe an examinee's *performance*, whereas standard scores, national percentile ranks, and *T*-scores provide different ways to describe an examinee's *relative standing in a peer group*. Before interpreting an individual's NIH Toolbox scores in clinical practice or analyzing scores at the group level in a research setting, you should understand the differences between the score metrics and how they are derived so that you can select the most appropriate score for your purpose.

PERFORMANCE METRICS

Raw scores, computed scores, theta scores, and CSSs are all metrics that describe how an examinee performed on a test or composite, independent of how others performed on the same test or composite. These scores are all derived using the examinee's item-level responses (correct or incorrect), although in some cases, they also account for the total amount of time the examinee took to complete the test items. Although performance metrics are valuable for evaluating an examinee's abilities in absolute terms, particularly in longitudinal studies, their usefulness in data analysis can vary depending on the metric. The following sections describe the performance metrics available from the NIH Toolbox Cognition domain tests and composites.

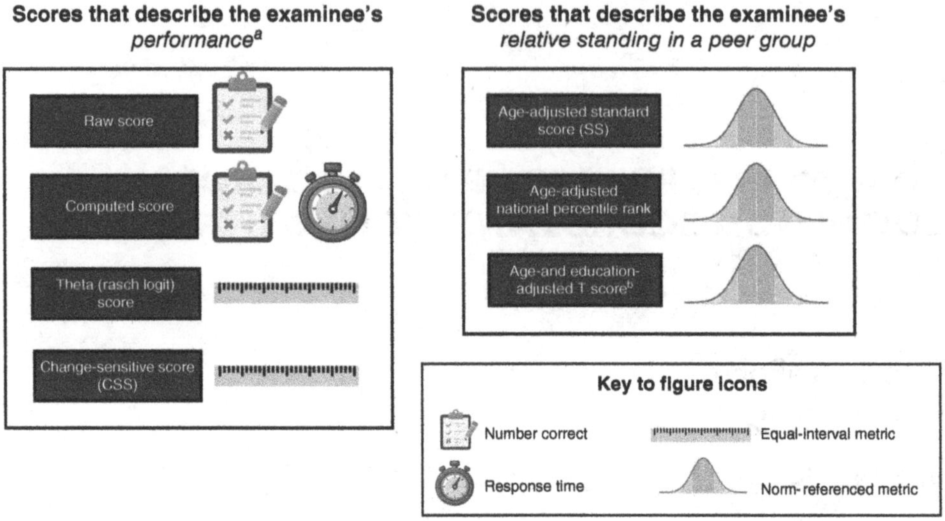

[a] Not all performance-related score metrics are reported for all tests and composites.
[b] Age- and education-adjusted T scores are available only for examinees ages 22 and older, if the examinee's education level is entered into the NIH Toolbox app prior to generating a report.

Figure 4.1 Available Scores from the NIH Toolbox V3 Cognition Domain Tests and Composites.

Raw Scores and Computed Scores: Some Interpretive Cautions

Generally, a raw score is the total number of items an examinee answers correctly from among the set of items the examinee encounters on a test. Historically, most tests in the social sciences—including tests in the NIH Toolbox—used raw scores to describe examinee test performance. In the NIH Toolbox Cognition domain, some scores are computed as the ratio of the total number of correct item responses over the sum of the item-level response times. While a raw score or a computed score is a necessary component for the calculation of other types of test scores (and this is the case for several of the NIH Toolbox Cognition tests), these metrics often have minimal interpretive value on their own for two reasons.

First, for raw scores to be comparable among examinees, all examinees would need to encounter an identical set of items during the test administration. With a few exceptions, this rarely happens on the NIH Toolbox Cognition tests. For example, on the Picture Sequence Memory test, examinees are routed to an age-appropriate sequence that contains 6, 9, or 15 pictures, and the test raw score is the total number of picture pairs that the examinee correctly places in adjacent positions on the grid across two trials of the same picture sequence. Whereas a raw score of 10 points on Picture Sequence Memory would represent perfect performance on a 6-picture sequence where the maximum possible score is 10 (i.e., 5 correct adjacent picture pairs on each of 2 trials), it would represent less-than-perfect performance on a 9-picture sequence (where the maximum possible raw score is 16), and even lower performance on a 15-picture sequence (where the maximum possible raw score is 28). In these three scenarios, the raw score of 10 has quite different interpretations depending on which picture sequence an examinee encounters during the test. Likewise, the NIH Toolbox Picture Vocabulary (PV), Oral

Reading Recognition (ORR), and Visual Reasoning (VR) tests are administered via a computerized adaptive testing (CAT) algorithm. For these tests, each examinee is administered a small subset of items from a large item pool, and the CAT algorithm selects items to administer based on the examinee's performance on the items that have already been administered. In this way, the test adapts to the examinee's ability and selects items that are appropriately challenging for the examinee. Therefore, each examinee who takes one of these CAT-administered tests encounters a unique set of items. Two examinees who obtain a raw score of, say, 12 correct on PV do not necessarily have the same ability because one examinee may have taken very easy items and the other may have taken very difficult items. For this reason, a raw score on these tests cannot be interpreted as an estimate of an examinee's ability; it is simply the number of correct responses from among the particular set of items selected by the CAT algorithm.

Second, a raw score is not an equal-interval metric; typically, it is an ordinal-level metric that is simply a *count of observations*, such as the number of items an examinee answered correctly or the sum of the Likert-type category scores endorsed by the examinee on a rating scale. While a raw number-correct score of 10 is generally considered "higher" than a score of 9, and a score of 9 is generally considered higher than a score of 8, the true magnitude of these raw score differences is unknown with respect to the underlying trait.

To illustrate this, we will use the example of a researcher who is studying the efficacy of different doses of a new medication developed to improve short-term memory for individuals in the early stages of Alzheimer's disease. In this study, participants are randomly assigned to receive either a high dose or a low dose of the medication for six months. The researcher administers a nine-item short-term recall test to all examinees at the outset of the study, and then administers the same nine-item test again after participants have been administered the medication for six months. On this particular short-term memory test, a test administrator reads a single-digit number or sequence of single-digit numbers aloud, and the examinee must immediately repeat the numbers back in the same order. Item 1 requires the participant to recall one number (e.g., "6"), item 2 requires the participant to recall 2 numbers (e.g., "7–4"), item 3 requires the participant to recall three numbers (e.g., "8–2–3"), and so on, up through 9 numbers. Participant 1, who is in the low-dose group, obtains a pretest raw score of 2 correct and a posttest raw score of 3 correct. Participant 2, who is in the high-dose group, obtains a pretest raw score of 5 correct and a posttest raw score of 6 correct. The researcher notes that participants 1 and 2 both experienced the same amount of improvement—1 raw-score point—on the short-term memory

DON'T FORGET 4.1

Ordinal-level scores have a logical order but are not necessarily equally spaced on the underlying metric. An example of an ordinal-level metric is the often-used rating scale category structure: *strongly disagree, disagree, agree*, and *strongly agree*. We know that *strongly agree* represents more "agreement" than *agree*, but we do not necessarily know *how much* more. *Equal-interval scores*, on the other hand, have a consistent and measurable spacing between each score on the underlying metric. Inches are examples of equal-interval metrics. A one-inch difference is the same, whether we are describing the difference between 11 and 12 inches or between 100 and 101 inches.

Table 4.1 Pre- and Posttreatment Memory Test Raw Scores for Participants 1 and 2

Participant	Condition	Pretreatment Raw Score	Posttreatment Raw Score	Raw Score Change
1	Low dose	2 correct	3 correct	+1 point
2	High dose	5 correct	6 correct	+1 point

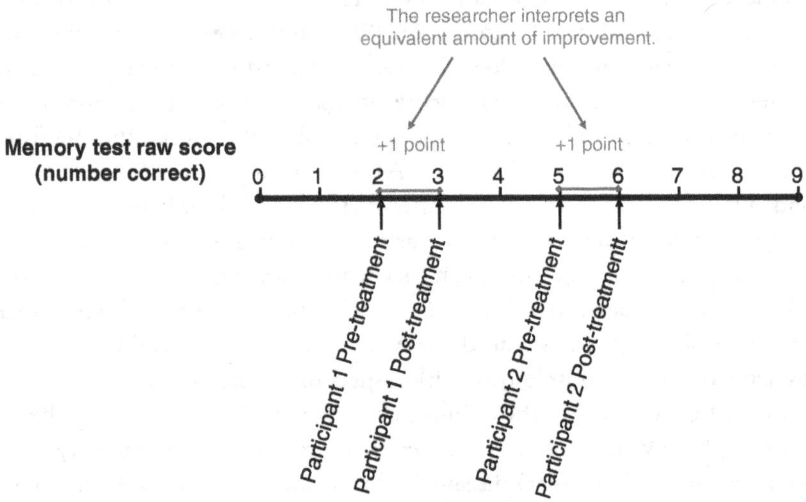

Figure 4.2 Interpretation of the Pre- and Posttreatment Memory Test Raw Scores for Participants 1 and 2.

test as a result of the new medication and concludes that the low dose of the new medication must be just as effective as the high dose for improving short-term memory (Table 4.1 and Figure 4.2).

In reality, our researcher has made a critical interpretive error by assuming that the memory test raw scores are equal-interval. Although each item is successively more difficult than the prior item, it is not the case that the difference between the difficulty of any two items is exactly the same. For example, it is not much more difficult to recall two single-digit numbers (item 2) than it is to recall one single-digit number (item 1), but it is much more difficult to recall 8 digits (item 8) than it is to recall 7 digits (item 7). In fact, as the number of digits in each item's sequence increases, the items become *exponentially* more difficult. This is shown by the location of the item difficulties below the horizontal axis in Figure 4.3. Imagine that the horizontal axis in Figure 4.3 represents a "ruler" describing the latent trait of *short-term memory functioning*, where the locations to the far left represent "very low functioning" and the locations to the far right represent "very high functioning." The arrows at each end of the horizontal axis convey the idea that there could be lower or higher levels of functioning than what is measured by the 9 items that happen to be on this test. For example, if an examinee obtains a raw score of 0, we are able to confidently state that the examinee's short-term memory functioning is low, but we are not able to accurately estimate *how low*, other than stating that it is lower than the

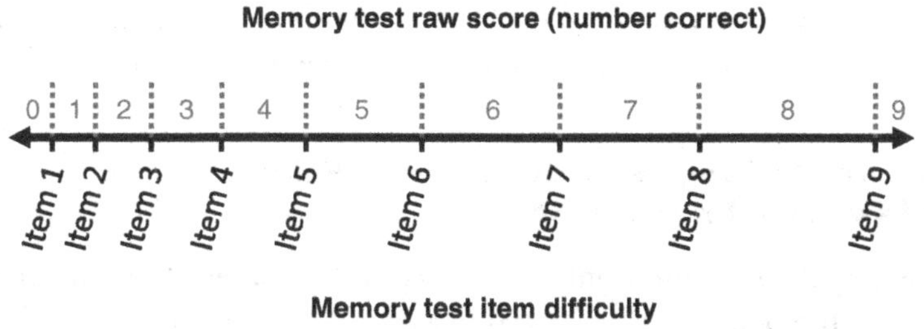

Figure 4.3 Memory Test Raw Scores Relative to the Difficulty of the Test Items.

functioning that can be measured by this particular test. On this scale, the item difficulties spread out to represent the *amount* of memory functioning that an examinee must display in order to obtain each raw score from 0 through 9 (the ranges labeled in red). For instance, if an examinee answers items 1 through 5 correctly but responds incorrectly to items 6 through 9, we can estimate that their short-term memory functioning lies somewhere in the range labeled "5" on the latent trait of short-term memory. Thinking about raw scores in this way, as simply *descriptions for ranges along a latent-trait continuum*, allows us to see why our researcher's original conclusion about his study data was erroneous.

DON'T FORGET 4.2

Do not be fooled by the fact that raw scores often masquerade around in number-correct form (i.e., 0, 1, 2, 3, etc.), giving them the appearance of equal-interval metrics. Although most of us would agree that a raw score of 3 correct is higher than a raw score of 2 correct, these numbers do not imply equal intervals in this context; they are counts and not measures.

The implication of the unequal item difficulty spacing shown in Figure 4.3 is that Participant 2 has actually experienced a much larger increase in memory functioning than Participant 1, because the functional short-term memory increase represented by the distance between raw scores of 5 and 6 is much greater than that represented by the distance between raw scores of 2 and 3. To put it another way, Participant 2's higher raw scores tell us that s/he generally exhibited higher memory functioning than Participant 1 at both the beginning of the study and after six months of medication, but because the raw scores are not equal-interval, we cannot assume that the amount of change from pretreatment to posttreatment was the same for both participants.

CAUTION 4.1

Raw scores and computed scores have limited utility for interpretation of an examinee's performance on the NIH Toolbox tests because they are not equal-interval. They should not be used to make comparisons between examinees or to compare changes in performance for individuals or groups over time.

In summary, while raw scores and computed scores are reported for many NIH Toolbox Cognition Domain tests, it would be a rare case in which one of these scores would be the best metric to use for interpreting an examinee's performance or the change in an examinee's ability over time. To more accurately interpret performance and change on the NIH Toolbox Cognition tests, it is better to rely on an equal-interval score metric such as those described in the next section.

Theta Scores and Change-Sensitive Scores: A Solution to the Pitfalls of Raw Score Interpretation

To avoid the pitfalls that arise from interpreting ordinal-level raw scores and computed scores, the NIH Toolbox tests are all scaled to a common, equal-interval CSS metric using the item response theory (IRT) family of measurement models. Whereas a raw score is a count of observations, such as the number correct or the sum of endorsed categories from rating scale items, CSSs describe levels of performance on a continuous latent-trait scale that incorporates the *difficulty* of the test items or rating scale categories as context. Using the example of our researcher who is interested in measuring change in short-term memory functioning following six months of either a low or high dose of a new medication, Figure 4.4 demonstrates how using CSSs allows the researcher to measure the change in equal-interval units. In Figure 4.4, the underlying short-term memory functioning latent-trait scale from Figure 4.3 now contains unit labels, ranging from 480 (very low functioning) to 570 (very high functioning). Participant 1 obtained raw scores of 2 and 3, corresponding respectively to CSSs of 491 and 497. Participant 2 obtained raw scores of 5 and 6, corresponding respectively to CSSs of 515 and 528. Whereas Participant 1 showed 6 points of improvement on the low-dose treatment, Participant 2 showed 13 points of improvement on the high-dose treatment. Therefore, Participant 2's absolute improvement when measured in CSS units was more than twice that of Participant 1.

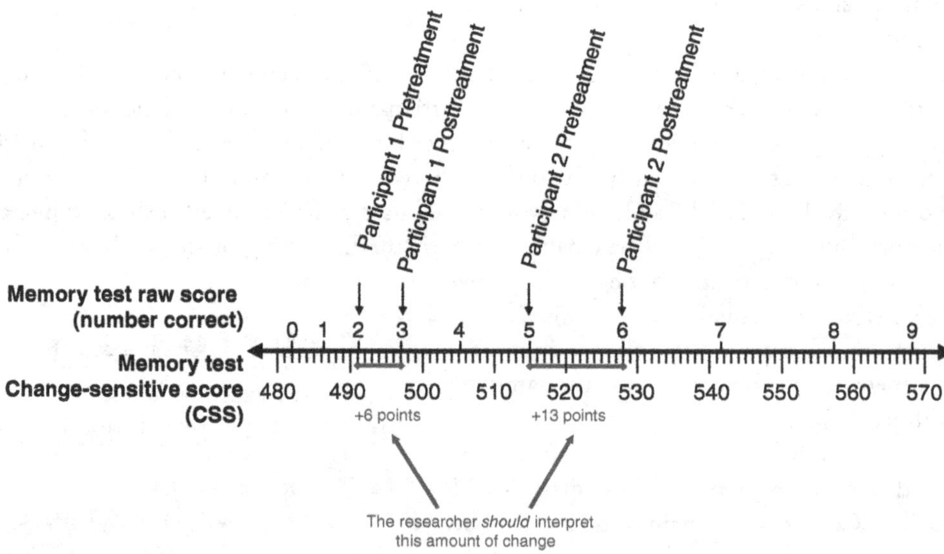

Figure 4.4 Interpretation of the Pre- and Posttreatment Memory Test CSSs for Participants 1 and 2.

Table 4.2 Pre- and Posttreatment Memory Test Change-Sensitive Scores (CSSs) for Participants 1 and 2

Participant	Condition	Pretreatment Change-Sensitive Score (CSS)	Posttreatment Change-Sensitive Score (CSS)	CSS Change
1	Low dose	491	497	+6 points
2	High dose	515	528	+13 points

Using CSSs in this context allows the researcher to reach a more accurate conclusion about the amount of improvement the new medication had on each participant's short-term memory functioning (Table 4.2). In addition to allowing users to track change over time in comparable (i.e., equal-interval) units, IRT-based scores offer several advantages over raw scores, including comparability across different test forms, greater precision in estimating ability levels, and estimation of score reliability that is conditional on the location of the score along the underlying latent trait scale.

Derivation of Test-Level Change-Sensitive Scores

The CSSs are the foundation for all other derived scores in the NIH Toolbox V3 Cognition domain, including the age-adjusted standard scores, national percentile ranks, and the age- and education-adjusted *T*-scores. For most tests, the CSSs are derived using the Rasch measurement model (Rasch, 1960/1980; Wright & Stone, 1979). The Rasch model is just one in the item-response theory (IRT) family of measurement models. While the various IRT models and their differences are beyond the scope of this chapter,[1] a gentle introduction to the Rasch model is warranted as it will facilitate understanding of other concepts introduced in this chapter.

The Rasch measurement model, introduced by Danish mathematician Georg Rasch (1960/1980), provides a way for test developers to calibrate, or locate, the ability of an examinee and the difficulty of an item on the same underlying scale. A key premise of the Rasch model is that comparisons between examinees' abilities should not depend on which particular test items they encountered, and comparisons between items' difficulties should not depend on which particular group of examinees took the test (Wright & Stone, 1979). The Rasch model uses a simple mathematical formula that predicts how likely it is that an examinee will answer a test item correctly (P_{ni}), based on the difference between the examinee's ability (B_n) and the difficulty of the test item (D_i):

$$P_{ni} = \frac{e^{(B_n - D_i)}}{1 - e^{(B_n - D_i)}} \tag{4.1}$$

Rasch scaling makes it possible to turn simple raw scores, or counts of correct responses, into *measures* of latent-trait abilities. When a set of test items is calibrated to a common Rasch scale, an examinee's ability can be estimated using only a subset of well-targeted

[1] Interested readers should consult the *Handbook of Item Response Theory* (Van der Linden, 2018) for a primer on IRT models.

DON'T FORGET 4.3

The Rasch-based theta scores and change-sensitive scores provide an estimate of the examinee's ability relative to the difficulty of the items the examinee encountered on the test. Because estimates of examinee ability and test item difficulty are on the same scale, these scores are very useful for estimating differences in ability among groups of examinees or between two time points for a single examinee.

items (as in CAT), and comparisons can be made between scores from two examinees who have taken different item sets (i.e., forms) or between individuals' scores from different points in time (i.e., as in longitudinal research).

While the Rasch model provides many important advantages to test developers and test users, the resulting examinee ability scores are not necessarily intuitive for users. Ability scores from Rasch-scaled tests are reported in *logits*, sometimes referred to as *theta scores* (θ). In their basic form, Rasch logit scales are centered so that the mean item difficulty is 0. When examinee ability scores are estimated on the logit scale, the resulting scores contain decimals and can be negative (e.g., 1.26 and −3.79). While the logit-based ability scores are equal-interval—which aids in the interpretation of differences between ability scores from different individuals or from the same individual at different time points—it is difficult for most researchers and clinicians to describe an examinee's ability in this frame of reference. Imagine trying to explain to an individual that their cognitive ability score is −3.79! For this reason, many test developers apply a linear transformation to the logit scale that removes decimals and negative values, resulting in a score scale that is easier to interpret—for example, a college admission test scale that runs from 400 to 1,600. In the NIH Toolbox, the CSSs are computed using the following linear transformation of the Rasch logit, or theta, scale:

$$CSS = (\theta \times 9.1024) + 500 \tag{4.2}$$

DON'T FORGET 4.4

Theta scores are equal-interval metrics but may be difficult to interpret or explain given the presence of decimals and negative values. Change-sensitive scores, on the other hand, are linear transformations of theta scores that are centered on a value of 500 and are reported as integers, making them easier to interpret and explain.

This transformation was first introduced by Woodcock and Dahl (1971) and is used widely today in educational and psychological testing. It produces ability scores that often range from the low-400s to the low-600s, but can vary depending on a test's range of difficulty. Further, the NIH Toolbox Cognition domain test-level CSS scales are centered so that a score of 500 always represents the approximate median ability of a 10-year-old individual from the norming sample.[2]

[2] The one exception in the NIH Toolbox is the Face Name Associative Memory Exam (FNAME) test, which is centered so that 500 represents the approximate median ability of an 18-year-old individual from the norming sample.

NIH Toolbox® (NIHTB) Cognition domain

Tests/ Composites	Raw score	Theta	Computed score	Change-sensitive score	Age-adjusted standard score	Age-adjusted standard score SE	National age-adjusted %ile	Age- and Education-Adjusted T-score
ORR	–	3.42	–	523	92	2.4	29	50
PV	–	2.48	–	520	95	2.2	36	52
Crystallized Composite	–	–	–	522	90	8.2	25	47
DCCS	–	–	1.41	503	85	5.4	15	41
Flanker	–	–	1.27	504	87	6.4	20	45
LSWM	14	1.03	–	513	95	5.8	37	49
PC	97	2.55	–	545	98	1.4	44	52
PSM Form A	–	7.55	–	513	102	3.4	55	53
Fluid Composite	–	–	–	516	90	8.2	25	47
Total Cognition Composite	–	–	–	519	89	7.4	22	48
FNAME Delay	27	0.32	–	500	97	7.6	41	49
OSD	77	2.00	–	538	90	2.2	26	46
RAVLT	18	−0.62	–	490	79	7.3	8	40
RAVLT Delay	5	−0.96	–	499	94	5.1	35	48
VR	–	1.55	–	506	101	4.5	52	53

Notes: DCCS = Dimensional Change Card Sort v3.1, FNAME Delay = Face Name Associative Memory Exam Delay, Flanker = Flanker Inhibitory Control and Attention v3.1, LSWM = List Sorting Working Memory, ORR = Oral Reading Recognition, OSD = Oral Symbol Digit, PC = Pattern Comparison Processing Speed, PSM Form A = Picture Sequence Memory Form A, PV = Picture Vocabulary, RAVLT = Rey Auditory Verbal Learning, RAVLT Delay = Rey Auditory Verbal Learning Delay, VR = Visual Reasoning v3.1.
Cells with "-" are intentionally blank.

Figure 4.5 NIH Toolbox Cognition Domain Score Table for a 24-Year-Old Male with a High School Education.

While the NIH Toolbox Cognition domain score report provides a CSS for every test and composite, the derivation of the CSS varies by test. Figure 4.5 contains a score report generated for a 19-year-old male study participant who was administered all age-appropriate NIH Toolbox Cognition domain tests. Note that the raw score, theta, and computed score columns are populated for some, but not all, tests. This is because the derivation of the CSS for each test is dependent upon the specific administration format of the test. Figure 4.6 shows how the NIH Toolbox app derives the CSS for each test.

- For List Sorting Working Memory (LSWM), Pattern Comparison (PC), Processing Speed, Speeded Matching (SM), Face Name Associative Memory Exam Delay (FNAME Delay), Oral Symbol Digit (OSD), Rey Auditory Verbal Learning Test (RAVLT), and Rey Auditory Verbal Learning Test Delay (RAVLT Delay), the app converts the examinee's raw (number correct) score to a Rasch ability (theta) score using either a lookup table or a scoring algorithm (varies by test), and then converts the theta score to a CSS using Eq. 4.2. The raw score, theta score, and CSS all appear in the score table.
- For Picture Sequence Memory (PSM), the app converts the examinee's raw (i.e., total number of correct adjacent pairs) score to a Rasch ability (theta) score using a lookup table that corresponds to the picture theme and sequence length the examinee encountered on the test (e.g., the 9-picture Fair sequence; the 15-picture Park sequence). The app then converts the theta score to a CSS using Eq. 4.2, and both of these scores are reported in the table of scores. The raw score is not reported because it is uninterpretable without the context of the particular picture sequence that was administered.

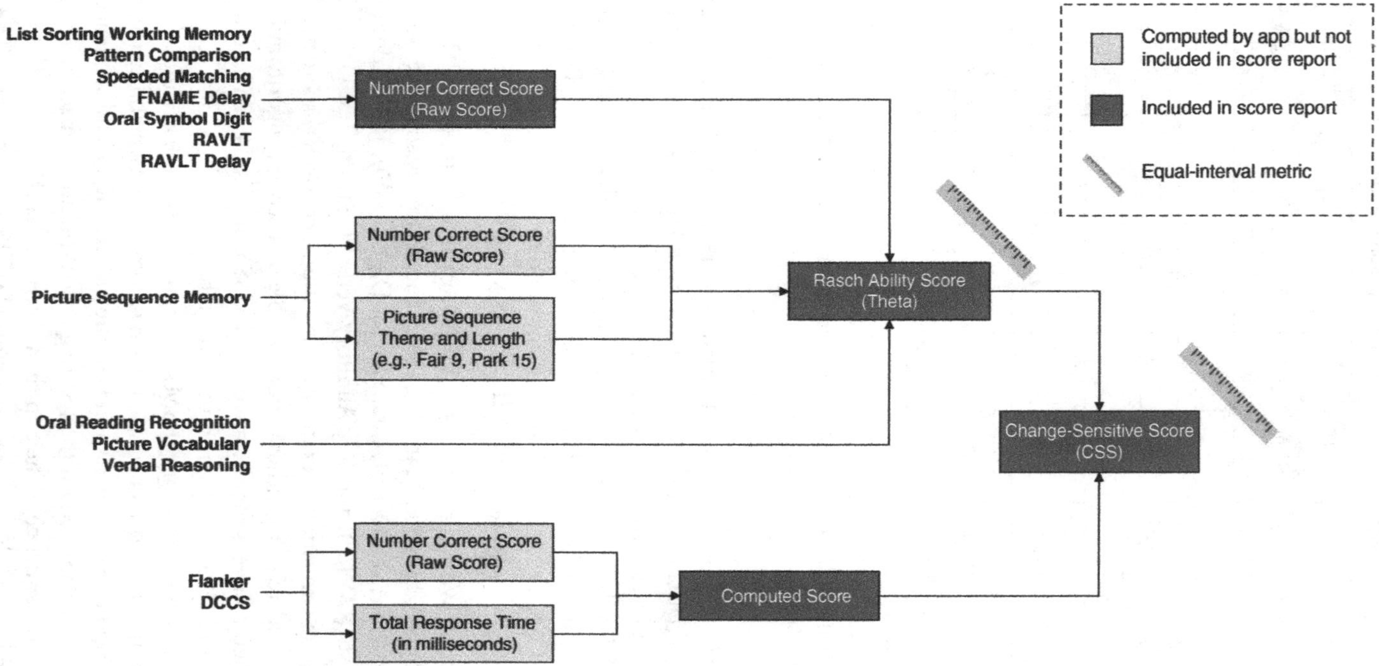

Figure 4.6 Derivation of the NIH Toolbox Cognition Test CSSs.

- The Oral Reading Recognition (ORR), Picture Vocabulary (PV), and Visual Reasoning (VR) tests are administered via a CAT algorithm. During these tests, the CAT estimates a Rasch (theta) ability score for the examinee after each item is administered. When the CAT reaches a designated stopping point, its theta ability estimate is the examinee's theta score for the test. The app then converts the theta score to a CSS using Eq. 4.2, and both scores appear in the score table. Because every examinee receives a potentially unique set of items on the CAT-administered tests, raw scores are not interpretable and are therefore not reported for these tests.
- The Flanker Inhibitory Control and Attention (Flanker) and Dimensional Change Card Sort (DCCS) test scores are computed as the ratio of the number of correct responses (out of 30 possible) over the sum of the item response times (in seconds). The app converts the examinee's computed score directly to a CSS using a built-in formula. The computed score and CSS appear in the score report.

CAUTION 4.2

While the NIH Toolbox Cognition Domain score report displays raw scores and computed scores for some tests, these scores are not interpretable without context and are not equal-interval. They should generally not be used for making intra-individual comparisons (as in longitudinal research) or making comparisons among examinees.

Derivation of Composite-Level Change-Sensitive Scores

The NIH Toolbox Cognition domain produces scores for up to five composites, though whether they are displayed in the score report depends on the age of the examinee and whether the requisite tests have been administered in that assessment. Table 4.3 includes the Cognition domain composites and the tests that must be administered to obtain the composites. Each composite contains a recommended age range and an extended age range. Composite scores will always be generated for an examinee whose age falls within the extended age range, though scores should generally be interpreted only for an examinee whose age falls into the recommended age range. However, exceptions can be made in some instances. The Total Cognition Composite, Crystallized Cognition Composite, and Fluid Cognition Composite are appropriate to interpret when you are administering NIH Toolbox V3 to a very high-functioning six-year-old child, and the Early Childhood Cognition Composite and Early Childhood Cognition CFPS Composite are appropriate to interpret when you are administering the tests to a very low-functioning child between the ages of 7 and 8-½.

Table 4.3 Composite Scores Reported for the NIH Toolbox Cognition Domain

			NIH TB V3 Cognition Tests								
NIH TB V3 Cognition Composites	Recommended Age Range (years)	Extended Age Range (years)	Oral Reading Recognition	Picture Vocabulary	Dimensional Change Card Sort	Flanker Inhibitory Control and Attention	List Sorting Working Memory	Pattern Comparison Processing Speed	Picture Sequence Memory	Speeded Matching	Visual Reasoning
Total Cognition Composite	7–90	6–90	●	●	●	●	●	●	●		
Crystallized Composite	7–90	6–90	●	●							
Fluid Composite	7–90	6–90			●	●	●	●	●		
Early Childhood Cognition Composite	4–6	4–8.5		●	●	●			●	●	
Early Childhood Crystallized-Fluid-Processing Speed (CFPS) Composite	3–6	3–8.5		●						●	●

Note: ● indicates that the test must be administered to obtain the composite score.

The NIH Toolbox V3 app computes the Crystallized Cognition Composite, Fluid Cognition Composite, Early Childhood Cognition Composite, and Early Childhood Cognition CFPS Composite CSSs as the arithmetic mean of the CSSs from the contributing tests. For example, the Crystallized Composite CSS is calculated as:

$$\text{Crystallized Composite CSS} = \frac{\text{Oral Reading Recognition CSS} + \text{Picture Vocabulary CSS}}{2} \tag{4.3}$$

The app computes the Total Cognition Composite as the arithmetic mean of the Crystallized Composite and Fluid Composite:

$$\text{Total Cognition Composite CSS} = \frac{\text{Crystallized Composite CSS} + \text{Fluid Composite CSS}}{2} \tag{4.4}$$

Computing the Total Cognition Composite CSS in this way, rather than as the arithmetic mean of the seven tests that contribute to the Crystallized Cognition Composite and Fluid Cognition Composites, ensures that the Total Cognition Composite calculation gives equal weight to the crystallized and fluid abilities it measures.

METRICS DESCRIBING RELATIVE STANDING IN A PEER GROUP

In addition to the performance metrics described in the prior section, the NIH Toolbox V3 Cognition domain score report also provides several metrics that describe an examinee's relative standing among a peer group (see Figure 4.1). These are often referred to as "norm-referenced" scores. The age-adjusted standard score(SS) and age-adjusted national percentile rank describe an examinee's performance relative to the individuals from the NIH Toolbox V3 norming study who were the same age as the examinee. The age- and education-adjusted *T*-score describes an examinee's performance relative to individuals from the NIH Toolbox V3 norming study who were the same age as the examinee and who also had the same level of education as the examinee.[3] Relative-standing scores are useful for making comparisons among individual examinees or groups of examinees.

The CSS scores serve as the basis for the NIH Toolbox V3 Cognition test and composite norms. This means that when an examinee is administered a test from the NIH Toolbox, his or her obtained CSS is compared to the median CSS obtained by the reference group (i.e., individuals of the same age, or same age and education) from the NIH Toolbox V3 norming study. Rapid Reference 4.1 describes the reference groups in the NIH Toolbox V3 norms. The NIH Toolbox V3 app performs all of the score comparisons and calculations automatically, but the derivations are described here to facilitate your understanding of these scores.

Rapid Reference 4.1

Reference Groups for NIH Toolbox V3 Norms

Reference Group	Age Reference Groups	Education Level Reference Groups
Age	• 3-month age groups for ages 3 years, 0 months through 10 years, 11 months • 6-month age groups for ages 11 years, 0 months through 17 years, 11 months • 1-year age groups for ages 18 years through 90 years	N/A
Age and Education	• 1-year age groups for ages 22 and older	• High school diploma or less • Some college or trade school • Bachelor's degree • Advanced degree

[3] The age- and education-adjusted *T*-scores are available only for examinees who are age 22 or older on the day of testing.

z-scores: The Nuts and Bolts of the Normal Curve

Although *z*-scores are not included in any NIH Toolbox V3 Cognition domain score report or score export, the *z*-score is a necessary interim step in the app's calculation of the other relative-standing metrics. The *z*-score scale has a mean of 0, representing the center of the normal curve or the mean of the score distribution from the reference group. A *z*-score, then, describes an examinee's performance relative to the mean performance of the reference peer group, where 1 *z*-score point equals 1 standard deviation unit. For this reason, z-scores are often referred to as *standard normal* units of measurement. A *z*-score of −1.00 represents test performance that is 1 standard deviation unit *below* the mean performance of the reference group, and a *z*-score of +1.00 represents test performance that is 1 standard deviation unit *above* the mean performance of the reference group. Approximately 68% of the individuals in any normal distribution have *z*-scores that fall between −1.00 and +1.00, and approximately 95% have *z*-scores that fall between −2.00 and +2.00. Rapid Reference 4.2 contains the percentage of individuals between several key values of *z*-score in the normal distribution. In the context of the NIH Toolbox V3 Cognition tests and composites, the *z*-score represents the distance of an examinee's obtained CSS from the mean CSS obtained by the examinee's reference group from the norming study, in standard deviation units.

The NIH Toolbox V3 norm tables contain reference values describing the mean and standard deviation of the score distribution from the V3 norming examinees for each age (for age-adjusted norms) and each age-and-education combination (for age- and education-adjusted norms). Under the hood, the NIH Toolbox V3 app compares the examinee's obtained CSS for each administered test and cluster to compute a *z*-score:

$$z\text{-score} = \frac{(\text{Obtained CSS} - \text{Reference CSS Mean})}{\text{Reference CSS Standard Deviation}} \quad (4.5)$$

Rapid Reference 4.2

Percentage of Individuals Between Key Values of *z*-Score in the Normal Distribution

z-score Range	Percentage of Individuals in the Standard Normal Distribution (%)
−3.00 to +3.00	99.7
−2.50 to +2.50	98.9
−2.00 to +2.00	95.4
−1.50 to +1.50	86.6
−1.00 to 1.00	68.3
−0.50 to +0.50	38.3

Similar to the challenges with the interpretation of theta scores described earlier, *z*-scores are not often used to describe examinee performance because they are expressed with decimals and may be negative. So, although they provide a simple way to describe an examinee's distance from the mean of a peer-group distribution, they are not often used for the interpretation of test performance and are not included in the NIH Toolbox V3 Cognition domain score reports or scores export.

Age-Adjusted Standard Scores

The age-adjusted standard score provides a mechanism for expressing the age-adjusted *z*-score in an easier-to-interpret frame of reference. The age-adjusted standard score has a mean of 100 and a standard deviation of 15, and is computed as a linear transformation of the *z*-score as follows:

$$\text{Age adjusted standard score} = 100 + \left(\text{Age-adjusted } z\text{-score} \times 15\right) \tag{4.6}$$

Following this transformation, an examinee whose obtained CSS is equal to the reference CSS for their age-peer group will receive an SS of 100, an examinee whose obtained CSS is one standard deviation below the mean will receive an SS of 85, and an examinee whose obtained CSS is one standard deviation above the mean will receive an SS of 115. The NIH Toolbox does not report exact values of SS below 40 or above 160 (i.e., scores more than four standard deviations from the mean). This is because the precision of those extreme scores is very low, given the small numbers of individuals in the population falling in those ranges of the normal distribution. For obtained SSs below 40, the NIH Toolbox V3 score report displays the value 39, and for obtained SSs above 160, the report displays the value 161.

CAUTION 4.3

If you are conducting longitudinal research that requires individual- or group-level comparisons of score changes over time, do not use relative standing metrics for this analysis. Relative standing metrics such as age-adjusted standard scores describe an individual's position in a distribution of peers, but do not necessarily capture growth or decline. For example, an individual who obtains a higher CSS score at Time 2 than Time 1 (suggesting positive growth) may actually obtain a lower age-adjusted standard score at Time 2 if the examinee's rate of growth during the study was slower than that of his peers.

Age-Adjusted National Percentile Ranks

The percentile rank of a test score is the percentage of scores in the distribution that fall *at or below* the given test score. Described in terms of the normal curve, it represents the area under the curve to the left of the given test score. For a score at the mean of the distribution, the percentile rank is 50% because half of the scores fall below it.

The NIH Toolbox V3 app computes the percentile rank as the cumulative frequency associated with the obtained *z*-score.

Age- and Education-Adjusted *T*-Scores

The age- and education-adjusted *T*-score is available only for examinees ages 22 and older and for whom the education level has been entered into the NIH Toolbox V3 app. It is a linear transformation of the age- and education-adjusted *z*-score that has a mean of 50 and a standard deviation of 10, and is computed as follows:

$$\text{Age- and education-adjusted } T\text{-score} = 500 + \left(\text{age-adjusted } z\text{-score} \times 10\right) \quad (4.7)$$

Following this transformation, an examinee whose obtained CSS is equal to the reference CSS for their age- and education-peer group will receive a *T*-score of 50, an examinee whose obtained CSS is one standard deviation below the mean will receive a *T*-score of 40, and an examinee whose obtained CSS is one standard deviation above the mean will receive a *T*-score of 60. Similar to the age-adjusted standard scores, the NIH Toolbox does not report exact values for *T*-scores that are more than four standard deviations from the mean (i.e., below 20 or above 80). For obtained *T*-scores below 20, the NIH Toolbox V3 score report displays the value 19, and for obtained *T*-scores above 80, the report displays the value 81.

QUANTIFYING AND INTERPRETING MEASUREMENT ERROR

Cognitive test scores are inherently imprecise; they must be interpreted with the understanding that they are *proxies* for describing *theoretical constructs* that cannot be *touched or seen*. This section provides some context for the imprecision of test scores in the cognitive and behavioral sciences in general, and a description of the estimates of measurement error that are available for the NIH Toolbox test and composite scores.

The Inherent Subjectivity and Ambiguity of Cognitive Assessments

The physical and biological sciences rely on a variety of tools to measure length, distance, mass, weight, temperature, time, and force. Tools vary with respect to their appropriate uses and their ability to make precise measurements. Some tools are readily available and require little training to use. For example:

- An elementary-age student who is studying the impact of sunlight on the growth of bean plants may use a standard 12-in. ruler to take daily measurements of the plants' heights.
- A mother may use a forehead thermometer to determine whether her child's fever warrants a day home from school.

Other tools are more highly calibrated, are less readily available to nonspecialists, and require expert knowledge or training for proper use. For example:

- Scientists who are studying cancer or other diseases may use a Positron Emission Tomography (PET) scanner to map metabolic processes in the body.
- Engineers who are designing a new bridge may use accelerometers and seismographs to detect the bridge's structural response to wind, traffic, and earthquakes.

> **DON'T FORGET 4.5**
>
> Cognition assessments are often the best tools we have at our disposal for understanding an individual's cognitive abilities—which cannot be seen or felt. Cognition assessments are proxies that help us understand how an individual's brain works based on the person's performance on various tasks.

Over the last century, the introduction of increasingly precise measurement tools that can detect, quantify, and visualize the physical world at precise levels of detail has enabled unprecedented progress in the physical and medical sciences. In contrast, advances in the behavioral and cognitive sciences have been slower, particularly because the objects of measurement in these fields (e.g., thinking and reasoning skills, learning capacity, and decision-making speed) are not clearly defined or directly observable. Instead of measuring physical properties like mass or force, researchers in behavioral and cognitive sciences often need to rely on *indirect indicators* such as surveys, performance tests, or self-reports, which are proxies for cognitive abilities and are laden with both subjectivity and ambiguity.

A clear example of this challenge can be seen in the measurement of working memory ability by tests such as the LSWM test in the NIH Toolbox. An individual's working memory ability, or the ability to maintain and manipulate information in active attention (Schneider & McGrew, 2018), is not a physical property of the human brain that can be directly observed; instead, it is a construct defined by researchers and test developers with varying definitions across theories and contexts. The NIH Toolbox LSWM test operationalizes working memory by presenting an individual with a list of foods and animals, and then measuring the individual's ability to mentally reorganize the list into separate size-order lists. While the LSWM stimuli are presented both orally (via audio recording) and visually (via pictures on the iPad screen), the test-taker must respond orally, providing a proxy for working memory that also relies upon—and may be confounded by—an individual's ability to communicate orally. In contrast, other working memory tests may include tasks that require an individual to remember and manipulate the placement of objects on a screen, requiring a visual-motor response. Any of these test tasks, however, are only proxies for the complex cognitive construct of "working memory." And since different working memory tests may emphasize different skills and rely on different response modes, they may also produce different outcomes, or scores, for the same individual. Moreover, external factors such as alertness, fatigue, hunger, anxiety, injury, or prior exposure to the testing format can even lead to different results for the same individual on the same test at different points in time. Until scientific advances allow us to peer into the human brain and "see" the processes happening there, cognitive and behavioral test developers will always face the challenges of construct subjectivity and ambiguity. And until measurement tools are available that will allow us to measure the physical aspects of these brain functions, our only tools will be the proxies that are available in cognitive assessment batteries such as the NIH Toolbox.

The Standard Error of Measurement

Because cognitive and behavioral measures are inherently imprecise, it is important that scores from these measures are interpreted and communicated in the context of this imprecision. In fact, in the *Standards for Educational and Psychological Testing* (AERA et al., 2014), Standard 2.3 states that, "For each total score, subscore, or combination of scores that is to be interpreted, estimates of relevant indices of reliability/precision should be reported." The *standard error of measurement* (*SEM*) is the mechanism that provides this context.

- Theoretically, the *SEM* is the standard deviation of the distribution of *observed* scores around an individual's (unknown) *true* score.
- Operationally, the *SEM* can be interpreted as the standard deviation of the distribution of an individual's observed scores from repeated administrations of a test under identical conditions (AERA et al., 2014). If we were able to administer the same test to one person many times under the same conditions without the confounding effects of practice, learning, or fatigue, the *SEM* is the standard deviation of the distribution of those scores.
- In practice, the *SEM* is presented as an interval, or *confidence band*, around an individual's obtained score, and is interpreted as the score range within which the individual's true score is very likely to fall.

DON'T FORGET 4.6

The standard error of measurement (*SEM*) describes the precision of the score. A test score with a relatively large corresponding *SEM* is not as precise as a test score with a relatively small SEM.

Test developers use various methods to calculate measurement error. In the NIH Toolbox V3 Cognition domain, the computation of *SEMs* is incidental to the IRT (Rasch) scaling of the tests described earlier in this chapter. In traditional (non-IRT) calculations, measurement error is hypothesized to be constant across all score levels. The IRT *SEMs*, on the other hand, are calculated uniquely for each ability estimate. For this reason, IRT-based estimates of *SEM* are referred to as "conditional *SEMs*" (i.e., they are *conditional* on a particular test score). Using the hypothetical CSS score scale described earlier in this chapter and shown in Table 4.4 as an example, the scores of 482, 486, 491, and 497 (corresponding to the raw scores of 0, 1, 2, and 3 on the hypothetical memory test) will have smaller *SEMs* than scores of 528, 542, 557, and 568 (corresponding to raw scores of 6, 7, 8, and 9) (see Table 4.4). This is because the measurement precision at the lower end of the CSS scale, where more test items are packed into a narrower range of difficulty, is higher than the measurement precision at the upper end of the scale, where there are fewer items spread across a much larger range of difficulty.

Although the NIH Toolbox V3 Cognition domain score report displays *SEMs* for the age-adjusted standard scores only (see Figure 4.5), the scores export also provides *SEMs*

Table 4.4 Standard Errors of Measurement (*SEMs*) corresponding to CSSs on a hypothetical memory test

Raw Score	CSS	SEM (CSS)
0	482	4
1	486	3
2	491	3
3	497	5
4	505	6
5	515	7
6	528	9
7	542	10
8	557	9
9	568	8

for theta scores (where applicable), CSSs, age-adjusted standard scores, and age- and education-adjusted *T*-scores (where applicable).

Interpretation of NIH Toolbox Test-Level Confidence Intervals

SEMs can be used to construct *confidence intervals* (sometimes also called "confidence bands") around an obtained score. A confidence interval is a range of scores within which the user can be fairly confident that the individual's true score is likely to fall. Often-used confidence levels in cognitive testing are 68%, 90%, and 95%, corresponding to intervals of ±1.00, ±1.65, and ±1.96 *SEMs* around an obtained test score. Examples of these confidence bands are shown in Figure 4.7 for a test score of 495 and a corresponding *SEM* of 4. The 68% confidence band extends from 491 to 499, the 90% confidence band extends from 488 to 502 (rounded to the nearest integer), and the 95% confidence band extends from 487 to 503 (rounded to the nearest integer). The higher the level of confidence, the wider the band.

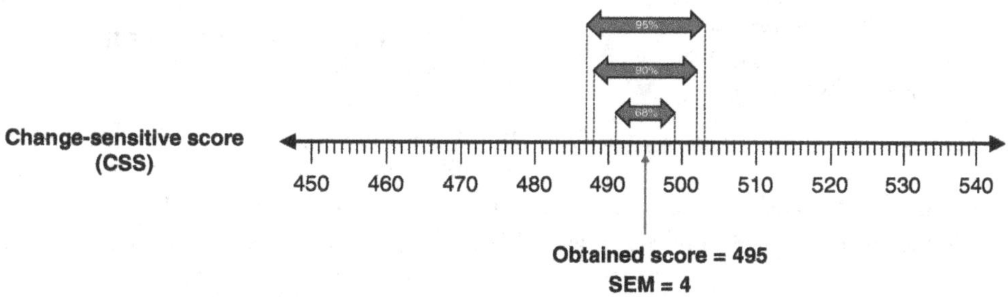

Figure 4.7 68%, 90%, and 95% Confidence Interval Bands Constructed from the *SEM* of an Obtained CSS.

Standard Score Profile Plot

The standard score profile plot contained in the NIH Toolbox V3 Cognition domain score report displays the 90% confidence interval around each test's age-adjusted standard score (see Figure 4.8). In this plot, the dots represent the individual's obtained age-adjusted standard score, and the endpoints of the lines represent the upper and lower bounds of the 90% standard score confidence intervals, or the range ±1.65 *SEMs* around the obtained scores. Note the large variation in the confidence interval widths in the plot; scores with narrower intervals have higher precision than those with wider intervals. Examples of interpretive statements that can be gleaned from the standard score profile plot include:

- While this individual obtained an age-adjusted standard score of 90 on this administration of the Flanker test, we can be 90% confident that his true score falls in the range between 78 and 101.
- This individual obtained an age-adjusted standard score on the OSD test of 66; however, we can be 90% confident that his true score falls in the range between 63 and 69.

> **DON'T FORGET 4.7**
>
> For IRT-scaled tests, measurement error is conditional on the test score. This means that a test may be highly precise for measuring at some ranges of ability and highly imprecise for measuring at other ranges of ability. When making clinical decisions with cognitive test scores, always evaluate the score's associated confidence interval to determine the likely range of the individual's ability, or true score. If a test score contains a wide confidence interval, interpret the score with caution as the test may lack adequate precision for clinical interpretation at that particular ability level.

Note in Figure 4.8 that the confidence intervals sometimes appear to be nonsymmetric around the obtained age-adjusted standard score (e.g., the PSM Form A confidence interval); this is due to rounding during the app's derivation of the upper and lower endpoints of the standard score intervals.

90% confidence intervals are not displayed in the standard score profile plot when an individual's obtained age-adjusted standard score is less than 40 or greater than 160, or when either endpoint of the confidence band around the obtained score is less than 40 or greater than 160.

COMPUTING OTHER CONFIDENCE INTERVALS

While the standard score profile plot contains the 90% confidence intervals defined as ±1.65 *SEMs* around the obtained scores, it is possible to compute intervals with other levels of confidence using information that is available in the NIH Toolbox V3 scores export.[4] For

[4] See "Options for Accessing NIH Toolbox V3 Cognition Domain Scores" later in this chapter for more information about the NIH Toolbox V3 exports.

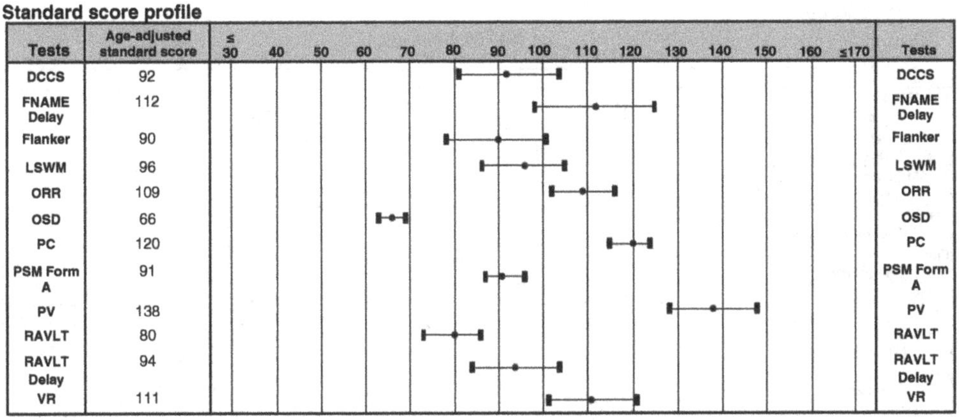

Notes: DCCS = Dimensional Change Card Sort v3.1, FNAME Delay = Face Name Associative Memory Exam Delay, Flanker = Flanker Inhibitory Control and Attention v3.1, LSWM= List Sorting Working Memory, ORR = Oral Reading Recognition, OSD = Oral Symbol Digit, PC = Pattern Comparison Processing Speed, PSM Form A = Picture Sequence Memory Form A, PV = Picture Vocabulary, RAVLT = Rey Auditory Verbal Learning, RAVLT Delay = Rey Auditory Verbal Learning Delay, VR = Visual Reasoning v3.1.
Profile ranges show the 90% confidence intervals.

Figure 4.8 A Standard Score Profile Plot from an NIH Toolbox V3 Cognition Domain Score Report Showing 90% Confidence Bands Around Obtained Standard Scores.

example, to compute the 68% confidence interval around a standard score, use the following equation:

$$\text{68\% SS confidence interval} = (\text{SS}) \pm \left(1.00 * SEM(\text{SS})\right) \tag{4.8}$$

where SS = the individual's obtained age-adjusted standard score and *SEM*(SS) = the corresponding age-adjusted standard score *SEM*. To compute the 95% confidence interval, substitute 1.96 for 1.00 in Eq. 4.8. Similar computations can be performed to obtain the confidence intervals around an individual's obtained age- and education-adjusted *T*-score:

$$T\text{-score confidence interval} = (T) \pm \left(C * \text{SEM}(T)\right) \tag{4.9}$$

where T = the individual's obtained age- and education-adjusted *T*-score, SEM(T) = the corresponding age- and education-adjusted *T*-score *SEM*, and C = either 1.00 (for 68% confidence), 1.645 (for 90% confidence), or 1.96 (for 95% confidence).

If you are conducting individual testing for clinical decision-making purposes, best practice is to include confidence bands when reporting derived scores.

PROCESS SCORES

In addition to the performance and relative standing metrics discussed up to this point, the NIH Toolbox Cognition domain also provides users with process scores for the DCCS, Flanker, PC, SM, FNAME Delay, RAVLT, and RAVLT Delay tests, if they are administered. Process scores can provide insight into how an individual approaches a task and can also uncover specific deficits in cognitive processing. Figure 4.9 contains an example of the process scores table from a score report.

Process scores:

Tests	Raw score	Median response time per item	Commission errors	Omission errors
DCCS	–	0.4	1	0
FNAME Delay (FSB)	10	–	–	–
FNAME Delay (FNL)	10	–	–	–
FNAME Delay (FNM)	11	–	–	–
Flanker (Congruent items)	–	0.84	0	–
Flanker (Incongruent items)	–	0.76	–	–
Flanker	–	–	–	0
PC	–	0.43	–	–
RAVLT (Trial 1)	4	–	–	–
RAVLT (Trial 2)	6	–	–	–
RAVLT (Trial 3)	8	–	–	–
RAVLT Delay	5	–	–	–

Notes: DCCS = Dimensional Change Card Sort v3.1, FNAME Delay = Face Name Associative Memory Exam Delay, Flanker = Flanker Inhibitory Cantral and Attention v3.1, PC = Pattem Comparison Processing Speed, RAVLT = Rey Auditory Verbal Learning, RAVLT Delay = Rey Auditory Verbal Learning Delay.
Cells with "-" are intentionally blank.

Figure 4.9 Process Scores from an NIH Toolbox V3 Cognition Domain Score Report.

The scores that are available in the process scores table include the following, if applicable, for each test:

- **Raw score:** The number-correct score; note that this is the same as the raw score displayed in the score table of the report.
- **Median response time per item (in seconds):** This is computed as the median response time across all live items encountered by the individual during the test administration. For the Flanker test, the median response time is reported separately for the congruent and incongruent items.
- **Commission errors:** For the DCCS test, a commission error is defined as an incorrect response to a live item, with a possible range of 0–30. For the Flanker test, a commission error is defined as an incorrect response to a congruent item only and has a possible range of 0–20.
- **Omission errors:** The number of trials for which an individual fails to select a response before the item time limit.

OPTIONS FOR ACCESSING NIH TOOLBOX V3 COGNITION DOMAIN SCORES

The NIH Toolbox V3 app allows you to access your Cognition domain scores in two different ways:

1. Via the score report for individual examinees; or
2. Via the scores export (.csv) for individual examinees or groups of examinees.

Additionally, the scores export is available in two different formats: *wide structure*, where each row contains score data from one examinee; and *narrow structure*, in which each row contains one type of score for one examinee (and the scores from each examinee appear in multiple rows in the data file). The wide structure file is usually appropriate for most statistical analyses, while the narrow structure file is often preferred by analysts for importing into other databases or creating pivot tables.

There are some differences in the types of information that are available in each of these files. For example, the 90% confidence interval plot appears in the score reports but not in the exports (although information in the exports *could* be used to create confidence interval plots in some statistical programs). Table 4.5 contains a comparison of the information that is included in the wide-format .csv export and in the score report. The first column contains the score (variable) name from the .csv export, and the second column contains the heading that corresponds to that score in the score report. Footnotes in the table provide additional information about the scores; for example, some standard errors are only displayed when a nonzero or nonperfect number-correct score on the test, and some scores are only available for examinees of certain ages.

CAUTIONS ABOUT INTERPRETING ZERO RAW SCORES

Often, a very young or very low-ability examinee will fail to respond correctly to any live test items on an NIH Toolbox V3 Cognition test. Other times, an examinee will fail to achieve a minimum level of accuracy on a test's practice items, and the test will end prior to the live items. In either of these scenarios, the test is said to have a *zero raw score*. When interpreting tests with zero raw scores, it is important to consider whether the examinee failed to understand the test task—which might indicate that the test is not developmentally appropriate for the examinee—or whether the examinee is simply functioning at a low level compared to age peers. To facilitate interpretation of zero raw test scores, the score report provides the following footnote to the table of scores:

> *Based on a raw score of 0; interpret with caution.*

When a composite contains one or more tests for which the test raw score is zero, the following footnote appears under the table of scores:

> *Includes at least one test with a raw score of 0; interpret with caution.*

DON'T FORGET 4.8

Always interpret zero raw scores with caution, regardless of whether the examinee scored 0 points on the live items or failed to achieve a minimum passing score on the practice items. A raw score of 0 may indicate that the examinee is not developmentally ready for the test or that the examinee is very low-functioning compared to typical peers.

Table 4.5 Scores Available in NIH Toolbox V3 Cognition Domain Scores Export and Score Report

		Tests													Composites				
Variable Name in the NIH Toolbox V3 "Wide" Scores Export (in order of appearance)	Column Heading in the NIH Toolbox V3 Score Report	Dimensional Change Card Sort	Flanker Inhibitory Control and Attention	List Sorting Working Memory	Pattern Comparison Processing Speed	Picture Sequence Memory	Picture Vocabulary	Oral Reading Recognition	Speeded Matching	Visual Reasoning	Face Name Associative Memory Exam	Rey Auditory Verbal Learning	Rey Auditory Verbal Learning Delay	Oral Symbol Digit	Total Cognition Composite	Crystallized Composite	Fluid Composite	Early Childhood Cognition Composite	Early Childhood Crystallized-Fluid-Processing Speed (CFPS) Composite
Raw Score	Raw Score			●	●						●	●	●	●					
Tscore[a]	—[a]																		
TScore Standard Error[a]	—[a]																		
Theta	Theta			●	●	●	●	●	●	●	●	●	●	●					
Theta Standard Error	—[b]			●[c]	●	●[c]	●	●	●[c]	●	●	●	●	●					
Change Sensitive Score	Change-Sensitive Score	●	●	●	●	●	●	●	●	●	●	●	●	●	●	●	●	●	●
Change Sensitive Score Standard Error	—[b]	●	●[d]	●[d]	●	●[d]	●[e]	●[e]	●[e]	●[e]	●	●[e]	●[e]	●	●[f]	●[f]	●	●[f]	●[f]
Age Adjusted Standard Score[g]	Age-Adjusted Standard Score[g]	●	●	●	●	●	●	●	●	●	●	●	●	●	●	●	●	●	●

Age Adjusted Standard Score Standard Error	Age-Adjusted Standard Score SE	●	●	●	●	●	●[c]	●[c]	●	●[c]	●	●[c]	●[c]	●	●[f]	●[f]	●	●[f]	●[f]
Age Edu Adjusted TScore[h,i]	Age- and Education-Adjusted T-Score[h,i]	●	●	●	●	●	●	●		●	●	●	●	●	●	●	●		
Age Edu Adjusted TScore Standard Error[h]	—[b]	●	●	●	●	●	●	●		●	●	●	●	●	●[f]	●[f]	●		
National Percentile Age Adjusted	National Age-Adjusted %ile	●	●	●	●	●	●	●	●	●	●	●	●	●	●	●	●	●	●
Computed Score	Computed Score	●	●																

Note: ● indicates that the score is provided in the Scores export for the test or composite.

[a] This score is not computed in NIH Toolbox V3. It has been replaced with the Age- and Education- Adjusted T Score.

[b] This score appears in the Scores Export but does not appear in the NIH Toolbox V3 Cognition Domain Score Report.

[c] This score will appear as 99 if the examinee fails out of the test after practice items and before any live items have been administered.

[d] This score is not computed if the examinee fails out of the test after practice items and before any live items have been administered.

[e] This score is only computed when the examinee obtains a non-zero or non-perfect number-correct score during the test administration.

[f] This score is only computed when the examinee obtains a non-zero or non-perfect number-correct score on all contributing tests during the administration.

[g] If this value is < 40, it will display as 39. If the value is > 160, it will display as 161.

[h] This score is only available for examinees ages 22 and older for whom education level was entered into the NIH Toolbox V3 app.

[i] If this value is < 20, it will display as 19. If the value is > 80, it will display as 81.

CHAPTER SUMMARY

The NIH Toolbox V3 Cognition domain score reports and exports provide a variety of score information to describe an individual's performance on the tests. Performance metrics describe an individual's absolute level of functioning, while relative standing metrics describe the individual's standing in a reference group of peers. Measurement error is inherent in all cognition tests, and scores should be interpreted in the context of confidence bands, which quantify the amount of error, or uncertainty, in the test or composite score.

TEST YOURSELF

1. **The age-adjusted standard score (SS) and age-adjusted national percentile rank describe an examinee's performance relative to the entire NIH Toolbox V3 norming sample.**
   True or False
2. **Ability scores from Rasch-scaled tests are reported in logits, which are sometimes also referred to as ___.**
   (a) Standard scores
   (b) Percentile Ranks
   (c) Composite scores
   (d) Theta scores
3. **The Total Cognition Composite CSS is computed as the arithmetic mean of the Crystallized Cognition Composite and Fluid Cognition Composite (rather than as the arithmetic mean of the seven tests that contribute to the Crystallized Cognition Composite and Fluid Cognition Composites).**
   True or False
4. **Raw scores, computed scores, theta scores, and change-sensitive scores provide different ways to describe an examinee's performance, whereas standard scores, national percentile ranks, and *T*-scores provide different ways to describe an examinee's relative standing in a peer group.**
   True or False
5. **To obtain an accurate estimate of ability, computerized adaptive testing (CAT) algorithms require examinees to take all the items in the item pool.**
   True or False
6. **Which score is the ideal metric to use for NIH Toolbox V3 Cognition score interpretation when you are interested in studying cognitive decline in aging individuals?**
   (a) Age-adjusted standard score
   (b) Raw score
   (c) Change-sensitive score (CSS)
   (d) Age- and education-adjusted *T*-score

7. Which of the following statements is true?
(a) Scores with narrower 90% confidence intervals have higher precision than those with wider intervals.
(b) Scores with wider 90% confidence intervals have higher precision than those with narrower intervals.
(c) Scores with narrower 90% confidence intervals have the same precision as those with wider intervals.
(d) Scores do not have differences in precision; they are all the same.

8. What do omission errors reflect?
(a) The number of trials for which an individual answers incorrectly and/or fails to select a response before the item time limit.
(b) The number of trials for which an individual fails to select a response before the item time limit.
(c) The number of incorrect responses on live items.
(d) The number of incorrect responses to congruent items.

9. Change-sensitive scores are the foundation for all other derived scores in the NIH Toolbox Cognition V3 domain.
True or False

10. Which of the following scores is an equal-interval metric?
(a) Computed score
(b) Raw score
(c) Commission errors score
(d) Change-sensitive score

Answers: 1. False; 2. (d); 3. True; 4. True; 5. False; 6. (c); 7. (a); 8. (b); 9. True; 10. (d).

REFERENCES

American Educational Research Association (AERA), American Psychological Association (APA), & National Council on Measurement in Education (NCME). (2014). *Standards for educational and psychological testing*. AERA.

Rasch, G. (1980). *Probabilistic models for some intelligence and attainment tests*. University of Chicago Press. (Original work published 1960).

Schneider, W. J., & McGrew, K. S. (2018). The Cattell-Horn-Carroll theory of cognitive abilities. In D. P. Flanagan & E. M. McDonough (Eds.), *Contemporary intellectual assessment: Theories, tests, and issues* (4th ed., pp. 73–163). Guilford Press.

Van der Linden, W. J. (2018). *Handbook of item response theory: Three volume set*. CRC Press.

Woodcock, R. W., & Dahl, M. N. (1971). *A common scale for the measurement of person ability and test item difficulty (AGS Paper No. 10). Pearson.*

Wright, B. D., & Stone, M. S. (1979). *Best test design: Rasch measurement*. MESA Press.

Five

A COMPREHENSIVE EVALUATION OF THE NIH TOOLBOX® VERSION 3 COGNITION DOMAIN: ADVANCEMENTS, CHALLENGES, AND FUTURE DIRECTIONS

Anson Kairys
Bruno Giordani

INTRODUCTION

In the era of advanced technologies, big data, and artificial intelligence, there is an impetus to develop efficient, reliable, easily transportable, and valid cognitive assessments using digital platforms, such as tablets or smartphones. A cursory review of available digital cognitive assessment platforms shows there are *at least* 40 different digital cognitive assessments available, ranging from self-administered smartphone evaluations with novel tasks to digitized versions of classic paper-and-pencil measures such as the clock drawing test or Montreal Cognitive Assessment (Chan et al., 2021; Staffaroni et al., 2020). While this is a much-needed advancement, it is imperative that these measures are grounded in neuropsychological principles such as reliability, validity, and sensitivity/specificity to different diseases. The NIH Toolbox Cognition domain is a prime example of an assessment suite that remains grounded in neuropsychological principles while adapting to the changing technological landscape. Like many of our traditional paper-and-pencil neuropsychological measures, there are fundamental limitations that are difficult to overcome even in the best circumstances. Issues such as cultural adaptability, representative normative samples, reliability, and validity are all difficult to establish without rigorous efforts to establish sound testing principles. The National Institutes of Health (NIH) Toolbox Cognition tests are not alone in the strengths they possess and challenges they face. Years of development have led to the release of Version 3 (V3) of the NIHTB Cognition domain (i.e., the full suite of tests that measure cognitive functioning), and, in particular, the seven tests that comprise the NIH Toolbox Total Cognition Battery (NIHTB-CB; a specific subset of tests in the Cognition domain): Dimensional Change Card Sort (DCCS), Flanker Inhibitory Control and Attention (Flanker), List Sorting Working Memory (LSWM), Oral Reading

Recognition (ORR), Pattern Comparison (PC) Processing Speed, Picture Sequence Memory (PSM) Form A, and Picture Vocabulary (PV). While it has significantly improved over previous versions, it still has some areas for improvement, which are discussed throughout this chapter. This chapter provides a comprehensive evaluation of the NIH Toolbox V3 Cognition domain, highlighting its psychometric strengths, delving into domain-specific features, operational advantages, and broad research applicability, while also critically examining its limitations and opportunities for future development. The foundation for understanding these innovations and their significance lies in examining the extensive research base that has been built with previous versions of the domain. Where available, V3-specific data will be presented; however, given the relatively recent release of V3, most studies reference earlier NIHTB-CB versions. Throughout this chapter, "V3" will be clearly specified to distinguish between historical findings and current V3 capabilities. This evidence base provides crucial insights into both the capabilities and constraints that have shaped the development of NIHTBV3-CB. In the end, the reader should come away with a balanced appraisal of the benefits and limitations of the NIH Toolbox V3 Cognition domain.

Rapid Reference 5.1

NIH Toolbox V3 has 15 tests in the Cognition domain. The NIH Toolbox Cognition Battery is a specific subset of Cognition tests that, when administered together, produce an NIHTB Total Cognition Composite score. This battery is often referred to as "NIHTB-CB" when referred to generally (e.g., any/all version of the battery), or as "NIHTBV3-CB" when specifically discussing the Total Cognition Battery in the NIH Toolbox V3 app.

BRIEF OVERVIEW OF THE NIH TOOLBOX COGNITION DOMAIN

The NIHTB Cognition domain is a widely used, standardized digital cognitive assessment tool designed to assess cognitive functions across individuals aged 3 to 85+ (Gershon et al., 2013; Weintraub et al., 2013). Now in its third version (V3), it was developed as a streamlined alternative to traditional paper-and-pencil neuropsychological assessments. Administered via iPad, the V3 Cognition domain evaluates key cognitive constructs of executive function, episodic memory, working memory, attention, processing speed, language, and visual reasoning in approximately 30 minutes (Hook & Giella, 2023), making it particularly valuable for large-scale research initiatives and clinical research settings where efficiency is paramount and reliability across sites is critical. The NIH Toolbox V3 Cognition domain has undergone refinements in V3 aimed at enhancing its precision, usability, and sensitivity to cognitive changes longitudinally. Key updates include new normative samples and continuous norming for more precise age-based scoring, change-sensitive scores (CSSs) for longitudinal monitoring, additional cognitive measures for broader domain coverage, and streamlined administration protocols (LaForte et al., 2024). While these advancements seek to address prior limitations, important challenges remain. These include limitations in clinical depth, cultural adaptability, sensitivity to subtle cognitive deficits, and technological accessibility. These constraints, which to varying degrees affect many digital cognitive assessment tools, warrant careful evaluation when considering the domain's appropriate applications and interpreting its results.

HISTORICAL CONTEXT AND DEVELOPMENT

Since its initial conception, the NIHTB-CB has addressed a fundamental need in cognitive assessment: providing a comprehensive yet efficient evaluation that can be administered across a broad range of ages and settings (Weintraub et al., 2013). The evolution of the NIHTB-CB reflects a continuous effort to refine cognitive assessment methodologies, balancing scientific rigor with practical utility in diverse research and clinical contexts (Fox et al., 2022). The development of the NIHTB-CB began as part of the NIH Blueprint for Neuroscience Research initiative, which sought to create a set of standardized measures for neurological and behavioral function assessment (Gershon et al., 2013). The battery was developed through collaborative efforts of multiple research teams who adapted well-established laboratory-based cognitive tasks into standardized and digitized formats suitable for widespread use. These tasks provided researchers with efficient, psychometrically sound instruments that could be used across diverse populations and settings. This standardization was particularly important for enabling cross-study comparisons and facilitating data sharing across research initiatives. The NIH Toolbox originally began as a desktop/laptop-based assessment platform before transitioning to tablet (iPad) administration. The early versions of the NIHTB-CB provided valuable cognitive insights, but they revealed some limitations, particularly in reliability and sensitivity to cognitive changes, ultimately leading to the release of V3, which incorporates targeted improvements in scoring models, norming methods, additional targeted tasks, and test administration protocols (LaForte et al., 2024), a number of which had been recommended by active users. The NIH Toolbox V3 Cognition domain has five new tests and has undergone rigorous validation across various demographic groups (LaForte et al., 2024), establishing its credibility as a reliable measurement tool.

A significant milestone in the NIH Toolbox Cognition battery's development has been its integration into major research initiatives. The V2 battery's adoption in the Adolescent Brain Cognitive Development (ABCD) study (Luciana et al., 2018), which follows over 10,000 children from ages 9 to 10 into early adulthood, has provided unprecedented opportunities to examine cognitive development in relation to brain maturation, environmental influences, and behavioral outcomes. Similarly, its use in the NIH's Environmental influences on Child Health Outcomes (ECHO) program signifies the importance of the NIHTB-CB as a useful measure of cognitive development across the lifespan (Morales et al., 2024). In the Human Connectome Project, the largest initiative to map brain structures and functions to date (Van Essen et al., 2012), the NIHTB-CB has enabled researchers to explore relationships between cognitive performance and vast neural connectivity patterns, solidifying its importance in our understanding of brain-behavior relationships.

Through its widespread use, the NIH Toolbox Cognition domain now serves as a central instrument for investigating cognition in both clinical populations and developmental contexts (Fox et al., 2022). Its evolution from initial conception to the current V3 represents a responsive approach to the needs of the research community, with each iteration addressing limitations identified through practical application and empirical investigation. The development trajectory of the NIH Toolbox Cognition domain illustrates the dynamic nature of cognitive assessment tools, which must continually evolve to incorporate methodological advancements, respond to user feedback, and align with emerging theoretical frameworks in cognitive science. As we examine the specific strengths and limitations of the NIH Toolbox V3 Cognition domain throughout this chapter, it is important to consider these features within this historical context of continuous refinement and expanding application. The domain's current form represents not an endpoint but rather a stage in an ongoing development process aimed at enhancing the precision, efficiency, and utility of a lifespan approach to cognitive assessment across diverse research and clinical contexts. Given this extensive development history and widespread research adoption, evaluating the psychometric foundation becomes essential for understanding the domain's scientific validity and practical utility. The NIH Toolbox V3 Cognition domain introduces several important advancements in its psychometric framework while still facing certain limitations that warrant consideration. This section examines both the strengths and limitations of the domain's psychometric properties, providing a balanced evaluation of its measurement capabilities based on available V3 technical documentation and research findings from earlier versions of the NIHTB-CB (i.e., the Cognition Battery from V1 and V2).

PSYCHOMETRIC STRENGTHS, LIMITATIONS, AND COMPARISON WITH OTHER DIGITAL ASSESSMENTS

Psychometric Strengths

The NIHTBV3-CB builds upon previous versions with substantial psychometric enhancements that strengthen its foundation for accurate and reproducible cognitive assessment. A key advancement is the updated normative sample, which now includes 3,904 participants representative of the US population (LaForte et al., 2024). This sample was designed to reflect national distributions across age, sex, race/ethnicity, and education, though race and ethnicity are no longer used as adjustment variables in normative scoring, a deliberate shift from prior versions aimed at improving fairness and scientific validity. Perhaps the most significant methodological improvement in V3 is the implementation of continuous norming, which allows for more precise age-based norms in three-month intervals for children and one-year intervals for adults (LaForte et al., 2024). Continuous norming uses regression-based modeling to generate normative values along a continuous age scale, avoiding the artificial jumps and drops seen with traditional age bins. This approach represents a substantial advancement over traditional block norming methods, which can create artificial gaps at age-group boundaries. Continuous norming provides smoother developmental trajectories and more accurate comparisons, particularly important when assessing individuals near the boundaries of traditional age blocks. For instance, an assessment with traditional age blocks might compare a child of five years and two months against the normative group of five-year-olds; continuous norming would compare that same child with the five years, zero months to five years, three months normative group. This approach improves on block norming by eliminating artificial score gaps at age boundaries, yielding smoother developmental trajectories and more accurate comparisons near those cutoffs.

The introduction of SSs based on item response theory (IRT) represents another important psychometric advancement. CSS values are derived from IRT-based models that capture both accuracy and, where relevant, response time, and are scaled to enhance sensitivity to within-individual cognitive change across repeated assessments. This feature is particularly valuable for research tracking developmental progressions or interventional outcomes, where detecting cognitive changes is essential. Extensive validation studies underscore the NIHTB-CB's robust test–retest reliability, construct validity, and discriminant validity, with strong convergence against traditional neuropsychological measures (LaForte et al., 2024). These psychometric properties establish the battery as a scientifically sound suite of tests that can be used with confidence in various research contexts, from developmental studies to clinical trials.

Rapid Reference 5.2

Change Sensitive Scores (CSSs) are derived from the examinee's raw score and do not rely on normative references. Therefore, it is sensitive to changes in that particular examinee's ability over time.

Psychometric Limitations

Despite its substantial psychometric strengths, the NIHTBV3-CB faces several important limitations that must be considered when interpreting results. Research with V2 raised some concerns about test–retest reliability (Taylor et al., 2022), and it remains to be seen whether V3 can fully overcome these challenges over extended testing periods. This issue is particularly important for large-scale, multisite research trials where cognitive assessment may only occur annually, making test–retest reliability and intraclass correlation coefficients (ICCs) paramount. V3 ICCs are generally acceptable for use at the group level, based on 14-day testing intervals (LaForte et al., 2024), but fall short of the generally accepted ICC level of 0.90 for individual diagnostic decisions (Koo & Li, 2016). This limitation is particularly relevant for clinical applications, where higher precision is required for individual-level decision-making compared to group-level research analyses.

The NIHTB-CB V2 also demonstrated limitations in detecting more subtle cognitive changes or relationships with key clinical biomarkers, particularly in high-functioning individuals at early stages of neurodegenerative diseases. Snitz et al. (2020) reported that although specific NIH Toolbox Fluid Cognition measures correlated with tau deposition in cognitively unimpaired older adults, the battery's overall sensitivity to early pathological changes was limited (Snitz et al., 2020). This finding suggests that while the NIHTB-CB may be effective for detecting more pronounced cognitive deficits, it may be less sensitive to the subtle changes that characterize preclinical stages of cognitive decline. Further, when compared with standardized cognitive composites in Alzheimer's research, such as the Preclinical Alzheimer Cognitive Composite (PACC; Donohue et al., 2014), other measures, such as the Cogstate Brief Battery, may have greater potential to identify subtle cognitive impairments (Buckley et al., 2017). These considerations highlight challenges for NIH Toolbox V3 Cognition research focused on early detection and precise tracking of cognitive changes in preclinical stages of neurodegeneration, though the introduction of CSS may improve this precision.

An additional psychometric limitation pertains to the factor structure of the battery when applied to diverse populations. Using earlier versions of the NIHTB-CB, studies have produced unexpected factor loadings for different demographic groups, such as Black individuals, suggesting that the NIHTB-CB's factor structure may vary depending on the level of cognitive impairment among diverse participants and how normative adjustments are applied (Kairys et al., 2022; Rigby et al., 2024; Rose et al., 2024). Kairys et al. (2022) found that in a sample of community-dwelling Black adults, the NIHTB-CB V2's (administered via laptop) crystallized ability tests, such as ORR and PV, were unexpectedly the most sensitive in differentiating MCI from healthy controls, suggesting potential cultural or educational biases in the battery's measurement approach. Similarly, Rose et al. (2024) noted that race influenced NIHTB-CB V2 scores when predicting brain amyloid status in older adults, with the List Sorting Working Memory (LSWM) Test showing sensitivity to amyloid positivity, indicating that demographic factors like race may affect the battery's diagnostic utility. This research team also observed cultural differences in test performance, specifically differences in factor structure for cognitively normal, but not MCI, Black participants compared to White participants, suggesting distinct cultural and impairment-associated interactions with the NIHTB-CB measures (Rose et al., 2024). Furthermore, they identified instability in the NIHTB-CB's factor structure across varying levels of cognitive impairment within Black participants, highlighting potential limitations when assessing cognitive decline longitudinally. This instability was particularly evident in the Crystallized Composite, challenging the assumption that crystallized measures consistently represent a cognitive "hold" factor across different racial groups. Additionally, Rigby et al. (2024) found that although the NIHTB-CB's overall discriminant accuracy did not significantly differ by race, the models showed notably poorer accuracy in identifying White individuals with amnestic MCI compared to Black participants, underscoring nuanced racial differences in cognitive assessment outcomes. These collective findings raise important questions about measurement invariance across diverse populations, leading to considerations of aspects such as educational quality versus comparisons on years of education and reading level alone, and highlight the need for continued psychometric evaluation in varied demographic groups. Again, these studies were conducted using previous versions of the NIHTB-CB, and it remains to be seen whether V3 will produce similar findings.

The psychometric limitations of the NIHTBV3-CB do not negate its value as a cognitive assessment tool but rather define the boundaries of its appropriate application and signal where particular attention should be spent to ensure accuracy of normative corrections and interpretations of results. Researchers and clinicians should be mindful of these constraints when selecting assessment methods, particularly for studies requiring high sensitivity to subtle cognitive changes or applications involving diverse populations where measurement invariance has not been fully established.

Comparison with Other Digital Measures

When compared to other widely used computerized cognitive assessments, the NIHTBV3-CB demonstrates both advantages and trade-offs. While the Cogstate Brief Battery (Maruff et al., 2013) has shown significant practice effects and performance discrepancies between clinic- and home-based testing (Stricker et al., 2020), it may offer superior sensitivity to subtle cognitive changes in preclinical populations, an area where the NIH Toolbox V2 Cognition domain has faced limitations (Buckley et al., 2017). The NIH Toolbox V3 Cognition domain addresses reliability concerns through standardized audio instructions, consistent task presentation, and continuous norming based on extensive in-person data collection, enhancing score comparability across diverse settings (LaForte et al., 2024). However, this approach sacrifices the flexibility of remote administration that Cogstate provides.

The Cambridge Neuropsychological Test Automated Battery (CANTAB; Barnett et al., 2016) offers greater precision in isolating specific cognitive processes through its neuroscience-based task design, potentially providing more detailed clinical information than the NIH Toolbox's efficiency-focused approach. While CANTAB does not offer the same level of comprehensive normative validation as the NIHTB-CB, with normative data only available for selected tests, its tasks may better capture subtle deficits in complex cases. Similarly, Creyos provides rapid, accessible screening with a large normative dataset (over 44,000 individuals), though its reliance on self-reported online data limits clinical precision compared to the NIH Toolbox's examiner-administered structure (Hampshire et al., 2012).

The NIH Toolbox V3 Cognition domain's primary competitive advantages lie in its comprehensive normative validation, standardized administration, and balance of efficiency with psychometric rigor, making it well-suited for large-scale research. However, this comparison highlights the inherent trade-offs between breadth and depth, efficiency and sensitivity, that characterize the digital assessment landscape.

CONSTRUCT-SPECIFIC STRENGTHS AND LIMITATIONS OF THE NIH TOOLBOX V3 COGNITION DOMAIN

While the broader psychometric considerations inform the appropriate use of the NIH Toolbox V3 Cognition domain, a more nuanced understanding emerges by examining how the domain performs across specific cognitive constructs. The V3 Cognition domain assesses six core areas: attention, episodic and delayed memory, executive function, language, processing speed, and working memory. This section reviews the strengths and limitations of each, highlighting construct-specific considerations that impact both research and clinical applications. As with previous sections, the domain-specific research base primarily reflects findings from earlier NIH Toolbox Cognition versions, with V3-specific improvements noted where available.

Attention

Attention is the capacity to selectively process relevant stimuli while ignoring distractions, sustain focus over time, and flexibly shift between tasks or mental sets. It is a foundational cognitive construct that supports learning, working memory, and executive functioning, and is commonly disrupted in a wide range of clinical conditions, including attention-deficit hyperactivity disorder (ADHD), traumatic brain injury, and neurodegenerative disorders.

Strengths

The NIH Toolbox assesses attention primarily through the Flanker test, which measures selective attention and inhibitory control. This task effectively captures the ability to focus on relevant stimuli while suppressing responses to irrelevant ones, a fundamental aspect of attentional processing. The task's design, which requires examinees to respond to a central target while ignoring flanking distractors, engages key neural networks involved in attentional control. The Flanker task demonstrates good psychometric properties, including adequate reliability and validity across diverse age groups. The task's design minimizes cultural and linguistic biases, enhancing its applicability across diverse populations. The attention measure shows sensitivity to developmental changes across the lifespan, capturing age-related improvements in children and adolescents and age-related changes in older adults. This developmental sensitivity positions it as a valuable tool for tracking attentional trajectories across the lifespan, contributing to our understanding of normal cognitive development and aging (LaForte et al., 2024; Zelazo et al., 2013). The integration of attention assessment with other cognitive constructs in the NIH Toolbox allows researchers to examine relationships between attentional processes and other cognitive functions, such as executive control, working memory, and processing speed. New to NIH Toolbox V3, Flanker also reports the median response time and commission errors for all congruent items (i.e., items in which all the fish point the same way), and reports median response time for all incongruent items (i.e., items in which the middle fish points in the direction opposite the other fish). This integrated approach enhances the battery's utility for comprehensive cognitive assessment and facilitates research on the interconnections between different cognitive systems.

Limitations

Despite these strengths, the NIH Toolbox's attention assessment faces several important limitations. The Flanker task effectively evaluates inhibitory control and selective attention but offers limited insight into other attentional processes, such as sustained attention or divided attention, functions critical for understanding conditions such as ADHD or post-stroke cognitive impairment (Fan et al., 2002; Mirsky et al., 1991).

Established theoretical models conceptualize attention as a multidimensional construct encompassing several distinct but interrelated processes, including selective attention, sustained attention, divided attention, and attentional switching (Mirsky et al., 1991). By focusing primarily on selective attention and inhibitory control, the NIH Toolbox provides only a partial assessment of the broader attentional system, potentially missing deficits in specific attentional processes that may be differentially affected in various clinical conditions. This relatively narrow focus limits the depth of attention assessment available through the NIH Toolbox Cognition domain, potentially necessitating supplementation with more specialized measures to achieve comprehensive assessment in certain populations. For example, sustained attention deficits, which involve maintaining attentional focus over extended periods, are particularly relevant for conditions like ADHD but may not be fully captured by the current assessment approach (Gu et al., 2018).

Executive Function

Executive function refers to higher-order cognitive processes essential for goal-directed behavior, including cognitive flexibility, inhibition, and planning.

Strengths

The NIH Toolbox's assessment of executive function primarily utilizes three well-established tasks representing the Cognition domain's three-component model: DCCS for set shifting; Flanker for inhibition; and VR, a new addition in V3, designed to evaluate nonverbal problem-solving. DCCS effectively measures cognitive flexibility, the ability to switch between different rules of mental sets, a fundamental component of executive function. DCCS has been validated across diverse age groups and demonstrates good sensitivity to developmental changes in cognitive flexibility (Zelazo et al., 2013). New to V3,

DCCS also reports the median response time per item, number of commission errors, and number of omission errors. The Flanker task complements this by assessing inhibitory control, another key executive function component, requiring examinees to focus on relevant stimuli while suppressing responses to irrelevant ones. The VR test fills a notable gap left by V2 by providing a dedicated measure of fluid reasoning that is minimally dependent on verbal skills, akin to traditional measures like Matrix Reasoning or Raven's Progressive Matrices (Raven & Raven, 2003). The computerized adaptive testing (CAT) format improves administration efficiency, typically completing within 10 minutes.

The standardized administration and scoring of these tasks represent significant strengths, ensuring consistency across different testing contexts and examiners. This standardization is particularly valuable for large-scale, multisite research initiatives where maintaining assessment uniformity is essential. Additionally, the tasks are designed to be engaging and accessible across the lifespan, making them suitable for developmental research spanning from early childhood through late adulthood. The NIH Toolbox V2 executive function measures are sensitive to age-related change, capturing both developmental gains in youth and declines in older adulthood (Mather et al., 2024). The VR task showed moderate convergent validity, correlating with the WAIS-IV Matrix Reasoning subtest and Perceptual Reasoning Index, and with the WISC-V Fluid Reasoning Index in children, providing evidence for its validity as a measure of nonverbal reasoning across the lifespan (LaForte et al., 2024). This developmental sensitivity positions these measures as valuable tools for tracking executive function trajectories across the lifespan, contributing to our understanding of normal cognitive development and aging.

Limitations

While the NIH Toolbox V3 Cognition domain offers several advantages, its coverage of executive function is somewhat constrained in terms of scope and depth. The domain captures inhibition, cognitive flexibility, and nonverbal reasoning but fails to adequately assess critical higher-order executive processes such as planning and complex goal-directed behaviors. Established theoretical models consistently emphasize executive functioning as multidimensional, encompassing not just flexibility and inhibition but also the ability to strategize, adaptively plan, and solve problems across diverse contexts (Miyake et al., 2000). By not including measures that require strategic planning and nuanced problem-solving, such as the Tower of London or similar paradigms, the NIHTB-CB potentially overlooks deficits that manifest predominantly during the execution of complex real-world tasks. This narrow assessment approach might prevent the accurate identification of impairments that impact essential activities of daily living, such as financial management or social interactions, underscoring the need for a more comprehensive evaluation of executive functioning or supplemental questionnaires surrounding daily functioning.

As an added task in V3, the VR task faces several specific limitations despite its psychometric strengths. Its item complexity is deliberately constrained to optimize administration time and accessibility, but this may reduce its sensitivity to subtle deficits in high-functioning populations or those with selective right-hemisphere dysfunction, such as constructional apraxia or spatial neglect (Chen et al., 2012). Like traditional measures of visual reasoning, the VR task does not independently control for lower-level perceptual and attentional processes such as visual scanning or processing speed, which could confound the interpretation of results. Unlike some traditional matrix reasoning tasks, there is no time pressure per item, potentially decreasing ecological validity when assessing rapid real-world visuospatial reasoning demands. Furthermore, although it shows moderate associations with other established measures of fluid intelligence, the VR task is the only nonverbal reasoning task in the Cognition domain, potentially limiting the breadth of the domain's measurement of visuospatial abilities (LaForte et al., 2024). Finally, while useful for large-scale research or screening, the VR test's brevity and constrained item formats may limit its clinical utility as a standalone diagnostic measure for detailed visuospatial dysfunction.

The ecological validity of the executive function measures—their ability to predict real-world functioning—remains a concern. As with many assessment techniques, including the NIHTBV3-CB, the tasks demonstrate good construct validity in laboratory settings, but their relationship to everyday executive challenges has not been fully established. This gap between test performance and functional outcomes represents an important limitation for clinical applications, where understanding the impact of cognitive deficits on daily functioning is essential for diagnosis and intervention planning.

Episodic and Delayed Memory

Episodic memory refers to the capacity to encode, store, and retrieve information about specific events, including the contextual details surrounding them. This form of memory is crucial for daily functioning and is often one of the earliest cognitive domains affected in neurodegenerative conditions such as Alzheimer's disease.

Strengths

The NIH Toolbox's approach to episodic memory assessment has been significantly improved over V2 with the addition of the Rey Auditory Verbal Learning Test (RAVLT), RAVLT Delay, Face Name Associative Memory Exam (FNAME), and FNAME Delay, which complement the existing Picture Sequence Memory (PSM) test. PSM utilizes a visual sequence learning paradigm, intended to reduce verbal and cultural biases, making it accessible across diverse populations. By requiring examinees to recall the sequence of images depicting everyday activities, the task engages memory processes that mirror real-world demands (LaForte et al., 2024). The addition of the RAVLT and RAVLT Delay, an extensively validated and widely used measure of verbal learning and memory across trials, represents a major enhancement by aligning the NIHTBV3-CB with well-known verbal memory paradigms. The FNAME tasks further expand the memory assessment by evaluating associative memory through an extensively validated paradigm where examinees remember 12 faces paired with names, then, after a 5–25-minute delay, complete face recognition, first letter recognition, and full name recognition components.

The combination of PSM (visual–spatial sequence learning), RAVLT (verbal learning), and FNAME (face name associative memory) provides a comprehensive evaluation of episodic memory across multiple modalities and memory processes. Additional strengths include the availability of raw scores for each FNAME phase, allowing clinicians to compare performance across face recognition, first letter recognition, and full name recognition components. The FNAME tasks represent an improvement from the experimental version present in V2, which lacked normative data. V3 now provides norm-referenced scores for both FNAME components (LaForte et al., 2024).

With NIH Toolbox V2, PSM demonstrated good sensitivity to developmental changes and age-related declines. Researchers have shown clear age-related improvements in younger populations on the PSM (Akshoomoff et al., 2013), providing important benchmarks for understanding memory development. Similarly, PSM showed sensitivity to normal age-related declines in older adults, with performance decreasing significantly after age 85 (Mather et al., 2024). These findings align with established models of cognitive aging (Park & Reuter-Lorenz, 2009; Salthouse, 2010) and highlight the battery's relevance for lifespan research. While specific developmental research on the FNAME tasks is limited, given the recent addition to V3 with normative data, the extensively validated paradigm suggests similar developmental sensitivity patterns (LaForte et al., 2024). The additions of RAVLT and FNAME in V3 will undoubtedly add to the lifespan applicability of these memory assessments. The standardized administration and scoring of these tasks improve reliability and comparability across research sites, making them suitable for large-scale, multisite studies focused on memory function in both normative and clinical populations.

Limitations

Despite these strengths, the NIH Toolbox's approach to episodic memory assessment faces important limitations. PSM, while valuable for assessing sequence learning, does not differentiate among core memory processes—encoding, storage, and retrieval—which are essential distinctions in clinical neuropsychology, particularly for diagnosing and staging neurodegenerative diseases (Bauer et al., 2013; McKhann et al., 2011).

Although the inclusion of the RAVLT with delayed recall enhances the depth of memory assessment and provides differentiation of core memory processes, its recognition trial must be administered separately and is not part of the standard V3 battery. This omission limits the tool's capacity to robustly assess memory storage in contrast to retrieval, thereby reducing diagnostic specificity for clinical applications. Recognition trials are particularly valuable for distinguishing between memory ***storage deficits***, such as those seen in AD, and ***retrieval deficits***, more common in conditions involving frontal-subcortical dysfunction. Individuals with medial temporal lobe damage, as in AD, typically show impairments on both recall and recognition tasks due to true storage failure (Salmon & Bondi, 2009). In contrast, patients with disorders like Huntington's disease or Parkinson's disease often exhibit poor free recall but relatively intact recognition, reflecting impaired retrieval processes rather than degraded memory traces (Butters et al., 1985; Higginson et al., 2005).

While the FNAME tasks provide valuable associative memory assessment, they are supplementary and are not included in any composite scores, limiting their integration with overall cognitive assessment. With multiple memory tests now available in V3 (PSM, RAVLT, RAVLT Delay, FNAME, and FNAME Delay), the absence of a dedicated memory composite score represents a missed opportunity to provide an integrated assessment of memory-related cognitive decline.

Finally, the sensitivity of the memory tasks to early-stage or subtle deficits, such as those seen in preclinical AD, is not yet well established. Although the RAVLT and FNAME tasks may offer improved detection of verbal and associative memory impairment, additional research is needed to determine whether the NIH Toolbox V3 Cognition domain can reliably identify the earliest signs of memory decline that precede clinical diagnosis, as this is a growing priority in both research and healthcare.

Language

Language functions refer to the cognitive processes that enable the comprehension, production, and manipulation of spoken and written language, encompassing skills such as vocabulary knowledge, semantic retrieval, syntactic processing, and verbal reasoning.

Strengths

The NIH Toolbox includes two measures in the language construct: PV, which assesses receptive vocabulary, and ORR, which evaluates single-word decoding and reading fluency. This dual approach allows for the assessment of both verbal knowledge (crystallized ability) and basic academic skills, which can help distinguish between developmental language delay and limited educational exposure in children or differentiate types of language decline in adults. In neuropsychological contexts, oral reading is often used as an estimate of premorbid functioning, while vocabulary scores provide insight into verbal intellectual abilities (Lezak et al., 2012). The inclusion of both measures enables a broader snapshot of language abilities than vocabulary alone, and the automated administration allows for consistent delivery across examinees.

Limitations

Although the necessary components to establish proxies of crystallized intelligence and educational attainment are covered, the NIH Toolbox language measures remain somewhat limited in diagnostic utility for many clinical populations. Expressive language, verbal fluency, syntactic comprehension, and discourse-level assessments are not included. These are critical areas for identifying aphasia, early semantic impairment in LD, or frontal language syndromes (Goodglass et al., 2001). Moreover, neither the vocabulary nor reading tasks assess the pragmatics of language use, such as coherence, social communication, or narrative ability, aspects which are often impaired in autism, right hemisphere stroke, or frontotemporal dementia (Ash et al., 2010). While reading recognition may offer some estimate of academic exposure, it lacks sensitivity to surface dyslexia or phonological impairments and may not detect subtle breakdowns in reading comprehension. The brevity and format of both language tasks risk reducing examiner flexibility and may prevent deeper probing of errors, limiting the ability to characterize the nature and source of language deficits, possibly limiting its use in comprehensive LD evaluations.

Processing Speed

Processing speed refers to the efficiency with which the brain can perceive, interpret, and respond to simple stimuli. It underlies performance across virtually all cognitive constructs and is particularly sensitive to neurological insult and typically declines with age.

Strengths

The NIH Toolbox V3 Cognition domain assesses processing speed through the PC Processing Speed test, Speeded Matching (SM) test, and the Oral Symbol Digit (OSD) test, which evaluate how quickly individuals can make simple perceptual judgments about visual stimuli. In PC (aged 5–85+), examinees determine whether two abstract patterns are the same or different, allowing the task to isolate core information processing speed while minimizing the influence of higher-order reasoning. This straightforward design enhances the measure's specificity and reduces confounding from more complex cognitive operations. The PC task has demonstrated good psychometric properties, and the use of culturally neutral visual stimuli minimizes language and cultural bias, increasing its applicability in demographically diverse samples. SM (aged three to six) is a match-to-sample task assessing processing speed (LaForte et al., 2024). It requires identifying which of the four images at the bottom matches the one at the top. Added to the NIHTBV3 Cognition domain, SM targets younger children who may struggle with the PC paradigm, as matching images is cognitively easier than judging image identity (LaForte et al., 2024). It appears in both the Early Childhood Cognition Battery and the new Crystallized-Fluid-Processing Speed (CFPS) Battery.

Rapid Reference 5.3

Pattern Comparison Processing Speed (PC) is a test of processing speed for ages five+, while Speeded Matching measures processing speed in examinees aged three to six.

OSD measures processing speed by having examinees pair and verbally match numbers and symbols within 120 seconds. It is particularly useful for individuals with upper extremity motor limitations who may be unable to complete the PC task (i.e., quickly tap the iPad screen; LaForte et al., 2024).

Limitations

While the PC, SM, and OSD tests efficiently measure basic perceptual speed, they do not capture higher-order demands such as task switching, working memory load, or sustained attention—factors often implicated in subtle deficits seen in early Alzheimer's disease, traumatic brain injury, or multiple sclerosis (Bryant et al., 2004; Fields, 2008). Although V3 introduces CSSs, the underlying task may lack the complexity needed to detect meaningful changes in functional speed, particularly in high-functioning or preclinical populations. Its abstract, decontextualized format minimizes cultural bias but reduces ecological validity, offering little insight into real-world challenges like managing time-sensitive tasks or driving (Royall et al., 2002). Moreover, as a single-task paradigm, it cannot disentangle cognitive slowing from motor or perceptual delays, and the absence of dual-task measures further constrains its interpretability in nuanced clinical profiles.

Working Memory

Working memory refers to the ability to temporarily hold and manipulate information for immediate use in cognitive tasks such as reasoning, problem-solving, and goal-directed behavior. It plays a foundational role in executive functioning, learning, and adaptive performance across the lifespan.

Strengths

The NIH Toolbox assesses working memory primarily through the List Sorting Working Memory (LSWM) Test, a task that requires examinees to temporarily hold and reorganize information according to category and size. This task effectively captures the core components of working memory, both maintenance and manipulation of information, making it a theoretically sound measure of this cognitive construct. LSWM demonstrates good psychometric properties, including adequate reliability and validity across diverse age groups. As with other measures in the battery, its standardized administration and scoring enhance consistency across different testing contexts. The task's design minimizes cultural and linguistic biases by using familiar objects as stimuli, enhancing its applicability across diverse populations.

The working memory measure shows sensitivity to developmental changes across the lifespan, capturing age-related improvements in children and adolescents and age-related declines in older adults. This developmental sensitivity positions it as a valuable tool for tracking working memory trajectories across the lifespan, contributing to our understanding of normal cognitive development and aging. The integration of working memory assessment with other cognitive constructs in the NIH Toolbox allows researchers to examine relationships between working memory and other cognitive functions, such as executive control, attention, and learning. This integrated approach enhances the battery's utility for comprehensive cognitive assessment and facilitates research on the interconnections between different cognitive systems.

Limitations

While functionally effective in many contexts, the NIH Toolbox's approach to working memory provides only a partial view of this complex cognitive construct. LSWM primarily focuses on one aspect of working memory (i.e., verbal working memory with executive components) but does not comprehensively assess other working memory systems, such as visuospatial working memory or more complex working memory processes involved in dual-task coordination or updating. This narrow scope reduces the comprehensiveness of the working memory evaluation. For instance, visuospatial working memory deficits are frequently observed in neurodevelopmental disorders such as ADHD (Bédard et al., 2014; Gu et al., 2018) and following posterior brain injury (Arciniega et al., 2021), but these may go undetected with the current verbal-only measure.

Additionally, LSWM may have a restricted sensitivity range that limits its utility at both ends of the cognitive spectrum. For high-functioning individuals, the task may not detect subtle inefficiencies, potentially leading to ceiling effects and underestimating early cognitive decline. Conversely, individuals with more advanced cognitive impairment may find the task too demanding, resulting in non-completion or floor effects that obscure meaningful differentiation in ability (Hackett et al., 2018). In some cases, examinees with dementia sometimes could not complete NIH Toolbox tasks, including LSWM, highlighting its limited applicability in later-stage cognitive decline and its need for adaptation or supplementation in both clinical and research settings (Hackett et al., 2018).

CULTURAL AND LINGUISTIC ADAPTATION

Cultural and linguistic inclusivity is a crucial consideration for any widely used cognitive assessment tool. An instrument that performs well in one population may produce biased or invalid results in another if not properly adapted. While not perfect, the NIH Toolbox V3 Cognition domain has made substantial efforts toward cultural adaptation to achieve fairness and applicability across diverse groups.

Strengths in Cultural Adaptation

The NIHTBV3-CB has made substantial progress toward cultural and linguistic inclusivity. There are currently available translations in Spanish, Italian, French, Hebrew, and Arabic (LaForte et al., 2024). Spanish-language versions of key measures, such as PV and ORR, were not merely translated but developed independently to ensure linguistic and contextual appropriateness (Weintraub et al., 2013). The NIHTBV3-CB also includes age- and education-adjusted normative data (LaForte et al., 2024), along with audio-recorded instructions and a standardized, fully digital administration platform that minimizes examiner variability. These features are major steps to expand accessibility and improve consistency across diverse populations spanning the globe. Internationally, the NIHTB-CB V2 has been successfully adapted and validated for use in populations speaking Swahili and Dholuo, using a rigorous process that included forward–back translation, local expert review, and cognitive interviewing to ensure cultural relevance (Duffey et al., 2022). This effort represents how to engage in the process of cultural adaptation while maintaining the scientific rigor of the assessment platform. Furthermore, improvements to stimuli for cultural relevance and other considerations place the NIHTB-CB as one of the most well-developed, culturally responsive digital measures on the market.

Limitations in Cultural Adaptation

Despite these meaningful advances, researchers have identified some notable limitations in the performance of the NIH Toolbox V2 Cognition tests when applied in different settings, particularly in diverse clinical research settings with minority populations. Despite separate normative corrections for English and Spanish speakers, cultural and linguistic background factors still affect NIH Toolbox performance. In a large community sample of Spanish-speaking and English-speaking Hispanic adults, Flores et al. (2017) found that Spanish-speaking examinees scored significantly lower on uncorrected fluid cognition measures (particularly in attention, processing speed, and working memory) than both English-speaking Hispanics and Non-Hispanic Whites. While demographically corrected norms attenuated these differences, some disparities persisted even when tested in their preferred languages, suggesting residual cultural and educational effects not fully captured by existing adjustments (Flores et al., 2017). Similarly, in a sample of community-dwelling Black adults, Kairys et al. (2022) found an unexpected pattern: tests of crystallized cognition (ORR and PV), rather than fluid tasks, were the strongest discriminators of MCI vs. healthy controls. This was contrary to clinical expectations and consensus diagnosis models, where memory and executive functioning typically drive group differentiation (Kairys et al., 2022). These findings raise questions about the influence of educational quality and literacy—variables not directly adjusted for in current NIH Toolbox norms (Manly et al., 2005). This pattern may reflect unmeasured structural disparities in educational experience that are particularly salient in historically marginalized populations. It also highlights the potential for crystallized measures to either mask or exaggerate impairment depending on the individual's educational history. While not a flaw unique to the NIH Toolbox, these findings underscore the need for continued refinement of norms and interpretive frameworks to ensure validity across populations with diverse educational and linguistic backgrounds.

TECHNOLOGICAL AND OPERATIONAL USABILITY

The shift to a digital platform for cognitive assessment, exemplified by the NIH Toolbox V3 Cognition's iPad-based delivery, brings both significant advantages and distinct challenges. The practical utility of a tool in real-world research and clinical settings depends not only on its psychometrics but also on its ease of use, accessibility, and integration into workflows. This section examines both the strengths and limitations of the Cognition domain's technological and operational usability.

Strengths in Technological and Operational Usability

The NIHTBV3-CB's computerized format and brief 30-minute administration time represent transformative advantages for research efficiency. This standardization minimizes variability across examiners and settings—a critical feature for multisite projects (Van Essen et al., 2012). The battery reduces examinee burden and logistical demands, allowing standardized assessment of large cohorts, a much-needed improvement upon traditional paper-and-pencil tests that are lengthy and prone to administrative inconsistencies (Miller & Barr, 2017). The streamlined workflows of the NIHTBV3-CB enhance efficiency by reducing examiner administration and scoring errors. The automated scoring system eliminates the potential for calculation errors that can occur with manual scoring methods, enhancing the reliability of assessment results. This automation is particularly valuable for large-scale research initiatives where maintaining scoring consistency across multiple examiners and sites is essential.

> **DON'T FORGET 5.1**
>
> After purchasing the iPad, wireless keyboard, and annual subscription, there is no additional cost to administer the NIH Toolbox V3 Cognition tests. Examiners can administer as many assessments and export data as many times as they would like.

> **CAUTION 5.1**
>
> User data remains securely stored in the app, on the iPad it was collected on. However, this also means the examiner should regularly export and back up their data, as the Toolbox Assessments team has no way to access/store/share that collected data.

As a native iPad app, once downloaded and set up, the NIH Toolbox Cognition tests run directly from the iPad without requiring Internet access for test administration. This offline functionality is advantageous for testing in remote or connectivity-limited locations, expanding the battery's utility beyond well-resourced research centers to diverse field settings. This feature is particularly valuable for community-based research or studies conducted in areas with limited technological infrastructure.

Compared to traditional assessment systems with numerous physical components, the NIH Toolbox V3 Cognition domain's administration requires minimal supplemental materials beyond the NIH Toolbox V3 Administration Manual, scoring keys for relevant tests, Bluetooth keyboard for relevant tests, and the iPad (Hook & Giella, 2023). This streamlined approach reduces logistical burdens, simplifies test administration, and minimizes the potential for missing or damaged test materials that can be costly to replace and compromise assessment validity if not present during administration.

The usability of the NIH Toolbox Cognition domain is further enhanced in V3 through several specific improvements. The removal of the "home base" requirement in speeded tests simplifies task administration and reduces potential confusion for both examiners and examinees. The implementation of pre-recorded audio instructions ensures standardized presentation of test directions, minimizing variability in how tasks are explained and enhancing consistency across different testing contexts (LaForte et al., 2024). The costs associated with the NIH Toolbox V3 present a mixed picture but include several advantageous aspects. The developers offer free access to Administration and Technical Manuals, which can significantly reduce expenses compared to other instruments. The app charges an annual subscription fee without additional costs for individual tests or reports. Once subscribed, examiners can administer unlimited tests and generate reports freely, offering substantial savings, especially with high-volume use.

Limitations in Technological and Operational Usability

Despite these benefits, NIH Toolbox V3 faces several limitations that impact accessibility, security, and collaborative workflow. A major technical constraint is the lack of interoperability between Toolbox apps; custom batteries and participant data cannot be shared across modules, requiring users to re-enter information and recreate workflows, an inefficiency that may be magnified in multi-app or multisite studies. This siloed approach prevents seamless information sharing, forcing users who purchase multiple apps to duplicate effort when creating custom batteries or participant lists, as each app operates independently without data integration capabilities. Additionally, the app employs an "all-or-nothing" access model with no role-based permissions, posing potential risks to data security in team-based environments (Filkins et al., 2016). When sharing the app with another clinician, research assistant, or technician, there is no mechanism to limit access to specific content or functionality, potentially exposing sensitive patient information or allowing unauthorized modifications to test protocols or data.

The absence of comprehensive audit tracking further complicates accountability in multiuser settings. While the system logs when actions occur, such as archiving content, it fails to identify which specific user performed these actions. This limitation makes it difficult to maintain proper oversight and accountability in research or clinical teams where multiple individuals access the same app account. Technological barriers can also limit adoption. Institutional device management policies may restrict certain functions, including data export or cloud integration, depending on local IT configurations. However, the Toolbox app performs all scoring and data storage locally on the iPad, without requiring data to be sent to external servers. This native processing can be advantageous in university settings concerned about third-party data access or compliance, in contrast to platforms that require external data submission for scoring. Although a secure cloud-based reporting system can be established, the local data handling structure minimizes concerns over data ownership and aligns well with university IT policies. Still, users must maintain compatibility with frequent iOS updates, and managed device settings may impose additional constraints, particularly in environments with limited IT support or technical staffing (Filkins et al., 2016).

The required iPad and wireless keyboard represent a modest initial investment that may be prohibitive for smaller clinics or educational programs, but are relatively modest as compared to other available assessments. Examiners and examinees with low digital literacy, particularly older adults, may struggle with navigation or experience added cognitive load, potentially distorting assessment results (Mitzner et al., 2016). Prior research indicates that cognitive abilities, educational background, ethnicity, computer self-efficacy, and computer anxiety significantly influence individuals' ability to engage with digital technologies (Czaja et al., 2006). This is particularly important for digital cognitive assessments like the NIH Toolbox V3 Cognition tests, where the very populations being evaluated—such as those with suspected neurodegenerative disease, lower educational attainment, or from historically underrepresented groups—may be among the most vulnerable to technology-related barriers in digital testing environments. While the app includes a touch screen tutorial and standardized instructions, the lack of real-time clarification limits examiner flexibility. Collectively, these challenges underscore the importance of evaluating institutional resources, staffing capacity, and participant demographics when considering NIH Toolbox V3 Cognition implementation.

CLINICAL UTILITY AND DIAGNOSTIC VALUE OF THE NIH TOOLBOX

Strengths in Clinical Utility for Diagnosis

The NIH Toolbox Cognition domain offers significant potential for clinical applications, particularly with the enhancements introduced in V3. The addition of the RAVLT, FNAME, SM, and VR represents a substantial improvement in the Cognition domain's clinical utility, providing well-established measures of verbal learning, memory, processing speed, and visual reasoning/executive functioning that align with traditional neuropsychological assessment approaches. This addition enhances the domain's sensitivity to memory impairments associated with conditions such as MCI and AD, addressing a significant limitation of previous versions (LaForte et al., 2024).

The implementation of continuous norming and CSSs in V3 further strengthens the domain's clinical applications, particularly for monitoring cognitive changes over time. These features provide a more precise measurement of cognitive trajectories, which is essential for tracking disease progression or treatment effects in clinical populations. The comprehensive normative data, stratified by age and education, enhances the accuracy of score interpretation across diverse patient groups, improving diagnostic precision. Notably, demographic adjustments in V3 no longer include race, consistent with a growing consensus that race is a sociocultural, not biological, variable and should not be used in normative corrections. This change reflects an effort to base scoring adjustments on factors with clearer empirical relevance to cognitive performance.

For clinicians working in memory disorders clinics or neurodegenerative disease research projects, the NIHTBV3-CB can serve as an efficient screening tool that provides standardized assessment across multiple cognitive constructs. Its brevity and comprehensive coverage make it particularly valuable for initial cognitive evaluation, potentially identifying areas that warrant more detailed assessment with specialized measures. The domain's standardized administration and scoring also facilitate communication among healthcare providers, enhancing continuity of care and enabling more consistent documentation of cognitive status.

Limitations in Clinical Utility for Diagnosis

While the NIHTBV3-CB offers notable advantages in efficiency and standardization, it faces important limitations when compared to comprehensive neuropsychological evaluations. Traditional assessments typically include a more detailed examination of specific cognitive processes, often employing multiple measures within each domain to capture different aspects of functioning. This depth allows for more nuanced a characterization of cognitive profiles, which can be crucial for differential diagnosis and treatment planning (Lezak et al., 2012). NIHTB-CB's breadth-over-depth approach may limit its utility for detailed clinical evaluation in several ways. The battery's assessment of executive functioning, while capturing inhibition and cognitive flexibility, lacks comprehensive measures of planning, problem-solving, and strategic thinking. This narrow focus may prevent the identification of executive deficits that significantly impact daily functioning, particularly in conditions affecting frontal-subcortical systems (Miyake et al., 2000).

Similarly, the battery's language assessment focuses primarily on vocabulary and reading recognition, omitting evaluation of expressive language, discourse, or higher-level language processing. This limitation restricts its utility for diagnosing or characterizing language disorders, which often require a more comprehensive assessment of various language components (Ash et al., 2010). The memory assessment, while strengthened by the addition of the RAVLT and FNAME tasks, still lacks integrated recognition trials for the RAVLT, which can be important for differential diagnosis of memory disorders. The FNAME task, which does offer recognition, is not included in the Fluid Composite Score and is supplemental, precluding a ready-made comprehensive memory composite. These limitations may reduce the battery's sensitivity to certain memory impairments and its ability to distinguish between different types of memory dysfunction.

Diagnostic Utility Compared to Other Digital Assessment Tools

When compared to other computerized cognitive assessment tools designed for clinical use, the NIHTB-CB demonstrates both advantages and limitations. Cogstate (Maruff et al., 2013), Cambridge Neuropsychological Test Automated Battery (CANTAB; Barnett et al., 2016), and Creyos (formerly known as Cambridge Brain Sciences; Hampshire et al., 2012) each offer different approaches to digital cognitive assessment, and each offers their own relative challenges.

Cogstate provides a brief, repeatable assessment battery specifically designed for detecting cognitive change in clinical trials and clinical practice. Its focus on sensitivity to change and minimization of practice effects makes it particularly valuable for longitudinal monitoring. Studies have indicated that Cogstate had greater potential than the NIHTB-CB V2 to identify subtle cognitive impairments in preclinical stages of Alzheimer's disease (Buckley et al., 2017). However, Cogstate's more narrow focus on specific cognitive processes may limit its utility for comprehensive cognitive profiling compared to the NIHTB-CB's broader approach.

CANTAB offers a comprehensive suite of computerized neuropsychological tests with strong foundations in cognitive neuroscience research. Its tasks are purportedly designed to isolate specific cognitive processes with greater precision than the NIHTB-CB, potentially enhancing its utility for detailed clinical assessment and differential diagnosis (Barnett et al., 2016). CANTAB has been extensively validated in various clinical populations and has demonstrated sensitivity to subtle cognitive deficits in conditions such as mild cognitive impairment and early-stage dementia (Barnett et al., 2016). However, CANTAB's normative data is more limited than the NIHTB-CB's, with normative information available only for selected tests, test variants, and outcome measures.

The NIH Toolbox V3 Cognition domain's primary advantage in the clinical context lies in its efficiency, standardization, and comprehensive normative data. These features make it particularly valuable for screening and general cognitive assessment, especially in settings where time constraints are significant. However, for detailed diagnostic evaluation, particularly in complex cases or early-stage cognitive decline, other digital assessment tools or traditional paper-and-pencil measures may offer greater depth and specificity in some instances. For clinical applications requiring differential diagnosis according to established criteria, such as the National Institute on Aging-Alzheimer's Association criteria for Alzheimer's disease (McKhann et al., 2011), the NIH Toolbox Cognition tests may need to be supplemented with additional measures to provide the necessary diagnostic information. This limitation reflects the inherent trade-off between efficiency and depth that characterizes many computerized cognitive assessment tools.

FUTURE DIRECTIONS

To address its current constraints and maximize its impact, the NIH Toolbox V3 Cognition domain could evolve through several strategic enhancements. This section explores potential future directions for the domain's development, focusing on opportunities to expand its cognitive coverage, enhance its accessibility, improve its sensitivity to subtle cognitive changes, and strengthen its connections to real-world outcomes.

Expanding Cognitive Process Specificity

Expanding tests to dissect specific cognitive processes would significantly enhance the domain's clinical utility and neuroscientific value. Separating memory tasks into distinct components that independently assess encoding, storage, and retrieval would provide a more precise characterization of memory deficits, particularly important given that various neurological conditions affect memory systems differently (Salmon & Bondi, 2009). Similarly, developing more nuanced attention measures that distinguish between selective, sustained, and divided attention would improve sensitivity to different attention systems.

The addition of recognition memory trials to the RAVLT would enhance the comprehensiveness of episodic memory assessment, providing important information about memory storage that complements recall measures. Further, a "memory composite" score combining RAVLT, FNAME, and PSM would make sense as well as adding FNAME to the Fluid Composite, assuming it adds incremental value. These additions would align the NIHTBV3-CB more closely with standard clinical memory assessment protocols and would enhance its utility for differential diagnosis of memory disorders (Lezak et al., 2012).

Incorporating Broader Executive Function Assessment

Adding a more explicit planning task, similar to the Tower of Hanoi or decision-making paradigms resembling the Iowa Gambling Task, could help rectify current gaps in higher-order executive function assessment. These additions would strengthen the Cognition domain's ecological validity by better capturing the cognitive processes that support independent functioning in daily activities. Expanding executive function assessment to include measures of strategic thinking, planning, and complex problem-solving would align the NIH Toolbox more closely with contemporary theoretical models of executive function (Miyake et al., 2000). This alignment would enhance the domain's construct validity and would improve its utility for identifying executive deficits that impact real-world functioning.

Expanding Accessibility

The developers of NIH Toolbox V3 Cognition domain have recently released a mobile platform for similar test administration via smartphone. This smartphone-friendly version, alongside cost-reduction strategies, would substantially broaden access, particularly in low-resource settings (Polk et al., 2025). Creating tiered licensing models or open-access versions for educational and low-resource settings could further democratize access. Additionally, expanding cross-cultural validation beyond translation to include stimulus adaptation, concept presentation, and interchangeable instruction sections by language would enhance the Cognition domain's global relevance and fairness.

Addressing technological barriers through simplified interfaces and alternative administration formats would enhance accessibility for populations with limited digital literacy or access to advanced technology (Staffaroni et al., 2020). These adaptations would support the battery's use in diverse settings and would align with broader efforts to reduce disparities in cognitive assessment and research participation.

Enhancing Sensitivity to Subtle Cognitive Changes

Refining sensitivity to subtle cognitive changes through adaptive testing approaches or additional fine-grained tasks could significantly improve utility for detecting early-stage cognitive decline. The incorporation of process-based metrics, such as intraindividual performance variability, response time distributions, and error pattern analyses (already begun in V3), will continue to enhance diagnostic sensitivity for early detection and intervention research (Salthouse, 2010).

Developing specialized modules for high-risk populations, such as those with genetic predisposition to neurodegenerative conditions or those with subjective cognitive complaints, would enhance the Cognition domain's utility for early detection and prevention research. These specialized applications would complement the domain's general assessment approach and would support its use in precision medicine initiatives focused on early intervention (Snitz et al., 2020).

Connecting Assessment to Real-World Outcomes

Establishing stronger connections between NIH Toolbox Cognition test performance and real-world functional outcomes would enhance clinical relevance and translational value. Linking cognitive data to ecological measures like the Everyday Cognition (ECog) scale would bridge laboratory assessment with everyday functioning (Farias et al., 2008). Developing functional composite scores to predict specific real-world abilities would also enhance the battery's practical utility for clinical decision-making, with empirical validation against actual functional outcomes rather than proxy measures. Integrating digital phenotyping approaches, such as passive monitoring of smartphone use or daily activities, with the NIH Toolbox Cognition assessment could provide a more comprehensive understanding of cognitive functioning in real-world contexts (Staffaroni et al., 2020). This integration would enhance the ecological validity of cognitive assessment and would support more personalized approaches to intervention and support.

Technological Innovations

Leveraging emerging technologies such as augmented reality and artificial intelligence could enhance the Cognition domain's assessment capabilities and user experience. Augmented reality environments could provide more naturalistic assessment contexts that better approximate real-world cognitive demands. Artificial intelligence algorithms could enhance adaptive testing approaches, optimize test selection based on individual characteristics, and identify subtle patterns in performance data that might indicate early cognitive changes (Chan et al., 2021). Developing cloud-based data integration systems would address current interoperability limitations, allowing seamless sharing of assessment data across different Toolbox modules and potentially with other assessment platforms. Simplifying download and backup procedures, particularly by enabling easy export of data to common research databases such as REDCap, would further ease implementation in both clinical and research contexts. These changes would enhance the domain's overall utility and streamline workflows. Implementation of role-based access controls and comprehensive audit tracking would strengthen data security and accountability in multiuser environments. These enhancements would address current limitations in access management and would support the battery's use in team-based research and clinical settings where data security and regulatory compliance are paramount. Expanding remote assessment capabilities through secure, HIPAA-compliant platforms would enhance the battery's utility for telehealth applications and distributed research designs. Remote assessment options would increase accessibility for individuals with mobility limitations or those in geographically remote areas, potentially reducing disparities in access to cognitive assessment services (Stricker et al., 2020). Further integration of the iPad's built-in camera and touchscreen sensors to record finger movements during extended motor tasks could enable more detailed measurement of upper limb mobility and its relationship to cognitive performance.

CONCLUSIONS

The NIH Toolbox V3 Cognition domain represents a significant advancement in the field of digital cognitive assessment, offering a standardized, efficient, and psychometrically robust tool for evaluating cognitive function across a wide age range (Gershon et al., 2013; Weintraub et al., 2013). Its development reflects a concerted effort to bridge traditional neuropsychological principles with modern technological capabilities, resulting in a domain well-suited for large-scale research initiatives and increasingly considered for clinical research applications (Fox et al., 2022). Key strengths include its brief administration time, automated scoring, continuous norming, CSSs for longitudinal tracking, and offline iPad functionality, which enhance its practicality and reach (LaForte et al., 2024).

However, the NIH Toolbox V3 Cognition domain is not without limitations. While efficient, its streamlined nature may lack the clinical depth required for nuanced diagnostic distinctions in complex cases, particularly concerning specific memory processes and higher-order executive functions like planning and problem-solving (Bauer et al., 2012; Miyake et al., 2000). Further research on performance across clinical populations is needed to support the transition of this measure from a research instrument to a clinically valid diagnostic tool. Cross-cultural adaptability requires ongoing refinement to ensure equitable assessment across diverse populations. Furthermore, significant technological and operational challenges persist, including a lack of interoperability between Toolbox apps, inadequate granular access control and audit tracking for multiuser environments, and potential barriers related to cost, required technical proficiency, and digital literacy (Torous et al., 2019).

Future directions for the NIH Toolbox Cognition domain should focus on addressing these limitations while leveraging its strengths. Enhancing cognitive process specificity, particularly in memory and executive function constructs, incorporating more ecologically valid tasks, and improving sensitivity to subtle cognitive changes are crucial for increasing its clinical utility (Lezak et al., 2012; Salmon & Bondi, 2009).

Expanding accessibility through mobile smartphone platforms, tiered pricing, and improved cross-cultural adaptation will broaden its reach. Technologically, implementing features like cloud-based data integration, role-based access controls, comprehensive audit logs, and enhanced remote assessment capabilities will be vital for improving workflow, security, and applicability in modern research and telehealth contexts (Stricker et al., 2020; Torous et al., 2019).

In summary, the NIH Toolbox V3 Cognition domain stands as a valuable and evolving instrument in the cognitive assessment landscape. Its strengths in efficiency, standardization, and psychometric grounding make it a powerful tool for research. Yet, realizing its full potential, especially in diverse clinical and global contexts, necessitates continued development focused on enhancing clinical depth, improving technological usability and security, expanding accessibility, and strengthening links to real-world functional outcomes. A balanced appraisal acknowledges both its significant contributions and the ongoing need for refinement to meet the complex demands of cognitive assessment in the 21st century.

TEST YOURSELF

1. **The psychometric foundation of any cognitive assessment tool is critical to its scientific validity and practical utility.**
   True or False
2. **Which of the following was introduced as a new feature to NIH Toolbox V3 Cognition?**
   (a) New tests
   (b) New normative data
   (c) Change Sensitive Scores (CSSs)
   (d) All of the above
3. **NIH Toolbox V3 Cognition builds upon previous versions with substantial psychometric enhancements that strengthen its foundation for accurate and reproducible cognitive assessment.**
   True or False
4. **NIH Toolbox V3 Cognition implemented continuous norming, which allows for more precise age-based norms in three-month intervals for children and one-year intervals for adults.**
   True or False
5. **Which of the following is a strength of the NIH Toolbox V3 Cognition tests?**
   (a) Administration of the NIH Toolbox V3 Cognition battery is brief
   (b) Test workflows have been streamlined and enhanced to reduce examiner errors
   (c) Availability on an iPad is advantageous for remote or connectivity-limited locations
   (d) All of the above

6. **Which of the following is a limitation of the NIH Toolbox V3 Cognition tests?**
   (a) Flanker and DCCS do not capture complex goal-directed behaviors.
   (b) Examiners are required to bring numerous manuals, stimulus books, and other materials to all administrations.
   (c) Attention is a construct that is not assessed by NIH Toolbox V3 Cognition tests.
   (d) Tests can only be administered while being online/connected to the Internet.
7. **The addition of the Face Name Associative Memory Exam, Face Name Associative Memory Exam Delay, Rey Auditory Verbal Learning Test Delay, Speeded Matching, and Visual Reasoning tests helps to further assess memory, processing speed, and visual reasoning.**
   True or False
8. **At the time of this book's publication, NIH Toolbox V3 Fluid Cognition tests have been translated into Spanish, French, Arabic, Hebrew, and ______.**
   (a) German
   (b) Portuguese
   (c) Italian
   (d) Japanese
9. **Which of the following is not listed as a "Future Direction"?**
   (a) Incorporating broader executive function assessment
   (b) Adding more physical components required for testing
   (c) Technological innovations
   (d) Expanding cognitive process specificity
10. **The NIH Toolbox V3 Cognition domain's primary advantage in the clinical context lies in its efficiency, standardization, and comprehensive normative data.**
    True or False

Answers: 1. True; 2. (d); 3. True; 4. True; 5. (d); 6. (a); 7. True; 8. (c); 9. (b); 10. True

REFERENCES

Akshoomoff, N., Beaumont, J. L., Bauer, P. J., Dikmen, S. S., Gershon, R. C., Mungas, D., … Heaton, R. K. (2013). VIII. NIH Toolbox Cognition Battery (CB): Composite scores of crystallized, fluid, and overall cognition. *Monographs of the Society for Research in Child Development*, *78*(4), 119–132. https://doi.org/10.1111/mono.12038

Arciniega, H., Shires, J., Furlong, S., Kilgore-Gomez, A., Cerreta, A., Murray, N. G., & Berryhill, M. E. (2021). Impaired visual working memory and reduced connectivity in undergraduates with a history of mild traumatic brain injury. *Scientific Reports*, *11*, 2789. https://doi.org/10.1038/s41598-021-80995-1

Ash, S., McMillan, C., Gunawardena, D., Avants, B., Morgan, B., Khan, A., … Grossman, M. (2010). Speech errors in progressive non-fluent aphasia. *Brain and Language*, *113*(1), 13–20. https://doi.org/10.1016/j.bandl.2009.12.001

Barnett, J. H., Blackwell, A. D., Sahakian, B. J., & Robbins, T. W. (2016). The Paired Associates Learning (PAL) Test: 30 years of CANTAB translational neuroscience from laboratory to bedside in dementia research. In T. W. Robbins & B. J. Sahakian (Eds.), *Translational neuropsychopharmacology* (pp. 449–474). Springer International Publishing. https://doi.org/10.1007/7854_2015_5001

Bauer, P. J., Dikmen, S. S., Heaton, R. K., Mungas, D., Slotkin, J., & Beaumont, J. L. (2013). III. NIH Toolbox Cognition Battery (CB): Measuring episodic memory. *Monographs of the Society for Research in Child Development, 78*(4), 34–48. https://doi.org/10.1111/mono.12033

Bauer, R. M., Iverson, G. L., Cernich, A. N., Binder, L. M., Ruff, R. M., & Naugle, R. I. (2012). Computerized neuropsychological assessment devices: Joint position paper of the American Academy of Clinical Neuropsychology and the National Academy of Neuropsychology. *Archives of Clinical Neuropsychology: The Official Journal of the National Academy of Neuropsychology, 27*(3), 362–373. https://doi.org/10.1093/arclin/acs027

Bédard, A. C. V., Newcorn, J. H., Clerkin, S. M., Krone, B., Fan, J., Halperin, J. M., & Schulz, K. P. (2014). Reduced prefrontal efficiency for visuospatial working memory in attention-deficit/hyperactivity disorder. *Journal of the American Academy of Child & Adolescent Psychiatry, 53*(9), 1020–1030.e6. https://doi.org/10.1016/j.jaac.2014.05.011

Bryant, D., Chiaravalloti, N. D., & DeLuca, J. (2004). Objective measurement of cognitive fatigue in multiple sclerosis. *Rehabilitation Psychology, 49*(2), 114–122. https://doi.org/10.1037/0090-5550.49.2.114

Buckley, R. F., Sparks, K. P., Papp, K. V., Dekhtyar, M., Martin, C., Burnham, S., … Rentz, D. M. (2017). Computerized cognitive testing for use in clinical trials: A comparison of the NIH toolbox and Cogstate C3 batteries. *Journal of Prevention of Alzheimer's Disease, 4*(1), 3–11. https://doi.org/10.14283/jpad.2017.1

Butters, N., Wolfe, J., Martone, M., Granholm, E., & Cermak, L. S. (1985). Memory disorders associated with Huntington's disease: Verbal recall, verbal recognition and procedural memory. *Neuropsychologia, 23*(6), 729–743. https://doi.org/10.1016/0028-3932(85)90080-6

Chan, J. Y., Yau, S. T., Kwok, T. C., & Tsoi, K. K. (2021). Diagnostic performance of digital cognitive tests for the identification of MCI and dementia: A systematic review. *Ageing Research Reviews, 72*, 101506. https://doi.org/10.1016/j.arr.2021.101506

Chen, P., Hreha, K., Fortis, P., Goedert, K. M., & Barrett, A. M. (2012). Functional assessment of spatial neglect: A review of the Catherine Bergego Scale and an introduction of the Kessler Foundation Neglect Assessment Process. *Topics in Stroke Rehabilitation, 19*(5), 423–435. https://doi.org/10.1310/tsr1905-423

Czaja, S. J., Charness, N., Fisk, A. D., Hertzog, C., Nair, S. N., Rogers, W. A., & Sharit, J. (2006). Factors predicting the use of technology: Findings from the

Center for Research and Education on Aging and Technology Enhancement (CREATE). *Psychology and Aging, 21*(2), 333–352. https://doi.org/10.1037/0882-7974.21.2.333

Donohue, M. C., Sperling, R. A., Salmon, D. P., Rentz, D. M., Raman, R., Thomas, R. G., ... Alzheimer's Disease Cooperative Study. (2014). The preclinical Alzheimer cognitive composite. *JAMA Neurology, 71*(8), 961–970. https://doi.org/10.1001/jamaneurol.2014.803

Duffey, M. M., Ayuku, D., Ayodo, G., Abuonji, E., Nyalumbe, M., Giella, A. K., ... McHenry, M. S. (2022). Translation and cultural adaptation of NIH toolbox cognitive tests into Swahili and Dholuo languages for use in children in western Kenya. *Journal of the International Neuropsychological Society, 28*(4), 414–423. https://doi.org/10.1017/S1355617721000497

Fan, J., McCandliss, B. D., Sommer, T., Raz, A., & Posner, M. I. (2002). Testing the efficiency and independence of attentional networks. *Journal of Cognitive Neuroscience, 14*(3), 340–347. https://doi.org/10.1162/089892902317361886

Farias, S. T., Mungas, D., Reed, B. R., Cahn-Weiner, D., Jagust, W., Baynes, K., & Decarli, C. (2008). The measurement of everyday cognition (ECog): Scale development and psychometric properties. *Neuropsychology, 22*(4), 531–544. https://doi.org/10.1037/0894-4105.22.4.531

Fields, R. D. (2008). White matter in learning, cognition and psychiatric disorders. *Trends in Neurosciences, 31*(7), 361–370. https://doi.org/10.1016/j.tins.2008.04.001

Filkins, B. L., Kim, J. Y., Roberts, B., Armstrong, W., Miller, M. A., Hultner, M. L., ... Steinhubl, S. R. (2016). Privacy and security in the era of digital health: What should translational researchers know and do about it? *American Journal of Translational Research, 8*(3), 1560–1580.

Flores, I., Casaletto, K. B., Marquine, M. J., Umlauf, A., Moore, D. J., Mungas, D., ... Heaton, R. K. (2017). Performance of Hispanics and non-Hispanic Whites on the NIH toolbox cognition battery: The roles of ethnicity and language backgrounds. *The Clinical Neuropsychologist, 31*(5), 783–797. https://doi.org/10.1080/13854046.2016.1276216

Fox, R. S., Zhang, M., Amagai, S., Bassard, A., Dworak, E. M., Han, Y. C., ... Gershon, R. C. (2022). Uses of the NIH toolbox® in clinical samples. *Neurology: Clinical Practice, 12*(3), 307–319. https://doi.org/10.1212/CPJ.0000000000200060

Gershon, R. C., Wagster, M. V., Hendrie, H. C., Fox, N. A., Cook, K. F., & Nowinski, C. J. (2013). NIH toolbox for assessment of neurological and behavioral function. *Neurology, 80*(Supplement 3), S2–S6. https://doi.org/10.1212/WNL.0b013e3182872e5f

Goodglass, H., Kaplan, E., & Barresi, B. (2001). *The assessment of aphasia and related disorders* (3rd ed.). Lippincott Williams & Wilkins.

Gu, C., Liu, Z. X., Tannock, R., & Woltering, S. (2018). Neural processing of working memory in adults with ADHD in a visuospatial change detection task with distractors. *PeerJ*, *6*, e5601. https://doi.org/10.7717/peerj.5601

Hackett, K., Krikorian, R., Giovannetti, T., Melendez-Cabrero, J., Rahman, A., Caesar, E. E., … Isaacson, R. S. (2018). Utility of the NIH Toolbox for assessment of prodromal Alzheimer's disease and dementia. *Alzheimer's & Dementia: Diagnosis, Assessment & Disease Monitoring*, *10*, 764–772. https://doi.org/10.1016/j.dadm.2018.10.002

Hampshire, A., Highfield, R. R., Parkin, B. L., & Owen, A. M. (2012). Fractionating human intelligence. *Neuron*, *76*(6), 1225–1237. https://doi.org/10.1016/j.neuron.2012.06.022

Higginson, C. I., Wheelock, V. L., Carroll, K. E., & Sigvardt, K. A. (2005). Recognition memory in Parkinson's disease with and without dementia: Evidence inconsistent with the retrieval deficit hypothesis. *Journal of Clinical and Experimental Neuropsychology*, *27*(4), 516–528. https://doi.org/10.1080/13803390490515469

Hook, J. N., & Giella, A. K. (2023). *National Institutes of Health (NIH) Toolbox® V3 administration manual.* Toolbox Assessments, Inc.

Kairys, A., Daugherty, A., Kavcic, V., Shair, S., Persad, C., Heidebrink, J., … Giordani, B. (2022). Laptop-administered NIH Toolbox and Cogstate Brief Battery in community-dwelling Black adults: Unexpected pattern of cognitive performance between MCI and healthy controls. *Journal of the International Neuropsychological Society*, *28*(3), 239–248. https://doi.org/10.1017/S135561772100028X

Koo, T. K., & Li, M. Y. (2016). A guideline of selecting and reporting intraclass correlation coefficients for reliability research. *Journal of Chiropractic Medicine*, *15*(2), 155–163. https://doi.org/10.1016/j.jcm.2016.02.012

LaForte, E. M., Hook, J. N., & Giella, A. K. (2024). *National Institutes of Health (NIH) Toolbox® V3 technical manual.* Toolbox Assessments, Inc.

Lezak, M. D., Howieson, D. B., Bigler, E. D., & Tranel, D. (2012). *Neuropsychological assessment* (5th ed.). Oxford University Press.

Luciana, M., Bjork, J. M., Nagel, B. J., Barch, D. M., Gonzalez, R., Nixon, S. J., & Banich, M. T. (2018). Adolescent neurocognitive development and impacts of substance use: Overview of the adolescent brain cognitive development (ABCD) baseline neurocognition battery. *Developmental Cognitive Neuroscience*, *32*, 67–79. https://doi.org/10.1016/j.dcn.2018.02.006

Manly, J. J., Schupf, N., Tang, M. X., & Stern, Y. (2005). Cognitive decline and literacy among ethnically diverse elders. *Journal of Geriatric Psychiatry and Neurology*, *18*(4), 213–217. https://doi.org/10.1177/0891988705281868

Maruff, P., Lim, Y. Y., Darby, D., Ellis, K. A., Pietrzak, R. H., Snyder, P. J., … Masters, C. L. (2013). Clinical utility of the Cogstate brief battery in identifying cognitive impairment in mild cognitive impairment and Alzheimer's disease. *BMC Psychology*, *1*, 30. https://doi.org/10.1186/2050-7283-1-30

Mather, M. A., Ho, E. H., Bedjeti, K., Karpouzian-Rogers, T., Rogalski, E. J., Gershon, R., & Weintraub, S. (2024). Measuring multidimensional aspects of health in the oldest old using the NIH toolbox: Results from the ARMADA study. *Archives of Clinical Neuropsychology, 39*(3), 535–546. https://doi.org/10.1093/arclin/acad105

McKhann, G. M., Knopman, D. S., Chertkow, H., Hyman, B. T., Jack, C. R., Kawas, C. H., ... Phelps, C. H. (2011). The diagnosis of dementia due to Alzheimer's disease: Recommendations from the National Institute on Aging-Alzheimer's Association workgroups on diagnostic guidelines for Alzheimer's disease. *Alzheimer's & Dementia, 7*(3), 263–269. https://doi.org/10.1016/j.jalz.2011.03.005

Miller, J. B., & Barr, W. B. (2017). The technology crisis in neuropsychology. *Archives of Clinical Neuropsychology, 32*(5), 541–554. https://doi.org/10.1093/arclin/acx050

Mirsky, A. F., Anthony, B. J., Duncan, C. C., Ahearn, M. B., & Kellam, S. G. (1991). Analysis of the elements of attention: A neuropsychological approach. *Neuropsychology Review, 2*(2), 109–145. https://doi.org/10.1007/BF01109051

Mitzner, T. L., Rogers, W. A., Fisk, A. D., Boot, W. R., Charness, N., Czaja, S. J., & Sharit, J. (2016). Predicting older adults' perceptions about a computer system designed for seniors. *Universal Access in the Information Society, 15*(2), 271–280. https://doi.org/10.1007/s10209-014-0383-y

Miyake, A., Friedman, N. P., Emerson, M. J., Witzki, A. H., Howerter, A., & Wager, T. D. (2000). The unity and diversity of executive functions and their contributions to complex "frontal lobe" tasks: A latent variable analysis. *Cognitive Psychology, 41*(1), 49–100. https://doi.org/10.1006/cogp.1999.0734

Morales, S., Bowers, M. E., Shuffrey, L., Ziegler, K., Troller-Renfree, S., Hernandez, A., Leach, S. C., McGrath, M., Ola, C., Leve, L. D., Nozadi, S. S., Swingler, M. M., Lai, J. S., Schweitzer, J. B., Fifer, W., Camargo Jr., C. A., Khurana Hershey, G. K., Shapiro, A. L. B., Keating, D. P., ..., & Elliott, A. J. (2024). Maternal education prospectively predicts child neurocognitive function: An environmental influences on child health outcomes study. Developmental Psychology, 60(7), 1028–1040. https://doi.org/10.1037/dev0001642

Park, D. C., & Reuter-Lorenz, P. (2009). The adaptive brain: Aging and neurocognitive scaffolding. *Annual Review of Psychology, 60*, 173–196. https://doi.org/10.1146/annurev.psych.59.103006.093656

Polk, S. E., Öhman, F., Hassenstab, J., König, A., Papp, K. V., Schöll, M., & Berron, D. (2025). A scoping review of remote and unsupervised digital cognitive assessments in preclinical Alzheimer's disease. *npj Digital Medicine, 8*, 266. https://doi.org/10.1038/s41746-025-01583-5

Raven, J., & Raven, J. (2003). Raven progressive matrices. In J. H. O. Smith (Ed.), *Handbook of nonverbal assessment* (pp. 223–237). Kluwer Academic/Plenum Publishers. https://doi.org/10.1007/978-1-4615-0153-4_11

Rigby, T., Gregoire, A. M., Reader, J., Kahsay, Y., Fisher, J., Kairys, A., ... Giordani, B. (2024). Identification of amnestic mild cognitive impairment among Black and White community-dwelling older adults using NIH toolbox cognition tablet battery. *Journal of the International Neuropsychological Society, 30*(5), 689–696. https://doi.org/10.1017/S1355617724000213

Rose, S., Gergoire, A., Pal, S., Reader, J., Bhaumik, A., Slotkin, J., ... Giordani, B. (2025). Evaluating the factor structure and construct validity of the NIH toolbox in older adults, with a focus on cognitive normalcy and amnestic mild cognitive impairment: Considerations for diversity, including insights from persons over 85 years of age and Black older Americans. *Journal of the International Neuropsychological Society, 31*. https://doi.org/10.1017/S1355617724000699, 53–58.

Royall, D. R., Lauterbach, E. C., Cummings, J. L., Reeve, A., Rummans, T. A., Kaufer, D. I., ... Coffey, C. E. (2002). Executive control function: A review of its promise and challenges for clinical research. A report from the committee on research of the American Neuropsychiatric Association. *Journal of Neuropsychiatry and Clinical Neurosciences, 14*(4), 377–405. https://doi.org/10.1176/jnp.14.4.377

Salmon, D. P., & Bondi, M. W. (2009). Neuropsychological assessment of dementia. *Annual Review of Psychology, 60*, 257–282. https://doi.org/10.1146/annurev.psych.57.102904.190024

Salthouse, T. A. (2010). Selective review of cognitive aging. *Journal of the International Neuropsychological Society, 16*(5), 754–760. https://doi.org/10.1017/S1355617710000706

Snitz, B. E., Tudorascu, D. L., Yu, Z., Campbell, E., Lopresti, B. J., Laymon, C. M., ... Cohen, A. D. (2020). Associations between NIH toolbox cognition battery and in vivo brain amyloid and tau pathology in non-demented older adults. *Alzheimer's & Dementia: Diagnosis, Assessment & Disease Monitoring, 12*, e12018. https://doi.org/10.1002/dad2.12018

Staffaroni, A. M., Tsoy, E., Taylor, J., Boxer, A. L., & Possin, K. L. (2020). Digital cognitive assessments for dementia. *Practical Neurology, 2020*, 24–45.

Stricker, N. H., Lundt, E. S., Alden, E. C., Albertson, S. M., Machulda, M. M., Kremers, W. K., ... Mielke, M. M. (2020). Longitudinal comparison of in clinic and at home administration of the Cogstate Brief Battery and demonstrated practice effects in the Mayo Clinic Study of Aging. *Journal of Prevention of Alzheimer's Disease, 7*(1), 21–28. https://doi.org/10.14283/jpad.2019.35

Taylor, B. K., Frenzel, M. R., Eastman, J. A., Wiesman, A. I., Wang, Y. P., Calhoun, V. D., ... Wilson, T. W. (2022). Reliability of the NIH toolbox cognitive battery in children and adolescents: A 3-year longitudinal examination. *Psychological Medicine, 52*(8), 1718–1727. https://doi.org/10.1017/S0033291720003487

Torous, J., Wisniewski, H., Bird, B., Carpenter, E., David, G., Elejalde, E., Fulford, D., Guimond, S., Hays, R., Henson, P., Hoffman, L., Lim, C., Menon, M., Noel, V., Pearson, J., Peterson, R., Susheela, A., Troy, H., Vaidyam, A., ..., & Keshavan, M. (2019). Creating a digital health smartphone app and digital phenotyping platform for mental health and diverse healthcare needs: An interdisciplinary and collaborative approach. Journal of Technology in Behavioral Science, 4(2), 73–85. https://doi.org/10.1007/s41347-019-00095-w

Van Essen, D. C., Ugurbil, K., Auerbach, E., Barch, D., Behrens, T. E. J., Bucholz, R., Chang, A., Chen, L., Corbetta, M., Curtiss, S. W., Della Penna, S., Feinberg, D.,

Glasser, M. F., Harel, N., Heath, A. C., Larson-Prior, L., Marcus, D., Michalareas, G., Moeller, S., …, & WU-Minn HCP Consortium. (2012). The Human Connectome Project: A data acquisition perspective. NeuroImage, 62(4), 2222–2231. https://doi.org/10.1016/j.neuroimage.2012.02.018

Weintraub, S., Dikmen, S. S., Heaton, R. K., Tulsky, D. S., Zelazo, P. D., Bauer, P. J., Carlozzi, N. E., Slotkin, J., Blitz, D., Wallner-Allen, K., Fox, N. A., Beaumont, J. L., Mungas, D., Nowinski, C. J., Richler, J., Deocampo, J. A., Anderson, J. E., Manly, J. J., Borosh, B., …, & Gershon, R. C. (2013). Cognition assessment using the NIH Toolbox. Neurology, 80(11 Suppl. 3), S54–S64. https://doi.org/10.1212/WNL.0b013e3182872ded

Zelazo, P. D., Anderson, J. E., Richler, J., Wallner-Allen, K., Beaumont, J. L., & Weintraub, S. (2013). II. NIH Toolbox Cognition Battery (CB): Measuring executive function and attention. *Monographs of the Society for Research in Child Development, 78*(4), 16–33. https://doi.org/10.1111/mono.12032

Six

CLINICAL APPLICATIONS OF THE NIH TOOLBOX® COGNITION TESTS

Julie N. Hook
Amy K. Giella
Abigail B. Sivan

INTRODUCTION

The National Institutes of Health (NIH) Toolbox Cognition tests represent a major advance in lifespan cognitive assessment, offering a scientifically validated, brief, and comprehensive approach to measuring brain health from ages 3 to 85+. Developed through rigorous psychometric research and field validation (Hook & Giella, 2023; LaForte et al., 2024), it serves not only as a tool for characterizing normative cognitive trajectories but also for identifying deviations associated with medical, neurological, and psychiatric conditions. Its increasing adoption in clinical, education, and research settings is largely due to its scalability, standardization, digital administration, and normative comparability across ages.

These tests assess key areas of cognition, including executive function, attention, episodic memory, language, working memory, and processing speed (Weintraub et al., 2013). Each of these areas is critical for independent functioning as well as academic or vocational success across the lifespan. Further, the NIH Toolbox is not restricted to the assessment of a specific disease state but is uniquely suited to assess both health and impairment. For example, in pediatric settings, these tests can support early developmental screening, while in adulthood, they can track cognition in chronic disease management, and in older adulthood, it serves as a sensitive tool for detecting early cognitive decline.

As a starting point, foundational brain–behavior relationships are reviewed, highlighting how large-scale cortical and subcortical systems broadly support cognition. Rather than focusing on fine anatomical details that go beyond the scope of this chapter, the emphasis is on how executive, memory, language, attentional, and perceptual functions emerge from coordinated neural networks. The NIH Toolbox V3 Cognition domain leverages these principles by aligning each test with the major systems most relevant to its construct, providing a useful framework for interpreting performance in the context of brain function. Following this overview, the chapter organizes clinical utility across developmental time points—beginning with fine-grained age bands during periods of rapid change (i.e., early childhood) and shifting to broader categories as trajectories stabilize. This review emphasizes not only disease burden but also healthy cognitive aging and developmental milestones, reflecting the NIH Toolbox's unique capacity to serve both clinical and wellness-oriented purposes.

BRAIN–BEHAVIOR FOUNDATIONS

A basic understanding of neuroanatomy is essential for interpreting cognitive assessment results. Please recall that the brain does not operate as a collection of isolated lobes, but as an integrated network in which certain regions are more strongly associated with particular functions. Figure 6.1 provides a schematic overview of the major lobes of the human brain.

- **Frontal lobe:** Critical for executive functions, including planning, inhibition, decision-making, working memory, and task-switching.
- **Temporal lobe:** Supports episodic memory (via medial temporal structures such as the hippocampus) and language comprehension.
- **Parietal lobe:** Involved in attention allocation, spatial reasoning, and integration of multimodal sensory input.
- **Occipital lobe:** Specialized in visual processing, which underpins rapid perceptual judgments required in many cognitive tests.

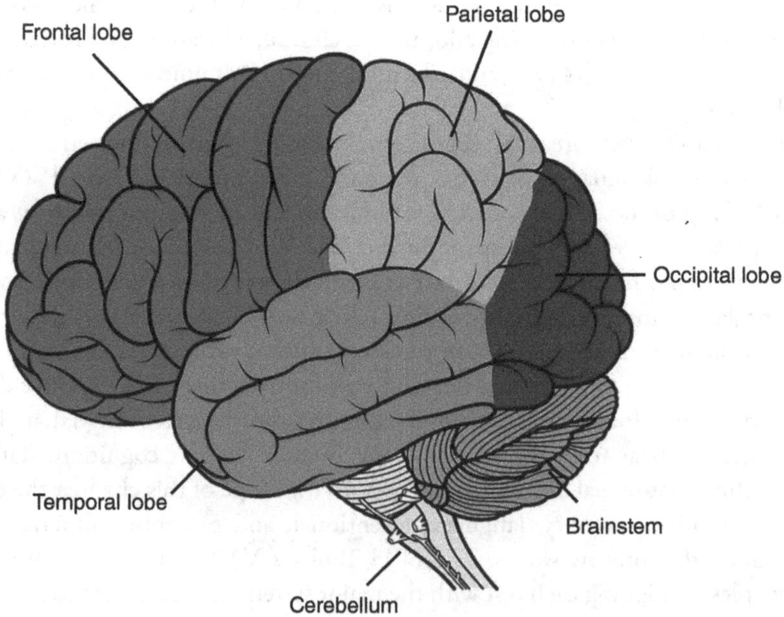

Figure 6.1 Basic Brain Lobes and Regions. Taleseedum / Adobe Stock Photo.

- **Subcortical structures and white matter:** The basal ganglia regulate processing speed and motor–cognitive integration, while white-matter tracts act as high-speed conduits linking distributed cortical regions (Turken et al., 2008).

Mapping NIH Toolbox Tests to Brain Regions

Within the NIH Toolbox Cognition Battery, each test is broadly linked to the neural systems most critical for its successful performance. This mapping offers a practical framework for interpreting how task performance reflects the functioning of different brain regions. It should be emphasized, however, that these associations are not one-to-one; rather, they highlight predominant neural contributions while recognizing that cognition arises from dynamic, distributed brain networks. Table 6.1 maps tests in the NIH Toolbox V3 Cognition domain with their relevant brain regions.

Table 6.1 Brain Regions of the NIH Toolbox V3 Cognition Tests

Test	Cognitive Domain	Brain Regions
Dimensional Change Card Sort	Executive function, set shifting	Frontal lobe (planning, inhibition), parietal lobe (flexibility, integration)
Face Name Associative Memory	Associative memory, delayed memory	Temporal lobe (face–name binding, memory), medial temporal structures (hippocampus)
Flanker Inhibitory Control and Attention	Selective attention, inhibition	Frontal lobe (inhibition), parietal lobe (attention allocation)
List Sorting Working Memory	Working memory (storage and manipulation)	Frontal lobe (working memory), parietal lobe (maintenance and manipulation)
Oral Reading Recognition	Reading/decoding	Frontal lobe (articulation), temporal lobe (phonology), parietal lobe (orthography)
Oral Symbol Digit	Processing speed without motor demands	Frontal lobe, basal ganglia, white matter (rapid integration)
Pattern Comparison Processing Speed	Processing speed, visual discrimination	Subcortical structures/white matter (processing efficiency), occipital lobe (visual input)
Picture Sequence Memory	Episodic memory, sequencing	Temporal lobe (episodic memory, sequencing)
Picture Vocabulary	Receptive language, crystallized knowledge	Temporal lobe (language comprehension), parietal lobe (semantic integration)
Rey Auditory Verbal Learning Test	Verbal learning and recall	Temporal lobe (verbal encoding and retrieval)
Speeded Matching	Early childhood processing speed	Occipital lobe (visual matching), parietal lobe (fast visual–spatial comparison)
Visual Reasoning	Nonverbal reasoning	Frontal lobe (problem-solving), parietal lobe (spatial reasoning), occipital lobe (visual analysis)

LIFESPAN ASSESSMENT

Cognitive trajectories across the lifespan reflect a dynamic interplay between typical developmental changes and age-related risks for neurodevelopmental and neurodegenerative conditions. This section outlines some of the most prevalent cognitive and neuropsychological disorders at each life stage, including estimated population prevalence, and associates these conditions with the relevant NIH Toolbox V3 Cognition measures.

Each age-based subsection provides:

- A brief overview of typical cognitive development
- Key disorders and their prevalence
- Recommended NIH Toolbox V3 Cognition tests for screening, monitoring, or intervention planning.

Recall that cognitive abilities do not change uniformly across the lifespan. Rather, they follow typical developmental trajectories while also reflecting periods of heightened vulnerability to neurodevelopmental and neurodegenerative disorders. The NIH Toolbox V3 Cognition domain accommodates age-related variability through its normed scoring system and also enables longitudinal tracking of individuals and populations, supporting early identification of atypical change. These features make it a valuable tool for both clinical decision-making and large-scale research initiatives aimed at understanding resilience, risk, and intervention outcomes across development and aging.

Early Childhood (Aged Three to Six Years)

Early childhood is marked by rapid development in attention regulation, language acquisition, memory formation, and foundational executive functions. While this is an exciting time for growth, this stage of development is also a critical period for the emergence of neurodevelopmental disorders. Among the most common disorders that first appear during this life stage include:

- **Autism spectrum disorder (ASD)**: 1.7% of children aged eight years, often with earlier developmental signs (Maenner et al., 2021).
- **Attention-deficit hyperactivity disorder (ADHD)**: 2.4% of preschool-aged children (Visser et al., 2014).
- **Specific language impairment (SLI)**: Estimated in 7%–10% of children (Norbury et al., 2016).
- **Global developmental delay (GDD)**: 1%–3% of children under age five (Shevell et al., 2003).

> **DON'T FORGET 6.1**
>
> A disorder is a disruption of normal physical, mental, or functional processes that causes distress, impairment, or dysfunction, but may not have a single identifiable cause or consistent biological markers. In contrast, a disease usually has a known etiology. A disease is a pathological condition of a body part, organ, or system that has a defined biological cause, characteristic signs and symptoms, and often measurable changes in anatomy or physiology.

- **Cerebral palsy (CP)**: 2.1 per 1,000 live births in the US (Centers for Disease Control and Prevention [CDC], 2020).
- **Sensory processing disorders**: Estimated prevalence of 5%–16% in preschool children (Ahn et al., 2004).

Table 6.2 summarizes how the NIH Toolbox V3 Cognition tests can align with specific cognitive features of early childhood disorders.

Table 6.2 Early Childhood (Ages Three to Six Years): NIH Toolbox V3 Cognition Tests for Screening Common Disorders in Early Childhood

Disorder	Core Cognitive Features	Relevant NIH Toolbox Tests	Screening Utility
Autism Spectrum Disorder (ASD)	Impaired social cognition, restricted flexibility, inhibitory control difficulties	DCCS, Flanker, PV, VR, parent-report socioemotional measures in the NIH Toolbox V3 Emotion domain	Identifies difficulties in set-shifting and inhibition; combined with socioemotional reports, can flag children for ASD-specific follow-up
Attention Deficit Hyperactivity Disorder (ADHD)	Executive dysfunction, inattention, impulsivity, poor inhibitory control	DCCS, Flanker, SM	Detects attentional lapses, inhibition deficits, and flexibility problems, which are early indicators of ADHD-related regulation difficulties
Specific Language Impairment (SLI)	Delayed expressive/ receptive language, narrative and verbal memory weaknesses	PV, ORR, PSM	PV and ORR highlight receptive and expressive language deficits; PSM captures narrative sequencing/ memory impairments, supporting early language intervention planning
Global Developmental Delay (GDD)	Broad deficits across multiple domains (language, memory, processing speed)	PV, PSM, SM, NIH Toolbox V3 Motor domain	Consistently low performance across tasks signals global cognitive risk and need for comprehensive evaluation
Cerebral Palsy (CP)	Motor impairments, with possible attention, executive, and processing speed deficits	OSD, SM, Flanker, DCCS	Detects processing inefficiency and co-occurring executive issues; tasks with minimal motor demand are especially useful for screening
Sensory Processing Disorder (SPD)	Over-/under-responsivity to sensory input; attentional instability	Flanker, SM, parent-report socioemotional measures in the NIH Toolbox V3 Emotion domain	Highlights attentional modulation difficulties and performance variability; parent reports complement task data for risk identification

Note. DCCS = Dimensional Change Card Sort, Flanker = Flanker Inhibitory Control and Attention, ORR = Oral Reading Recognition, OSD = Oral Symbol Digit, PC = Pattern Comparison Processing Speed, PSM = Picture Sequence Memory, PV = Picture Vocabulary, SM = Speeded Matching, VR = Visual Reasoning.

DON'T FORGET 6.2

Though the main focus of this book is Cognition, tests from the Emotion, Motor, and Sensation domains can also provide valuable insight about the examinee. For example, there are nearly 50 tests in the Emotion domain that explore psychological well-being, stress and self-efficacy, social relationships, and negative affect. Tests such as the Fear/Anxiety CAT, Sadness/Depression CAT, and General Life Satisfaction CAT may help uncover emotional health deficiencies. Performance on Motor and Sensation tests can also reveal physiological, sensory-perceptual, biochemical, and neurologic issues, to name a few, and may provide a clearer overall picture of the individual being tested.

The value of these screening measures is in providing a profile of cognitive strengths and weaknesses that can guide early referrals, interventions, and longitudinal tracking. For example, ASD rarely presents isolated deficits. Executive function, language, and social-cognitive processes often interact in complex ways (Kenworthy et al., 2008). NIH Toolbox V3 Cognition tests, such as Dimensional Change Card Sort (DCCS), Flanker Inhibitory Control and Attention (Flanker), and Picture Vocabulary (PV), can show atypical flexibility and inhibition, which, in combination with language tasks and parent-report measures, can provide a preliminary assessment of social cognition. As a test of nonverbal and visual reasoning, Visual Reasoning (VR) is also a valuable tool in measuring executive function without relying on verbal or motor processes. Measuring a variety of aspects of cognitive functioning often impacted by ASD will assist in early identification, particularly when behavioral symptoms may still be emerging.

Patients with Attention-Deficit Hyperactivity Disorder (ADHD) often show variability in their profile of cognitive scores. For instance, inconsistent performance across Flanker, DCCS, and Speeded Matching (SM) can highlight attentional lapses, a hallmark of ADHD in preschoolers (Pauli-Pott & Becker, 2011). Other sources of information, such as behavioral observations during the evaluation or parent/caregiver report, will also be helpful in speaking to attentional difficulties.

The NIH Toolbox V3 Cognition tests can also be useful in screening for Specific Language Impairment (SLI) in children. Scores on PV, Oral Reading Recognition (ORR), and Picture Sequence Memory (PSM) would be useful in understanding how their language is developing. In addition, these language scores can serve as baseline measures to monitor the impact of targeted interventions, supporting evidence-based educational planning.

Children with Global Developmental Delay (GDD) frequently show weaknesses across multiple tests of cognitive function and other domains such as motor development. Due to this presentation, the examiner may wish to select from tests in the NIH Toolbox V3 Motor domain in addition to the Cognition domain. For children with GDD, PV, PSM, and SM test results can be used to detect low, flat performance profiles spanning language, memory, and processing speed (Weintraub et al., 2013; Zelazo et al., 2013). This profile may not diagnose GDD directly, but it provides strong evidence to support a comprehensive multidisciplinary evaluation. Furthermore, given the briefer nature of these tests, it is often more easily tolerated by patients with GDD. The *NIH Toolbox V3 Cognition Battery Supplemental Administration Manual for Intellectual and Developmental Disabilities* (McKenzie et al., 2023) would also be important to consult for more guidance on testing patients with significant intellectual impairments.

Cognition tasks used in the assessment of patients with cerebral palsy are particularly valuable when carefully selected to minimize confounding motor demands. For example, tasks such as DCCS, Flanker, Oral Symbol Digit (OSD), and SM emphasize processing speed and executive control, which can reveal cognitive inefficiencies that might otherwise be masked by motor challenges (Bax et al., 2005). This highlights the flexibility of the NIH Toolbox in accommodating children with heterogeneous physical and cognitive presentations.

Although Sensory Processing Disorder (SPD) is not a diagnosis in the *Diagnostic and Statistical Manual of Mental Disorders* (5th ed.; DSM–5; American Psychiatric Association, 2013), sensory modulation differences are common in ASD and ADHD (Miller et al., 2007). Performance on some Cognition tests (e.g., Flanker, SM) may reveal secondary effects of sensory dysregulation, such as attentional instability or inconsistent task engagement. Coupling these findings with the child's history, parent-report socioemotional scales enhance ecological validity and support case formulation in clinical and school contexts.

Summary: Early Childhood (Ages Three to Six Years)

The NIH Toolbox offers a structured approach for identifying early cognitive vulnerabilities during a period when many neurocognitive and behavioral concerns first emerge. By assessing foundational domains such as attention, language, memory, and executive function, it enables clinicians and educators to recognize children who may be diverging from expected milestones. When interpreted alongside medical history and behavioral observations, NIH Toolbox V3 Cognition test results can improve the precision of early identification, support timely referrals for comprehensive evaluation, and help to inform tailored intervention strategies. Given the quick digital and standardized nature of the tests as well as the age-normed scoring, these characteristics make the assessments well-suited for repeat administration, providing a reliable framework for tracking growth, monitoring response to interventions (RTIs), and detecting the emergence of new concerns across the preschool years.

School-Age and Adolescence (Aged 7–17 Years)

During school-age years and adolescence, cognitive development accelerates in areas of working memory, processing speed, executive control, and literacy. Increasing academic and social demands can reveal vulnerabilities in attention, learning, and emotional regulation. Schools and clinics often evaluate children in this age band for both learning and behavioral difficulties. Some of the more common cognitive conditions that can arise during this period are:

- **ADHD:** 9.8% of children aged 3–17 (Danielson et al., 2018).
- **ASD:** Ongoing assessment is often required to support educational and functional planning.

- **Anxiety disorders:** 7.1% prevalence in children and adolescents (Ghandour et al., 2019).
- **Depressive disorders:** 3.2% of adolescents aged 12–17 (Ghandour et al., 2019).
- **Learning disorders (LDs):** 5%–15% prevalence depending on diagnostic criteria (American Psychiatric Association, 2013).
- **Traumatic brain injury (TBI):** 1.8% of children experience TBI before age 16 (Langlois et al., 2006).

Table 6.3 provides a more detailed review of how the NIH Toolbox V3 Cognition tests may be of assistance in the assessment of these disorders.

Table 6.3 School Age and Adolescence (Ages 7–17 Years): NIH Toolbox V3 Cognition Tests for Screening Common Disorders

Disorder	Core Cognitive Features	Relevant NIH Toolbox Tests	Screening Utility
ADHD	Inattention, poor inhibition, executive dysfunction	Flanker, DCCS, LSWM	Captures attentional lapses, inhibitory failures, and cognitive inflexibility characteristic of ADHD
ASD	Persistent executive and social-cognitive differences	DCCS, Flanker, PV, VR	Supports monitoring of executive control and language to guide academic support
Anxiety Disorders	Impaired attention under stress, working memory disruption	Flanker, LSWM, parent- and self-report socioemotional measures in the NIH Toolbox V3 Emotion domain	Highlights difficulties in sustaining focus and managing load when anxious
Depression	Processing inefficiency, memory retrieval challenges	PC, PSM, parent- and self-report socioemotional measures in the NIH Toolbox V3 Emotion domain	Detects slowed performance and episodic recall issues linked to mood symptoms
LDs	Deficits in reading, working memory, and processing speed	ORR, LSWM, PC	Identifies literacy challenges, memory weaknesses, and slowed processing that underlie academic struggles
TBI	Slowed processing, working memory deficits, executive dysfunction	PC, Flanker, DCCS	Sensitive to post-concussive slowing and executive difficulties

Note. DCCS = Dimensional Change Card Sort, Flanker = Flanker Inhibitory Control and Attention, LSWM = List Sorting Working Memory, ORR = Oral Reading Recognition, PC = Pattern Comparison Processing Speed, PSM = Picture Sequence Memory, PV = Picture Vocabulary, VR = Visual Reasoning.

As noted earlier, ADHD in preschoolers often presents as inconsistent performance and attentional lapses across cognitive measures such as Flanker, DCCS, and SM (Pauli-Pott & Becker, 2011); however, the school-age years bring additional cognitive and academic challenges. At this stage, ADHD is characterized not only by variability in attention but also by persistent deficits in inhibitory control, working memory, and cognitive flexibility that interfere with classroom learning and behavior (Kofler et al., 2011). The executive tasks, such as Flanker and DCCS, are well-suited to flagging these regulatory difficulties, and List Sorting Working Memory (LSWM) provides insight into verbal working memory weaknesses that often underlie academic problems. These screening results can highlight patterns consistent with ADHD, but they are best understood in combination with behavioral reports and classroom observations. Children demonstrating significant variability or inefficiency should be referred for a comprehensive evaluation to confirm the diagnosis and guide intervention (Hook et al., 2022).

In school-age children and adolescents, ASD is often characterized by ongoing differences in executive function and language-related processes. For many individuals, these difficulties represent a continuation of patterns first observed in early childhood. While early assessments emphasize the interaction of cognitive flexibility, inhibitory control, language, and emerging social-cognitive abilities, later developmental stages tend to reveal the broader impact of these challenges. By adolescence, difficulties in these domains are more clearly expressed through academic performance and social functioning, where their effects are both measurable and clinically significant (Demetriou et al., 2018). Executive function tasks (such as DCCS, Flanker, and VR) remain useful for tracking cognitive flexibility and inhibitory control, while PV provides an estimate of receptive language comprehension. Taken together, these measures offer objective data that can complement teacher observations and parent input, serving as a valuable screening tool for educational teams, who may choose to refer the child for more comprehensive testing in order to design or adapt individualized education plans (IEPs).

Anxiety in childhood and adolescence often presents with impaired attentional control and working memory under conditions of stress (Eysenck & Derakshan, 2011). While NIH Toolbox V3 Cognition measures such as Flanker and LSWM are not specific to anxiety disorders, they sometimes reveal reduced efficiency in cognitive control systems, especially in tasks requiring interference resolution. This performance profile complements clinical interviews and emotional health and mood questionnaires, illustrating how emotional dysregulation disrupts cognitive functioning in academic contexts (Moran, 2016).

Rapid Reference 6.1

Interference resolution is the brain's ability to resolve conflict between competing stimuli or responses. For example, the Flanker test asks children to indicate the direction of a central arrow while ignoring surrounding "flanker" arrows that may point in the opposite direction. This requires interference resolution because the distractors can conflict with the correct answer.

Adolescent depression is often associated with processing speed inefficiencies and memory retrieval difficulties, which can lead to academic impairment (Rock et al., 2014). The Pattern Comparison (PC) and PSM tests capture slowed processing and episodic recall problems, respectively. These measures may be useful in offering quantitative evidence of cognitive impact of depression even in subclinical cases. Such measures are also important because cognitive symptoms often persist beyond mood recovery, serving as targets for intervention and rehabilitation. These tests may be paired with tests from the NIH Toolbox V3 Emotion domain, such as Sadness/Depression CAT Ages 8–17, Sadness/Depression Parent Report CAT Ages 8–12, and Loneliness FF Ages 8–17.

LDs encompass difficulties in reading, written expression, or mathematics, with impairments in reading (e.g., dyslexia) being one of the most prevalent. In addition, deficits in working memory and processing speed are well-documented in children with LDs (Yeates et al., 2000). The ORR test provides a brief, standardized indicator of literacy skills that align with core academic competencies. When considered together with tasks such as PC and LSWM, it can offer a preliminary sense of whether reading challenges may reflect language-based weaknesses or broader processing inefficiencies. These results should be viewed as part of a screening process, useful for flagging potential areas of concern and supporting referral for more comprehensive psychoeducational or clinical evaluation when needed.

TBI, even in mild forms, can produce persistent deficits in processing speed and executive functioning (Anderson et al., 2011). Given the nature of the PC, DCCS, and Flanker tasks, they can be particularly useful in measuring possible post-concussive slowing and executive inefficiencies. These tests may also be useful for Return-to-Learn or Return-to-Play protocols. Beyond acute care, longitudinally, these tests can be used to provide valuable data on recovery trajectories, highlighting whether deficits normalize or persist over time, which is critical for educational planning.

Summary: School-Age and Adolescence (Aged 7–17 Years)

The NIH Toolbox V3 Cognition Battery is particularly useful in school-aged populations because it can help differentiate between domain-specific weaknesses (e.g., phonological deficits in LDs) and domain-general inefficiencies (e.g., processing speed in TBI, ADHD, and depression). By pairing objective screening measures with classroom and clinical data, these tests can provide a scalable, norm-referenced system for identifying children who may benefit from a more comprehensive assessment, educational planning, mental health interventions, and longitudinal monitoring across adolescence.

Young Adults (Aged 18–29 Years)

Young adulthood is a developmental period frequently marked by peak cognitive performance in reasoning, processing speed, and episodic memory (Hartshorne & Germine, 2015). However, it is also a high-risk period for the emergence of psychiatric illness, persistent effects of neurodevelopmental disorders, and sequelae of earlier injuries. The combination of increased autonomy, academic and professional demands, as well as social stressors makes cognitive screening particularly valuable in this group. More common conditions in young adults are:

- **Adult ADHD:** Symptoms persist in ~60% of those diagnosed in childhood (Faraone et al., 2006).
- **Bipolar disorder:** 2.6% prevalence, often with onset in young adulthood (Merikangas et al., 2007).
- **Generalized anxiety disorder (GAD):** Lifetime prevalence of 6.2% (Kessler et al., 2005).
- **Major depressive disorder (MDD):** 13.1% prevalence among US young adults (National Institute of Mental Health [NIMH], 2022).
- **Post-concussion syndrome:** Persistent symptoms in up to 30% of mild TBI cases (McCrea et al., 2004).
- **Substance use disorders:** 8.1% of adults aged 18–25 (Substance Abuse and Mental Health Services Administration [SAMHSA], 2021).

Table 6.4 provides a more detailed review of how the NIH Toolbox V3 Cognition tests may assist in diagnosis of these disorders and understanding of their symptoms.

Table 6.4 Young Adults (Aged 18–29 Years): NIH Toolbox V3 Cognition Tests for Screening Common Disorders

Disorder	Core Cognitive Features	Relevant NIH Toolbox Tests	Screening Utility
Adult ADHD	Executive dysfunction, persistent inattentiveness	Flanker, DCCS, LSWM	Objectively documents continued regulation difficulties
Bipolar Disorder	Executive variability, episodic memory disruption during episodes	Flanker, DCCS, PSM, self-report emotional measures in the NIH Toolbox V3 Emotion domain	Provides tracking of mood-state-related fluctuations
GAD	Attentional bias, reduced working memory under stress	Flanker, LSWM, self-report emotional measures in the NIH Toolbox V3 Emotion domain	Sensitive to attentional instability and reduced working memory capacity
MDD	Slowed processing, episodic memory inefficiency	PC, PSM, self-report emotional measures in the NIH Toolbox V3 Emotion domain	Captures subtle psychomotor slowing and retrieval inefficiencies
Post-Concussion Syndrome	Processing speed decline, executive inefficiency, memory complaints	PC, Flanker, PSM, VR	Tracks residual slowing and executive difficulties
Substance Use Disorders	Working memory deficits, slowed processing	LSWM, PC	Detects impairments linked to long-term substance exposure

Note. DCCS = Dimensional Change Card Sort, Flanker = Flanker Inhibitory Control and Attention, LSWM = List Sorting Working Memory, PC = Pattern Comparison Processing Speed, PSM = Picture Sequence Memory.

ADHD persisting into adulthood remains characterized by inhibitory control failures, attentional variability, and working memory inefficiency (Barkley & Murphy, 2010). Flanker, DCCS, and LSWM provide evidence of these deficits in young adults, assisting in the facilitation of documentation for educational or workplace accommodations.

Cognitive impairments in bipolar disorder often persist during euthymic states, including executive dysfunction and episodic memory deficits (Bora et al., 2009). Executive and memory tasks such as Flanker, DCCS, and PSM provide a quick and easy way to track fluctuations in cognition across mood states. Monitoring impairment with these tasks and measures from the NIH Toolbox V3 Emotion domain may help identify cognitive predictors of relapse risk and functional outcomes.

In GAD, attentional control deficits and working memory overload under stress are common (Eysenck & Derakshan, 2011). Flanker can highlight inhibitory control instability, while LSWM demonstrates reduced working memory efficiency during anxiety episodes. These results are clinically relevant because they reflect real-world challenges with sustained academic and work performance (Moran, 2016).

MDD in young adults is consistently associated with psychomotor slowing and inefficiencies in memory retrieval, which can predict long-term occupational outcomes (Rock et al., 2014). PC is particularly sensitive to reduced processing speed, while PSM highlights memory inefficiencies that may persist even after mood recovery (Bora & Berk, 2016). These measures can also be used to quickly monitor cognition even beyond symptom remission.

Post-Concussion Syndrome frequently leads to slowed processing speed, reduced executive control, and memory complaints long after injury resolution (McInnes et al., 2017). PC can measure slowing processing speed, VR can measure executive function, and Flanker and PSM help document deficits that align with self-reported cognitive complaints. These tasks can contribute to Return-to-Work protocols and provide objective evidence of ongoing deficits, if needed.

Chronic substance use in young adults is associated with working memory deficits and slowed processing speed, particularly in individuals with cannabis and alcohol use disorders (Squeglia et al., 2009). LSWM and PC can quantify these impairments, supporting both clinical monitoring and intervention planning.

Summary: Young Adults (Aged 18–29 years)

The NIH Toolbox offers sensitive markers for psychiatric and neurological conditions that often peak in young adulthood. Its strength lies in quantifying subtle inefficiencies in speed, attention, and memory at a developmental stage when cognition should be at its best. Deviations from this can be clinically meaningful and informative for understanding what may be impacting the young adult's cognition.

Adults (Aged 30–59 Years)

Cognition is generally stable in midlife, though subtle declines in fluid abilities (e.g., processing speed, working memory) can emerge while crystalized abilities remain strong

(Schaie, 2005). Chronic illness and neurological disease become more prominent and contribute to cognitive variability in this stage of life. Some of the more common conditions prevalent in this age group include:

- **Epilepsy:** 1.2% prevalence; cognitive deficits occur in 30%–40% (Helmstaedter & Elger, 2009).
- **Mood and anxiety disorders:** Often persist or recur in midlife.
- **Multiple sclerosis (MS):** Cognitive impairment in 40%–65% of patients (Chiaravalloti & DeLuca, 2008).
- **Stroke:** Affects 2.7% of adults aged 45–64 (Benjamin et al., 2019).
- **Sleep apnea:** Linked to executive dysfunction and memory problems (Wallace & Bucks, 2013).
- **Type 2 diabetes mellitus:** Affects around 10.5% of US adults, with associated cognitive slowing (Biessels & Despa, 2018).

See Table 6.5 for a review of these common conditions in adults and relevant NIH Toolbox V3 Cognition tests.

Table 6.5 Adults (Aged 30–59 Years): NIH Toolbox V3 Cognition Tests for Screening Common Disorders

Disorder	Core Cognitive Features	Relevant NIH Toolbox Tests	Screening Utility
Epilepsy	Memory disruption, executive dysfunction	PSM, LSWM, RAVLT, FNAME, Flanker	Highlights episodic memory, delayed recall, and control deficits
Mood and Anxiety Disorders	Processing inefficiency, working memory overload	PC, LSWM, self-report emotional measures in the NIH Toolbox V3 Emotion domain	Screens for subtle declines linked to psychiatric symptoms
MS	Slowed processing, executive dysfunction	PC, Flanker, DCCS	Detects speed and executive function inefficiencies
Stroke	Focal deficits, executive and working memory impairments	LSWM, Flanker, DCCS	Captures executive deficits related to vascular injury
Sleep Apnea	Memory retrieval and attention problems	PSM, RAVLT, FNAME, Flanker	Sensitive to hypoxia-related impairments
Type 2 Diabetes Mellitus	Slowed processing, executive inefficiency	PC, Flanker	Identifies systemic disease effects on cognition

Note. DCCS = Dimensional Change Card Sort, FNAME = Face Name Associative Memory Exam, Flanker = Flanker Inhibitory Control and Attention, LSWM = List Sorting Working Memory, PC = Pattern Comparison Processing Speed, PSM = Picture Sequence Memory, PV = Picture Vocabulary, RAVLT = Rey Auditory Verbal Learning.

Adults with epilepsy frequently experience deficits in episodic memory, delayed recall, and executive functioning, even in well-controlled cases (Helmstaedter & Elger, 2009). Face Name Associative Memory Exam (FNAME), Rey Auditory Verbal Learning Test (RAVLT), PSM, and LSWM are particularly relevant for quantifying memory disruptions, while Flanker can highlight inhibitory control difficulties. Results on these can be used to screen for disturbances and can contribute to both clinical care and disability evaluations, albeit additional testing may be warranted for both, depending on the patient's needs.

Chronic mood and anxiety disorders contribute to processing inefficiency and working memory issues, even in remission (Semkovska et al., 2019). NIH Toolbox V3 Cognition tests (particularly PC and Flanker) can objectively measure these inefficiencies, complementing self-report measures of emotional functioning, both of which can aid in treatment planning.

Rapid Reference 6.2

In some cases (e.g., chronic mood and anxiety disorders, mild cognitive impairment), administering certain tests over time and comparing the results can help detect improvement or decline. When significant changes in scores are identified, the individual's healthcare team might consider alternative treatment (e.g., decreased dosage of a specific medication, increased occupational therapy).

Cognitive impairment is present in up to 65% of MS patients, often with early declines in processing speed and executive function (Benedict et al., 2020). PC is highly sensitive to slowed processing, while Flanker and DCCS can capture executive dysfunction tied to demyelination in fronto-striatal circuits. These measures can be used longitudinally to track disease-modifying treatment effects, and results can contribute to a larger work that may be needed.

Cognitive outcomes following stroke vary depending on lesion location, but executive dysfunction, attention deficits, and working memory impairments are common (Nys et al., 2005). LSWM and executive measures such as Flanker and DCCS provide efficient tools to identify executive focal deficits and track rehabilitation progress. Age-adjusted norms allow clinicians to distinguish stroke-related impairment from age-expected variability.

Sleep apnea is linked to memory retrieval and attention deficits due to intermittent hypoxia (Wallace & Bucks, 2013). Tasks such as FNAME, RAVLT, PSM, and Flanker can be sensitive to these impairments and useful in monitoring cognitive changes following continuous positive airway pressure (CPAP) treatment.

Type 2 diabetes is associated with slowed processing speed and executive dysfunction, reflecting vascular and metabolic contributions to brain health (Biessels & Despa, 2018). NIH Toolbox V3 speed and executive tasks such as PC and Flanker provide a validated method of tracking disease impact over time.

Summary: Adults (Aged 30–59 Years)

While crystallized intelligence is often maintained or improves during these years, the NIH Toolbox V3 Cognition domain, in part or in its entirety, can sensitively detect non-normative declines in working memory, processing speed, and flexibility, which can serve as early indicators of disease-related cognitive decline in midlife. NIH Toolbox V3 Cognition tests' utility lies in differentiating system and neurological disease effect from normative aging and providing brief, psychometrically sound measures for longitudinal monitoring.

Older Adults (Aged 60–85+ Years)

Cognitive abilities in later life are marked by heterogeneity. While some older adults maintain cognitive resilience, others experience neurodegenerative disease. Early detection and monitoring are, thus, essential in this stage for planning and intervention. Some common conditions for older adults are:

- **Alzheimer's disease (AD):** Prevalence of 11.3% among adults 65+ (Alzheimer's Association, 2023).
- **Hearing loss-associated cognitive decline:** Observed in 32% of older adults (Lin et al., 2013).
- **Mild cognitive impairment (MCI):** Affects 15%–20% of adults over 65 (Petersen et al., 2009).
- **Parkinson's disease (PD):** 1% prevalence in adults over 60 (Tysnes & Storstein, 2017).
- **Vascular cognitive impairment (VCI):** Represents 25%–30% of dementia cases (O'Brien & Thomas, 2015).

See Table 6.6 for more information, including an overview of cognitive features and NIH Toolbox V3 Cognition tests that would be useful in assessing those areas of cognitive ability.

Although many older adults maintain adequate cognitive functioning into their 80s, baseline and repeat assessments can assist in monitoring cognitive functions and detecting decline, should it occur. Specifically, the NIH Toolbox Change-Sensitive Scores (CSSs) and age-corrected standard scores are particularly valuable in geriatric care, wellness assessments, and longitudinal aging studies.

Table 6.6 Older Adults (Aged 60–85+ Years): NIH Toolbox V3 Cognition Tests for Screening Common Disorders

Disorder	Core Cognitive Features	Relevant NIH Toolbox Tests	Screening Utility
AD	Episodic memory loss, language impairment, executive dysfunction	PSM, PV, LSWM, RAVLT, FNAME, Flanker, VR	Identifies impairments of AD
Hearing Loss-Associated Cognitive Decline	Reduced efficiency and memory decline	PC, PSM, WiN (Sensation domain), HT (Sensation domain)	Distinguishes auditory versus cognitive contributions
MCI	Early memory decline	PSM, LSWM, RAVLT	Detects subtle changes preceding dementia
PD	Executive dysfunction, slowed processing	Flanker, PC, LSWM	Tracks fronto-striatal dysfunction
VCI	Processing speed, executive dysfunction	PC, Flanker, DCCS	Captures vascular-related slowing and control deficits

Note. DCCS = Dimensional Change Card Sort, FNAME = Face Name Associative Memory Exam, Flanker = Flanker Inhibitory Control and Attention, HT = Hearing Threshold, LSWM = List Sorting Working Memory, PC = Pattern Comparison Processing Speed, PSM = Picture Sequence Memory, PV = Picture Vocabulary, RAVLT = Rey Auditory Verbal Learning, WiN = Words in Noise, VR = Visual Reasoning.

AD is characterized by prominent episodic memory loss, language impairment, and executive dysfunction (Jack et al., 2018). NIH Toolbox tasks spanning memory (PSM, RAVLT, FNAME, and LSWM), language (PV), and executive function (Flanker, VR) provide a multidomain approach to capturing hallmark deficits associated with AD. Their digital format allows repeated use in clinical trials and longitudinal studies.

Hearing loss is increasingly recognized as a modifiable risk factor for dementia (Livingston et al., 2020). Tasks such as PC and PSM can help distinguish cognitive inefficiency due to sensory loss versus primary neurodegenerative processes, which can be assessed with tests from the Sensation domain, such as Words-in-Noise and Hearing Threshold.

MCI represents a transitional stage between normal aging and dementia, with deficits most evident in episodic memory (Petersen et al., 2009). PSM, LSWM, and RAVLT can detect subtle memory declines, offering sensitive indicators for early intervention.

PD involves progressive executive dysfunction and slowed processing speed linked to fronto-striatal circuits (Kehagia et al., 2010). Flanker, PC, and LSWM can track these deficits and complement motor assessments in clinical practice.

VCI accounts for 25%–30% of dementia cases and often presents with slowed processing speed and executive dysfunction (O'Brien & Thomas, 2015). PC and executive tasks such as Flanker and DCCS are well-suited for tracking these deficits, particularly in patients with vascular risk factors.

Summary: Older Adults (60–85+ Years)

In older adulthood, NIH Toolbox tasks provide sensitive markers for distinguishing healthy aging from neurodegeneration. Though the focus of this book is on the Cognition domain, tests from the Emotion, Motor, and Sensation domains can provide a wealth of information about each person and can be especially helpful if used longitudinally to track change over time. Their brevity, digital administration, and norm-referenced scoring make them well-suited for early detection, monitoring, and clinical trial applications.

NIH TOOLBOX V3 COGNITION DOMAIN IN APPLIED SETTINGS AND DIVERSE CONTEXTS

The NIH Toolbox V3 Cognition tests can and have been deployed across a variety of real-world settings, including (but not limited to) education, inpatient/outpatient rehabilitation services, multicultural contexts, accessibility and disability use cases, remote/hybrid delivery, and research. In fact, proven scalability of these measures in research has lent credibility to them becoming increasingly interesting to clinics and schools (LaForte et al., 2024). For example, one advantage of the NIH Toolbox tests is that they offer common metrics across the lifespan, which supports screenings, triage, progress monitoring, and longitudinal follow-up without sacrificing rigor.

Test Applications Across Educational Settings (Pre-K through College)

Academic demands naturally stress attention, working memory, processing speed, language, and executive control. Because these areas are measured efficiently by NIH Toolbox, these tests can be used to assist in defining workflows for a multitiered system of supports (MTSS) and RTI, as well as special education screens and assistance with accommodation decisions (Bailey et al., 2020; Zelazo et al., 2013). Table 6.7 provides an overview of the NIH Toolbox Cognition V3 measures that would be some of the most impactful in making decisions at different levels of education.

When using the NIH Toolbox Cognition V3 tests in a school setting, the examiner should consider use of age-corrected scores and CSSs for progress and combining them with other sources of information about the student, such as attendance in school, in class observation, grades, teacher ratings, and any other neuropsychological testing, as inclusion of any of this information can help improve ecological validity of the evaluation.

In preschool and early elementary years, rapid growth in attention, language, memory, and early executive skills creates both opportunity and vulnerability. Brief, engaging tasks such as SM (processing speed), PV (receptive language), PSM (episodic memory), as well as Flanker and DCCS (selective attention and cognitive flexibility) provide a quick, standardized snapshot to flag children who may diverge from expected milestones and to inform early intervention or RTI/MTSS Tier 1–2 decisions (Bailey et al., 2020; Berkeley et al., 2020; Zelazo et al., 2013). Repeated administrations with age-corrected scores and CSSs support progress monitoring in IEPs.

Table 6.7 A Guide for Helping Select NIH Toolbox V3 Cognition Measures for Educational Assessments

Grade Bands	Purposes	NIH Toolbox V3 Cognition Measures	Decisions Supported
Pre-K–grade 1	Universal screening, early risk flags, baseline for progress monitoring	SM, PV, PSM, Flanker, DCCS	MTSS Tier 1–2 supports, early referrals, parent feedback
Elementary–middle school	Differentiate domain-specific vs. domain-general issues	ORR, LSWM, PC	Literacy supports vs. processing-speed/working memory interventions, psychoeducational referral
High school	Return-to-Learn, accommodations, monitoring mood/anxiety impacts	Flanker, DCCS, LSWM, PC, VR	Section 504/IEP accommodations, concussion care pathways
College	Wellness screening, chronic condition monitoring, documentation for disability services	PC, LSWM, PSM, Flanker, DCCS	Academic accommodations, medication/therapy effectiveness tracking

In elementary school through middle school years, there is an increasing academic load, which often highlights specific and general challenges. ORR can aid in literacy screening, while the LSWM and PC tests can assist in understanding the student's underlying cognitive capacities that impact classroom performance across multiple subjects. When integrated with teacher observations and curriculum-linked assessments, the NIH Toolbox V3 profiles help differentiate skill deficits (e.g., phonological decoding) from other, broader processing inefficiencies, guiding targeted support and referrals for comprehensive evaluation (Danielson et al., 2018; Peterson et al., 2013).

During high school and the transition to college, executive demands and independent study place a premium on working memory, cognitive control, and processing speed. Flanker, DCCS, LSWM, PC, and VR can document functional limitations associated with ADHD, LDs, mood/anxiety symptoms, or post-concussion effects, particularly if the student needs testing accommodations, Return-to-Learn planning, or disability services. Because the NIH Toolbox V3 app spans adolescence into adulthood on a common metric, results provide continuity as students transition to college settings (Kofler et al., 2011; Rock et al., 2014).

In undergraduate studies (i.e., college) and professional training, the NIH Toolbox V3 measures can be administered as part of wellness screening, following campus injuries (e.g., concussion clinics), or to monitor cognitive load in students with chronic medical conditions (e.g., diabetes, sleep apnea). The brevity of the tests and the app's automated scoring facilitate integration into clinic visits, while longitudinal comparisons help evaluate the efficacy of accommodations or treatments over a term or academic year (Chiaravalloti & DeLuca, 2008; Biessels & Despa, 2018).

Use of Cognition Composite Scores in Educational Settings

When using the NIH Toolbox V3 Cognition tests in school settings, the composite scores can also be of assistance (i.e., Early Childhood Composite, Early Childhood CFPS Composite, Fluid Composite, Crystallized Composite, and Total Cognition Composite). These composites aggregate across multiple subtests to provide more robust, reliable estimates of broad cognitive abilities, which can be valuable in educational settings to detect more general patterns or to monitor change over time. The Fluid Cognition Composite captures capacities such as working memory, processing speed, attention, inhibitory control, and episodic memory, which are sensitive to developmental changes, adversities (e.g., stress, injury, illness), or learning difficulties. The Crystallized Cognition Composite reflects accumulated learning in language and reading skills, providing a benchmark of prior academic or environmental exposure to this information. Thus, as a union of the Fluid Cognition Composite and the Crystallized Cognition Composite, the Total Cognition Composite offers a summary metric that is useful when broad functioning (rather than specific subskills) is of interest.

Research shows these composite scores have strong psychometric properties: good test–retest reliability and internal consistency (LaForte et al., 2024). They also show robust developmental effects. For example, Fluid Cognition Composite scores tend to increase through childhood, peak in early adulthood, then decline. Comparatively, Crystallized Cognition scores tend to increase more gradually and remain more stable over time.

When deciding whether to administer the full set of tests required for composite scores, the examiner must weigh several factors. These include the additional time needed to complete more measures and the potential value gained from a broader assessment. In cases where a student shows inconsistent performance across individual NIH Toolbox tasks or between classroom functioning and test results, administering the full battery to generate composite scores may provide a more comprehensive and reliable picture of the student's cognitive profile. If a fuller assessment of the student is warranted, the resulting composites can enhance decision-making in several ways. First, they simplify interpretation when subtest scores are inconsistent. Second, they may help in screening or progress monitoring as composite scores are often more robust to change than individual subtests (i.e., reducing false positives and false negatives). Third, in high school, college, or transitions to postsecondary settings, composite scores (e.g., Total Cognition Composite) may aid in documentation for accommodations by adding a more holistic picture of cognitive functioning. Lastly, in longitudinal tracking (e.g., across years, through transitions), composite scores allow more comparability over time and lessen the measurement error that might occur if only individual subtests are used.

Inpatient, Rehabilitation, and Specialty Outpatient Medical Settings

Many medical conditions affect speeded processing, interference control, memory, or working memory. NIH Toolbox tasks are ideal in these settings because, as mentioned, they are brief, device-based, and normed, facilitating bedside screens, clinic triage, and rehab outcome tracking (Anderson et al., 2011; Chiaravalloti & DeLuca, 2008; Helmstaedter & Elger, 2009; Nys et al., 2005; O'Brien & Thomas, 2015).

Frequently in medical settings, short, repeatable batteries (10–15 minutes) at intake, midpoint, and discharge are useful to measure change and cognitive status. See Table 6.8 for suggested NIH Toolbox tests for common conditions in different medical settings.

During acute inpatient settings, when clinical availability and patient stamina are typically limited, the NIH Toolbox offers indices of attention, processing speed, working memory, and episodic memory that can be administered at bedside or in short sessions. For example, PC and Flanker are sensitive to generalized slowing and executive control issues common after stroke, TBI, hypoxia, or delirium. Age-corrected scores help distinguish medical effects from age-expected variability and can support discharge planning (Anderson et al., 2011; Nys et al., 2005).

In neurorehabilitation, repeated administrations can help to quantify recovery curves from admission to discharge and beyond. For stroke and TBI, combinations of PV, PC, Flanker, DCCS, LSWM, and PSM are useful for goal setting, tracking response to therapies, and informing multidisciplinary team conferences. In addition, standardized administration across sites allows for data aggregation for quality improvement studies and other clinical research, if desired (Langlois et al., 2006).

Table 6.8 A Guide for Helping Select NIH Toolbox V3 Cognition Measures in Medical Settings

Setting	Common Conditions	NIH Toolbox Cognition Measures	Typical Use
Acute Inpatient/ Consult-Liaison	Stroke, TBI, hypoxia/delirium, systemic illness	PC, Flanker, DCCS, PSM; add OSD when minimal motor evaluation is needed	Bedside screening, discharge planning, therapy targets
Outpatient Neurology	MS, epilepsy, PD, vascular cognitive impairment	PC, Flanker, DCCS, LSWM, PSM; FNAME and RAVLT are optional	Cognitive phenotyping, tracking disease-modifying therapies, risk counseling
Outpatient Psychiatry/ Primary Care	MDD, GAD, bipolar, sleep apnea, diabetes	PC, LSWM, Flanker, PSM; add ORR when there are literacy concerns	Psychotropic monitoring, documenting residual cognitive burden, behavioral sleep/ metabolic care
Inpatient/Day Rehab	Stroke, TBI, polytrauma	PV, PC, Flanker, DCCS, LSWM, PSM, RAVLT	Admission → discharge trajectories, goal setting, multidisciplinary rounds

In MS, epilepsy, Parkinson's disease, and mood/anxiety disorders, the NIH Toolbox assists with efficient cognitive screening, phenotyping, and longitudinal follow-up. PC is particularly sensitive to slowing seen in MS and vascular disease; LSWM and PSM quantify working and episodic memory, respectively; and Flanker/DCCS capture interference control and flexibility relevant to fronto-striatal dysfunction (Chiaravalloti & DeLuca, 2008; Helmstaedter & Elger, 2009; Kehagia et al., 2010; O'Brien & Thomas, 2015).

Multicultural and Multilingual Use

The NIH Toolbox development team emphasized cultural validity and multilingual access by combining language-independent tasks (e.g., Flanker and PC) with translated and culturally reviewed measures (e.g., LSWM and PSM). Translation and adaptation followed structured workflows, including but not limited to forward translation by a native speaker, back-translation, reconciliation, thorough review by the NIH Toolbox translation team, and cognitive debriefing when possible, to maximize conceptual rather than literal equivalence. In addition, an independent native speaker who is both familiar with the target culture and familiar with NIH Toolbox tests reviewed the text translations, audio, and the translated app to confirm that it is linguistically and culturally appropriate while remaining true to the original NIH Toolbox content (Giella & Hook, 2024). All NIH Toolbox V3 tests are available in Spanish, and many of the Cognition tests are available in French, Italian, Hebrew, and Arabic, with ongoing cultural review and recalibration when needed (Hook & Giella, 2023).

Research suggests that in diverse communities, pairing language-neutral tasks with language measures aids in distinguishing limited language exposure from primary cognitive impairment, while age- and education-adjusted norms improve diagnostic accuracy across SES and linguistic backgrounds (Livingston et al., 2020; Manly, 2008).

When using any of the translated versions of the NIH Toolbox V3 app, please use the following guidance:

- When feasible, use language-neutral measures if the examinee's language proficiency is uncertain, and interpret language-dependent tasks in the context of exposure and educational history.
- Use available translated interfaces and instructions for both examinees and examiners to reduce construct-irrelevant variance.
- When feasible, supplement collected data with collateral information (e.g., acculturation, literacy history) to support fair interpretation.

Accessibility and Use with Individuals with Disabilities

The V3 redesign incorporated accessibility features and examiner workflows aligned with the Revised Section 508 Standards for Information Communication and Technology accessibility (US Access Board, 2017), with the dual goal of examiner usability and participant access. Examples include:

- **Visual accessibility:** Scalable fonts, high-contrast displays, reduced visual clutter, and support for external assistive technologies where appropriate.
- **Hearing concerns:** On-screen instructions were added wherever possible so those with hearing concerns can read the instructions.
- **Motor accessibility:** Tasks with minimal motor demands (e.g., OSD); guidance on positioning devices and allowing alternate response methods consistent with test intent. For pediatric motor disorders (e.g., cerebral palsy) and acquired motor limitations, prioritizing measures with low motor demands and clear timing rules reduces confounds.
- **Cognitive accessibility:** Simplified on-screen instructions, consistent iconography, and examiner scripts to maintain standardization while minimizing memory load.
- **IDD and neurodiversity:** An NIH Toolbox V3 IDD Supplemental Administration Manual provides concrete guidance on administration, pacing, environmental modifications, and interpretation in individuals with intellectual and developmental disabilities, preserving standardized administration while maximizing tolerability (McKenzie et al., 2023).

Record any permitted accommodations and context (fatigue, environment) in reports to preserve interpretability across sites and improve transparency reporting (Bax et al., 2005).

Remote, Hybrid, and Decentralized Testing

Propelled by the social isolation imposed during COVID-19, remote administration has shifted from an emergency contingency to an established mainstream approach in both multicenter research and routine clinical care. Validation work supports the feasibility and reliability of remotely administered NIH Toolbox measures when protocols control device variability, audio and visual quality, ambient distractions, and examiner supervision (Remote Administration Guidelines for the NIH Toolbox: Response to COVID-19, 2021; Slotkin et al., 2021).

There is also a two-app beta version of the NIH Toolbox being used in remote settings, in which both the examiner and the participant have access to iPads and the Internet. Currently, this beta version of the examiner and participant apps is in use for a large research study and offers remote sessions allowing for synchronous observation, standardized prompts, and secure scoring. Another option for pragmatic and decentralized designs is a separate measurement system, the Mobile Toolbox, which extends assessment to smartphones for frequent, brief cognitive sampling between clinic visits or for research studies. This allows for a link between lab-quality tasks to everyday contexts and enables sensitive within-person change detection (Slotkin, 2024).

When assessing individuals remotely, examiners must establish the minimum device and connectivity requirements (e.g., stable internet access). Conducting presession checks helps reduce attrition and variance. Examiners should maintain visual confirmation of the examinee's engagement and their environment, and they should document deviations from standard conditions.

CONCLUSION

The NIH Toolbox V3 Cognition tests demonstrate their greatest value not only through psychometric rigor but also through adaptability across applied settings. From schools and community programs to inpatient rehabilitation, outpatient clinics, and large-scale research networks, it provides a lifespan-appropriate framework for assessing core areas of cognitive functioning.

Equally important are equity and accessibility. Translation initiatives, cultural reviews, and adherence to accessibility standards ensure that the measures remain responsive to diverse populations. As neuropsychology advances in the digital era, the NIH Toolbox V3 Cognition Domain occupies a unique position, balancing scientific rigor with scalability and inclusivity.

TEST YOURSELF

1. **Young adulthood is a developmental period frequently marked by peak cognitive performance in reasoning, processing speed, and episodic memory.**
   True or False
2. **Tapping on selective attention and inhibition, the Flanker Inhibitory Control and Attention test is most relevant to which brain regions?**
   (a) Occipital lobe and Frontal lobe
   (b) Temporal lobe and Basal ganglia
   (c) Frontal lobe and Parietal lobe
   (d) Parietal lobe and Occipital lobe
3. **In school-age children and adolescents, ASD is often characterized by ongoing differences in executive function and language-related processes. Which of the following is true?**
   (a) Executive function tasks (DCCS and Flanker) are useful for tracking cognitive flexibility and inhibitory control, while PV provides an estimate of receptive language comprehension.
   (b) ORR is the quickest and most informative test to diagnose ASD because it measures reading ability and language processing.
   (c) The Face Name Associative Memory Exam (FNAME), which measures associative and delayed memory, and OSD, which measures speeded processing, are effective in diagnosing ASD.
   (d) All of the above

4. **The Picture Vocabulary test measures selective attention and inhibition, and maps onto:**
   (a) Executive function
   (b) Receptive language
   (c) Fluid knowledge
   (d) Occipital lobe
5. **Which of the following are among the more common conditions prevalent in adults (aged 30–59 years) that are presented in this chapter?**
   (a) AD, Hearing loss-associated cognitive decline, MCI, PD, VCI
   (b) Type 2 diabetes, stroke, sleep apnea, TBI, ASD
   (c) Mood and anxiety disorders, stroke, type 2 diabetes, SLI, ADHD
   (d) Epilepsy, mood and anxiety disorders, MS, stroke, sleep apnea, type 2 diabetes
6. **The NIH Toolbox is suited for monitoring cognitive function across typical and atypical development in which of the following settings?**
   (a) Clinical and hospital
   (b) Research and university
   (c) Schools and education
   (d) All of the above
7. **Early childhood is marked by rapid development in attention regulation, language acquisition, memory formation, and foundational executive functions.**
   True or False
8. **Which of the following is not true?**
   (a) The NIH Toolbox is a valuable tool that can be used to measure functioning across the lifespan.
   (b) The NIH Toolbox measures specific disease states and provides diagnostic codes when all tests in the app are administered.
   (c) The NIH Toolbox is not restricted to the assessment of a specific disease state but is uniquely suited to assess both health and impairment.
   (d) NIH Toolbox Cognition tests are broadly linked to the neural systems most critical for their successful performance.
9. **Which of the following are not among the common conditions for older adults that are discussed in this chapter?**
   (a) Attention-deficit hyperactivity disorder (ADHD)
   (b) Parkinson's disease (PD)
   (c) Hearing loss-associated cognitive decline
   (d) Vascular cognitive impairment
10. **Tests in the NIH Toolbox V3 app are designed to be extensive diagnostic tools that, after full evaluation, provide DSV and ICD diagnostic codes.**
   True or False

Answers: 1. True; 2. (c); 3. (a); 4. (b); 5. (d); 6. (d); 7. True; 8. (b); 9. (a); 10. False

REFERENCES

Ahn, R. R., Miller, L. J., Milberger, S., & McIntosh, D. N. (2004). Prevalence of parents' perceptions of sensory processing disorders among kindergarten children. *American Journal of Occupational Therapy, 58*(3), 287–293. https://doi.org/10.5014/ajot.58.3.287

Alzheimer's Association. (2023). *2023 Alzheimer's disease facts and figures*. https://www.alz.org/media/documents/alzheimers-facts-and-figures.pdf

American Psychiatric Association. (2013). *Diagnostic and statistical manual of mental disorders* (5th ed.). APA. https://doi.org/10.1176/appi.books.9780890425596

Anderson, V., Brown, S., Newitt, H., & Hoile, H. (2011). Long-term outcome from childhood traumatic brain injury: Intellectual ability, personality, and quality of life. *Neuropsychology, 25*(2), 176–184. https://doi.org/10.1037/a0021217

Bailey, T. R., Colpo, A., & Foley, A. (2020). *Assessment practices within a multi-tiered system of supports* (Document No. IC-18). University of Florida, Collaboration for Effective Educator, Development, Accountability, and Reform Center. https://ceedar.education.ufl.edu/wp-content/uploads/2020/12/Assessment-Practices-Within-a-Multi-Tiered-System-of-Supports-1.pdf

Barkley, R. A., & Murphy, K. R. (2010). Impairment in occupational functioning and adult ADHD: The predictive utility of executive function (EF) ratings versus EF tests. *Archives of Clinical Neuropsychology, 25*(3), 157–173. https://doi.org/10.1093/arclin/acq014

Bax, M., Goldstein, M., Rosenbaum, P., Leviton, A., & Paneth, N. (2005). Proposed definition and classification of cerebral palsy. *Developmental Medicine & Child Neurology, 47*(8), 571–576.

Benedict, R. H. B., Amato, M. P., DeLuca, J., & Geurts, J. J. G. (2020). Cognitive impairment in multiple sclerosis: Clinical management, MRI, and therapeutic avenues. *The Lancet Neurology, 19*(10), 860–871. https://doi.org/10.1016/S1474-4422(20)30277-5

Benjamin, E. J., Muntner, P., Alonso, A., Bittencourt, M. S., Callaway, C. W., Carson, A. P., Chamberlain, A. M., Chang, A. R., Cheng, S., Das, S. R., Delling, F. N., Djousse, L., Elkind, M. S. V., Ferguson, J. F., Fornage, M., Jordan, L. C., Khan, S. S., Kissela, B. M., Knutson, K. L., …, & American Heart Association Council on Epidemiology and Prevention Statistics Committee and Stroke Statistics Subcommittee. (2019). Heart disease and stroke statistics—2019 update: A report from the American Heart Association. *Circulation, 139*(10), e56–e528. https://doi.org/10.1161/CIR.0000000000000659

Berkeley, S., Scanlon, D., Bailey, T., Sutton, J., & Sacco, D. (2020). A snapshot of RTI implementation a decade later: New picture, same story. *Journal of Learning Disabilities, 53*(5), 332–342. https://doi.org/10.1177/0022219420915867

Biessels, G. J., & Despa, F. (2018). Cognitive decline and dementia in diabetes mellitus: Mechanisms and clinical implications. *Nature Reviews Endocrinology, 14*(10), 591–604. https://doi.org/10.1038/s41574-018-0048-7

Bora, E., & Berk, M. (2016). Theory of mind in major depressive disorder: A meta-analysis. *Journal of Affective Disorders, 191*, 49–55. https://doi.org/10.1016/j.jad.2015.11.023

Bora, E., Yücel, M., & Pantelis, C. (2009). Cognitive endophenotypes of bipolar disorder: A meta-analysis of neuropsychological deficits in euthymic patients and their first-degree relatives. *Journal of Affective Disorders, 113*, 1–20. https://doi.org/10.1016/j.jad.2008.06.009

Centers for Disease Control and Prevention (CDC). (2020). *Cerebral palsy data and statistics*. https://www.cdc.gov/cerebral-palsy/index.html

Chiaravalloti, N. D., & DeLuca, J. (2008). Cognitive impairment in multiple sclerosis. *The Lancet Neurology, 7*(12), 1139–1151. https://doi.org/10.1016/S1474-4422(08)70259-X

Danielson, M. L., Bitsko, R. H., Ghandour, R. M., Holbrook, J. R., Kogan, M. D., & Blumberg, S. J. (2018). Prevalence of parent-reported ADHD diagnosis and associated treatment among U.S. children and adolescents, 2016. *Journal of Clinical Child & Adolescent Psychology, 47*(2), 199–212. https://doi.org/10.1080/15374416.2017.1417860

Demetriou, E. A., Lampit, A., Quintana, D. S., Naismith, S. L., Song, Y. J. C., Hickie, I., & Guastella, A. J. (2018). Autism spectrum disorders: A meta-analysis of executive function. *Molecular Psychiatry, 23*(5), 1198–1204. https://doi.org/10.1038/mp.2017.75

Eysenck, M. W., & Derakshan, N. (2011). New perspectives in attentional control theory. *Personality and Individual Differences, 50*(7), 955–960. https://doi.org/10.1016/j.paid.2010.08.019

Faraone, S. V., Biederman, J., & Mick, E. (2006). The age-dependent decline of attention deficit hyperactivity disorder: A meta-analysis of follow-up studies. *Psychological Medicine, 36*(2), 159–165. https://doi.org/10.1017/S003329170500471X

Ghandour, R. M., Sherman, L. J., Vladutiu, C. J., Ali, M. M., Lynch, S. E., Bitsko, R. H., & Blumberg, S. J. (2019). Prevalence and treatment of depression, anxiety, and conduct problems in U.S. children. *Journal of Pediatrics, 206*, 256–267. https://doi.org/10.1016/j.jpeds.2018.09.021

Giella, A. K., & Hook, J. N. (2024). *Streamlining the translation of the NIH Toolbox® cognition domain*. NIH Toolbox® Assessments Conference, Bethesda, MD.

Hartshorne, J. K., & Germine, L. T. (2015). When does cognitive functioning peak? The asynchronous rise and fall of different cognitive abilities across the life span. *Psychological Science, 26*(4), 433–443. https://doi.org/10.1177/0956797614567339

Helmstaedter, C., & Elger, C. E. (2009). Chronic temporal lobe epilepsy: A neurodevelopmental or progressively dementing disease? *Brain, 132*(10), 2822–2830. https://doi.org/10.1093/brain/awp182

Hook, J. N., & Giella, A. K. (2023). *National Institutes of Health (NIH) Toolbox® V3 administration manual*. Toolbox Assessments, Inc.

Hook, J. N., Kuentzel, J. G., Hodges, E. K., Hodges, E. K., Kuentzel, J. G., & Hook, J. N. (2022). Attention deficit hyperactivity disorder. In E. K. Hodges, J. G. Kuentzel, & J. N. Hook (Eds.), *Pediatric neuropsychology: Perspectives from the ambulatory care setting* (pp. 29–59). Routledge Taylor & Francis Group.

Jack, C. R., Jr., Bennett, D. A., Blennow, K., Carrillo, M. C., Dunn, B., Haeberlein, S. B., … Sperling, R. (2018). NIA-AA research framework: Toward a biological definition of Alzheimer's disease. *Alzheimer's & Dementia, 14*(4), 535–562. https://doi.org/10.1016/j.jalz.2018.02.018

Kehagia, A. A., Barker, R. A., & Robbins, T. W. (2010). Neuropsychological and clinical heterogeneity of cognitive impairment and dementia in patients with Parkinson's disease. *Lancet Neurology, 9*(12), 1200–1213. https://doi.org/10.1016/S1474-4422(10)70212-X

Kenworthy, L., Yerys, B. E., Anthony, L. G., & Wallace, G. L. (2008). Understanding executive control in autism spectrum disorders in the lab and in the real world. *Neuropsychology Review, 18*(4), 320–338. https://doi.org/10.1007/s11065-008-9077-7

Kessler, R. C., Berglund, P., Demler, O., Jin, R., Merikangas, K. R., & Walters, E. E. (2005). Lifetime prevalence and age-of-onset distributions of DSM-IV disorders in the National Comorbidity Survey Replication. *Archives of General Psychiatry, 62*(6), 593–602. https://doi.org/10.1001/archpsyc.62.6.593

Kofler, M. J., Rapport, M. D., Bolden, J., Sarver, D. E., Raiker, J. S., & Alderson, R. M. (2011). Working memory deficits and social problems in children with ADHD. *Journal of Abnormal Child Psychology, 39*, 805–817. https://doi.org/10.1007/s10802-011-9492-8

LaForte, E. M., Hook, J. N., & Giella, A. K. (2024). *National Institutes of Health (NIH) Toolbox® V3 technical manual.* Toolbox Assessments, Inc.

Langlois, J. A., Rutland-Brown, W., & Thomas, K. E. (2006). *Traumatic brain injury in the United States: Emergency department visits, hospitalizations, and deaths.* CDC.

Lin, F. R., Yaffe, K., Xia, J., Xue, Q. L., Harris, T. B., Purchase-Helzner, E., … Health ABC Study Group. (2013). Hearing loss and cognitive decline in older adults. *JAMA Internal Medicine, 173*(4), 293–299. https://doi.org/10.1001/jamainternmed.2013.1868

Livingston, G., Huntley, J., Sommerlad, A., Ames, D., Ballard, C., Banerjee, S., Brayne, C., Burns, A., Cohen-Mansfield, J., Cooper, C., Costafreda, S. G., Dias, A., Fox, N., Gitlin, L. N., Howard, R. H., Kales, H. C., Kivimäki, M., Larson, E. B., Ogunniyi, A., …, & Mukadam, N. (2020). Dementia prevention, intervention, and care: 2020 report of the Lancet Commission. *The Lancet, 396*(10248), 413–446. https://doi.org/10.1016/S0140-6736(20)30367-6

Maenner, M. J., Shaw, K. A., Bakian, A. V., Bilder, D. A., Durkin, M. S., Esler, A. Furnier, S. M., Hallas, L., Hall-Lande, J., Hudson, A., Hughes, M. M., Patrick, M., Pierce, K., Poynter, J. N., Salinas, A., Shenouda, J., Vehorn, A., Warren, Z., Constantino, J. N., …, & Cogswell, M. E. (2021). Prevalence and characteristics of autism spectrum disorder among children aged 8 years—Autism and developmental disabilities monitoring network, 11 sites, United States, 2018. *MMWR Surveillance Summaries, 70*(11), 1–16. https://doi.org/10.15585/mmwr.ss7011a1

Manly, J. J. (2008). Critical issues in cultural neuropsychology: Profit from diversity. *Neuropsychology Review, 18*(3), 179–183. https://doi.org/10.1007/s11065-008-9068-8

McCrea, M., Hammeke, T., Olsen, G., Leo, P., & Guskiewicz, K. (2004). Unreported concussion in high school football players. *Clinical Journal of Sport Medicine, 14*(1), 13–17.

McInnes, K., Friesen, C. L., MacKenzie, D. E., Westwood, D. A., & Boe, S. G. (2017). Mild traumatic brain injury (mTBI) and chronic cognitive impairment: A scoping review. *Neuroscience & Biobehavioral Reviews, 84*, 131–148. https://doi.org/10.1371/journal.pone.0174847

McKenzie, F. J., Drayton, A., Shields, R. H., Dakopolos, A., Glassman, D., Kaat, A., Coleman, J., Thompson, T., Sansone, S., Riley, K., Berry-Kravis, E., Gershon, R. C., & Hessl, D. (2023). *National Institutes of Health Toolbox® V3 cognition battery supplemental administration manual for intellectual and developmental disabilities: A guide on administration and scoring standards* [Supplemental material]. NIH Toolbox. https://nihbabytoolbox.org/wp-content/uploads/2023/07/NIHTB-V3-CB-IDD-Supplemental-Manual_07052023.pdf

Merikangas, K. R., Akiskal, H. S., Angst, J., Greenberg, P. E., Hirschfeld, R. M., Petukhova, M., & Kessler, R. C. (2007). Lifetime and 12-month prevalence of bipolar spectrum disorder in the National Comorbidity Survey Replication. *Archives of General Psychiatry, 64*(5), 543–552. https://doi.org/10.1001/archpsyc.64.5.543

Miller, L. J., Anzalone, M. E., Lane, S. J., Cermak, S. A., & Osten, E. T. (2007). Concept evolution in sensory integration: A proposed nosology for diagnosis. *American Journal of Occupational Therapy, 61*(2), 135–140. https://doi.org/10.5014/ajot.61.2.135

Moran, T. P. (2016). Anxiety and working memory capacity: A meta-analysis and narrative review. *Psychological Bulletin, 142*(8), 831–864. https://doi.org/10.1037/bul0000051

National Institute of Mental Health (NIMH). (2022). *Major depression.* https://www.nimh.nih.gov/health/statistics/major-depression.shtml

Norbury, C. F., Gooch, D., Wray, C., Baird, G., Charman, T., Simonoff, E., … Pickles, A. (2016). The impact of nonverbal ability on prevalence and clinical presentation of language disorder: Evidence from a population study. *Journal of Child Psychology and Psychiatry, 57*(11), 1247–1257. https://doi.org/10.1111/jcpp.12573

Nys, G. M. S., van Zandvoort, M. J. E., de Kort, P. L. M., van der Worp, H. B., Jansen, B. P. W., Algra, A., … Kappelle, L. J. (2005). The prognostic value of domain-specific cognitive abilities in acute first-ever stroke. *Neurology, 64*(5), 821–827. https://doi.org/10.1212/01.WNL.0000152984.28420.5A

O'Brien, J. T., & Thomas, A. (2015). Vascular dementia. *The Lancet, 386*(10004), 1698–1706. https://doi.org/10.1016/S0140-6736(15)00463-8

Pauli-Pott, U., & Becker, K. (2011). Neuropsychological basic deficits in preschoolers at risk for ADHD: A meta-analysis. *Clinical Psychology Review, 31*(4), 626–637. https://doi.org/10.1016/j.cpr.2011.02.005

Petersen, R. C., Roberts, R. O., Knopman, D. S., Boeve, B. F., Geda, Y. E., Ivnik, R. J., … Jack, C. R. (2009). Mild cognitive impairment: Ten years later. *Archives of Neurology, 66*(12), 1447–1455. https://doi.org/10.1001/archneurol.2009.266

Peterson, R. L., Pennington, B. F., & Olson, R. K. (2013). Subtypes of developmental dyslexia: Testing the predictions of the dual-route and connectionist frameworks. *Cognition, 126*(1), 20–38. https://doi.org/10.1016/j.cognition.2012.08.007

Remote Administration Guidelines for the NIH Toolbox®: Response to COVID-19. (2021, January 25). *Remote administration guidelines for the NIH Toolbox®: Response to COVID-19.* https://resources.nihtoolbox.org/wp-content/uploads/2022/05/COVID-19-Remote-Administration-Guidelines-01.25.2021.pdf

Rock, P. L., Roiser, J. P., Riedel, W. J., & Blackwell, A. D. (2014). Cognitive impairment in depression: A systematic review and meta-analysis. *Psychological Medicine, 44*(10), 2029–2040. https://doi.org/10.1017/S0033291713002535

Schaie, K. W. (2005). *Developmental influences on adult intelligence: The Seattle longitudinal study.* Oxford University Press.

Semkovska, M., Quinlivan, L., O'Grady, T., Johnson, R., Collins, A., O'Connor, J., … Gload, T. (2019). Cognitive function following a major depressive episode: A systematic review and meta-analysis. *The Lancet Psychiatry, 6*(10), 851–861. https://doi.org/10.1016/S2215-0366(19)30291-3

Shevell, M., Ashwal, M. D., Donley, D., Flint, J., Gingold, M., Hirtz, D., … Practice Committee of the Child Neurology Society. (2003). Practice parameter: Evaluation of the child with global developmental delay. *Neurology, 60*(3), 367–380.

Slotkin, J. (Ed.). (2024). *Mobile toolbox technical manual.* Toolbox Assessments.

Slotkin, J., Nowinski, C., & Gershon, R. C. (2021). Validation of NIH toolbox cognitive assessments in remote settings. *Neuropsychology Review, 31*(4), 507–523.

Squeglia, L. M., Jacobus, J., & Tapert, S. F. (2009). The influence of substance use on adolescent brain development. *Clinical EEG and Neuroscience, 40*(1), 31–38.

Substance Abuse and Mental Health Services Administration (SAMHSA). (2021). *Key substance use and mental health indicators in the United States: Results from the 2020 National Survey on Drug Use and Health.* https://www.samhsa.gov/data/

Turken, A. U., Whitfield-Gabrieli, S., Bammer, R., Baldo, J. V., Dronkers, N. F., & Gabrieli, J. D. E. (2008). Cognitive processing speed and the structure of white matter pathways: Convergent evidence from normal variation and lesion studies. *NeuroImage, 42*(2), 1032–1044. https://doi.org/10.1016/j.neuroimage.2008.03.057

Tysnes, O. B., & Storstein, A. (2017). Epidemiology of Parkinson's disease. *Journal of Neural Transmission, 124*(8), 901–905. https://doi.org/10.1007/s00702-017-1686-y

U.S. Access Board. (2017). *Revised 508 standards and 255 guidelines.* https://www.access-board.gov/ict/

Visser, S. N., Danielson, M. L., Bitsko, R. H., Holbrook, J. R., Kogan, M. D., Ghandour, R. M., ... Blumberg, S. J. (2014). Trends in the parent-report of health care provider-diagnosed and medicated attention-deficit/hyperactivity disorder: United States, 2003–2011. *Journal of the American Academy of Child & Adolescent Psychiatry, 53*(1), 34–46. https://doi.org/10.1016/j.jaac.2013.09.001

Wallace, A., & Bucks, R. S. (2013). Memory and obstructive sleep apnea: A meta-analysis. *Sleep, 36*(2), 203–220. https://doi.org/10.5665/sleep.2374

Weintraub, S., Dikmen, S. S., Heaton, R. K., Tulsky, D. S., Zelazo, P. D., Bauer, P. J., Carlozzi, N. E., Slotkin, J., Blitz, D., Wallner-Allen, K., Fox, N. A., Beaumont, J. L., Mungas, D., Nowinski, C. J., Richler, J., Deocampo, J. A., Anderson, J. E., Manly, J. J., Borosh, B., ..., & Gershon, R. C. (2013). Cognition assessment using the NIH Toolbox. *Neurology, 80*(11 Suppl 3), S54–S64. https://doi.org/10.1212/WNL.0b013e3182872ded

Yeates, K. O., Ris, M. D., & Taylor, H. G. (2000). *Pediatric neuropsychology: Research, theory, and practice.* The Guilford Press.

Zelazo, P. D., Anderson, J. E., Richler, J., Wallner-Allen, K., Beaumont, J. L., & Weintraub, S. (2013). NIH Toolbox Cognition Battery: Measuring executive function and attention. *Monographs of the Society for Research in Child Development, 78*(4), 16–33.

Seven

CLINICAL AND RESEARCH CASE CONCEPTUALIZATIONS USING THE NIH TOOLBOX® COGNITION TESTS

Julie N. Hook
Amy K. Giella
Abigail B. Sivan

INTRODUCTION

Contemporary neuropsychological assessment balances multiple competing demands: psychometric rigor, clinical utility, developmental appropriateness, cultural fairness, and practical efficiency. The NIH Toolbox Cognition tests address these requirements through a theoretically grounded, empirically validated measurement system applicable across the human lifespan (Weintraub et al., 2013). Moving beyond traditional fixed batteries that prioritize comprehensive depth, the NIH Toolbox offers a focused assessment of core cognitive domains with demonstrated sensitivity to both typical developmental and clinical deviation.

The transition from a theoretical framework to clinical applications requires understanding how standardized metrics inform real-world decision-making. Cognitive test scores, while quantitatively important, gain meaning only through integration with multiple data streams, such as behavioral observation, developmental trajectory, symptom history, functional impact, and contextual factors. This integrative approach is fundamental to neuropsychological practice and transforms numerical data into clinically actionable formulations.

The cases presented in this chapter exemplify this integration. Each follows a consistent organizational structure that mirrors clinical reasoning and includes (1) characterization of typical symptom presentation for the relevant condition, (2) detailed background including developmental and medical history, (3) systematic behavioral observation during assessment, (4) presentation of NIH Toolbox Cognition test performance, and (4) interpretive synthesis culminating in (5) specific recommendations. This structure reflects how professionals work, by gathering information systematically, observing carefully, testing strategically, and synthesizing thoughtfully.

Several interpretive principles recur across these presentations and are reviewed here:

1. **Pattern recognition over isolated scores:** Individual test scores, while informative, are rarely the sole determinant in a diagnosis. Instead, patterns across multiple measures reveal cognitive architecture. For example, a patient showing strong vocabulary skills alongside weak working memory presents differently than one showing uniformly low scores, despite potentially similar single-test results (e.g., poor working memory score).
2. **Developmental calibration:** The same numerical score carries different clinical significance depending on age, educational background, and expected developmental trajectory. For instance, declining memory skills in a 75-year-old require different interpretation than similar performance in a 45-year-old.
3. **Neural systems thinking:** Cognitive deficits reflect disruption in specific brain networks, such as the frontal-executive circuits, temporal-limbic memory systems, subcortical processing networks, and parietal attention systems. Mapping cognitive patterns to neural substrates aids in differential diagnosis and treatment planning.
4. **Convergence and consilience:** Diagnostic confidence increases when multiple data sources point toward the same conclusion. When cognitive testing, behavioral observation, symptom history, and functional impairment all converge, clinical formulations become more defensible. Discrepancies between data sources can be equally important and can signal the need for additional investigation.
5. **Functional significance:** Test scores matter because they predict and explain real-world functioning, such as academic performance, occupational achievement, success in independent living, and quality of life. Thus, clinical assessment may serve the function of helping individuals understand cognitive strengths and weaknesses to optimize outcomes.

The cases selected represent prototypical rather than unusual presentations. While every individual brings unique characteristics, certain patterns recur with sufficient frequency to merit recognition as distinct clinical phenotypes. These cases, while entirely fictional, reflect collective clinical experience and are designed to illustrate principles applicable to similar presentations encountered in practice.

CASE ONE: ATTENTION REGULATION DIFFICULTIES IN MIDDLE CHILDHOOD

Typical Clinical Presentation

Attention-deficit hyperactivity disorder (ADHD) affects approximately 5%–7% of school-age children, conceptualized as fundamentally an executive function disorder involving impaired cognitive control and self-regulation (Hook et al., 2022). Core symptoms cluster into recognizable patterns, including difficulty sustaining attention during effortful tasks, apparent forgetfulness, organizational failures, physical restlessness, impulsive responding, and difficulty waiting turns. That is, ADHD is distinguished from normal variations in attention and activity by the degree, pervasiveness, and functional impact of symptoms. Individuals with ADHD demonstrate these behaviors with sufficient frequency, intensity, and cross-situational consistency to cause measurable impairment in daily functioning, rather than transient or context-specific difficulties.

Executive function deficits represent the cognitive substrate. Meta-analyses demonstrate significant impairment across working memory, inhibitory control, cognitive flexibility, and planning, with effect sizes in the medium-to-large range (Friedman et al., 2017; Pievsky & McGrath, 2018). Working memory deficits deserve particular emphasis given robust replication and functional significance.

Rapid Reference 7.1

Working Memory is the capacity to hold and manipulate information, and this underlies the ability to follow multistep instructions, complete complex tasks, and sustain goal-directed behavior.

Neurobiologically, ADHD reflects disruption across multiple brain networks. Structural neuroimaging reveals volumetric reductions in frontal regions, basal ganglia, and cerebellum (Hoogman et al., 2019). Functional imaging demonstrates reduced dorsolateral prefrontal activation during executive tasks, altered frontoparietal connectivity, and insufficient default mode network suppression (Cortese et al., 2021). Dopamine and norepinephrine dysregulation in frontostriatal circuits contributes substantially to symptom expression, explaining stimulant medication efficacy (Rubia et al., 2014).

Background Summary

Matthew, a nine-year, three-month-old fourth grader, was referred for testing due to repeated teacher concerns about classroom attention, lack of work completion, and difficulties with organization despite apparent intellectual capability. Teachers describe him as "bright but scattered," and noted that he contributes insightfully during discussions yet fails to complete written work consistently. Academic underperformance relative to perceived ability prompted this screen of his cognitive abilities. Matthew's developmental history was unremarkable, and he met all his developmental milestones on time. Medical history includes routine childhood illnesses without complications. Family psychiatric history is significant, as his father has a history of ADHD in childhood with ongoing attention difficulties, and his mother suffers from generalized anxiety disorder. The patient's sleep, diet, and physical activity patterns are adequate. Matthew attends public school and lives with both parents and older sister, Carolann.

Assessment Observations

Matthew presented as articulate and socially appropriate with a sophisticated vocabulary, given his age. However, sustaining attention during testing required active engagement. He initially attended to instructions but frequently began scanning the room or fidgeting before the instructions concluded; this behavior necessitated redirection. He frequently fidgeted and repositioned himself during the evaluation. Task engagement varied considerably, as novel, game-like computerized tasks elicited better attention than other, more traditional paper-and-pencil forms.

Response style was marked by impulsivity, with Matthew frequently initiating responses before item presentation was complete. He required a reminder to slow down, after which and following a brief break, accuracy improved modestly. Frustration tolerance appeared moderately reduced, evidenced by visible signs of irritation during more challenging items; however, he remained responsive to encouragement and redirection. Speech, language, mood, and affect were age-appropriate. There was no indication during testing to suggest that his performance did not accurately reflect his true abilities (Figure 7.1).

Tests / Composites	Raw Score	Theta	Computed Score	Change-Sensitive Score	Age-Adjusted Standard Score	Age-Adjusted Standard Score SE	National Age-Adjusted %ile	Age- and Education-Adjusted T-Score
ORR	–	1.86	–	509	108	4	71	–
PV	–	1.55	–	512	114	6	83	–
Crystallized Composite	–	–	–	510	114	6	82	–
DCCS	–	–	0.57	478	78	6	8	–
Flanker	–	–	0.57	469	71	7	3	–
LSWM	8	-2.65	–	480	82	6	12	–
PC	51	-3.32	–	492	92	2	29	–
PSM Form A	–	4.98	–	490	94	4	34	–
Fluid Composite	–	–	–	482	76	11	5	–
Total Cognition Composite	–	–	–	496	93	7	32	–

Notes: DCCS = Dimensional Change Card Sort v3.1, Flanker = Flanker Inhibitory Control and Attention v3.1, LSWM = List Sorting Working Memory, ORR = Oral Reading Recognition, PC = Pattern Comparison Processing Speed, PSM Form A = Picture Sequence Memory Form A, PV = Picture Vocabulary.
Cells with "–" are intentionally blank.

Standard Score Profile

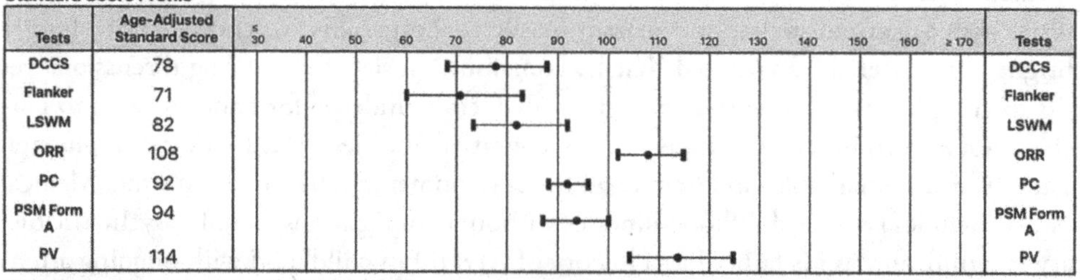

Notes: DCCS = Dimensional Change Card Sort v3.1, Flanker = Flanker Inhibitory Control and Attention v3.1, LSWM = List Sorting Working Memory, ORR = Oral Reading Recognition, PC = Pattern Comparison Processing Speed, PSM Form A = Picture Sequence Memory Form A, PV = Picture Vocabulary.
Profile ranges show the 90% confidence intervals.

Figure 7.1 Case One NIH Toolbox Score Profile.

Assessment Results

Interpretation

Matthew's profile reveals a large difference between knowledge-based abilities and executive control functions, which is characteristic of attention regulation disorders. His Crystalized Composite (Age-Adjusted Standard Score of 114, 82nd percentile) reflects well-developed vocabulary and verbal knowledge, while his Fluid Composite (Age-Adjusted Standard Score of 76, 5th percentile) indicates significant executive difficulty. This 38-point split occurs in fewer than 5% of typically developing children, representing a clinically meaningful difference (Casaletto et al., 2015).

> **CAUTION 7.1**
>
> Composite scores can mask clinically meaningful patterns. While composite scores provide convenient summary metrics, they can obscure the specific cognitive patterns essential for accurate diagnosis. A low average Fluid Composite could result from uniformly weak performance across all executive functions, or from severely impaired working memory with intact processing speed and cognitive flexibility, yet these patterns suggest entirely different diagnoses and interventions. Always examine individual subtest scores and their relationships before interpreting composites. The composite tells you there's a problem; the pattern tells you what the problem is.

Picture Vocabulary (PV) (Age-Adjusted Standard Score of 114, 83rd percentile) and Oral Reading Recognition (ORR) (Age-Adjusted Standard Score of 108, 71st percentile) are both high average, confirming strong verbal conceptual development and establishing baseline cognitive capacity. This preserved crystallized ability excludes global developmental delay. However, it likely creates a frustrating capability-performance gap for Matthew, such that he can acquire and demonstrate knowledge in optimal circumstances but struggles to access it independently in less structured environments.

Measure of his working memory shows impairment with List Sorting Working Memory (LSWM) (Age-Adjusted Standard Score of 82, 12th percentile), falling a standard deviation below expectations. This limitation likely contributes to his difficulty following multistep instructions, losing place during complex tasks, and organizational failures.

Results on Flanker Inhibitory Control and Attention (Flanker) (Age-Adjusted Standard Score of 71, 3rd percentile) show significantly reduced sustained selective attention and response inhibition. His performance revealed both slower response times and increased response variability. Of note, trial-to-trial inconsistency frequently emerges as one of the most sensitive ADHD markers, reflecting attentional fluctuations (Karalunas et al., 2014). Dimensional Change Card Sort (DCCS) (Age-Adjusted Standard Score of 78, 8th percentile) suggests difficulty when the task requires change or variability between activities.

Importantly, Pattern Comparison Processing Speed (Age-Adjusted Standard Score of 92, 29th percentile) falls within normal limits, indicating Matthew can process information efficiently when properly focused. This distinguishes his presentation from conditions where generalized slowing predominates. Picture Sequence Memory (PSM) (Age-Adjusted Standard Score of 94, 34th percentile) similarly documents intact episodic memory, indicating apparent "forgetfulness" likely reflects attention failures during encoding rather than true memory dysfunction.

Matthew's overall pattern of difficulties in working memory, inhibitory control, and cognitive flexibility, in the context of preserved processing speed and memory, aligns with current published understanding of ADHD cognitive test profiles (Pievsky & McGrath, 2018). These findings are reflective of frontostriatal network disruptions with relative preservation of temporal memory systems.

Results suggest that Matthew meets DSM-5-TR criteria for Attention-Deficit/Hyperactivity Disorder, Combined Presentation (314.01/F90.2), supported by his chronic pervasive symptoms across settings, symptom onset before age 12, clear functional impairment, characteristic cognitive profile, and family history.

Recommendations

- **Academic:** Matthew should have a Section 504 plan implemented to include preferential seating closer to the teacher and away from distractors, frequent breaks, extended time on tests (1.5x), visual supports when possible, and organizational systems. Teacher consultation regarding evidence-based ADHD management would be helpful to ensure they understand the implementation of this plan and can comment on what may be possible within the classroom.
- **Home-based:** Matthew's parents would benefit from evidence-based programs focusing on positive attention, clear expectations, and effective reinforcement (see Sibley et al., 2016). Programs like these typically emphasize structured homework routines with interval-based work periods and external organizational support.
- **Medical:** Given symptom severity and functional impairment, medication evaluation is appropriate. Referral to his pediatrician or to a child psychiatrist would be warranted to see if a trial of stimulant medication is indicated.
- **Monitoring:** Continued monitoring of Matthew's functioning is recommended through regular parent–teacher communication and periodic behavioral rating scales. Collaboration between home and school environments will help track changes in attention, organization, and emotional regulation over time. A repeat screen of his functioning is recommended in about 12 months to evaluate cognitive development, executive functioning, and treatment response. Readministration of the NIH Toolbox Cognition tests is recommended at that time, utilizing change-sensitive scores (CSSs) to detect meaningful improvements or emerging difficulties.

CASE TWO: MILD TRAUMATIC BRAIN INJURY (mTBI) IN A COLLEGIATE ATHLETE

Typical Clinical Presentation

Mild traumatic brain injury represents the most common form of head injury, with cognitive symptoms including mental fog, slowed thinking, attention difficulties, and memory complaints (McCrea et al., 2003). Most individuals demonstrate substantial recovery within 7–10 days, though 10%–20% experience prolonged symptoms (Silverberg & Iverson, 2011). The characteristic cognitive profile involves selective processing speed impairment with relatively preserved memory and executive functions, which can be helpful in distinguishing mTBI from other conditions.

Pathophysiology involves a neurometabolic cascade following biomechanical forces including ionic flux disturbances, altered neurotransmission, reduced cerebral blood flow, and disrupted cellular metabolism (Giza & Hovda, 2014). White matter tracts and subcortical structures are particularly vulnerable, which explains the characteristic processing speed deficits. Furthermore, advanced imaging techniques (e.g., Diffusion Tensor Imaging) reveal subtle white matter disruption despite normal conventional neuroimaging (Shenton et al., 2012).

Common differential or contributing diagnoses to consider include post-traumatic stress, sleep disturbance, depression, anxiety, and suboptimal effort. Each of these diagnoses suggests different management approaches. The key discriminator for true mTBI cognitive impact is selective processing speed impairment with preserved higher-order functions and documented acute injury mechanism (Iverson et al., 2012).

Background Summary

Ricky, a 20-year-old Division II soccer player, presented for cognitive evaluation two weeks post-concussion sustained during competition when he was struck in the temporal region during a header attempt. He experienced momentary disorientation (<one minute) without loss of consciousness. Following the standard protocol, he was removed from play immediately. Over subsequent days, he developed persistent headaches, photophobia, phonophobia, and subjective "mental fog." He noticed particular difficulty reading textbooks and found himself rereading paragraphs without retention.

Rapid Reference 7.2

Photophobia: sensitivity or discomfort when exposed to light.
Phonophobia: sensitivity or discomfort when exposed to sound.

Medical history is unremarkable with no prior concussions. Brain MRI three days post-injury revealed no hemorrhage, contusion, or structural abnormality; these findings are consistent with uncomplicated mTBI where functional impairment exists despite normal structural imaging (Bigler & Maxwell, 2012). At the time of the evaluation, he was attending partial classes under gradual return-to-learn protocol.

Rapid Reference 7.3

No prior concussions is a positive prognostic indicator based on the literature (Iverson, 2005).

Assessment Observations

Ricky arrived appropriately dressed, polite, cooperative, and was fully orientated (×3). His processing speed, however, was noticeably deliberate with frequent three to five second pauses before responding to straightforward questions. Speech was coherent and goal-directed, but the rate was mildly reduced. Affect was neutral to mildly constricted though appropriate to context. He expressed understandable concern about academic performance and return-to-sport timeline but did not appear depressed or anxious.

Rapid Reference 7.4

Orientation refers to a person's awareness of key aspects of their surroundings and themselves. In clinical and neuropsychological contexts, it is typically assessed across three or four domains:

Orientation to person: Knowing who you are (name, age, personal identity).
Orientation to place: Knowing where you are (city, building, setting).
Orientation to time: Knowing the date, day of the week, season, or approximate time.

(Sometimes assessed) Orientation to situation: Understanding why you are in a given setting (e.g., "I'm here for a testing appointment").

Being "oriented ×3" means the person is oriented to person, place, and time, which indicates intact basic awareness and attention.

Motor behavior was unremarkable with no tremor, imbalance, or vestibular dysfunction observed. Attention fluctuated somewhat over the evaluation, with best focus during the beginning of the assessment and some increased fidgeting during the middle portion. He spontaneously requested a brief break during testing due to a developing headache; this can be common during sustained cognitive exertion post-concussion (Kontos et al., 2012). He appeared to put forth adequate effort on the assessment (Figure 7.2).

Assessment Results

Interpretation

Ricky's results show isolated processing speed inefficiency with otherwise intact cognitive abilities; these findings are consistent with the prototypical mTBI signature (Belanger et al., 2005). Pattern Comparison Processing Speed (Age-Adjusted Standard Score of 77, sixth percentile) represents a significant departure from expected premorbid functioning.

This difference between his impaired speed alongside relatively preserved episodic memory (Picture Sequence Memory; Age-Adjusted Standard Score of 90, 25th percentile), working memory (List Sorting Working Memory; Age-Adjusted Standard Score of 95, 38th percentile), and cognitive flexibility (Dimensional Change Card Sort;

Tests / Composites	Raw Score	Theta	Computed Score	Change-Sensitive Score	Age-Adjusted Standard Score	Age-Adjusted Standard Score SE	National Age-Adjusted %ile	Age- and Education-Adjusted T-Score
DCCS	–	–	1.07	493	80	6	9	–
Flanker	–	–	1.58	520	98	7	45	–
LSWM	14	1.03	–	513	95	6	38	–
PC	58	-2.4	–	500	77	2	6	–
PSM Form A	–	5.93	–	498	90	3	25	–
Fluid Composite	–	–	–	505	80	8	9	–

Notes: DCCS = Dimensional Change Card Sort v3.1, Flanker = Flanker Inhibitory Control and Attention v3.1, LSWM = List Sorting Working Memory, PC = Pattern Comparison Processing Speed, PSM Form A = Picture Sequence Memory Form A.
Cells with "–" are intentionally blank.

Standard Score Profile

Tests	Age-Adjusted Standard Score
DCCS	80
Flanker	98
LSWM	95
PC	77
PSM Form A	90

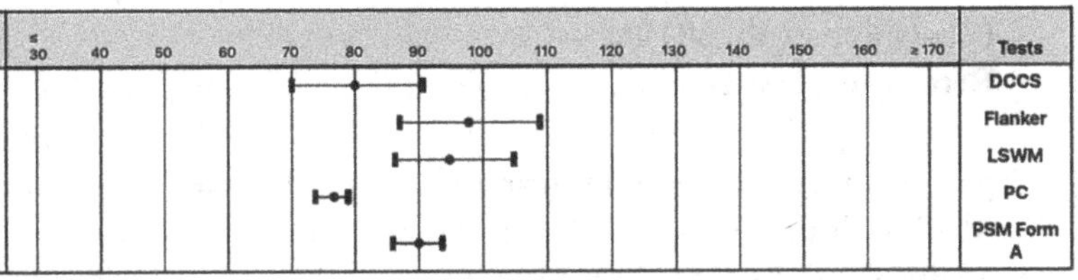

Notes: DCCS = Dimensional Change Card Sort v3.1, Flanker = Flanker Inhibitory Control and Attention v3.1, LSWM = List Sorting Working Memory, PC = Pattern Comparison Processing Speed, PSM Form A = Picture Sequence Memory Form A.
Profile ranges show the 90% confidence intervals.

Process Scores:

Tests	Raw Score	Median Response Time Per Item	Commission Errors	Omission Errors
DCCS	–	0.95	3	0
Flanker (Congruent Items)	–	0.52	0	–
Flanker (Incongruent Items)	–	0.71	–	–
Flanker	–	–	–	0
PC	–	0.89	–	–

Notes: DCCS = Dimensional Change Card Sort v3.1, Flanker = Flanker Inhibitory Control and Attention v3.1, PC = Pattern Comparison Processing Speed.
Cells with "–" are intentionally blank.

Figure 7.2 Case Two NIH Toolbox Score Profile.

Age-Adjusted Standard Score of 80, 9th percentile) reflects white matter tract vulnerability to biomechanical forces. Diffusion tensor imaging studies consistently demonstrate microstructural changes in corpus callosum, internal capsule, and frontal white matter following mTBI, manifesting functionally as slowed processing and reduced efficiency (Hulkower et al., 2013).

The relative preservation of Flanker (Age-Adjusted Standard Score of 98, 45th percentile) may seem contradictory but is actually common in mTBI. Ricky's accuracy was strong with few errors, but response time was slowed; the "accurate but slow" pattern typifying mTBI and differing from "fast but inaccurate" patterns in ADHD (Carmona et al., 2005).

Intact episodic memory and working memory indicate medial temporal structures and dorsolateral prefrontal-parietal networks supporting these functions sustained no significant injury. This preservation argues strongly against severe or diffuse traumatic brain injury and suggests a favorable recovery prognosis (Iverson, 2005).

Recommendations

- **Academic:** Extended time on exams (1.5×), allow lecture recordings, note-taking assistance, and reduced course load during weeks two to four post-injury. Progressive return-to-learn with 20–30-minute study blocks and mandatory rest breaks. Taper accommodations as symptoms improve based on cognitive retesting.
- **Symptom management:** Structured sleep (seven to nine hours nightly), consistent sleep–wake schedule, hydration, regular balanced meals, and limited recreational screen time. Physical therapy referral if vestibular symptoms emerge (Alsalaheen et al., 2010).
- **Return-to-play:** Gradual progression through five-stage protocol (aerobic exercise → sport-specific exercise → non-contact drills → full-contact practice → game play) with 24-hour minimum at each stage, advancing only if asymptomatic. Medical clearance required before contact activities (Patricios et al., 2018).
- **Monitoring:** Readminister NIH Toolbox at six weeks to document recovery using CSSs. If symptoms persist beyond six weeks, refer to a concussion specialist.

CASE THREE: COGNITIVE INEFFICIENCY IN MIDLIFE DEPRESSION

Typical Clinical Presentation

Major depressive disorder (MDD) is increasingly recognized as impacting cognition, with cognitive impairment representing a core feature affecting occupational and social functioning (Rock et al., 2014). Adults with MDD typically present with slowed processing speed, diminished attention, and reduced cognitive efficiency rather than frank memory loss, described subjectively as "mental cloudiness" or "thinking through molasses" (Snyder, 2013).

The cognitive profile typically includes psychomotor slowing (reduced processing speed), executive dysfunction (planning, organization, task initiation difficulties), attention deficits (sustained attention, distractibility), memory complaints (often reflecting attention failures during encoding rather than true retrieval deficits), and preserved crystallized knowledge (Castaneda et al., 2008). Severity varies considerably, with some patients experiencing impairment comparable to mild traumatic brain injury or mild cognitive impairment (MCI) (Bora et al., 2013).

Neurobiologically, depression involves disruption of prefrontal-striatal circuits (reduced dorsolateral prefrontal cortex activation correlating with executive dysfunction), anterior cingulate abnormalities (contributing to cognitive flexibility difficulties), hippocampal volume reduction (in chronic/recurrent depression), and white matter integrity disruption (Pizzagalli & Roberts, 2022). Serotonin, norepinephrine, and dopamine dysregulation can also contribute to cognitive symptoms.

Critical differential diagnosis distinguishes depression-related cognitive impairment from early neurodegenerative disease. Key differentiating features include acute onset temporally linked to mood episode, prominent subjective complaints potentially disproportionate to objective deficits, and improvement with treatment, which distinguishes depression from progressive neurodegenerative conditions (Butters et al., 2004).

Background Summary

Anna, a 44-year-old bilingual (English/Spanish) office administrator, reported six months of progressive forgetfulness, multitasking difficulty, and reduced energy. She has a 15-year history of recurrent MDD with the current episode beginning eight months ago, coinciding with work stress and her mother's cancer diagnosis. Current symptoms include pervasive low mood, anhedonia, reduced energy, hypersomnia (10–11 hours nightly), appetite increase with a 15-pound weight gain, concentration difficulty, and feelings of worthlessness. Patient Health Questionnaire-9 (PHQ-9; Kroenke et al., 2001) score of 18 (out of 27 points) indicates moderately severe depression.

Cognitive complaints qualitatively differ from prior episodes: slowed thinking ("brain moving through mud"), work task completion taking twice as long, multitasking impairment, word-finding difficulties, and forgetfulness. These changes significantly impacted work performance, with her supervisor noting slowed completion and missed deadlines after years of excellent evaluations. She feels intense shame about potentially losing her job.

Medical history includes controlled hypertension and hypothyroidism with recent normal thyroid function tests. She currently takes sertraline 150 mg daily for five months with partial mood improvement but persistent cognitive complaints. Recent workup including brain MRI, comprehensive metabolic panel, and vitamin levels was unremarkable. Family history is significant for depression but not dementia.

Assessment Observations

Anna appeared alert and cooperative but exhibited reduced spontaneity and flattened affect. Speech was soft and notably slowed with frequent 5–10 second pauses before responding; pauses appeared to reflect slowed cognitive processing rather than guardedness. She occasionally became tearful when discussing work performance concerns. Speech contained occasional word-finding pauses, though she would circumlocute or substitute less precise words when unable to retrieve targets.

Comprehension appeared intact for straightforward conversation, though she required repetition for complex multistep instructions. Her effort and engagement appeared adequate throughout testing. Psychomotor slowing was evident in her movements and task initiation. Performance validity remained adequate, supporting obtained results as valid representation of current functioning despite attention and processing challenges.

Tests / Composites	Raw Score	Theta	Computed Score	Change-Sensitive Score	Age-Adjusted Standard Score	Age-Adjusted Standard Score SE	National Age-Adjusted %ile	Age- and Education-Adjusted T-Score
Flanker	–	–	1.12	497	87	6	19	41
LSWM	12	-0.2	–	502	93	6	32	44
PC	57	-2.53	–	499	87	2	19	42
PSM Form A	–	6.12	–	500	101	2	52	51
PV	–	3.89	–	533	108	5	71	54

Notes: Flanker = Flanker Inhibitory Control and Attention v3.1, LSWM = List Sorting Working Memory, PC = Pattern Comparison Processing Speed, PSM Form A = Picture Sequence Memory Form A, PV = Picture Vocabulary.
Cells with "–" are intentionally blank.

Standard Score Profile

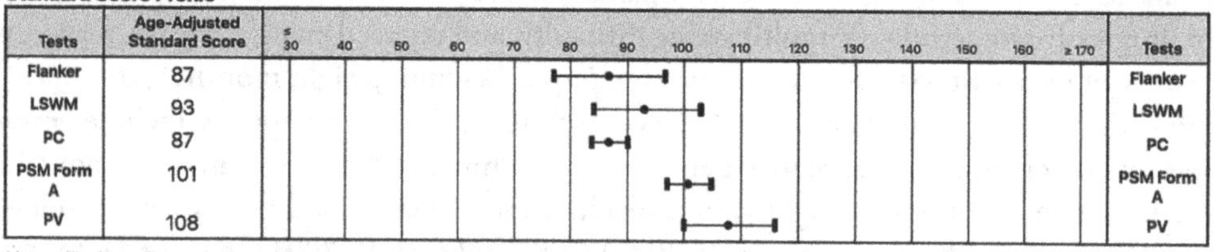

Notes: Flanker = Flanker Inhibitory Control and Attention v3.1, LSWM = List Sorting Working Memory, PC = Pattern Comparison Processing Speed, PSM Form A = Picture Sequence Memory Form A, PV = Picture Vocabulary.
Profile ranges show the 90% confidence intervals.

Figure 7.3 Case Three NIH Toolbox Score Profile.

Anna reported that while she speaks both English and Spanish, she would prefer testing in English as this is the language she uses most often (Figure 7.3).

> **CAUTION 7.2**
>
> Bilingualism can impact test interpretation. For bilingual individuals, always clarify which language they use most frequently and consider testing in their dominant language. Scores on tests of vocabulary and other language-based tests may underestimate cognitive capacity when tested in a non-dominant language.

Assessment Results

Interpretation

Anna's profile demonstrates slowed processing and mild working memory inefficiency with preserved language and learning. This is consistent with cognitive slowing typical of depression (Rock et al., 2014; Snyder, 2013). Pattern Comparison (Age-Adjusted Standard Score of 87, 19th percentile) shows marked psychomotor slowing, while PV (108, 71st percentile) shows preserved ability. This pattern suggests frontal-striatal circuit disruption affecting psychomotor speed and cognitive control; these circuits are particularly sensitive to depressive pathophysiology.

List Sorting Working Memory (Age-Adjusted Standard Score of 93, 32nd percentile) falls in the low-average range, reflecting the mild executive inefficiency common in depression. However, Picture Sequence Memory (Age-Adjusted Standard Score of 101, 52nd percentile) documents intact encoding and retrieval. This finding suggests that Anna can learn and remember new information. Her subjective "memory problems" likely reflect attention failures during initial learning due to reduced processing speed and working memory rather than fundamental memory system dysfunction.

The absence of progressive decline, preserved vocabulary, and strong insight argues against early neurodegenerative processes. The pattern reflects a functional cognitive slowing that typically improves with mood treatment rather than the structural brain changes characteristic of dementia (Butters et al., 2004). Anna reported that her bilingual proficiency remained intact in both English and Spanish, further supporting functional rather than degenerative etiology.

From a neuroanatomical perspective, this profile implicates disruption primarily in frontal-striatal circuits mediating psychomotor speed and cognitive control, with relative preservation of medial temporal lobe memory systems and posterior cortical language networks. This selective pattern aligns with neuroimaging findings in depression showing reduced prefrontal activation and altered frontal-striatal connectivity (Pizzagalli & Roberts, 2022).

Recommendations

- **Medical/psychiatric:** Optimize antidepressant regimen with psychiatrist; consider adjunctive agents targeting cognition (e.g., bupropion augmentation). Screen again for thyroid dysfunction and for sleep apnea if not recently evaluated. Consider psychiatric consultation for medication adjustment or augmentation strategies.
- **Cognitive-behavioral:** Implement behavioral activation to improve initiation and engagement. Employ external aids (structured checklists, digital reminders, simplified task breakdowns) to reduce cognitive load. Cognitive-behavioral therapy focusing on executive strategy training may benefit (Herrera-Guzmán et al., 2010).
- **Workplace:** Request flexible scheduling or reduced cognitive demands during particularly symptomatic periods if possible. Break large projects into smaller, manageable segments. Use external organization tools and frequent breaks during sustained cognitive work.
- **Monitoring:** Reassess cognition with NIH Toolbox 8–12 weeks posttreatment adjustment to objectively quantify recovery using CSSs. Combined with the NIH Toolbox Emotion Battery, clinicians can map cognition-emotion interactions supporting integrated treatment (Rock et al., 2014).

CASE FOUR: EARLY COGNITIVE DECLINE IN AN OLDER ADULT

Typical Clinical Presentation

MCI involves cognitive decline exceeding normal aging expectations while functional independence remains largely preserved. Amnestic MCI, the most common subtype, features memory difficulties as the predominant complaint. For example, patients frequently repeat questions, misplace items, experience reduced recall of recent events, and suffer from word-finding issues (Petersen et al., 2014). For MCI patients, their insight typically remains preserved in early stages; this preserved ability is one way in which MCI can be distinguished from dementia.

At times, it can be difficult to differentiate MCI from normal cognitive aging. While both can involve some memory changes, MCI-associated memory impairment is typically significant enough that it is an apparent decline on standardized testing, falling about 1–1.5 standard deviations below age expectations; notably, some researchers use this threshold to assist in distinguishing expected variation from pathological change (Jak et al., 2009). Informant reports from a spouse or friend are also helpful when possible, to better assess if they too see an apparent change.

Neurobiologically, amnestic MCI is frequently the prodromal phase to Alzheimer's disease. Neuropathological studies demonstrate that most individuals meeting MCI criteria show Alzheimer's pathology (e.g., amyloid plaques, neurofibrillary tangles) on autopsy, but not to the degree that would warrant a dementia diagnosis (Jack et al., 2018). In addition, neuroimaging results show hippocampal atrophy and temporoparietal hypometabolism, which are characteristic of early Alzheimer's disease (Chételat et al., 2020). On average, approximately 10%–15% of individuals with MCI experience symptom progression to dementia each year. Some patients remain clinically stable or even revert to normal cognition, particularly if cognitive difficulties are secondary to depression, medication effects, sleep disturbance, or other reversible factors.

Differential diagnosis requires careful consideration of normal aging, depression, medication effects, sleep disorders, vitamin deficiencies, thyroid dysfunction, and other medical conditions that can impair memory. Depression deserves particular attention as it frequently co-occurs with MCI and produces overlapping symptoms; both involve memory complaints, slowed thinking, and reduced cognitive efficiency. Key differentiators include depression's acute onset, prominence of mood symptoms, and cognitive improvement with antidepressant treatment (Butters et al., 2004).

Background Summary

Dr. Butler, a 75-year-old retired physicist, was referred to a memory disorders clinic for evaluation after he complained to his internist of progressive memory loss over the last two years and received 24 out of 30 points on the Mini-Mental State Exam (Folstein et al., 1975). He described increasing reliance on written reminders, difficulty recalling names of acquaintances, and occasional disorientation regarding appointment times despite previously managing complex schedules without assistance. His wife corroborated these concerns, noting he frequently asks repeated questions, particularly about upcoming plans, and sometimes forgets conversations from the previous day.

Dr. Butler remains functionally independent, as he manages personal finances, drives without incident, maintains social engagements, and lives independently with his wife. However, he has begun relying heavily on compensatory strategies, such as maintaining detailed daily schedules, using smartphone reminders extensively, and keeping written notes for important information. He expresses frustration with these changes, stating he "used to remember everything effortlessly."

In terms of education and occupation, Dr. Butler earned a PhD in physics from the University of Michigan and enjoyed a successful 40-year career conducting theoretical physics research. He published extensively, mentored graduate students, and received recognition for his contributions. His wife describes him as having had exceptional intellectual abilities throughout their 50-year marriage; she said he is "the smartest person I've ever known," making his current memory difficulties particularly striking by contrast.

Medical history includes well-controlled hypertension (Lisinopril 10 mg daily) and hyperlipidemia (Atorvastatin 20 mg daily) without a history of stroke, transient ischemic attack, or cardiovascular events. He underwent prostate cancer treatment five years ago (radiation therapy) and is currently in remission. He takes no medications with known cognitive effects. A recent comprehensive medical evaluation, including vitamin B12, folate, thyroid function, and metabolic panel, documented no abnormalities. Brain MRI revealed mild bilateral hippocampal volume loss and scattered periventricular white matter hyperintensities consistent with chronic small vessel ischemic changes; while these findings may be nonspecific, they are also not inconsistent with early neurodegenerative disease.

Family history is significant for Alzheimer's disease in his mother, who developed dementia in her late 70s and died at age 83. His father died at age 68 from a myocardial infarction without cognitive impairment. Two siblings (aged 72 and 70) remain cognitively intact.

Mood screening revealed mild depressive symptoms, as assessed by the Geriatric Depression Scale (Yesavage et al., 1983) score 8/15; he endorsed decreased interest in activities, reduced energy, and worry about memory problems. However, he denied pervasive sadness, hopelessness, suicidal ideation, or significant anhedonia. Sleep is adequate (seven to eight hours nightly) and there are no reported sleep disturbances (e.g., disordered breathing). He remains socially engaged, participating in book clubs and recreational tennis, though he notes some decreased enjoyment due to memory concerns.

Rapid Reference 7.5

Anhedonia refers to a reduced or absent capacity to experience pleasure, joy, or interest in activities that are typically enjoyable.

Assessment Observations

Dr. Butler arrived punctually for his evaluation, accompanied by his wife, appearing well-groomed and appropriately dressed. He was cooperative, engaged, and demonstrated excellent social graces throughout the assessment. His demeanor was pleasant, though he expressed mild concern regarding test performance. He made several self-deprecating comments about his memory, such as "I used to be able to remember phone numbers after hearing them once, and now I can barely remember my own phone number."

Rapport was easily established. His speech was fluent, grammatically complex, and reflected sophisticated vocabulary consistent with his educational background. He used technical terminology appropriately when describing his former research. No word-finding difficulties, paraphasias, or language comprehension problems were evident during conversational speech. His thought processes were linear and goal-directed.

Rapid Reference 7.6

Paraphasias are speech production errors involving the unintentional use of incorrect or distorted words or sounds. These may include the substitution of a word that sounds similar to the intended target (phonemic paraphasia) or one that is semantically related in meaning (semantic paraphasia).

During cognitive testing, however, subtle difficulties emerged. On learning trials requiring encoding of new information, Dr. Butler demonstrated effortful processing with visible concentration. After the word list presentation, he remarked, "I'm not sure I got all of those," showing awareness of encoding difficulties. He employed organizational strategies spontaneously (e.g., attempting to group words semantically and rehearse them aloud), which suggests preserved metacognitive awareness and compensatory strategy use.

On a delayed recall trial, he showed significant difficulty retrieving previously learned information despite recognition that items had been presented. He would say, "I know we talked about that, but I can't quite recall the word." This pattern of impaired free recall with preserved recognition that information was encountered suggests retrieval inefficiency rather than complete encoding failure, though retrieval deficits can also reflect consolidation problems.

CAUTION 7.3

High premorbid ability can mask early decline. Individuals with superior premorbid intellectual abilities often score in the "average" range even after significant cognitive decline. For example, a person with a 130 IQ who now tests at 110 has lost cognitive capacity despite a normal score. Always consider premorbid functioning when interpreting current test performance.

On more complex executive tasks requiring cognitive flexibility and abstract reasoning, he performed adequately, though more slowly than might be expected, given his superior premorbid intellectual abilities.

Attention and concentration appeared generally adequate during testing, with Dr. Butler maintaining focus across the evaluation. He did not appear distractible or demonstrate significant attention lapses. Processing speed was mildly reduced relative to age expectations but

Tests / Composites	Raw Score	Theta	Computed Score	Change-Sensitive Score	Age-Adjusted Standard Score	Age-Adjusted Standard Score SE	National Age-Adjusted %ile	Age- and Education-Adjusted T-Score
ORR	–	6.22	–	549	117	4	88	57
PV	–	5.44	–	547	116	4	85	56
Crystallized Composite	–	–	–	548	119	5	89	58
DCCS	–	–	1.13	495	90	6	25	44
Flanker	–	–	1.08	495	96	6	39	45
LSWM	10	-1.38	–	491	93	6	33	44
PC	45	-4.08	–	485	88	3	22	43
PSM Form A	–	-0.95	–	436	72	5	3	32
Fluid Composite	–	–	–	480	80	14	10	36
Total Cognition Composite	–	–	–	514	101	9	54	46
RAVLT	12	-1.5	–	477	78	5	8	34
RAVLT Delay	1	-2.71	–	472	72	20	3	36

Notes: DCCS = Dimensional Change Card Sort v3.1, Flanker = Flanker Inhibitory Control and Attention v3.1, LSWM = List Sorting Working Memory, ORR = Oral Reading Recognition, PC = Pattern Comparison Processing Speed, PSM Form A = Picture Sequence Memory Form A, PV = Picture Vocabulary, RAVLT = Rey Auditory Verbal Learning, RAVLT Delay = Rey Auditory Verbal Learning Delay.
Cells with "–" are intentionally blank.

Standard Score Profile

Tests	Age-Adjusted Standard Score
DCCS	90
Flanker	96
LSWM	93
ORR	117
PC	88
PSM Form A	72
PV	116
RAVLT	78
RAVLT Delay	72

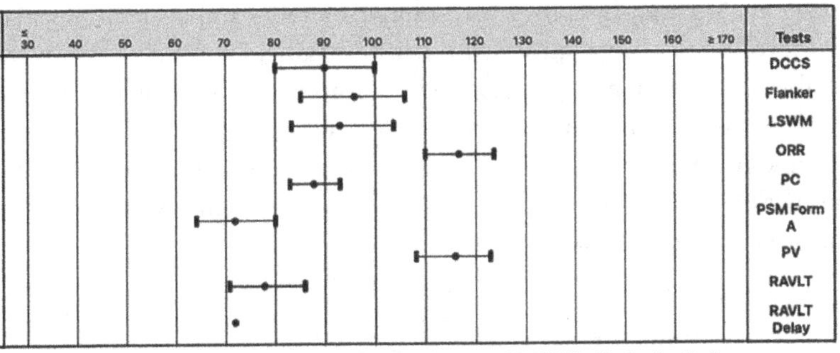

Notes: DCCS = Dimensional Change Card Sort v3.1, Flanker = Flanker Inhibitory Control and Attention v3.1, LSWM = List Sorting Working Memory, ORR = Oral Reading Recognition, PC = Pattern Comparison Processing Speed, PSM Form A = Picture Sequence Memory Form A, PV = Picture Vocabulary, RAVLT = Rey Auditory Verbal Learning, RAVLT Delay = Rey Auditory Verbal Learning Delay.
Profile ranges show the 90% confidence intervals.

Figure 7.4 Case Four NIH Toolbox Results.

not dramatically slowed. Mood remained stable throughout testing without significant frustration intolerance, though he did express disappointment when informed he had missed items.

Dr. Butler was motivated to perform well, and there was no apparent evidence of symptom exaggeration or suboptimal effort. The obtained scores, therefore, appear to represent valid estimates of his current cognitive functioning (Figure 7.4).

Assessment Results

Interpretation

Dr. Butler's cognitive profile reveals a clinically significant difference between crystallized and fluid cognitive abilities. His Crystallized Composite (Age-Adjusted Standard Score of 119, 89th percentile) falls in the high average range, documenting well-preserved verbal knowledge, vocabulary, and reading ability. This finding confirms his high premorbid intellectual functioning and indicates that semantic memory networks and language systems remain largely intact.

In contrast, his Fluid Composite (Age-Adjusted Standard Score of 80, 10th percentile) falls below average; a split this large between crystallized and fluid abilities occurs infrequently in healthy older adults (Casaletto et al., 2015). Thus, this pattern of well-preserved knowledge alongside impaired new learning and cognitive flexibility is consistent with early neurodegenerative disease, particularly Alzheimer's disease pathophysiology (Weintraub et al., 2018).

Based on a comprehensive evaluation including cognitive testing, clinical interview, informant report, neuroimaging findings, family history and exclusion of alternative etiologies, Dr. Butler meets diagnostic criteria for DSM-V-TR Mild Cognitive Impairment due to Alzheimer's Disease, Amnestic Presentation (G31.84). Evidence to support this diagnosis: (1) subjective cognitive complaints corroborated by reliable informant; (2) objective episodic memory impairment (>1.5 SD below age norms); (3) preserved functional independence in daily activities; (4) absence of dementia; (5) cognitive profile consistent with Alzheimer's pathophysiology (prominent memory impairment with crystallized preservation); (6) hippocampal atrophy on neuroimaging; (7) positive family history; (8) exclusion of alternative etiologies (depression, medications, and metabolic disorders).

The 'due to Alzheimer's disease' specifier reflects a high likelihood that Alzheimer's pathology underlies cognitive impairment, though definitive confirmation would require biomarker testing (amyloid PET or CSF analysis) demonstrating Alzheimer's pathological changes (Jack et al., 2018).

Recommendations

- **Medical:**
  - A neurology referral is recommended for a comprehensive dementia evaluation, which may include consideration of Alzheimer's disease biomarker testing (e.g., amyloid PET imaging or CSF analysis of amyloid-β42, total tau, and phosphorylated tau). Biomarker confirmation can help increase diagnostic confidence, guide therapeutic planning, inform prognosis, and, when appropriate, facilitate participation in clinical research or disease-modifying trials.
  - Given the MRI evidence of white matter changes, aggressive vascular risk management remains essential. Continued attention to blood pressure control, lipid management, and diabetes screening is advised, along with encouragement of a Mediterranean-style diet and regular physical activity. Optimizing vascular health may help slow cognitive decline, even in the context of Alzheimer's pathology (Livingston et al., 2020).
- **Lifestyle:**
  - **Exercise:** Weekly exercise has been found to improve cerebral blood flow and promote neuroplasticity, and is associated with slower cognitive decline in observational studies (Livingston et al., 2020).

- **Diet:** Emphasize vegetables, fruits, whole grains, legumes, fish, and olive oil, limiting red meat and processed foods. Mediterranean diet adherence has been found to be associated with reduced Alzheimer's risk and slower cognitive decline (Scarmeas et al., 2018).
- **Cognitive engagement:** Maintain intellectually stimulating activities, such as reading, puzzles, learning new skills, and social interactions. Dr. Butler is encouraged to continue with his book club and may also consider adding new cognitively challenging hobbies.
- **Social engagement:** Maintain robust social networks and meaningful relationships. Social isolation accelerates cognitive decline while engagement provides cognitive stimulation and emotional support.

- **Compensatory strategies and safety:**
  - Leverage Dr. Butler's preserved organizational abilities and metacognitive awareness to implement systematic compensatory strategies
  - Maintain detailed calendar systems (e.g., paper and electronic with alerts)
  - Use smartphone medication reminders
  - Establish designated locations for important items (e.g., keys, wallet, and glasses)
  - Implement written checklists for complex tasks
  - Continue external memory aids that he is already using successfully
  - Discuss driving safety proactively. While Dr. Butler currently drives without reported incidents, and cognitive testing does not suggest immediate concern, monitoring remains important. Consider a formal driving evaluation if the family expresses concerns or if cognitive decline progresses.
  - Review medication management systems, ensuring no missed doses. Consider a medication organizer or automated dispensing systems if adherence difficulties emerge.
- **Family education and support:**
  - Provide comprehensive education about MCI and Alzheimer's disease including:
    - Natural history and expected progression (annual 10%–15% dementia conversion risk)
    - Symptom management strategies
    - Available resources (e.g., Alzheimer's Association, local support groups, respite care)
    - Importance of advance care planning while capacity remains intact
  - Encourage completion of legal documents while Dr. Butler retains decision-making capacity:
    - Healthcare proxy and advance directives specifying treatment preferences
    - Durable power of attorney for financial management
    - Consider discussing long-term care preferences and financial planning

- **Monitoring:**
  - Schedule clinical follow-up in 6–12 months. Consider repeated NIH Toolbox administration to document the trajectory. If cognitive decline accelerates or functional impairment progresses from MCI to dementia, revisit pharmacological treatment options and adjust care planning accordingly. A dementia diagnosis may trigger additional interventions.

REVIEW AND ANALYSIS ACROSS CASES

Across the four cases, Matthew (ADHD), Ricky (mTBI), Anna (MDD), and Dr. Butler (MCI), consistent interpretive principles emerge that demonstrate how the NIH Toolbox enhances diagnostic understanding when embedded within a clinical evaluation.

Pattern Recognition Over Isolated Scores

> **CAUTION 7.4**
>
> An isolated low score rarely justifies a diagnosis. A single low test score, even a very low one, rarely justifies a clinical diagnosis without supporting evidence from multiple sources. Measurement error, temporary distraction, task-specific difficulties, or cultural factors can all produce spuriously low individual scores. Always look for a pattern across multiple measures before reaching diagnostic conclusions.

Individual test scores provide limited diagnostic value in isolation. Rather, patterns across multiple cognitive domains reveal the underlying cognitive architecture distinguishing between conditions with superficial similarities.

Matthew and Ricky both demonstrated selective fluid cognitive deficits with preserved crystallized abilities, yet their specific patterns differentiated their diagnoses. Matthew showed impaired working memory and inhibitory control with intact processing speed. This pattern is consistent with ADHD. Ricky, however, showed the opposite: isolated processing speed impairment with preserved working memory and executive control. This selective deficit, emerging acutely post-trauma and gradually improving, characterized his mTBI sequelae.

Anna and Dr. Butler both showed processing inefficiency, but accompanying deficits distinguished depression from neurodegeneration. Anna demonstrated slowed processing with executive inefficiency while memory remained relatively preserved. This pattern of psychomotor slowing with preserved memory is consistent with depression-related cognitive dysfunction. Dr. Butler showed relatively preserved processing efficiency with marked memory impairment. This memory-predominant pattern helped distinguish neurodegenerative disease from psychiatric etiologies.

Developmental Calibration

The same cognitive performance carries different clinical significance depending on developmental stage, educational attainment, and expected trajectory.

Working memory deficits illustrate this principle. Matthew's lower working memory score raised concerns about neurodevelopmental conditions affecting prefrontal cortex maturation (e.g., ADHD, learning disabilities). Identical performance at age 75 prompts different considerations, such as normal cognitive aging, vascular disease, medication effects, or early neurodegenerative change. The same numerical score at different ages generates entirely different differential diagnoses.

Other memory impairments similarly require developmental calibration. Dr. Butler's memory inefficiencies raised neurodegenerative concerns (i.e., a cardinal Alzheimer's disease feature). Equivalent memory impairment in Anna at age 44 would shift differential diagnosis toward depression (which she had), sleep disorders, medication effects, or metabolic disturbances before considering early-onset neurodegeneration.

Developmental context also shapes trajectory expectations. Matthew's ADHD symptoms may improve with prefrontal maturation through adolescence. Ricky's mTBI-related deficits showed expected recovery as white matter inflammation resolved. Anna's depression-related dysfunction should resolve with treatment. Dr. Butler's MCI represents progressive deterioration, with decline rate informing prognosis and treatment urgency.

Neural Systems Thinking

Cognitive deficits reflect disruption in specific brain networks. Mapping patterns onto neural substrates enhances differential diagnosis and treatment planning.

Matthew's executive deficits, including impaired working memory, inhibitory control, and cognitive flexibility, alongside preserved processing speed, mapped onto frontoparietal network dysfunction characteristic of ADHD. Disruption in dorsolateral prefrontal cortex and anterior cingulate altered dopaminergic neurotransmission and likely contributed to this profile. Preserved processing speed suggested intact white matter and subcortical networks.

Ricky's isolated processing speed impairment reflected white matter and subcortical network disruption from traumatic axonal injury. This diffuse damage slowed information transmission while preserving grey matter structures (prefrontal cortex, medial temporal lobes). Gradual recovery aligned with resolution of white matter inflammation, guiding return-to-learn and return-to-play decisions.

Anna's psychomotor slowing reflected frontostriatal circuit dysfunction from depression-related neurochemical dysregulation. Her preserved memory and crystallized abilities, alongside impaired processing efficiency, suggested network dysfunction rather than structural damage, which suggests she should recover her cognitive functioning with effective treatment.

Dr. Butler's memory-predominant impairment is likely localized to medial temporal lobe structures vulnerable to early Alzheimer's pathology. His preserved processing speed and crystallized abilities, alongside prominent memory impairment characterized amnestic MCI, signaling high progression risk to Alzheimer's dementia.

Convergence and Consilience

Diagnostic confidence strengthens when multiple independent data sources point toward the same conclusion. Discrepancies signal the need for additional investigation.

Matthew's case demonstrated strong convergence. NIH Toolbox showed executive deficits, classroom observations revealed attention difficulties, academic records showed underachievement relative to potential, and developmental history documented early symptom onset. This convergence across cognitive testing, behavioral ratings, observations, academic records, and history created strong diagnostic confidence for ADHD.

Anna's case showed how discrepancies can be diagnostically informative. Her NIH Toolbox profile showed mild processing inefficiency with preserved memory. However, subjective cognitive complaints were more severe than objective findings, as she reported profound memory difficulties, yet episodic memory remained average on testing. This discrepancy pointed toward depression rather than neurological disease, where objective deficits typically match or exceed subjective awareness.

Dr. Butler's case also showed convergence. NIH Toolbox documented memory impairment, his wife reported daily functioning difficulties, and Dr. Butler reported concern. Further, his MRI showed atrophy. This multilevel convergence provided strong diagnostic confidence for MCI due to Alzheimer's disease.

Functional Significance

Cognitive test scores derive clinical importance from their relationship to real-world functioning, such as academic achievement, occupational performance, independent living, and quality of life.

Matthew's cognitive profile directly predicted academic struggles. Strong vocabulary indicated intellectual capacity to understand material, but working memory deficits impaired holding multistep instructions and organizing ideas during writing. Inhibitory control deficits reduced sustained focus and increased impulsive responding. These specific cognitive-functional linkages guided targeted interventions: accommodations addressing functional impairments (assignment checklists, extended time) and strategies teaching compensation (external memory aids, organizational systems).

Ricky's processing speed deficit, though numerically modest, produced significant functional impairment. Academically, completing assignments requires substantially more time despite understanding the material. Further, reduced processing speed can delay his reaction times and potentially increase injury risk on the soccer field. Understanding cognitive-functional relationships guided a graduated return with accommodations during recovery and delayed sports participation until processing normalized.

Anna's relatively modest cognitive inefficiency produced significant occupational impairment in a demanding environment. As depression is treated, her cognitive efficiency should improve, and occupational performance should recover, demonstrating state-dependence rather than fixed impairment.

Dr. Butler maintained apparent independence despite substantial memory impairment. However, functional dependence was increasing through reliance on compensatory strategies. This illustrates that "functional independence" exists on a continuum, and individuals with cognitive impairment often maintain apparent independence through increasing environmental support.

Although the NIH Toolbox provides efficient, psychometrically sound measurement supporting these interpretive processes, clinician expertise in integrating cognitive data with developmental history, behavioral observations, medical context, and functional assessment transforms test scores into meaningful clinical formulations. Standardized assessment enhances rather than replaces clinical judgment, providing objective quantification supporting diagnostic reasoning while enabling communication across providers through common measurement language.

DON'T FORGET 7.1

Clinical expertise remains irreplaceable. Standardized scores aid reasoning; they do not substitute for it.

RESEARCH APPLICATIONS OF THE NIH TOOLBOX IN CLINICAL PRACTICE: IMPLEMENTATION FRAMEWORKS AND METHODOLOGICAL CONSIDERATIONS

The NIH Toolbox Cognition tests have evolved from their origins as a research standardization tool into a more versatile clinical and translational research instrument (Gershon et al., 2013). This evolution raises important questions about optimal implementation across different research paradigms. The following section presents two examples of research frameworks: one examining intervention efficacy in educational settings and the other exploring longitudinal cognitive trajectories. These examples illustrate key conceptual and methodological considerations that can guide the design of studies aimed at obtaining more robust and meaningful results using the NIH Toolbox.

These examples were selected because they represent different measurement considerations and challenges. For instance, educational intervention research operates within constrained timelines with predictable measurement occasions, making it easier to examine acute cognitive change. Longitudinal cohort studies, on the other hand, introduce complexities of developmental maturation, practice effects, and the distinction between absolute change and change relative to peers (McArdle, 2009). Together, these frameworks illustrate how the same assessment battery requires different implementation strategies depending on the underlying research question.

Research Application One: Educational Intervention Research

Conceptual Framework

Educational intervention research examines whether deliberately introduced experiences produce measurable cognitive changes beyond those expected from typical development, practice, and maturation. The fundamental challenge lies in isolating intervention-specific effects from multiple confounding sources of change. Children naturally develop cognitively during any intervention period, repeatedly taking the same tests improves performance independent of cognitive growth (Calamia et al., 2012), and measurement error can also create change that reflects statistical noise rather than genuine ability shifts. One benefit of the NIH Toolbox is that it offers standardized administration, reducing examiner-introduced variability (Weintraub et al., 2013).

Theoretical Considerations in Study Design

Transfer of Skill

> **Rapid Reference 7.7**
>
> **Proximal vs. Distal Outcomes**
>
> Proximal outcomes reflect improvement on tasks closely aligned with training, capturing practice effects or task-specific learning.
>
> Distal outcomes assess untrained but related abilities, indicating generalization of cognitive change.
>
> Interpreting both levels clarifies whether an intervention improves specific performance or underlying cognitive capacity.

Executive function interventions face well-documented challenges, such that trained skills often improve on measures that closely resemble training tasks while showing minimal transfer to related but distinct cognitive abilities or real-world functioning (Melby-Lervåg & Hulme, 2013; Sala & Gobet, 2017). This phenomenon necessitates distinguishing between proximal and distal outcomes when selecting NIH Toolbox measures.

Proximal outcomes assess cognitive abilities directly targeted by the intervention. If a training program focuses on inhibitory control through repeated stop-signal tasks, the Flanker test represents a proximal outcome, i.e., similar enough to training tasks to detect intervention effects if they exist. The Dimensional Change Card Sort, measuring cognitive flexibility, represents a moderately proximal outcome; these are theoretically related to inhibition but distinct enough to test whether training benefits generalize beyond the specific trained ability (Diamond & Ling, 2016).

Distal outcomes assess cognitive abilities not directly targeted but theoretically connected through broader executive function networks. Pattern Comparison serves this purpose; executive function theories suggest that better attentional control might improve processing efficiency, but the connection is indirect. If intervention effects emerge only on proximal outcomes, this suggests training enhanced specific task performance rather than underlying cognitive capacity (Shipstead et al., 2012). If effects extend to distal outcomes and real-world academic performance, evidence for meaningful cognitive enhancement strengthens.

This proximal-distal distinction shapes the entire interpretive framework. Investigators should articulate theoretical predictions about which abilities should improve, which should show partial transfer, and which should remain unchanged. Without this framework, any pattern of results can be interpreted as supporting intervention efficacy, reducing scientific rigor.

Control Condition Challenges

Comparing intervention to "no treatment" can confound intervention-specific effects with nonspecific factors, such as expectancy effects, time engaged in structured activity, and novelty (Boot et al., 2013). Active control conditions addressing these factors present their own challenge, as well. For example, they must provide equivalent nonspecific benefits without providing cognitive training benefits. An ideal active control matches:

- Interaction time and quality
- Expectancy for improvement
- Setting and scheduling
- Digital interaction (for digitally administered interventions)
- Engagement and interest level

Yet it must avoid strengthening the cognitive abilities under investigation. Selecting appropriate control activities requires careful theoretical consideration of which activities might inadvertently train target abilities. Educational content (science videos, history lessons) often serves well because it engages attention and provides structure while minimizing overlap with executive function training.

> **DON'T FORGET 7.2**
>
> Change-sensitive scores (CSSs): Best for detecting absolute change over time; a 10-point gain reflects equal improvement across ages but includes both intervention and developmental effects.
>
> Age-adjusted scores: Best for evaluating relative standing among peers; scores stay stable (~100) if development is typical.
>
> Tip: Report both; CSS for capacity change, age-adjusted scores for context.

Measurement Considerations

Score Selection

The NIH Toolbox provides multiple score types, each optimized for different purposes. This choice represents more than technical preference; it fundamentally shapes what research questions can be answered and how results are interpreted (LaForte et al., 2024; Tulsky et al., 2014).

CSSs provide interval-scaled metrics optimized for detecting individual change. A 10-point CSS increase represents the same magnitude of cognitive improvement regardless of the child's starting point or age. This property makes CSS ideal for intervention research where the focus is on detecting change magnitude. However, CSS does not account for developmental expectations. All children naturally improve over time through maturation and learning, so CSS increases reflect both intervention effects and natural development.

Age-adjusted standard scores place children relative to same-age peers, with scores normed to remain stable (around 100) across development for children progressing typically. This property creates challenges for intervention research. Consider a child who improves substantially in absolute terms but whose age-adjusted score remains stable or declines slightly because peers improved even more. Has the intervention succeeded (absolute improvement occurred) or failed (relative standing unchanged)? The answer depends on the intervention's purpose. If the goal is to enhance cognitive capacity, absolute improvement matters. If the goal is improving academic competitiveness, relative standing matters (LaForte et al., 2024; Lichtenberger & Kaufman, 2009).

This conceptual tension suggests that reporting both metrics serves different interpretive purposes. CSS quantifies intervention impact on cognitive capacity, while age-adjusted scores contextualize whether improvements are sufficient to alter children's standing relative to peers.

Practice Effect Phenomenon

Practice effects pose universal challenges for repeated-measures research. The NIH Toolbox minimizes but does not eliminate practice effects through alternate forms and CAT-administered tests. However, examinees still become familiar with test formats, instructions, and task demands, improving performance through procedural learning rather than cognitive enhancement (Zelazo et al., 2013).

Rapid Reference 7.8

Practice effects: performance improves from repeated test exposure independent of cognitive change.

Active control designs address this challenge by providing equivalent test exposure to intervention and control groups. Any practice effects should affect groups equally, allowing between-group comparisons to isolate intervention-specific effects. However, interpretation becomes complex when control groups show substantial improvement. If controls improve 8 CSS points over 12 weeks while the intervention group improves 12 points, is the 4-point difference meaningful? This requires considering:

- Measurement error magnitude
- Expected developmental change
- Clinical significance thresholds
- Percentage of children showing reliable improvement exceeding measurement error

These considerations suggest that intervention research requires multiple complementary metrics, such as mean group differences, effect sizes, reliable change percentages, and academic outcome transfers, to help build evidence for intervention efficacy.

Analytical and Interpretive Framework

DON'T FORGET 7.3

Effect size ≠ clinical significance. Always contextualize statistics within meaningful functional outcomes.

Beyond Statistical Significance

Statistical significance indicates whether observed differences are unlikely to reflect sampling error, but provides limited information about intervention value (Wasserstein & Lazar, 2016).

Several considerations contextualize statistical findings:

- **Effect size magnitude:** Even statistically significant effects may be substantively small. Cohen's conventions ($d = 0.2$ small, 0.5 medium, 0.8 large) provide rough guidelines (Cohen, 1988), but clinical significance requires considering whether effects are large enough to meaningfully impact children's functioning.
- **Reliable change:** What percentage of children show improvement exceeding measurement error? An intervention showing statistically significant group differences, but only 35% of children demonstrating reliable improvement (versus 28% of controls), may lack practical utility despite statistical significance (Jacobson & Truax, 1991).
- **Transfer patterns:** Do effects extend beyond trained abilities to untrained cognitive domains and academic outcomes? Intervention science increasingly emphasizes transfer as the critical benchmark distinguishing meaningful cognitive enhancement from task-specific learning (Barnett & Ceci, 2002).

Interpretation Matrix

Three broad result patterns emerge, each suggesting different interpretation.

Broad Transfer

Intervention effects emerge on trained abilities, related cognitive abilities, and academic outcomes. This pattern provides the strongest evidence that intervention enhanced cognitive capacity in ways generalizing beyond the specific training context. The intervention impacted underlying cognitive processes, supporting learning across domains (Diamond & Ling, 2016).

Selective Transfer

Large effects on directly trained abilities, moderate effects on closely related cognitive abilities, and minimal effects on academic outcomes. This pattern, most common in intervention literature, suggests training enhanced specific cognitive processes, but benefits did not generalize sufficiently to impact real-world functioning (Sala & Gobet, 2017). The intervention successfully targeted specific abilities, but these abilities either contribute less to academic success than theorized, or insufficient training intensity was provided to produce educationally meaningful changes.

Null Findings

No differences between intervention and control groups. This pattern requires process evaluation: Was the intervention implemented with sufficient fidelity? Did children engage meaningfully with training content? Were outcome measures adequately sensitive? Was the sample sufficiently powered? Null findings may reflect intervention inefficacy, implementation failure, or measurement inadequacy, and distinguishing between these requires examining implementation data (Durlak & DuPre, 2008).

Methodological Pitfalls

Several common design and analysis decisions undermine intervention research and should be considered:

Inappropriate Score Metrics

Using age-adjusted scores as primary outcomes can obscure genuine improvements when intervention benefits occur, but children remain below peer averages. Conversely, using only CSS without considering age-adjusted changes can overstate intervention value when improvements are too small to meaningfully alter children's relative standing.

Inadequate Control Conditions

Comparing intervention to "no treatment" or usual care confounds intervention-specific effects with nonspecific factors (Boot et al., 2013). Results become less interpretable because multiple explanations exist for any observed differences.

Within-group pre-post comparisons: Interpreting within-group improvement without comparison to controls conflates intervention effects with practice, development, and regression to the mean. All groups typically improve over time, making between-group comparisons essential (Singer & Willett, 2003).

Publication Bias

Selectively reporting "significant" outcomes while ignoring null findings on other measures creates misleading impressions of intervention efficacy (Franco et al., 2014). Transparent reporting of all planned analyses strengthens scientific integrity.

Research Application Two: Longitudinal Developmental Research

Conceptual Framework

Longitudinal research examines how cognitive abilities unfold across development and how early abilities predict later outcomes. Unlike intervention research focusing on induced change within relatively brief periods, longitudinal research must disentangle multiple interacting processes unfolding across years, such as biological maturation, experiential learning, practice effects from repeated assessment, and measurement error. The fundamental question shifts from "Does an intervention cause change?" to "What is the nature of developmental change, what factors influence it, and how do early abilities relate to later functioning?" (Singer & Willett, 2003).

The NIH Toolbox's design offers specific advantages for developmental research; for example, continuous norming across ages minimizes measurement discontinuities that affect research using different tests at different ages (Akshoomoff et al., 2013), and standardized administration reduces examiner-introduced variability across long time periods. However, longitudinal research introduces methodological challenges that are not typically encountered in shorter studies.

Theoretical Considerations

Developmental Trajectory Question

Rapid Reference 7.9

Developmental Trajectories of Cognitive Abilities

Crystallized abilities (G_c): Reflect accumulated knowledge such as vocabulary and factual information. Growth is steady and largely linear across childhood and adolescence as language and learning experiences expand (Cattell, 1963; Horn & Cattell, 1967).

Research focus: Factors accelerating vocabulary growth and how early language predicts later academic outcomes.

Fluid abilities (G_f): Encompass reasoning, processing speed, and working memory. Development follows a curvilinear path: rapid gains in childhood, continued growth into adolescence, plateauing in early adulthood, and decline in later years (Kail & Ferrer, 2007; McArdle et al., 2002).

Research focus: Biological and experiential drivers of change (e.g., myelination, learning efficiency) and their links to academic progress.

Interplay with achievement: Language and reasoning support learning, while schooling further refines cognitive skills – creating bidirectional influences over time (Ferrer & McArdle, 2004). Early advantages may compound through "Matthew effects," where stronger early skills foster continued growth (Stanovich, 1986).

Cognitive abilities follow distinct developmental patterns. Crystallized abilities (i.e., language, acquired knowledge) show steady, relatively linear growth throughout childhood as children accumulate vocabulary and factual knowledge (Cattell, 1963; Horn & Cattell, 1967). Fluid abilities (i.e., reasoning, processing speed, working memory) show more complex trajectories, improving rapidly during early childhood, continuing growth through adolescence, plateauing in early adulthood, then declining in later adulthood (McArdle et al., 2002). These different patterns suggest different measurement and analysis strategies.

For crystallized abilities, longitudinal research should document growth rates, identify factors accelerating or decelerating vocabulary development, and examine how early language abilities predict later academic achievement. The prediction is straightforward such that more vocabulary supports reading comprehension, which supports learning across domains, creating cascading effects where early language advantages compound over time (sometimes termed "Matthew effects" in educational research; Stanovich, 1986).

For fluid abilities, research questions have become more complex. Does processing speed improvement during elementary school reflect myelination of white matter pathways, or practice-related efficiency, or both (Kail & Ferrer, 2007)? Do children showing faster processing speed development also show steeper growth in academic skills? The relationship between cognitive ability growth and academic achievement growth tests whether cognitive abilities cause academic learning or whether bidirectional relationships exist (cognitive abilities support learning, but academic learning also develops cognitive abilities; Ferrer & McArdle, 2004).

Developmental Timing Question

When during development do cognitive abilities most strongly predict academic outcomes? Several theoretical perspectives suggest different answers:

Critical Period Hypothesis

Cognitive abilities during specific sensitive periods exert disproportionate influence on later development (Knudsen, 2004). Early language abilities may particularly matter because they shape reading acquisition, which becomes the gateway for later learning. This perspective suggests early cognitive assessment may provide maximum predictive power.

Cumulative Advantage Hypothesis

Early advantages amplify over time as better cognitive abilities support learning, which develops cognitive abilities further, creating positive feedback loops (DiPrete & Eirich, 2006). This perspective predicts that cognitive ability differences present at school entry will widen over time unless interventions address them.

Compensatory Hypothesis

Educational experiences can offset early disadvantages, and children who start behind can catch up with adequate support. This perspective predicts that cognitive ability differences might narrow over time, particularly for children receiving high-quality instruction (Crosnoe et al., 2010).

Testing these competing hypotheses requires modeling not just baseline cognitive abilities but also growth rates and how they relate to contextual factors like school quality, family resources, and intervention exposure.

Practice Effect Challenge Revisited

In longitudinal research spanning multiple years, practice effects manifest differently than in brief intervention studies. Initial exposures to NIH Toolbox tests can produce practice effects, but these effects plateau with repeated administration (Zelazo et al., 2013). The question becomes: Do all children show similar practice effects, or do practice effects vary systematically by cognitive ability, demographic factors, or educational experiences?

If practice effects vary systematically, this introduces measurement bias. For example, if higher-ability children show larger practice effects because they better remember previous test exposures and strategize for subsequent administrations, then longitudinal change estimates will be distorted. Distinguishing practice effects from genuine developmental change requires careful modeling, examining whether patterns observed in the normative data (where practice effects are quantified through test–retest reliability studies) match patterns observed in the research sample.

Measurement and Design Decisions

Assessment Frequency Question

How frequently should children be assessed? More frequent assessment captures developmental change with greater temporal precision but increases participant burden, costs, and practice effects. Several factors inform this decision:

> **CAUTION 7.5**
>
> More assessment isn't always better. In longitudinal research, the temptation exists to assess children as frequently as possible to capture developmental change precisely. However, more frequent assessment increases participant burden (reducing retention), multiplies practice effects, inflates costs, and may not meaningfully improve measurement precision. Match assessment frequency to the rate of developmental change in the abilities being studied.

Rate of Developmental Change

During periods of rapid change (early elementary years for many abilities), more frequent assessment captures growth patterns. During periods of slower change (later elementary years), less frequent assessment suffices (McArdle, 2009).

Research Question

If the goal is predicting later outcomes from early abilities, intensive early assessment with sparse later assessment may be optimal. If the goal is characterizing growth trajectories, consistent assessment density across the studied period matters more.

Practical Constraints

School-based research often aligns assessment with academic calendars, testing at academic milestones (end of kindergarten, end of third grade when standardized testing typically occurs) rather than at regular chronological intervals.

The example design (kindergarten fall and spring, then spring annually through 5th grade) reflects these considerations: more frequent early assessment during rapid change, then annual assessment at consistent points in the academic year.

Score Metric Decision Revisited

Longitudinal research faces unique challenges in selecting score metrics. CSSs provide interval-scaled metrics ideal for modeling growth, but all children's CSSs increase over time through development. This creates analytic complexity where growth curve models must distinguish between:

- Average developmental change (how much do children improve on average?)
- Individual variation in starting points (how much do children differ at baseline?)
- Individual variation in growth rates (do some children develop faster than others?)

Age-adjusted scores address developmental expectations by design; that is, a stable age-adjusted score indicates a child is developing at the typical rate for their age. However, age-adjusted scores become problematic for examining absolute change because the metric shifts as the reference group changes. A child maintaining a standard score of 100 from ages 5–10 has improved substantially in absolute cognitive ability (evidenced by rising CSS) but remained average relative to peers (constant age-adjusted score).

This suggests that longitudinal research benefits from examining both metrics serving different purposes: CSS for modeling developmental trajectories, age-adjusted scores for examining relative standing and identifying children who gain or lose ground compared to peers (McArdle et al., 2002).

Attrition Challenge

Longitudinal research spanning multiple years inevitably loses participants through family relocation, withdrawal of consent, loss of contact, or inability to schedule assessments. Attrition creates problems beyond reduced sample size if it occurs non-randomly. Children from more disadvantaged backgrounds, lower-performing students, and families experiencing instability are disproportionately likely to drop out. This selective attrition biases remaining samples toward higher-functioning children from more stable families (Miller & Wright, 1995).

Modern statistical approaches address missing data through multiple imputation or maximum likelihood estimation, generating plausible values for missing observations based on observed data patterns (Graham, 2009; Little & Rubin, 2002). However, these methods rest on assumptions about missingness mechanisms. If missingness relates only to observed variables (e.g., children with lower baseline scores are more likely to drop out), statistical corrections work well. If missingness relates to unobserved factors (e.g., children developing learning problems are more likely to drop out, but learning problems are not fully captured by baseline measures), statistical corrections may inadequately address bias.

This suggests that longitudinal research requires: (1) retention efforts minimizing attrition, (2) careful documentation of attrition patterns and participant characteristics predicting dropout, (3) sensitivity analyses examining whether conclusions change under different missing data assumptions, and (4) transparent reporting of attrition rates and patterns.

DON'T FORGET 7.4

Don't infer causality from correlation. Even with temporal order, unmeasured variables can drive relationships.

Methodological Considerations

Causality Limitation

Longitudinal prediction does not establish causality, despite temporal precedence sometimes creating that impression. Early cognitive abilities predicting later academic achievement could reflect:

- Cognitive abilities causing academic learning (stronger cognitive foundations support skill acquisition)
- Common causes (family resources, genetic factors, educational experiences) affect both cognitive abilities and academic achievement

- Bidirectional relationships (cognitive abilities support learning, but learning experiences also develop cognitive abilities)

Distinguishing between these requires experimental intervention (establishing causality through manipulation) or sophisticated statistical approaches controlling for confounds (Shadish et al., 2002). Longitudinal observational research primarily describes developmental patterns and identifies factors associated with different trajectories, generating hypotheses for experimental testing rather than establishing causal mechanisms.

Longitudinal Strengths

Despite challenges, longitudinal designs provide unique insights:

- **Temporal precedence:** Establishing that cognitive abilities precede academic outcomes strengthens (though does not prove) causal inferences.
- **Developmental mechanisms:** Examining how change in one domain relates to change in another domain (e.g., do processing speed improvements predict reading growth?) illuminates developmental mechanisms (McArdle, 2009).
- **Critical periods:** Identifying when cognitive abilities most strongly predict later outcomes informs optimal intervention timing (Knudsen, 2004).

Overarching Themes and Recommendations

Matching Measurement to Theory

Both intervention and longitudinal research require explicit theoretical frameworks specifying what should change (or predict), how much, when, and why. The NIH Toolbox provides measurement tools, but theoretical frameworks guide which tests to administer, which score metrics to analyze, and how to interpret findings. Without clear theoretical predictions, any pattern of results can be retrospectively interpreted as meaningful, reducing scientific rigor (Meehl, 1990).

For example, individual-differences research accepts moderate measurement error because aggregating across many people reduces its impact. Change detection research examines smaller effects (within-person shifts) where measurement error constitutes larger proportions of observed variance (Cronbach & Furby, 1970). Understanding standard error of measurement and reliable change indices becomes important. In addition, single-administration research avoids practice effects entirely, whereas repeated-measures research must account for score improvements from test familiarity independent of cognitive change (Calamia et al., 2012).

Context of Development

Cognitive abilities develop within social, educational, and family contexts that both shape development and are shaped by children's cognitive characteristics (Bronfenbrenner & Morris, 2006). Longitudinal research increasingly emphasizes bidirectional relationships: high-quality instruction develops cognitive abilities, but children with stronger cognitive abilities may also elicit more stimulating instruction from teachers. Family resources support cognitive development, but children demonstrating strong cognitive abilities may also prompt families to provide more learning opportunities.

These bidirectional relationships complicate causal interpretation but enrich understanding of developmental processes (Sameroff, 2009). They suggest that examining contextual factors (school quality, teacher characteristics, and family practices) alongside cognitive trajectories illuminates how environments support or constrain development. This broader perspective moves beyond a narrow focus on cognitive test scores toward an understanding of how cognition develops in context.

Interpretation Framework

Research using the NIH Toolbox requires careful interpretation grounded in multiple converging indicators rather than single metrics:

- **Statistical significance alone is insufficient:** Effect sizes, confidence intervals, and practical significance thresholds contextualize whether statistically significant effects are meaningful (Wasserstein & Lazar, 2016).
- **Absolute versus relative change:** CSS quantifies absolute cognitive change while age-adjusted scores indicate change relative to peers. Both matter for different purposes.
- **Pattern consistency:** Do findings cohere across multiple cognitive measures, academic outcomes, and functional indicators? Consistent patterns across multiple indices strengthen interpretive confidence (Campbell & Fiske, 1959).
- **Comparison to normative expectations:** Do observed changes align with patterns in the normative sample (expected practice effects, developmental trajectories)? Large deviations suggest either meaningful intervention effects (if intervention research) or potential data quality concerns.

Methodological Transparency

Research quality depends not only on design sophistication but also on transparent reporting, allowing readers to evaluate design decisions and interpretive choices (Simmons et al., 2011). This includes:

- Clear articulation of theoretical frameworks and predictions
- Detailed description of implementation procedures and fidelity
- Complete reporting of all planned analyses
- Discussion of limitations and alternative interpretations
- Provision of sufficient detail for replication attempts

The increasing emphasis on preregistration (documenting analysis plans before seeing data) reflects recognition that analytical flexibility (choosing which analyses to conduct after seeing results) inflates false positive rates (Nosek et al., 2018).

CONCLUSION

The NIH Toolbox Cognition tests represent a significant advancement in standardized cognitive assessment, offering researchers efficient, psychometrically sound measurement across broad age ranges (Gershon et al., 2013). However, maximizing its research utility requires thoughtful consideration of study design, theoretical framework, measurement properties, and interpretive approach. The intervention and longitudinal research paradigms discussed here illustrate how identical assessment tools require substantially different implementation strategies depending on research questions. Several guiding principles informed measurement decisions to ensure that scientific objectives, not convenience, shaped the research design and interpretation. These principles are: scores should be selected based on what the research question requires; designs should incorporate appropriate control conditions or comparison groups; analyses should employ statistical methods suited to data structure; and interpretation should consider multiple explanations.

The NIH Toolbox provides powerful measurement tools, but tools are only as valuable as the conceptual frameworks guiding their application. Research that carefully matches measurement approach to theoretical questions, appropriately handles methodological challenges, and interprets findings cautiously will yield insights advancing both basic understanding of cognitive development and practical applications improving educational and clinical outcomes.

As the NIH Toolbox evidence base continues expanding across diverse research contexts (Fox et al., 2022), the field will develop an increasingly nuanced understanding of optimal implementation approaches for different research questions, populations, and settings. This chapter's integration of methodological considerations and theoretical frameworks aims to accelerate that process, helping researchers design studies that maximize the NIH Toolbox's considerable strengths while appropriately addressing its limitations.

TEST YOURSELF

1. **Examiners should use results from NIH Toolbox testing in tandem with other examinations, observations, and information from other health care professionals to make any diagnoses and recommendations.**

   True or False

2. **Diagnostic confidence ___ when multiple data sources point toward the same conclusion.**

   (a) increases
   (b) decreases
   (c) remains the same/unchanged
   (d) cannot be determined

3. **Test scores matter because they predict and explain real-world functioning, such as academic performance, occupational achievement, success in independent living, and quality of life.**

   True or False

4. **If an individual's test scores indicate low crystallized cognitive abilities and high fluid cognitive abilities, that person likely has Attention-Deficit Hyperactivity Disorder (ADHD).**

   True or False

5. **The key discriminator for true mTBI cognitive impact is selective processing speed impairment with preserved higher-order functions and ___.**
   (a) Unhindered, fully understandable speech
   (b) Focused gaze and responsive motor abilities
   (c) Documented acute injury mechanism
   (d) Increased attention to detail

6. **Being "oriented x3" means:**
   (a) The examinee is oriented to person, oriented to place, oriented to time, and oriented to situation.
   (b) The examinee is oriented to situation, oriented to place, and oriented to time.
   (c) The examinee is oriented to situation, oriented to place, and oriented to person.
   (d) The examinee is oriented to person, oriented to place, and oriented to time.

7. **Which of the following was NOT among the recommendations in this chapter's mild traumatic brain injury (mTBI) case example?**
   (a) Structured sleep
   (b) Monitoring via readministration of the NIH Toolbox
   (c) Extended time on exams and allowing lecture recordings
   (d) Prescribing stimulant medication

8. **Cognitive test scores derive clinical importance from their relationship to real-world functioning, such as ___, occupational performance, independent living, and quality of life.**
   (a) Social relationships
   (b) Academic achievement
   (c) Locomotor abilities
   (d) Visual acuity

9. **Which of the following is incorrect?**
   (a) Proximal outcomes reflect improvement on tasks closely aligned with training, capturing practice effects or task-specific learning.
   (b) Proximal outcomes assess cognitive abilities directly targeted by the intervention.
   (c) Proximal outcomes assess untrained abilities, while distal outcomes assess practice effects.
   (d) Distal outcomes assess untrained but related abilities, indicating generalization of cognitive change.

10. **Both intervention and longitudinal research require explicit theoretical frameworks specifying what should change (or predict), how much, when, and why.**

    True or False

Answers: 1. True; 2. (a); 3. True; 4. False; 5. (c); 6. (d); 7. (d); 8. (b); 9. (c); 10. True

REFERENCES

Akshoomoff, N., Beaumont, J. L., Bauer, P. J., Dikmen, S. S., Gershon, R. C., Mungas, D., … Heaton, R. K. (2013). VIII. NIH Toolbox Cognition Battery (CB): Composite scores of crystallized, fluid, and overall cognition. *Monographs of the Society for Research in Child Development, 78*(4), 119–132. https://doi.org/10.1111/mono.12038

Alsalaheen, B. A., Mucha, A., Morris, L. O., Whitney, S. L., Furman, J. M., Camiolo-Reddy, C. E., … Sparto, P. J. (2010). Vestibular rehabilitation for dizziness and balance disorders after concussion. *Journal of Neurologic Physical Therapy, 34*(2), 87–93. https://doi.org/10.1097/NPT.0b013e3181dde568

Barnett, S. M., & Ceci, S. J. (2002). When and where do we apply what we learn? A taxonomy for far transfer. *Psychological Bulletin, 128*(4), 612–637. https://doi.org/10.1037/0033-2909.128.4.612

Belanger, H. G., Curtiss, G., Demery, J. A., Lebowitz, B. K., & Vanderploeg, R. D. (2005). Factors moderating neuropsychological outcomes following mild traumatic brain injury: A meta-analysis. *Journal of the International Neuropsychological Society, 11*(3), 215–227. https://doi.org/10.1017/S1355617705050277

Bigler, E. D., & Maxwell, W. L. (2012). Neuropathology of mild traumatic brain injury: Relationship to neuroimaging findings. *Brain Imaging and Behavior, 6*(2), 108–136. https://doi.org/10.1007/s11682-011-9145-0

Boot, W. R., Simons, D. J., Stothart, C., & Stutts, C. (2013). The pervasive problem with placebos in psychology: Why active control groups are not sufficient to rule out placebo effects. *Perspectives on Psychological Science, 8*(4), 445–454. https://doi.org/10.1177/1745691613491271

Bora, E., Harrison, B. J., Yücel, M., & Pantelis, C. (2013). Cognitive impairment in euthymic major depressive disorder: A meta-analysis. *Psychological Medicine, 43*(10), 2017–2026. https://doi.org/10.1017/S0033291712002085

Bronfenbrenner, U., & Morris, P. A. (2006). The bioecological model of human development. In R. M. Lerner & W. Damon (Eds.), *Handbook of child psychology: Theoretical models of human development* (pp. 793–828). John Wiley & Sons.

Butters, M. A., Whyte, E. M., Nebes, R. D., Begley, A. E., Dew, M. A., Mulsant, B. H., … G., Reynolds, C. F., & Becker, J. T. (2004). The nature and determinants of neuropsychological functioning in late-life depression. *Archives of General Psychiatry, 61*(6), 587–595. https://doi.org/10.1001/archpsyc.61.6.587

Calamia, M., Markon, K., & Tranel, D. (2012). Scoring higher the second time around: Meta-analyses of practice effects in neuropsychological assessment. *The Clinical Neuropsychologist, 26*(4), 543–570. https://doi.org/10.1080/13854046.2012.680913

Campbell, D. T., & Fiske, D. W. (1959). Convergent and discriminant validation by the multitrait-multimethod matrix. *Psychological Bulletin, 56*(2), 81–105. https://doi.org/10.1037/h0046016

Carmona, S., Vilarroya, O., Bielsa, A., Tremols, V., Soliva, J. C., Rovira, M., ... Bulbena, A. (2005). Global and regional gray matter reductions in ADHD: A voxel-based morphometric study. *Neuroscience Letters, 389*(2), 88–93. https://doi.org/10.1016/j.neulet.2005.07.020

Casaletto, K. B., Umlauf, A., Beaumont, J., Gershon, R., Slotkin, J., Akshoomoff, N., & Heaton, R. K. (2015). Demographically corrected normative standards for the English version of the NIH Toolbox Cognition Battery. *Journal of the International Neuropsychological Society, 21*(5), 378–391. https://doi.org/10.1017/S1355617715000351

Castaneda, A. E., Tuulio-Henriksson, A., Marttunen, M., Suvisaari, J., & Lönnqvist, J. (2008). A review on cognitive impairments in depressive and anxiety disorders with a focus on young adults. *Journal of Affective Disorders, 106*(1–2), 1–27. https://doi.org/10.1016/j.jad.2007.06.006

Cattell, R. B. (1963). Theory of fluid and crystallized intelligence: a critical experiment. *Journal of Educational Psychology, 54*(1), 1–22. https://doi.org/10.1037/h0046743

Chételat, G., Arbizu, J., Barthel, H., Garibotto, V., Law, I., Morbelli, S., ... Drzezga, A. (2020). Amyloid-PET and ^{18}F-FDG-PET in the diagnostic investigation of Alzheimer's disease and other dementias. *The Lancet Neurology, 19*(11), 951–962. https://doi.org/10.1016/S1474-4422(20)30314-8

Cohen, J. (1988). *Statistical power analysis for the behavioral sciences* (2nd ed.). Lawrence Erlbaum Associates. https://doi.org/10.4324/9780203771587

Cortese, S., Aoki, Y. Y., Itahashi, T., Castellanos, F. X., & Eickhoff, S. B. (2021). Systematic review and meta-analysis: Resting-state functional magnetic resonance imaging studies of attention-deficit/hyperactivity disorder. *Journal of the American Academy of Child & Adolescent Psychiatry, 60*(1), 61–75. https://doi.org/10.1016/j.jaac.2020.08.014

Cronbach, L. J., & Furby, L. (1970). How we should measure "change": Or should we? *Psychological Bulletin, 74*(1), 68–80. https://doi.org/10.1037/h0029382

Crosnoe, R., Leventhal, T., Wirth, R. J., Pierce, K. M., Pianta, R. C., & NICHD Early Child Care Research Network. (2010). Family socioeconomic status and consistent environmental stimulation in early childhood. *Child Development, 81*(3), 972–987. https://doi.org/10.1111/j.1467-8624.2010.01446.x

Diamond, A., & Ling, D. S. (2016). Conclusions about interventions, programs, and approaches for improving executive functions that appear justified and those that, despite much hype, do not. *Developmental Cognitive Neuroscience, 18*, 34–48. https://doi.org/10.1016/j.dcn.2015.11.005

DiPrete, T. A., & Eirich, G. M. (2006). Cumulative advantage as a mechanism for inequality: A review of theoretical and empirical developments. *Annual Review of Sociology, 32*, 271–297. https://doi.org/10.1146/annurev.soc.32.061604.123127

Durlak, J. A., & DuPre, E. P. (2008). Implementation matters: A review of research on the influence of implementation on program outcomes and the factors affecting implementation. *American Journal of Community Psychology, 41*(3), 327–350. https://doi.org/10.1007/s10464-008-9165-0

Ferrer, E., & McArdle, J. J. (2004). An experimental analysis of dynamic hypotheses about cognitive abilities and achievement from childhood to early adulthood. *Developmental Psychology, 40*(6), 935–952. https://doi.org/10.1037/0012-16.9.40.6.935

Folstein, M. F., Folstein, S. E., & McHugh, P. R. (1975). "Mini-mental state": A practical method for grading the cognitive state of patients for the clinician. *Journal of Psychiatric Research, 12*(3), 189–198. https://doi.org/10.1016/0022-3956(75)90026-6

Fox, R. S., Zhang, M., Amagai, S., Bassard, A., Dworak, E. M., Han, Y. C., … Gershon, R. C. (2022). Uses of the NIH toolbox® in clinical samples: A scoping review. *Neurology: Clinical Practice, 12*(4), 307–319. https://doi.org/10.1212/CPJ.0000000000200060

Franco, A., Malhotra, N., & Simonovits, G. (2014). Publication bias in the social sciences: Unlocking the file drawer. *Science, 345*(6203), 1502–1505. https://doi.org/10.1126/science.1255484

Friedman, L. M., Rapport, M. D., Raiker, J. S., Orban, S. A., & Eckrich, S. J. (2017). Reading comprehension in boys with ADHD: The mediating roles of working memory and orthographic conversion. *Journal of Abnormal Child Psychology, 45*, 273–287. https://doi.org/10.1007/s10802-016-0171-7

Gershon, R. C., Wagster, M. V., Hendrie, H. C., Fox, N. A., Cook, K. F., & Nowinski, C. J. (2013). NIH toolbox for assessment of neurological and behavioral function. *Neurology, 80*(11 Supplement 3), S2–S6. https://doi.org/10.1212/WNL.0b013e3182872e5f

Giza, C. C., & Hovda, D. A. (2014). The new neurometabolic cascade of concussion. *Neurosurgery, 75*(Suppl 4), S24–S33. https://doi.org/10.1227/NEU.0000000000000505

Graham, J. W. (2009). Missing data analysis: Making it work in the real world. *Annual Review of Psychology*, 60, 549–576. https://doi.org/10.1146/annurev.psych.58.110405.085530

Herrera-Guzmán, I., Herrera-Abarca, J. E., Gudayol-Ferré, E., Herrera-Guzmán, D., Gómez-Carbajal, L., Pẽna-Olvira, M., … Guàrdia-Olmos, J. (2010). Effects of selective serotonin reuptake and dual serotonergic-noradrenergic reuptake treatments on attention and executive functions in patients with major depressive disorder. *Psychiatry Research, 177*(3), 323–329. https://doi.org/10.1016/j.psychres.2010.03.006

Hoogman, M., Muetzel, R., Guimaraes, J. P., Shumskaya, E., Mennes, M., Zwiers, M. P., … Franke, B. (2019). Brain imaging of the cortex in ADHD: A coordinated analysis of large-scale clinical and population-based samples. *American Journal of Psychiatry, 176*(7), 531–542. https://doi.org/10.1176/appi.ajp.2019.18091033

Hook, J. N., Kuentzel, J. G., & Hodges, E. K. (2022). Attention deficit hyperactivity disorder. In E. K. Hodges, J. G. Kuentzel, & J. N. Hook (Eds.), *Pediatric neuropsychology* (pp. 2–16). Routledge.

Horn, J. L., & Cattell, R. B. (1967). Age differences in fluid and crystallized intelligence. *Acta Psychologica, 26*, 107–129. https://doi.org/10.1016/0001-6918(67)90011-X

Hulkower, M. B., Poliak, D. B., Rosenbaum, S. B., Zimmerman, M. E., & Lipton, M. L. (2013). A decade of DTI in traumatic brain injury: 10 years and 100 articles later. *American Journal of Neuroradiology*, *34*(11), 2064–2074. https://doi.org/10.3174/ajnr.A3395

Iverson, G. L. (2005). Outcome from mild traumatic brain injury. *Current Opinion in Psychiatry*, *18*(3), 301–317. https://doi.org/10.1097/01.yco.0000165601.29047.ae

Iverson, G. L., Lange, R. T., Waljas, M., Liimatainen, S., Dastidar, P., Hartikainen, K. M., … Öhman, J. (2012). Outcome from complicated versus uncomplicated mild traumatic brain injury. *Rehabilitation Research and Practice*, 2012, 415740. https://doi.org/10.1155/2012/415740

Jack, C. R., Jr., Bennett, D. A., Blennow, K., Carrillo, M. C., Dunn, B., Haeberlein, S. B., Holtzman, D. M., Jagust, W., Jessen, F., Karlawish, J., Liu, E., Molinuevo, J. L., Montine, T., Phelps, C., Rankin, K.P ., Rowe, C. C., Scheltens, P., Siemers, E., Snyder, H. M., …, & Silverberg, N. (2018). NIA-AA Research Framework: Toward a biological definition of Alzheimer's disease. Alzheimer's & Dementia, *14*(4), 535–562. https://doi.org/10.1016/j.jalz.2018.02.018

Jacobson, N. S., & Truax, P. (1991). Clinical significance: A statistical approach to defining meaningful change in psychotherapy research. *Journal of Consulting and Clinical Psychology*, *59*(1), 12–19. https://doi.org/10.1037/0022-006X.59.1.12

Jak, A. J., Bondi, M. W., Delano-Wood, L., Wierenga, C., Corey-Bloom, J., Salmon, D. P., & Delis, D. C. (2009). Quantification of five neuropsychological approaches to defining mild cognitive impairment. *The American Journal of Geriatric Psychiatry*, *17*(5), 368–375. https://doi.org/10.1097/JGP.0b013e31819431d5

Kail, R. V., & Ferrer, E. (2007). Processing speed in childhood and adolescence: Longitudinal models for examining developmental change. *Child Development*, *78*(6), 1760–1770. https://doi.org/10.1111/j.1467-8624.2007.01088.x

Karalunas, S. L., Geurts, H. M., Konrad, K., Bender, S., & Nigg, J. T. (2014). Annual research review: Reaction time variability in ADHD and autism spectrum disorders: Measurement and mechanisms of a proposed trans-diagnostic phenotype. *Journal of Child Psychology and Psychiatry*, *55*(6), 685–710. https://doi.org/10.1111/jcpp.12217

Knudsen, E. I. (2004). Sensitive periods in the development of the brain and behavior. *Journal of Cognitive Neuroscience*, *16*(8), 1412–1425. https://doi.org/10.1162/0898929042304796

Kontos, A. P., Elbin, R. J., Schatz, P., Covassin, T., Henry, L., Pardini, J., & Collins, M. W. (2012). A revised factor structure for the post-concussion symptom scale: Baseline and postconcussion factors. *The American Journal of Sports Medicine*, *40*(10), 2375–2384. https://doi.org/10.1177/0363546512455400

Kroenke, K., Spitzer, R. L., & Williams, J. B. (2001). The PHQ-9: Validity of a brief depression severity measure. *Journal of General Internal Medicine*, *16*(9), 606–613. https://doi.org/10.1046/j.1525-1497.2001.016009606.x

LaForte, E. M., Giella, A. K., & Hook, J. N. (2024). *National Institutes of Health (NIH) Toolbox® V3 technical manual.* Toolbox Assessments, Inc.

Lichtenberger, E. O., & Kaufman, A. S. (2009). *Essentials of WAIS-IV assessment.* John Wiley & Sons.

Little, R. J., & Rubin, D. B. (2002). *Statistical analysis with missing data* (2nd ed.). John Wiley & Sons. https://doi.org/10.1002/9781119013563

Livingston, G., Huntley, J., Sommerlad, A., Ames, D., Ballard, C., Banerjee, S., … Mukadam, N. (2020). Dementia prevention, intervention, and care: 2020 report of the Lancet Commission. *The Lancet, 396*(10248), 413–446. https://doi.org/10.1016/S0140-6736(20)30367-6

McArdle, J. J. (2009). Latent variable modeling of differences and changes with longitudinal data. *Annual Review of Psychology, 60*, 577–605. https://doi.org/10.1146/annurev.psych.60.110707.163612

McArdle, J. J., Ferrer-Caja, E., Hamagami, F., & Woodcock, R. W. (2002). Comparative longitudinal structural analyses of the growth and decline of multiple intellectual abilities over the life span. *Developmental Psychology, 38*(1), 115–142. https://doi.org/10.1037/0012-1649.38.1.115

McCrea, M., Guskiewicz, K. M., Marshall, S. W., Barr, W., Randolph, C., Cantu, R. C., … Kelly, J. P. (2003). Acute effects and recovery time following concussion in collegiate football players: The NCAA Concussion Study. *JAMA, 290*(19), 2556–2563. https://doi.org/10.1001/jama.290.19.2556

Meehl, P. E. (1990). Why summaries of research on psychological theories are often uninterpretable. *Psychological Reports, 66*(1), 195–244. https://doi.org/10.2466/pr0.1990.66.1.195

Melby-Lervåg, M., & Hulme, C. (2013). Is working memory training effective? A meta-analytic review. *Developmental Psychology, 49*(2), 270–291. https://doi.org/10.1037/a0028228

Miller, R. B., & Wright, D. W. (1995). Detecting and correcting attrition bias in longitudinal family research. *Journal of Marriage and the Family, 57*(4), 921–929. https://doi.org/10.2307/353412

Nosek, B. A., Ebersole, C. R., DeHaven, A. C., & Mellor, D. T. (2018). The preregistration revolution. *Proceedings of the National Academy of Sciences of the United States of America, 115*(11), 2600–2606. https://doi.org/10.1073/pnas.1708274114

Patricios, J. S., Ardern, C. L., Hislop, M. D., Aubry, M., Bloomfield, P., Broderick, C., … Raftery, M. (2018). Implementation of the 2017 Berlin Concussion in Sport Group Consensus Statement in contact and collision sports: A joint position statement from 11 national and international sports organisations. *British Journal of Sports Medicine, 52*(10), 635–641. https://doi.org/10.1136/bjsports-2018-099079

Petersen, R. C., Roberts, R. O., Knopman, D. S., Geda, Y. E., Cha, R. H., Pankratz, V. S., … Rocca, W. A. (2010). Prevalence of mild cognitive impairment is higher in men: The Mayo Clinic Study of Aging. *Neurology, 75*(10), 889–897. https://doi.org/10.1212/WNL.0b013e3181f11d85

Pievsky, M. A., & McGrath, R. E. (2018). The neurocognitive profile of attention-deficit/hyperactivity disorder: A review of meta-analyses. *Archives of Clinical Neuropsychology, 33*(2), 143–157. https://doi.org/10.1093/arclin/acx055

Pizzagalli, D. A., & Roberts, A. C. (2022). Prefrontal cortex and depression. *Neuropsychopharmacology, 47*(1), 225–246. https://doi.org/10.1038/s41386-021-01101-7

Rock, P. L., Roiser, J. P., Riedel, W. J., & Blackwell, A. D. (2014). Cognitive impairment in depression: A systematic review and meta-analysis. *Psychological Medicine, 44*(10), 2029–2040. https://doi.org/10.1017/S0033291713002535

Rubia, K., Alegría, A. A., Cubillo, A. I., Smith, A. B., Brammer, M. J., & Radua, J. (2014). Effects of stimulants on brain function in attention-deficit/hyperactivity disorder: A systematic review and meta-analysis. *Biological Psychiatry, 76*(8), 616–628. https://doi.org/10.1016/j.biopsych.2013.10.016

Sala, G., & Gobet, F. (2017). Does far transfer exist? Negative evidence from chess, music, and working memory training. *Current Directions in Psychological Science, 26*(6), 515–520. https://doi.org/10.1177/0963721417712760

Sameroff, A. (2009). *The transactional model of development: How children and contexts shape each other.* American Psychological Association. https://doi.org/10.1037/11877-000

Scarmeas, N., Anastasiou, C. A., & Yannakoulia, M. (2018). Nutrition and prevention of cognitive impairment. *The Lancet Neurology, 17*(11), 1006–1015. https://doi.org/10.1016/S1474-4422(18)30338-7

Shadish, W. R., Cook, T. D., & Campbell, D. T. (2002). *Experimental and quasi-experimental designs for generalized causal inference.* Houghton Mifflin.

Shenton, M. E., Hamoda, H. M., Schneiderman, J. S., Bouix, S., Pasternak, O., Rathi, Y., … Zafonte, R. (2012). A review of magnetic resonance imaging and diffusion tensor imaging findings in mild traumatic brain injury. *Brain Imaging and Behavior, 6*, 137–192. https://doi.org/10.1007/s11682-012-9156-5

Shipstead, Z., Redick, T. S., & Engle, R. W. (2012). Is working memory training effective? *Psychological Bulletin, 138*(4), 628–654. https://doi.org/10.1037/a0027473

Sibley, M. H., Campez, M., Perez, A., Morrow, A. S., Merrill, B. M., Altszuler, A. R., … Yeguez, C. E. (2016). Parent management of organization, time management, and planning deficits among adolescents with ADHD. *Journal of Psychopathology and Behavioral Assessment, 38*, 216–228. https://doi.org/10.1007/s10862-015-9515-9

Silverberg, N. D., & Iverson, G. L. (2011). Etiology of the post-concussion syndrome: Physiogenesis and psychogenesis revisited. *NeuroRehabilitation, 29*(4), 317–329. https://doi.org/10.3233/NRE-2011-0708

Simmons, J. P., Nelson, L. D., & Simonsohn, U. (2011). False-positive psychology: Undisclosed flexibility in data collection and analysis allows presenting anything as significant. *Psychological Science, 22*(11), 1359–1366. https://doi.org/10.1177/0956797611417632

Singer, J. D., & Willett, J. B. (2003). *Applied longitudinal data analysis: Modeling change and event occurrence.* Oxford University Press. https://doi.org/10.1093/acprof:oso/9780195152968.001.0001

Snyder, H. R. (2013). Major depressive disorder is associated with broad impairments on neuropsychological measures of executive function: A meta-analysis and review. *Psychological Bulletin, 139*(1), 81–132. https://doi.org/10.1037/a0028727

Stanovich, K. E. (1986). Matthew effects in reading: Some consequences of individual differences in the acquisition of literacy. *Reading Research Quarterly, 21*(4), 360–407. https://doi.org/10.1598/RRQ.21.4.1

Tulsky, D. S., Carlozzi, N., Chiaravalloti, N. D., Beaumont, J. L., Kisala, P. A., Mungas, D., ... Gershon, R. (2014). NIH Toolbox Cognition Battery (NIHTB-CB): List sorting test to measure working memory. *Journal of the International Neuropsychological Society, 20*(6), 599–610. https://doi.org/10.1017/S135561771400040X

Wasserstein, R. L., & Lazar, N. A. (2016). The ASA statement on p-values: context, process, and purpose. *The American Statistician, 70*(2), 129–133. https://doi.org/10.1080/00031305.2016.1154108

Weintraub, S., Dikmen, S. S., Heaton, R. K., Tulsky, D. S., Zelazo, P. D., Bauer, P. J., Carlozzi, N. E., Slotkin, J., Blitz, D., Wallner-Allen, K., Fox, N. A., Beaumont, J. L., Mungas, D., Nowinski, C. J., Richler, J., Deocampo, J. A., Anderson, J. E., Manly, J. J., Borosh, B., ..., & Gershon, R. C. (2013). Cognition assessment using the NIH Toolbox. Neurology, 80(11 Supplement 3), S54–S64. https://doi.org/10.1212/WNL.0b013e3182872ded

Weintraub, S., Salmon, D., Mercaldo, N., Ferris, S., Graff-Radford, N. R., Chui, H., ... Morris, J. C. (2009). The Alzheimer's Disease Centers' Uniform Data Set (UDS): The neuropsychologic test battery. *Alzheimer Disease & Associated Disorders, 23*(2), 91–101. https://doi.org/10.1097/WAD.0b013e318191c7dd

Yesavage, J. A., Brink, T. L., Rose, T. L., Lum, O., Huang, V., Adey, M., & Leirer, V. O. (1983). Development and validation of a geriatric depression screening scale: A preliminary report. *Journal of Psychiatric Research, 17*(1), 37–49. https://doi.org/10.1016/0022-3956(82)90033-4

Zelazo, P. D., Anderson, J. E., Richler, J., Wallner-Allen, K., Beaumont, J. L., & Weintraub, S. (2013). II. NIH Toolbox Cognition Battery (CB): Measuring executive function and attention. *Monographs of the Society for Research in Child Development, 78*(4), 16–33. https://doi.org/10.1111/mono.12032

Appendix A

FREQUENTLY ASKED QUESTIONS ABOUT THE NIH TOOLBOX

WHAT ARE THE HARDWARE REQUIREMENTS?

Technology is an ever-improving medium and is, by nature, constantly being updated. As an iPad-only app, NIH Toolbox® V3 must be compatible with Apple's current hardware (i.e., iPad) and software (i.e., iOS) requirements. To see a current list of iPads that are officially supported to run NIH Toolbox® V3, please refer to the *Hardware Requirements* article available on https://nihtoolbox.org/. Further, NIH Toolbox users are strongly encouraged to regularly update their NIH Toolbox app when a new version is released to not miss out on new and updated features.

WHAT ADDITIONAL EQUIPMENT OR MATERIALS ARE REQUIRED?

Most NIH Toolbox tests can be administered using only the iPad and the NIH Toolbox® V3 app. Before administering any test, examiners should review the NIH Toolbox® V3 Administration Manual for test-specific instructions and refer to Appendix B for a list of equipment that is needed to administer each test. There are only three Cognition tests that require additional materials. List Sorting Working Memory requires a Bluetooth wireless keyboard and the List Sorting Working Memory Answer Sheet. Oral Reading Recognition requires a Bluetooth wireless keyboard and the Oral Reading Recognition Pronunciation Guide. Oral Symbol Digit requires the Oral Symbol Digit Examination Sheet.

HOW SHOULD EXAMINERS BE TRAINED?

The NIH Toolbox® V3 Cognition Tests were developed and are made available in accordance with the *Standards for Educational and Psychological Testing* developed jointly by the American Psychological Association, the American Educational Research Association, and the National Council on Measurement in Education (2014). Consistent with these standards, test users must have the appropriate knowledge, skills, training, and experience to responsibly use NIH Toolbox measures.

"Test users" are those persons responsible for the selection, administration, scoring, and interpretation of tests and the communication of results. The NIH Toolbox Cognition measures are considered C-Level tests (similar to the Wechsler Adult Intelligence Scales; Weschler, 2008). C-Level tests require a high degree of expertise in test interpretation, and thus access is restricted to individuals with state licensure or certification to practice in a field related to the request, or a doctorate degree in psychology, education, or a closely related field, with formal training in the ethical administration, scoring, and interpretation of clinical assessments related to the intended use of the assessment.

Any users of C-Level assessments must be supervised by one or more users with C-Level qualifications. Please note that the NIH Toolbox offers a number of free online resources for learning about the administration of these tests, including the administration manual, administration videos, and e-learning. However, review of these materials alone (in the absence of any other training as indicated earlier) does not replace the education and training requirements for C-Level access.

HOW MUCH DOES THE NIH TOOLBOX SUBSCRIPTION COST?

The NIH Toolbox® V3 app is free to download and explore, but a valid subscription is required to save data and access results. At the time of this book's publication, an annual app subscription from the Apple App Store for two iPads is $599.99. It is $1499.99 per year to use the NIH Toolbox® V3 subscription on up to six iPads, and it is $2499.99 per year to use the subscription on up to 10 iPads. Please check the Apple App Store for current subscription costs.

For those who are not able to purchase through the App Store, such as those using a managed device, the app can be purchased and distributed using alternative methods. The user must contact Help@NIHToolbox.org for more information about cost (App Store pricing may not apply) and deployment.

Please note that in addition to the NIH Toolbox subscription cost, you must have an iPad that meets the minimum hardware and software requirements. Please refer to the *Hardware Requirements* article available on https://nihtoolbox.org/. A wireless keyboard is required to administer the List Sorting Working Memory test and Oral Reading Recognition test.

CAN I ADMINISTER THE NIH TOOLBOX REMOTELY?

At the time of this book's publication, the NIH Toolbox is available as a face-to-face iPad app only. A remote administration version of NIH Toolbox® V3 is currently being developed as part of a larger research study. One remote alternative for some users may be the Mobile Toolbox system, which contains similar test paradigms to the NIH Toolbox. Of note, the Mobile Toolbox tests are administered via a smartphone (iPhone or Android) and are self-administered. Currently, the Mobile Toolbox system is free for use and is accessed exclusively through RedCap.

HOW CAN I GET ACCESS TO COGNITION TESTS?

Results of the NIH Toolbox Cognition tests can be used to inform diagnoses or other decisions. To preserve NIH Toolbox Cognition test integrity and ensure the tests are being administered in accordance with the Standards for Educational and Psychological Testing developed jointly by the American Psychological Association, the American Educational Research Association, and the National Council on Measurement in Education (2014), examiners must be adequately trained and experienced in general test administration and must be knowledgeable about the specific tests they use. First, examiners should create a free user account at https://nihtoolbox.org/, then apply for access, for free, at www.NIHToolbox.org/get-the-toolbox/#approval-for-cognition-measures-1. C-Level qualifications are required for all Cognition tests except for Picture Vocabulary, which requires B-Level or C-Level access.

It is important to note that a paid NIH Toolbox subscription does not automatically grant access to the Cognition tests, nor does having access to Cognition tests circumvent the need for an NIH Toolbox subscription.

After access has been granted, examiners can go to the User Resources section at https://nihtoolbox.org/ to view and download supplemental materials that are required to administer some Cognition tests (i.e., List Sorting Working Memory, Oral Reading Recognition, and Oral Symbol Digit).

Approved users can share credentials with members of their team, but it is that approved user's responsibility to oversee any data collection efforts and interpretation of results. Approved users are responsible for preserving test integrity by not sharing NIH Toolbox materials beyond their immediate team.

CAN I ASSESS EXAMINEES BELOW THE AGE OF 3?

NIH Toolbox® V3 tests were designed and validated to assess examinees aged 3 to 85+. Examiners and clinicians who are interested in assessing younger examinees may be interested in the NIH Baby Toolbox. The NIH Baby Toolbox features 30+ tests specifically designed to assess cognitive, behavioral, motor, and social functioning from infancy to early childhood (1 to 42 months). The NIH Baby Toolbox website has more information: https://nihbabytoolbox.org/.

WHERE IS MY DATA STORED?

The NIH Toolbox App stores the participant information and assessment data in the app, on the iPad it was collected, and will remain there until the examiner exports it. Please be aware that if the iPad is lost or if the user deletes the app, the data collected on that device is lost. We strongly recommend users regularly export/back up their data to prevent data loss. Please note that Apple's operating system, iOS, allows for automatic backups of all apps, and as such, this would include the data on the NIH Toolbox App. If users do not want this functionality, which is part of Apple's iOS, then users will need to turn off this automatic backup.

HOW CAN I VIEW MY SCORES/RESULTS?

After an assessment has been completed, the app automatically scores each completed test and any applicable composites. Examiners can view those results in two formats: score reports or exports.

Score reports are PDFs that show demographic information and test-level scores for tests that were completed in the selected assessment. It is a view into the examinee's performance during that single assessment. Score reports can be viewed directly in the app, either from that participant's assessment card or from the Results section on the left sidebar. Examiners can also email individual score reports to themselves so they can review the results at a later time.

Exports are a series of CSV spreadsheets that each contain different information: Registration (demographic details), Scores (test-level scores), and Item (item-level scores). All three of these export files (i.e., Registration spreadsheet, Scores spreadsheet, and Item spreadsheet) should be reviewed together, using the PID (Participant ID) to link participant-specific data across the files. Examiners select which assessments they would like to review in each export; a given export can contain data for a single assessment or for hundreds. Exports can be viewed directly in the app, or they can be sent externally via four export methods: iPad file sharing, email, upload to iCloud, and upload to your web server.

Of note, the NIH Toolbox offers wide exports and narrow exports. Wide exports show information for each examinee, test, or item across numerous columns. Narrow exports are modeled on key-value tables that pivot the data across numerous rows; this format is generally more helpful for analysts using statistical computing software, such as R. In other words, there are a total of 6 CSV export file types: wide Registration export, wide Scores export, wide Item export, narrow Registration export, narrow Scores export, and narrow Item export.

CAN YOU EXPLAIN MY SCORES/RESULTS?

An overview of available scores and what those scores indicate is available throughout this book, and Chapter 4 explains in detail how to interpret acquired scores. NIH Toolbox Cognition test results should be interpreted by professionals who have C-level qualifications and appropriate training and experience in test interpretation. Users are welcome to contact the NIH Toolbox support team at help@NIHToolbox.org with specific questions or to request special consultation services from the NIH Toolbox data scientists.

WHICH SCORE/RESULT SHOULD I BE USING?

NIH Toolbox® V3 Cognition tests provide different types of scores, and each score provides different information. For example, Change-Sensitive Scores (CSS) are ideal for measuring change over time and would be ideal for tracking an examinee's progress from the beginning of the school year to the end of the school year. Another consideration is whether to use test-level or composite-level scores. Test-level scores are more informative in evaluating performance in a specific construct; Picture Vocabulary test scores, for instance, provide information about that examinee's crystallized receptive vocabulary. Alternatively, composite scores reveal a more comprehensive view of the examinee's overall performance; Fluid Composite scores, for example, provide insight into the examinee's overall ability to process new information to make quick or complex decisions.

WHY CAN'T I EXPORT DATA COLLECTED DURING FREE TRIAL?

Users are welcome to download the NIH Toolbox® V3 app for free and explore the tests and features the system has to offer. It is free for examiners to administer mock assessments to experience the test workflows, but data from free-trial administrations are not saved. A paid and valid subscription is required for the app to save any data or for that data to be available for export.

ARE ANY TRANSLATIONS AVAILABLE?

At the time of this book's publication, the NIH Toolbox® V3 app is available in six languages: English, Arabic, French, Hebrew, Italian, and Spanish. The NIH Toolbox® V3 Spanish app is fully translated and has the same tests that are available in the NIH Toolbox® V3 English app. The NIH Toolbox® V3 Arabic, NIH Toolbox® V3 French, NIH Toolbox® V3 Hebrew, and NIH Toolbox® V3 Italian apps have an English examiner interface and translations of the Fluid Cognition tests (i.e., Dimensional Change Card Sort, Flanker Inhibitory Control and Attention, List Sorting Working Memory, Pattern Comparison Processing Speed, Picture Sequence Memory Form A, and Picture Sequence Memory Form B). Supplemental materials, such as the Administration Manual, and user support are currently available in English only.

REFERENCES

American Educational Research Association and National Council on Measurement in Education (2014). *Standards for educational and psychological testing*. American Psychological Association.

Wechsler, D. (2008). *Wechsler Adult Intelligence Scale—Fourth Edition (WAIS-IV) [Database record]*. APA PsycTests. https://doi.org/https://doi.org/10.1037/t15169-000

Appendix B

AVAILABLE ONLINE RESOURCES

Supplemental resources and documentation about the NIH Toolbox can be found at the main NIH Toolbox website (https://nihtoolbox.org/) or the NIH Toolbox Help Desk (https://nihtoolbox.zendesk.com/hc/en-us).

The main NIH Toolbox website houses information about how to access the apps, details about each test, a wealth of publications, and the User Resources (https://resources.nihtoolbox.org/).

- Test-level information: https://nihtoolbox.org/test-finder/
  - The Test Finder allows users to search for tests by name, domain, participant age, and administration format. By default, all tests appear. Clicking on a test displays the relevant details such as the test description, appropriate ages, estimated time to administer each test, supplies needed, and training videos.
  - The NIH Toolbox has an abundance of tests across four domains. The Cognition domain requires the examiner to have special credentials before they can view or administer any Cognition tests. To obtain C-Level access, users must complete the online form to request access at https://resources.nihtoolbox.org/apply-for-access/. If granted, users will have access to the Cognition tests in the app, as well as additional supplemental materials through the User Resources on https://nihtoolbox.org/.
- Training videos (https://nihtoolbox.org/training/)
  - This section of the website includes various instructional videos that demonstrate how users can complete certain actions within the app. Videos include demonstrations on how to create participants, how to create assessments, how to export results, and general best practices during test administration.
  - Information about live workshops and training sessions can also be found here.
  - E-learning is also available for the NIH Toolbox tests. In the e-learning test modules, the user can test their knowledge and understanding of the administration of the tests, as well as the area they are assessing.
- Publications (https://nihtoolbox.org/publication-finder/)
  - The regularly maintained Publications Finder contains over 600 published resources that focus on the NIH Toolbox. Users can filter by domain,

participant age, year of publication, and tags. This list of predominantly journal articles covers topics from traumatic brain injury to dementia to depression and beyond.

- User Resources
  - It is free to sign up for an account on https://resources.nihtoolbox.org/. Doing so grants access to the available NIH Toolbox® V3 Administration and Technical Manuals, brochures, informational PowerPoints, and a sample of results outputs.
  - Users who have been granted C-Level access to Cognition tests also gain access to the supplemental materials that are required to administer those tests. For instance, C-Level access is required to administer the List Sorting Working Memory test, and the "NIH Toolbox® V3 List Sorting Working Memory Answer Sheet" can only be downloaded from the User Resources if that user has been granted special access.

To view additional support documentation and articles, please visit the NIH Toolbox Help Desk at https://nihtoolbox.zendesk.com/hc/en-us. Over 200 articles detail the NIH Toolbox in general, troubleshooting advice, and frequently asked questions. It is likely that user questions are already addressed there.

Lastly, please note that technology is an ever-developing medium, and while the URLs listed here are accurate at the time of this book's publication, it is possible that some may be updated or changed. To this end, please know that the NIH Toolbox user support team is always happy to help address any issues or answer any questions. If you cannot easily find the answer to a question in this book or the resources mentioned earlier, please do not hesitate to email help@NIHToolbox.org with any questions.

Appendix C

STANDARD SCORES TO PERCENTILES

NIHTB SS	Percentile
≤61	<1
62	1
63	1
64	1
65	1
66	1
67	1
68	2
69	2
70	2
71	3
72	3
73	4
74	4
75	5
76	5
77	6
78	7
79	8
80	9
81	10
82	12
83	13
84	14
85	16
86	18
87	19
88	21
89	23
90	25
91	27
92	30
93	32
94	34
95	37
96	39
97	42
98	45
99	47
100	50
101	53
102	55
103	58
104	61
105	63
106	66
107	68
108	70
109	73
110	75
111	77
112	79
113	81
114	82
115	84
116	86
117	87
118	88
119	90
120	91
121	92
122	93
123	94
124	95
125	95
126	96
127	96
128	97
129	97
130	98
131	98
132	98
133	99
134	99
135	99
136	99
137	99
138	99
≥161	>99

Appendix D

GLOSSARY OF TERMS

Adjacent-Pairs Score: Adjacent-pairs scores are only produced by the Picture Sequence Memory (PSM) test. In PSM, a series of pictures are displayed in a specific order, then jumbled in the middle of the screen. Examinees are meant to move the pictures back into the correct boxes, in the order they were initially presented. When two pictures are placed in the correct order (regardless of position), they receive an adjacent-pairs score of 1. For example, placing the first and second pictures in the correct order (i.e., picture 1 followed by picture 2) would earn an adjacent-pairs score of 1, regardless of whether they were placed in the first and second boxes (e.g., versus close to the last of the boxes).

Administration: As a verb, "administration" is used to refer to a testing session, during which the examiner presents a predefined selection of tests to an examinee, and the examinee responds to the tasks as instructed. See Figure 1.

"Administration" is also often used as a noun, in reference to the collection of tests that were administered to the examinee during the testing session, also referred to as "assessment."

Age-Adjusted National Percentile: A norm-referenced score that details an individual's performance relative to their same-age peers. It is reported on a scale of 1 to 99 and can be interpreted as the percentage of same-age peers in the population who would obtain a score that is equal to or less than the individual's obtained score.

Age-Adjusted Standard Score: A norm-referenced score that describes an individual's performance relative to their same-age peers in the NIH Toolbox® V3 norming sample. It is based on a normal distribution of change-sensitive scores where the mean is set equal to 100, and the standard deviation is set equal to 15. Extreme Age-Adjusted Standard Scores that fall four standard deviations above or below the mean are rounded (i.e., scores below 40 are rounded to 39, and scores above 160 are rounded to 161). Age-Adjusted Standard Scores are useful for describing the performance of an individual or comparing the performance of multiple individuals at a single point in time.

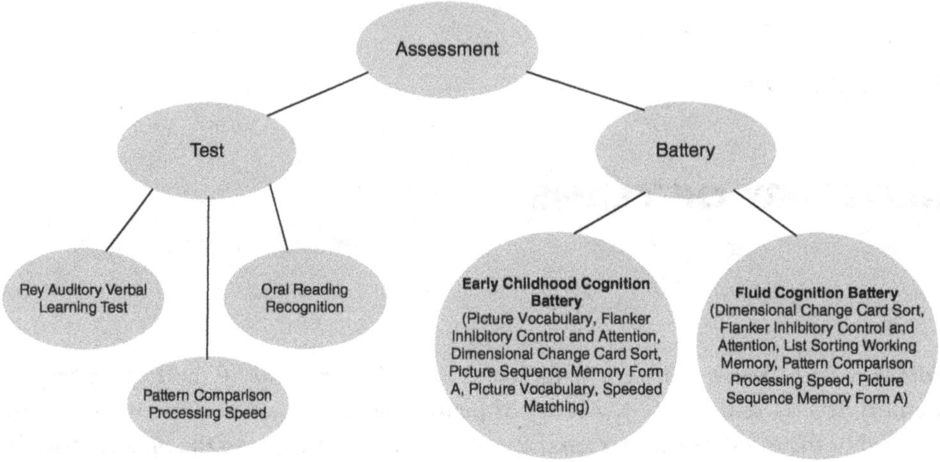

Figure 1 Relationship of Assessments, Tests, and Batteries in the NIH Toolbox® V3 App.

Age- and Education-Adjusted T-Score: A norm-referenced score that describes an individual's performance relative to their same-age peers in the NIH Toolbox® V3 norming sample who also have the same level of education. It is based on a T-score metric, with a mean of 50 and a standard deviation of 10. Age- and Education-Adjusted T-Scores are only reported for adults ages 22 and older in NIH Toolbox® V3 Cognition tests.

Anhedonia: A reduced or absent capacity to experience pleasure, joy, or interest in activities that are typically enjoyable.

Assessment: A set of tests that are administered to an examinee (e.g., "Assessment 1" might be the name of a specific set of tests to be administered).

Assessment also refers to when something is being examined in close detail (e.g., the examinee can undergo an assessment for a specific illness).

Attention: A person's capacity to selectively process relevant stimuli while ignoring distractions, sustain focus over time, and flexibly shift between tasks or mental sets. Attention is a critical cognitive construct that supports numerous higher-order functions, including learning, memory, and executive processes.

Basal: A predetermined number of live items on some fixed-form tests that are ordered by increasing item difficulty, which the examinee must answer correctly before they are permitted to continue onto more difficult items. A basal is sometimes present when a fixed-form test begins on an item that is not Item 1, with the purpose of determining whether the examinee should go backward to respond to easier items or continue forward to more difficult items.

For instance, a 20-year-old might be asked to begin a fixed-form test ordered by increasing difficulty on Item 16, and the basal rule for that test might be to answer the first three items correctly. If the examinee answers Items 16, 17, and 18 correctly, they can move forward to Item 19 and beyond. If this examinee answers any of Items 16, 17, or 18 incorrectly, the "reverse rule" would be implemented until a basal of three consecutive items is answered correctly. That is, the examinee would be presented with Item 15, then Item 14, then Item 13, and so forth, until they provide three consecutive correct responses. Then, they would move forward to Item 19 and continue the test.

Generally, credit is given to pre-basal items, even if they were not administered. For instance, if the basal was met at Item 10, the examinee would not be required to respond to Items 1–10, but would be given credit as if they had answered those items correctly.

Battery: A specific set of tests that are saved in a specific order. For instance, the "Early Childhood Cognition Battery—CFPS" is a preset battery that, when administered, always presents the same tests in the same order (i.e., Picture Vocabulary, Visual Reasoning, and Speeded Matching). See Figure 1. Examiners can use the preset batteries that are preprogrammed in the NIH Toolbox app, or they can create their own custom batteries with any tests in the app.

"Battery" can also be used as an overarching term for a full suite of tests (e.g., to assess someone's general health, clinicians might use a battery of multiple tests and assessments, often from different products/measurement systems).

Behavioral Observation: Aspects of the examinee that the examiner has taken note of and ideally recorded somewhere. Observations include, but are certainly not limited to, fatigue, inattention, irritability, carelessness, motor disturbances (e.g., tremor at rest), and visual or auditory complaints (e.g., excessive squinting). Observing the examinee's behaviors during a testing session can provide essential context for interpreting performance and unexpected scores.

Ceiling: A predetermined number of live items on which some fixed-form tests that are ordered by increasing item difficulty, which the examinee must answer incorrectly before the test ends. If an examinee answers incorrectly to numerous consecutive items on a fixed-form test ordered by increasing item difficulty, there is a point at which, statistically, they are unlikely to answer more difficult items correctly than at a better-than-chance level. To spare that examinee from taking many more items, the test ends when the ceiling is met. Ceilings can reduce test fatigue and examinee discouragement while reducing the overall testing time. A ceiling is sometimes also referred to as a "stop point."

C-Level Cognition Access: Tests in the NIH Toolbox Cognition domain are classified as Level C measures, which is the highest classification level used in test security protocols. Level C assessments require users to possess a doctoral degree in psychology, education, or a closely related field, or to hold current state licensure or national certification to practice independently in a relevant professional capacity. Furthermore, users must have formal training in the administration, scoring, and interpretation of standardized assessments. Individuals who do not meet these qualifications must be supervised by a qualified professional to ensure test integrity and ethical standards are upheld. Restricting access to these assessments also serves to protect the validity and reliability of the measures by preventing overexposure of test content.

Change-Sensitive Score (CSS): A linear transformation of the Theta score, where CSS = 500 + (9.1024 * Theta). The resulting value is rounded to the nearest integer to remove decimals. This transformation produces scores that are always positive integers, making them easier to explain and interpret; a typical range of CSS on the NIH Toolbox tests and composites is approximately 400 to 600. CSS is the recommended metric for use cases where the amount of change over time (i.e., growth or decline) is of interest. Because it is an equal-interval metric (like tick marks on a ruler), differences in CSS can be compared within and across examinees.

Cognition: Mental processes involved in gaining knowledge and comprehension, and includes concepts such as thinking, understanding, recalling, and problem-solving. In the NIH Toolbox® V3 app, the Cognition domain features tests that measure specific constructs of the individual's cognitive functioning.

Cognition Battery: A preset battery that contains the following tests, in the following order: Picture Vocabulary, Flanker Inhibitory Control and Attention, List Sorting Working Memory, Dimensional Change Card Sort, Pattern Comparison Processing Speed, Picture Sequence Memory Form A, and Oral Reading Recognition. This battery is appropriate for examinees aged 7 and older.

Commission Errors: The number of incorrect responses on a specific subset of items. Commission errors are only available for Dimensional Change Card Sort (DCCS) and Flanker Inhibitory Control and Attention (Flanker). The DCCS commission errors score reflects the number of incorrect responses on live items, while the Flanker commission errors score represents the number of congruent trials (i.e., all the fish pointing the same way) that are answered incorrectly.

Composite: A combination of scores from specific tests that measure a specific set of constructs.

Computed Score: A special type of Raw Score that takes into account the participant's speed and accuracy in answering the test items. A Computed Score describes how the examinee performed on a test or composite, independent of how others performed on the same test or composite. Computed Scores are reported only for the Dimensional Change Card Sort and Flanker Inhibitory Control and Attention tests.

Computerized Adaptive Test (CAT): When measuring constructs with more nuanced knowledge, test takers can accurately identify their ability level either by responding to a large number of items or by responding to a customized subset of the larger item pool. CAT measures are adaptive in that the examinee's response to the current item determines the difficulty of the next item; correct answers lead to more difficult items, while incorrect responses move to easier items. When the test has internally calculated the examinee's ability level, the test automatically ends. Generally, CATs are shorter in length than if the full item bank were to be administered to the examinee.

Confidence Interval: A range of scores within which the user can be fairly confident that the individual's true score is likely to fall. Confidence intervals are sometimes also called "confidence bands."

Construct: A theoretical concept that encompasses, explains, and/or interprets human behavior. NIH Toolbox® V3 Cognition constructs include attention, delayed memory, episodic memory, executive function, immediate memory, language, processing speed, and working memory. Each NIH Toolbox® V3 Cognition test is designed to measure a specific construct or two (e.g., the Picture Sequence Memory test assesses episodic memory).

Crystallized Abilities (Gc): Accumulated knowledge, such as vocabulary and factual information. Growth is generally steady from childhood and adolescence as language and learning experiences expand.

Crystallized Cognition Composite: An overall score that combines test-level scores from the following tests: Oral Reading Recognition and Picture Vocabulary. This composite score is appropriate for examinees aged 7 years and older and reflects the individual's language-based knowledge and skills acquired through experience.

Delayed Memory: A person's ability to recall short-term information. Memorizing a shopping list at home and recalling it at the grocery store is an example of delayed memory.

Diagnosis: When a professional with adequate training indicates that an individual has met a specific set of criteria that has been predefined by experts in that field.

Disease: A pathological condition of a body part, organ, or system that has a defined biological cause, characteristic signs and symptoms, and often measurable changes in anatomy or physiology. A disease usually has a known etiology.

Disorder: A disruption of normal physical, mental, or functional processes that causes distress, impairment, or dysfunction but may not have a single identifiable cause or consistent biological markers.

Distal Outcomes: Assesses untrained but related abilities, indicating generalization of cognitive change.

Domain: In the NIH Toolbox app, there are four domains—Cognition, Emotion, Motor, and Sensation—that encompass a subset of tests and measure a specific set of relevant constructs.

Early Childhood Cognition Battery: A preset battery that contains the following tests, in the following order: Picture Vocabulary, Flanker Inhibitory Control and Attention, Dimensional Change Card Sort, Picture Sequence Memory Form A, and Speeded Matching. This battery is appropriate for examinees aged 4 to 6 years, though extended normative data are available through age 8-½ years.

Early Childhood Cognition Battery—Crystallized-Fluid-Processing Speed (CFPS): A preset battery that contains the following tests, in the following order: Picture Vocabulary, Visual Reasoning, and Speeded Matching. This battery is appropriate for examinees aged 3 to 6 years old, though extended normative data are available through age 8-½ years.

Early Childhood Cognition CFPS Composite: An overall score that combines test-level scores from the following tests: Picture Vocabulary, Visual Reasoning, and Speeded Matching. This composite represents the child's overall capacity for executive function, processing speed, and language.

Early Childhood Cognition Composite: An overall score that combines test-level scores from the following tests: Picture Vocabulary, Flanker Inhibitory Control and Attention, Dimensional Change Card Sort, Picture Sequence Memory Form A, and

Speeded Matching. This composite represents the child's overall attention, episodic memory, executive function, processing speed, and language.

Episodic Memory: A person's capacity to encode, store, and retrieve information about specific events. The ability to recall what you did last weekend taps into episodic memory.

Examinee: A person who is to be assessed. Often, this term is used interchangeably with "participant," "test-taker," and "patient," though certain terms may be more applicable in specific situations (e.g., "patient" is generally only used by clinicians or pharmaceutical researchers). Also see "*Participant.*"

Examiner: The individual who sits with and guides the examinee through the tests during an administration. Examiners must have formal training in test administration, as well as a strong understanding of the NIH Toolbox app and the specific tests that are to be administered.

Examiner Interface: The screens in the NIH Toolbox app that only the examiner (i.e., not the examinee) sees. This includes the test list, list of batteries, participant information, assessment results, and app settings. In other words, the examiner interface is the part of the app that the examiner uses to navigate the app and set up administrations. The examiner interface is sometimes also referred to as the "examiner shell" or "shell."

Executive Function: A higher-order cognitive process essential for goal-directed behavior, cognitive flexibility, shifting between tasks, inhibition, and planning. The ability to plan your day and flexibly navigate distractions is an example of executive function.

Exports: The NIH Toolbox® V3 app has six CSV export files: Registration Export, Scores Export, Item Export, Registration Export (Narrow Structure), Scores Export (Narrow Structure), and Item Export (Narrow Structure). The Registration Export includes participant-level information, such as their name, date of birth, and other demographics. The Scores Export contains test-level information, such as the overall raw score for the Flanker test. The Item Export has item-level information, such as responses to each item. Examiners can export data for as many assessments as they would like (i.e., a single assessment, multiple assessments, or all completed assessments). For a comprehensive view of an assessment, the examiner should use the PID (Participant ID) to connect data from the Registration, Scores, and Item exports.

Expressive Language: A cognitive process that reflects an individual's ability to convey thoughts by producing language to communicate with others. Generally, language is expressed verbally (e.g., spoken words) or nonverbally (e.g., facial expressions, hand gestures).

Fluid Abilities (Gf): Encompasses reasoning, processing speed, and working memory. Development generally follows a curvilinear path with rapid advances in childhood, continued growth into adolescence, evening out in adulthood, and decline in later adulthood.

Fluid Cognition Composite: An overall score that combines test-level scores from the following tests: Dimensional Change Card Sort, Flanker Inhibitory Control and Attention, List Sorting Working Memory, Pattern Comparison Processing Speed, and Picture Sequence Memory. This composite score, appropriate for examinees aged 4 years and older, represents the capacity for problem-solving, reasoning, and novel information processing.

Frontal lobe: A part of the brain that is critical for executive functions, including planning, inhibition, decision-making, working memory, and task-switching.

Immediate Recall: A person's ability to immediately recall information. For example, if you were presented with a verbal list of ten grocery items, could you immediately repeat all ten items correctly?

Interpretation: The action and/or result of a trained professional's comprehensive review of an individual's information. Interpretation generally refers to the full picture that is formed by the examinee's data, referral information, test results, and behavioral observations.

Intervention: A response plan, therapy, or treatment designed to address a specific concern or set of concerns identified by various methods of evaluation (e.g., behavioral observation, parent-report and teacher-report surveys, psychological testing). Interventions should be tailored to individuals by their healthcare and/or academic team to ensure effective and efficient improvement.

Item Response Theory (IRT): A psychometric framework used to analyze and determine specific details and parameters about test items and their relationships with each other. IRT estimates the difficulty of each item and the ability of each test-taker on a common scale, allowing for more precise and adaptive measurement of latent traits (such as cognitive ability, personality, or skill).

Live Item: One of the numerous questions, problems, or prompts that are presented to the examinee as part of a test. The examinee's response is scored—most often as correct or incorrect—and often summed with all other live items in that test and/or has some additional calculation (e.g., response time) that relays the examinee's performance.

Logit: The metric in which Rasch-scaled tests report ability scores. Logits are also sometimes referred to as theta scores. These scores can contain decimals and can be negative (e.g., –3.79). Also see "Theta."

Median Response Time Per Item (in seconds): This is computed as the median response time across all live items encountered by the individual during the test administration. Median Response Time Per Item is available for the following tests: Dimensional Change Card Sort, Face Name Associative Memory Exam Delay, Flanker Inhibitory Control and Attention, Pattern Comparison Processing Speed, Rey Auditory Verbal Learning Test, and Rey Auditory Verbal Learning Test Delay.

Neurodegenerative Disease: This type of disease refers to a condition characterized by progressive structural and functional deterioration of neurons and neural networks, leading to gradual loss of cognitive, motor, or behavioral abilities over time. Unlike neurodevelopmental disorders, which arise from atypical formation, neurodegenerative diseases reflect pathological processes such as protein misfolding, synaptic dysfunction, oxidative stress, and neuronal death occurring after normal brain development. These diseases are typically age-associated, chronic, and irreversible, with symptoms that worsen as neuronal damage accumulates. Examples include Alzheimer's disease, Parkinson's disease, frontotemporal dementia, and amyotrophic lateral sclerosis.

Neurodevelopmental Disorder: This disorder refers to a condition characterized by atypical brain development that emerges during early childhood and affects the acquisition or organization of cognitive, behavioral, motor, or social functions. These disorders result from disruptions in the formation, growth, or connectivity of neural systems during critical periods of brain maturation. They are typically evident early in development, often before school age, and manifest as enduring patterns of functional impairment in domains such as attention, language, executive function, or social communication. Examples include attention-deficit hyperactivity disorder (ADHD), autism spectrum disorder, and specific learning disorders. Neurodevelopmental disorders are generally stable or improve with maturation and intervention rather than showing progressive decline.

Normative Scores: Numerical values that describe an individual's relative standing in a group of peers. For instance, an individual with a raw score of 12 on List Sorting Working Memory indicates how many items they answered correctly, but it does not provide any indication of whether that person performed well compared to their peers (e.g., is a raw score of 12 high? Low? Average?). However, a 21-year-old with a raw score of 12 on LSWM might have an Age-Adjusted Standard Score of 86, which is based on the normative sample and indicates that the individual's performance on LSWM was nearly a full standard deviation below their normative representation's mean (i.e., that person performed poorly on that test compared to similar-aged peers).

Normative scores are often also referenced as "normed scores" or "norm-referenced scores." Normative scores are generally less useful for describing relative change in ability between two time points.

Occipital Lobe: A part of the brain that specializes in visual processing, which underpins rapid perceptual judgments required in many cognitive tests.

Omission Errors: The number of live items on which the examinee does not respond or runs out of time before entering a response. Omission errors are only available for Dimensional Change Card Sort and Flanker Inhibitory Control and Attention.

Orientation: In clinical and neuropsychological contexts, "orientation" refers to a person's awareness of key aspects of their surroundings and themselves, and is typically assessed across three or four domains:

- Orientation to person: Knowing who you are (name, age, personal identity).
- Orientation to place: Knowing where you are (city, building, setting).
- Orientation to time: Knowing the date, day of the week, season, or approximate time.
- *(Sometimes assessed)* Orientation to situation: Understanding why you are in a given setting (e.g., "I'm here for a testing appointment").

Being "oriented ×3" means the person is oriented to person, place, and time, which indicates intact basic awareness and attention.

Paraphasia: Speech production error(s) involving the unintentional use of incorrect or distorted words or sounds. These may include the substitution of a word that sounds similar to the intended target (phonemic paraphasia) or one that is semantically related in meaning (semantic paraphasia).

Parietal lobe: A part of the brain that is involved in attention allocation, spatial reasoning, and integration of multimodal sensory input.

Participant: An individual who is to be assessed. In the NIH Toolbox app, the examiner must create a "participant" in the app for each person to be tested and may include demographic information such as education, sex assigned at birth, and ethnicity. Also see "*Examinee.*"

Phonophobia: Sensitivity or discomfort when exposed to sound.

Photophobia: Sensitivity or discomfort when exposed to light.

Practice Effect: When an examinee's performance improves from repeated test exposure, independent of cognitive change.

Practice Item: An item that is presented after the test's instructions, before the live items. Practice items offer the examinee the opportunity to see the layout of the upcoming live items (e.g., there are two response options at the bottom of the screen) and to ensure they adequately understand the task they are meant to complete. Responses to practice items do not contribute to the final test-level score, though for some tests, very poor performance on the practice items exposes poor comprehension of the task and, based on that test's fail rules, may immediately end the test.

Processing Speed: The efficiency with which the brain can perceive, interpret, and respond to stimuli. If someone says, "Quick! Think of a number between one and ten," your ability to promptly understand the command and think of a number within that range is an example of processing speed.

Proximal Outcomes: Reflects improvement on tasks closely aligned with training, capturing practice effects or task-specific learning.

Psychometrics: A field of study that explores theories and techniques involved with measuring mental processes related to psychological testing.

Rapport: A trusting and respectful social connection between the examiner and the examinee, which is a critical component of successful cognitive and neuropsychological assessment. Establishing a good rapport is the examiner's responsibility, as it can influence examinee engagement, effort, comfort, and overall data validity.

Raw Score: An unadjusted score that describes how the examinee performed on a test or composite, independent of how others performed on the same test or composite. For the Face Name Associative Memory Exam Delay, Pattern Comparison Processing Speed, Oral Symbol Digit, Rey Auditory Verbal Learning, Rey Auditory Verbal Learning Delay, and Speeded Matching tests, the Raw Score represents the total number of test items the participant answers correctly. For the List Sorting Working Memory test, the Raw Score is the total number of lists the participant correctly responds to, plus one point for each unadministered sequence below the basals in the 1-List and 2-List portions of the test. No Raw Scores are reported for the Dimensional Change Card Sort, Flanker Inhibitory Control and Attention, Face Name Associative Memory Exam, Oral Reading Recognition, Picture Sequence Memory, Picture Vocabulary, or Visual Reasoning tests.

Receptive Language: Involves the comprehension of structured verbal information, including identifying pieces of language and deriving meaning from them. An example of receptive language includes following instructions, such as "point to the green ball."

Recognition: In cognitive testing, recognition is the ability to correctly identify previously presented information from a list. For instance, if the examinee is shown a picture of a face and is later shown three faces, 'recognition' is the ability to select the specific face that was shown before.

Referral Question: The reason the examinee was recommended for testing. To select the most appropriate test(s) and to address the examinee's concerns, the examiner must have a clear understanding of why the examinee is being assessed.

Reliability: A test's ability to measure a construct consistently over time. For instance, if a person takes a test today and again in a week, during which no significant changes have occurred, that person's scores at Time 1 and Time 2 should be relatively unchanged. If that person takes a test of verbal memory, extensively practices verbal memory games, and then is again tested for verbal memory a week later, those scores are more likely to show an improvement between Time 1 and Time 2 than those of someone who had not practiced.

Score Report: A PDF file with information about a specific assessment. The Score Report can be viewed in the app or exported (e.g., emailed) and contains demographic information about the participant, as well as test-level scores for the selected assessment.

Sensitivity: A test's ability to accurately assess whether the examinee exhibits signs of the construct that is being tested. For example, a test of depression should reliably and accurately identify an individual who presents with depression.

Standard Error of Measurement (SEM): Error is inherent in all test scores; the standard error of measurement (SEM) quantifies the amount of variation in a distribution of observed test scores that is due to measurement error. A large standard error implies that a test score has less precision, or reliability, than a test score with a smaller standard error. Any observed test score is an estimate of the "true" score; the ±1 SEM interval around an observed test score provides a range within which the "true" score lies, with 68% probability. NIH Toolbox® V3 Cognition provides standard errors of measurement for the Theta score, CSS, Age-Adjusted Standard Score, and Age- and Education-Adjusted Standard Score.

Standardization: In testing, 'standardization' refers to uniformity and the ability of the test to be administered consistently across multiple administrations. NIH Toolbox® V3 Cognition tests are standardized by having a single set of instructions that are displayed on the screen and read aloud by prerecorded audio; no matter how many examinees take those tests, they will all see and hear the same instructions. The exception is Oral Symbol Digit, which requires the examiner to train the examinee on a physical "Oral Symbol Digit Examination Sheet," and therefore has standardized instructions for the examiner to read aloud while demonstrating to the "Oral Symbol Digit Examination Sheet."

Start Point: A predetermined live item on which the examinee will start the test. Some tests have a variable start point that is based on age and/or education, which allows the examinee to skip over the easiest items and instead begin on items that, based on the normative sample, are more likely attuned to their ability level. All but two IRT tests in the NIH Toolbox® V3 Cognition domain start on Item 1; List Sorting Working Memory and Picture Sequence Memory use the examinee's age to determine the start point (e.g., a 10-year-old will begin LSWM on Item E, skipping Items A, B, C, and D). All NIH

Toolbox® V3 Cognition CAT tests (i.e., Oral Reading Recognition, Picture Vocabulary, and Visual Reasoning) have start points based on the examinee's age (if age 18 or younger) or education (if 19 years or older).

Supplemental Tests: Optional tests that are part of a domain or product that can provide helpful information about specific constructs but do not contribute to a particular battery or composite. At the time of publication, NIH Toolbox® V3 Cognition has 6 supplemental tests: Face Name Associative Memory Exam, Face Name Associative Memory Exam Delay, Picture Sequence Memory Form B, Oral Symbol Digit, Rey Auditory Verbal Learning, and Rey Auditory Verbal Learning Delay. As a note, the NIH Toolbox team is considering additional composites that may incorporate these tests.

Temporal Lobe: A part of the brain that supports episodic memory (via medial temporal structures such as the hippocampus) and language comprehension.

Test: A series of items centered around a specific task. Tests are designed to measure something specific (e.g., List Sorting Working Memory is a test that assesses the examinee's working memory). In general, tests include a series of instructions that explain the task, practice items to allow the examinee to confirm they understand what to do, and then a series of live items that are scored and which contribute to the overall test-level score. A test is commonly also referred to as a "measure," "task," or "instrument." See Figure 1.

Theta: Theta scales are equal-interval metrics, which means that a change of 1 theta point has the same meaning across the entire scale range. Theta scores describe how the examinee performed on a test or composite, independent of how others performed on the same test or composite. Theta scores are reported for all NIH Toolbox® V3 Cognition tests except for Dimensional Change Card Sort and Flanker Inhibitory Control and Attention. A typical range of test Theta Scores on the NIH Toolbox is –8.0 to +8.0, but varies by test. Although Theta Scores can be useful for tracking growth or decline over time, they are less interpretable than change-sensitive scores because they can be negative and can contain decimals.

Total Cognition Composite: An overall score that combines test-level scores from the following tests: Dimensional Change Card Sort, Flanker Inhibitory Control and Attention, List Sorting Working Memory, Oral Reading Recognition, Pattern Comparison Processing Speed, Picture Sequence Memory, and Picture Vocabulary. This composite is available for examinees aged 7 and older and represents the capacity for attention, episodic memory, executive function, language, processing speed, and working memory.

User Experience (UX): The overall experience the user (i.e., examiner) has with the app. A primary goal for NIH Toolbox® V3 was to improve the UX by streamlining workflows for smooth, intuitive, and easy navigation throughout the app.

User Interface (UI): The app's visual elements and interface with which the users interact. A primary goal for NIH Toolbox® V3 was to improve the UI by implementing consistent colors, fonts, buttons, and overall style throughout the app to make it visually engaging.

Validity: A test's ability to distinctly measure the construct (i.e., specific concept) it was designed to explore. For instance, the Pattern Comparison Processing Speed test should only measure processing speed (i.e., not be confounded by other constructs or theories).

Working Memory: A person's ability to temporarily hold and manipulate information for immediate use. Working memory is essential for reasoning, comprehension, problem-solving, and goal-directed behavior. Mentally calculating a multistep math problem is an example of working memory; it's important to briefly store information from each step to solve the equation, but once the solution has been identified, the steps taken to get there can be forgotten.

z-score: z-scores have a mean of 0 and describe the examinee's performance relative to the mean performance of the reference peer group, where 1 z-score point equals 1 standard deviation unit. z-scores are used to calculate other scores in the NIH Toolbox® V3 Cognition domain, though they are not present in the Score Report or score exports. z-scores in the NIH Toolbox® V3 Cognition domain are derived by subtracting the reference CSS mean from the obtained CSS, then dividing by the CSS standard deviation. See Chapter 4 for more information.

Index